Understanding Autism For Dummies

Inquiring about Interventions

Many "entrepreneurs" are only too happy to accept your money for their "miracle cures" or interventions. Keep your eyes open, and ask these questions about all those sellers and their interventions:

- What evidence supports the intervention's effectiveness? Is the evidence *independent* research or just case studies? What's the success rate of the intervention? Are there side effects or interactions?
- Who else is offering the intervention, and how is yours better?
- What other interventions are available? Can they be combined?
- What's the total cost? Will my health insurance or a government program cover the cost, or is it tax deductible?
- Can I speak with other people who have tried this already?
- How will the treatment help, specifically? How can I measure progress? What time frame does the treatment call for?

Deciphering Important Acronyms

The following table helps you translate some acronyms that you'll see and hear over and over during your life as a caregiver of or a person with autism.

Acronym	What It Stands For
ABA	Applied Behavioral Analysis
AS	Asperger Syndrome
ASD	Autism Spectrum Disorder
BIP	Behavior Intervention Plan
BMP	Behavior Management Plan
ESY	Extended School Year
FAPE	Free and Appropriate Public Education
FERPA	Family Educational Rights and Privacy Act
IDEA	Individuals with Disabilities Education Act
IEP	Individualized Education Program
IFSP	Individualized Family Service Plan
IPP	Individual Program Plan
ISP	Individual Service Plan
LRE	Least Restrictive Environment
NT	Neurotypical

Logging On to Helpful Autism Web Sites

- www.autism-society.org
- www.autismlink.com
- www.autism-resources.com

Carrying an Emergency ID Card

Cut out this card and educate the person with autism to keep it on hand to share with people in confusing situations, such as when they're approached by a uniformed person or when they have difficulty interacting with others they don't know.

AUTISM AUTISM AUTISM AUTISM

My name is _____ and I have autism, which causes me to behave in unexpected ways. Please contact one of the following:

Name   Phone

_____   _____

_____   _____

_____   _____

More information about autism on the other side.

Understanding Autism For Dummies®

Getting the Most Out of Your Child's Education

- Insist on specific and measurable goals for your child's IEP. Involve your child in the process.
- Develop strong relationships with educational professionals. Keep it friendly, not adversarial.
- Stay informed about educational laws, your district's policies, and your child's progress. Know your options.
- Visit your child's classroom to confirm that it's an effective learning environment. It should have distinct areas for different subjects, comfortable lighting, good ventilation, appropriate noise level, and right-sized furniture, and the teacher should be approachable and fair.
- Support your child at home by reinforcing what educators are teaching at school. Develop your child's strengths; don't just remediate.
- If possible, get at least 25 hours a week of early intervention before age 3.

Preparing for Emergencies

- Consider attaching an identification sticker to the door or window of an autistic person's home to prepare a person coming in to help.
- Create or purchase a medical alert tag, bracelet, or other notification that identifies a person with autism.
- Network with relatives, friends, and others to establish a web of contacts for assistance if needed.
- Register the person on the autism spectrum with the community 911 service as a person with a disability.
- Have an evacuation plan, and review and practice it frequently with the person on the autism spectrum.
- Project a sense of calm. People with autism often sense and reflect your emotion.
- View more on disaster preparedness at the following locations:
  - **FEMA:** www.fema.gov/hazard/index.shtm
  - **NOAA:** www.aoml.noaa.gov/hrd/links.html
  - **American Red Cross:** www.redcross.org

Communicating with Autistic People

- Speak slowly and clearly, and don't expect an immediate response.
- Be gentle, persistent, and patient. Don't rush the person.
- Provide direct instruction in social rules. Teach an emotional vocabulary.
- Keep your communications simple. Don't overwhelm.
- Don't force eye contact or touch.
- Encourage special interests, but teach give-and-take in conversation.
- Demonstrate behaviors, allowing time for observation and reflection.
- Pay attention to non-verbal signals.

AUTISM INFORMATION

I may:
- Not understand what you say
- Appear deaf
- Suddenly dart away
- Have difficulty speaking
- Flap my hands or rock
- Not understand legal issues
- Be overly sensitive to shiny objects, sounds, touch, or smells

Please help by:
- Not shouting
- Speaking slowly and softly
- Using concrete terms
- Giving me time to respond
- Explaining before doing
- Employing visual aids for communication when possible
- Making no sudden movements
- Warning me first if you must touch me

For Dummies: Bestselling Book Series for Beginners

Understanding Autism FOR DUMMIES®

by Stephen M. Shore and Linda G. Rastelli

Foreword by Temple Grandin, author of *Thinking in Pictures*

WILEY

Wiley Publishing, Inc.

Understanding Autism For Dummies®

Published by
Wiley Publishing, Inc.
111 River St.
Hoboken, NJ 07030-5774
www.wiley.com

WILEY

About the Authors

Stephen M. Shore received a regressive autism diagnosis at age 18 months, became nonverbal, and was deemed "too sick" to be treated on an outpatient basis. Today, he's finishing a doctoral degree focused on helping people with autism lead fulfilling and productive lives. When not teaching college-level courses in special education and teaching children with autism how to play musical instruments, he consults and presents on autism-related issues internationally. Some topics of particular interest to him include comparative approaches for helping people with autism, education, and disaster preparedness for people with disabilities. He also focuses on challenges faced by adults in terms of self-advocacy, disclosure, post-secondary education, employment, interdependent living, and relationships.

Stephen holds bachelor degrees in music and accounting and information systems from the University of Massachusetts at Amherst. He also holds a masters degree in music education and is on the cusp of finishing his doctorate in education from Boston University. Although he seems to spend most of his time traveling in airplanes (Boeing 747-400 preferred), he resides in Brookline, Massachusetts, with his wife on the rare occasions when he's home.

Linda G. Rastelli is an award-winning journalist, instructional designer, and author with 20 years of experience in writing and designing instruction for health, education, and business topics. In her career, she has focused on making complex and technical information understandable to the layperson. Although she has covered subjects ranging from financial ratio analysis to educational reform, her most challenging inquiry to date — an undertaking that has made her other projects look like finger painting in comparison — has been autism.

Linda holds a bachelor of arts degree from the University of Delaware and a masters degree from Columbia University. She lives on the New Jersey coast with her husband and her cat, who have reached a blissful state of detente. She hopes to keep her day job.

Dedication

From co-author Stephen M. Shore: This book is dedicated to my wife, Yi Liu, my parents and siblings, and to all people on the autism spectrum.

From co-author Linda G. Rastelli: This book is dedicated to my husband, Bob Galante, and to Robert Rastelli, in memoriam.

Authors' Acknowledgments

This book is a wonderful collaboration between many generous souls, without whom we couldn't have written it. Temple Grandin, PhD, read every chapter and made helpful suggestions. We're also indebted to Peter Wright, Bart Stevens, Nadine Vogel, and Jaime Parent for their astute insights into financial and legal matters.

Our everlasting gratitude goes to Dr. David Holmes, Dr. Brenda Smith Myles, Dr. Joanne Cafiero, Bill Hayes, Donna Walters, and Dr. Peter Gerhardt for their educational expertise.

We also want to acknowledge Dr. Stephen Edelson, Dr. Bernard Rimland, Brad Middlebrook, Dr. Betty Jarusiewicz, Teresa Mankin, Tony Martin, and Dr. Craig Erickson for their all-around acumen.

Dr. Margaret Bauman, Dr. Jane M. El-Dahr, Dr. Lauren Underwood, Dr. Tapan Audhya, Dr. Jeff Bradstreet, Dr. Daniel Rosenn, and Dr. David J. Posey gave us much-appreciated medical guidance, for which we can't thank them enough. And many thanks to all the others who gave up their time and shared their personal experiences to make this book happen: Janet and Steve Cobourn (co-presidents of the Maryland chapter of the Autism Society of America), Meghan Cobourn and the rest of our focus group, Rebecca and Keith Sorenson, Ben Dorman, and Catriona Johnson. Also Nancy Cale, Kathy Grant, Chris Collins, Sharon Mendoza, Dr. Arnold Miller, Dr. Ann Roberts, Rosemary Littlefield, Kassiane Sibley, Dena Gassner, Jonathon Mitchell, Alex Freer, Charmaine Getz, and Toni Dunbar.

And a big thank you goes to our outstanding editorial team at Wiley, who went the extra mile for us: Kathy Cox, Alissa Schwipps, Josh Dials, and the Composition Services folks working on the book behind the scenes.

To those whom we may have inadvertently left out, only to remember them after the book goes to print, please accept our apologies, along with our heartfelt thanks. Your contributions were also vital to making this book what it is today.

Publisher's Acknowledgments

We're proud of this book; please send us your comments through our Dummies online registration form located at www.dummies.com/register/.

Some of the people who helped bring this book to market include the following:

Acquisitions, Editorial, and Media Development

Senior Project Editor: Alissa Schwipps

Acquisitions Editors: Kathy Cox, Lindsay Lefevere

Copy Editor: Josh Dials

Editorial Program Coordinator: Hanna K. Scott

Technical Editors: Tony Martin; David J. Posey, MD; Bart Stevens, ChLAP, AzCLDP; Peter W. D. Wright, Esq.

General Reviewer: Teresa Mankin

Senior Editorial Manager: Jennifer Ehrlich

Editorial Assistants: Nadine Bell, Erin Calligan, David Lutton

Cover Photo: © Ghislain & Marie David de Lossy/Getty Images

Cartoons: Rich Tennant (www.the5thwave.com)

Composition Services

Project Coordinator: Adrienne Martinez, Patrick Redmond

Layout and Graphics: Carl Byers, Andrea Dahl, Denny Hager, Stephanie D. Jumper, Jake Mansfield, Shelley Norris, Lynsey Osborn

Proofreaders: Christy Pingleton, Techbooks

Indexer: Techbooks

Special Help: Sarah Westfall

Publishing and Editorial for Consumer Dummies

Diane Graves Steele, Vice President and Publisher, Consumer Dummies

Joyce Pepple, Acquisitions Director, Consumer Dummies

Kristin A. Cocks, Product Development Director, Consumer Dummies

Michael Spring, Vice President and Publisher, Travel

Kelly Regan, Editorial Director, Travel

Publishing for Technology Dummies

Andy Cummings, Vice President and Publisher, Dummies Technology/General User

Composition Services

Gerry Fahey, Vice President of Production Services

Debbie Stailey, Director of Composition Services

Contents at a Glance

Table of Contents

Foreword

. . . .

*T*here are many different educational programs and treatments for autism, and their originators all claim that their methods are the best. The purpose of this book is to provide parents, teachers, therapists, and others who care for individuals with autism with a guidebook that offers objective, balanced information, thereby enabling you to make intelligent decisions. Like the original *DOS For Dummies* (Wiley), *Understanding Autism For Dummies* is meant to be a user-friendly manual that cuts through the load of information you find out there and helps you make the decision that's best for your situation.

Autism is a neurological disorder caused by abnormalities in the brain. Researchers have discovered that the parts of the brain that process emotions don't develop normally in autistic people. Further research has shown that some of the long-distance circuits that connect different regions in the brain may fail to connect. For example, one person may be sensitive to fluorescent lights, and another person may be sickened by strong smells. One individual may be more socially and emotionally related than another. It all depends upon which circuits connect.

The autism spectrum is very broad and ranges from severe autism, where the child never learns to speak, to mild Asperger Syndrome, where the child has no obvious speech delay. Doctors and caregivers don't often diagnose children with Asperger's until they have problems socializing with other children. An Asperger's child may play alone and have few friends. Some individuals with Asperger's are very intelligent; many eccentric, famous scientists, musicians, and artists probably had Asperger's. The spectrum is continuous, ranging from a person who needs lifetime help with basic living skills to a college professor. The great variability on the autism spectrum may be due to the extent of the abnormalities in the brain.

Co-author Stephen Shore is a college professor who has autism. As one who's been there, he will walk you step-by-step through the complicated world of autism spectrum disorders. An author who's on the autism spectrum can provide an insightful perspective that many academic authors may lack. Co-author Linda Rastelli is an experienced writer who brings unusual clarity to some of the most confusing issues surrounding autism and its treatment. Throughout the book, the authors use quotes and statements from other autistic individuals so you can appreciate the varied nature of the effects of this condition on the people who have it. I support this book and both these authors because in addition to writing a badly needed resource on autism, I, too, am an individual with autism.

To help you better understand how far we've come, and how far we still need to go, I would like to discuss some of my own early childhood experiences as a child with autism.

I had no speech until I was age 3½. For hours, I dribbled sand though my hand. Loud noises, such as the school bell, hurt my ears the way a dentist's drill hits a nerve. Fortunately, I had a great early educational program that started at age 2½. All autism specialists agree that an intensive educational program is most effective if started shortly after symptoms of autism occur. Specialists disagree on which program to use, but everybody agrees that waiting is the worst thing you can do.

Having good teachers is also vital with young children. I've observed that effective teachers know how to be gently insistent so as to draw a child with autism out of his/her world and improve both language and social interaction.

More than 50 years ago, the teacher who worked with me used methods that were similar to some of the best autism programs today. I had structured-speech therapy that resembled the behavioral programs used now. My mother hired a nanny who spent hours each day playing games with me and my sister. She had us take turns coasting down the hill on a single sled or playing board games. Every day I had to sit through three family meals where I had to behave and use good table manners. All these activities added up to over 40 hours a week where I was kept tuned in to the world and wasn't allowed to tune out and retreat into my autistic world of humming, twirling things, and rocking.

Today, I, too, am a college professor who has made contributions to animal science and who has been able to offer hope and perspective to others with autism and to those who care for individuals with autism.

Another important function of this book is to lead you through the maze of the different medical and biomedical treatments. This is often an area of controversy. Stephen Shore and Linda Rastelli explain all the methods in an even-handed manner, which enables you to make rational decisions. Due to the great variability of autism, a medication or biomedical intervention that works for one individual may not work for another. It's usually best to carefully try different things. Keep using those things that seem to work, and stop using things that don't work. In very young children, it's often best to try the safest methods first, such as diets and supplements. Some older children and adults may need to take conventional medication to control anxiety, aggression, or obsessive-compulsive behaviors. In some individuals, a combination of conventional medication and biomedical treatment may be most beneficial. For other individuals, we have yet to discover what helps. But every day, scientists, researchers, therapists, parents, behavioral specialists, nutritionists, and individuals with autism are contributing to the growing body of knowledge about autism spectrum disorders with the goal that, some day, all individuals with autism can make their place in the world and help make it better for everyone. Don't give up hope. Trust your instincts, and use the network of parents, teachers, and others devoted to the care of people with autism to help you cope and provide the best environment you can for you and your family.

Temple Grandin
Author of *Thinking in Pictures*

Introduction

• •

*T*he Centers for Disease Control in Atlanta estimates that as many as half a million children in the United States alone have some form of autism. Still, some doctors inform the parents of the diagnosis, hand them some pamphlets, and tell them, in effect, good luck! Many pediatricians have never seen an autistic patient, so they don't know what to look for, and uninformed doctors may tell parents who have concerns that they're overreacting and that they need to wait and see. Such an approach is risky if your child is displaying symptoms of an autism spectrum disorder, because time is so crucial; we explain why in this book.

If you're reading this book, you probably have a child or other loved one who's received a diagnosis of autism or developmental disability, or maybe you suspect that your child is showing symptoms that you've heard associated with the disorder before, and you want to find out more. Maybe you've received such a diagnosis yourself. The diagnosis of autism can be a devastating and confusing experience, and you want answers fast. You have so many questions, and you don't even know which ones to ask first. How do you put it all together? What do you do tomorrow? Next week? We designed this book to help you answer those questions. If you don't have an autistic relative or dependent, but you do have questions about how to educate, advocate for, or communicate with the autistic people in your life, this book can help you, too.

But first, you need to understand what autism is and isn't. Autism is a neurobiological condition that may come with many challenges, but also imparts great gifts. Autism isn't a mental illness, a result of bad parenting, or a death sentence for fulfilling and productive lives. Many autistic people have made great strides personally and have given amazing contributions to the understanding of autism, including the author of our foreword, Dr. Temple Grandin, who teaches animal science at Colorado State University. Grandin is a sought-after professional speaker on autism and the inventor of numerous livestock-handling innovations. I (co-author Stephen Shore) was diagnosed with atypical development and strong autistic tendencies when I was 2½, but with much help from my parents, friends, teachers, wife, and other professionals, I've gone on to the finishing stages of my doctoral dissertation, and I teach college courses and other activities. I'm honored to be able to contribute to the autism community.

Autism isn't new, but professionals no longer consider it rare. Autism touches the lives of more people than ever before, yet — and maybe because of this frequency — we have much reason for hope.

About This Book

You have in your hands an introductory reference to get you started in your quest to know what to do and where to turn in order to help people with autism. We provide plans and suggestions that we hope are useful to you, whether you're a parent, caregiver, family member, child-care worker, teacher, therapist, or other person supporting an individual with autism.

Understanding Autism For Dummies is designed to provide accessible, practical, user-friendly information in a format that's easy to navigate and follow. We designed each chapter to be self-contained so that you don't have to read the book sequentially or read the first parts to understand any later chapters. You should concentrate only on what you need. The table of contents and the index can help guide your search.

Because the topic of autism is so broad, we rely on many contributions from experienced professionals, experienced caregivers, and people with autism, such as Dr. Temple Grandin. We feel fortunate to have their input, and we believe you will, too. Along the way, we also share quotes and insights from parents of kids with autism and people who live with autism. These people may or may not have stories that are similar to your own, but you can be confident that they've all come through the fire and want to help others to understand what it's like and what they can do to help people with autism.

This book will help you sort out the bad ideas from the good and to understand that each child's plan for intervention is as different as each child's symptoms. And above all, we hope not to insult our audience. We've taken care not to make light of what can be a challenging and heart-wrenching disability. "Dummies" are people approaching a new subject who want clear, concise explanations and guidance. We're confident this book will serve your wants and needs.

Conventions Used in This Book

To help you navigate the waters of this book, we've set up a few conventions:

- We use *italics* for emphasis and to highlight new words or terms that we define.
- We use **boldface** text to indicate the action part of numbered steps and to highlight key words or phrases in bulleted lists.
- We put all Web addresses in `monofont` for easy identification.

Also, we're aware that some people with autism prefer to be called just that, "people with autism," whereas others on the spectrum prefer "autistic people." Although we respect each individual's preference and understand that nobody wants the label "autistic" to define a person, for purposes of clarity and simplicity, we use various constructions throughout this book.

Likely, you'll read the terms *low functioning,* which describes people with severe autism who have great difficulty in successful communication and just making sense of their environment, and *high functioning,* which describes people with mild autism or Asperger Syndrome who have greater verbal ability and increased success with interactions and their environment.

And although the word "autism" itself may not be as precise as terms like "communication disorder," "Pervasive Developmental Disorder," or even "autism spectrum disorder," we think it's a useful term, so we use it to describe the set of symptoms we outline in Part I.

No matter what terms you use, it's important to remember that although some people use labels to limit others, you can use labels to encourage greater awareness, cooperation, and understanding. An autism label can be useful in terms of obtaining services, for example.

What You're Not to Read

You don't absolutely, positively have to read every word in this book, but that doesn't mean that you shouldn't. The bottom line is that if you're in a hurry, you can skip some topics and still not miss the important stuff you need. Sections you can skip include the following:

- ✔ **Text in sidebars:** Sidebars are shaded boxes of text that appear throughout the book. They contain personal stories and observations, along with more technical discussions, provided for your enjoyment.

- ✔ **Any text with the Technical Stuff icon attached:** These paragraphs provide further explanation about autism, but the information isn't necessary for your general understanding of the subject.

Foolish Assumptions

We assume that you're affected by autism or an autism spectrum disorder, either personally, professionally, or both. You've probably heard the term Pervasive Developmental Disorder or autism spectrum disorder, but nobody has explained what it has to do with autism. You can attribute the lack of common knowledge to the fact that researchers still disagree about how to classify autism-related conditions.

We assume you have a brain, but that you don't perform brain surgery. Because you're not a brain surgeon, this book avoids the kind of terms only a doctor completely understands. When we include technical terms, we provide explanations.

We assume that if you're a parent or caregiver to a person with autism, you've come to this book to find out how to understand and relate to that person more effectively. Or maybe you want to understand yourself better, having been diagnosed with Asperger Syndrome or autism at some point in your life. If this is the case, we assume that you want to explore what makes you neurologically different and how people like you have coped with it and gone on to find ways to leverage their strengths.

Although we write many chapters with early intervention of children in mind, we assume that some of you want information about adult issues. Many adults may not be attending school, but they have questions pertaining to work, health, and relationships, and we try to address these concerns as well.

How This Book Is Organized

We set up *Understanding Autism For Dummies* in self-contained chapters that deal with many different topics. You can read the chapters out of order, or you can consume the book cover to cover. The following sections describe the parts of this book so you can pick and choose your spots.

Part 1: Understanding Autism

Part I provides the basics — what autism is, what may cause it, what symptoms you should be aware of, and where to go from there. In this part, we begin by exploring the behavioral symptoms of autism and how medical doctors typically diagnose — or misdiagnose — autism spectrum disorders. We explain the many forms autism can take and give you a checklist of behavioral symptoms. We discuss why people often confuse autism with other disorders and how you can sort them out. We include info on how you can plan ahead after you get a diagnosis and what steps to take to get help. Finally, we devote a whole chapter to Asperger Syndrome, autism's often-misunderstood cousin.

Part 11: Addressing Physical Needs

In Part II, we lay out the options for medical treatment — from medications that may alleviate some symptoms associated with autism to complementary biomedical treatments breaking new ground today.

Healthcare can be very difficult when the patient can't explain what's bothering him. This part goes into depth about what medical science has discovered about treating autism, what medications to consider, and health issues, such as food intolerances and digestive problems, many autistic people face. And because food intolerances are so common, we devote an entire chapter to helping you understand what dietary changes you may need to make. Another chapter stresses boosting the immune system. We also strive to answer some important questions you may have: What symptomatic relief do drugs offer, and is it okay to prescribe them for children? What does the emerging biomedical research show? How do you find a doctor you can trust?

Part III: Enhancing Learning and Social Skills

Learning and social skills often go hand in hand, so we group these topics together in Part III. We begin by presenting some interventions you can try with your loved one. We help you understand educational/behavioral treatments, from the Lovaas method, the original and still the most common standard of intervention in many places, to newer options gaining in popularity, such as Greenspan's Floortime, the Miller Method, and Daily Life Therapy. We also do our best to present some nonmedical interventions you may want to explore to help with sensory, social, or other challenges.

Children with autism can learn, but in different ways than you may think, and they can be very different from one another. Switching the focus to education, we lead you through the process of finding an appropriate classroom or program for your loved one and developing a proper educational plan tailored to his or her needs. We're also there to help protect your child's educational rights — what state or district you live in can make a big difference in how people interpret and implement the law.

Finally, we give you some tips on managing your loved one's sensory issues and on fostering good relationships with autistic children and others.

Part IV: Living with Autism as an Adult

What happens after childhood? Many autistic individuals go on to live independently. Other adults may require permanent care or some combination of supervision and partial independence. In Part IV, we address many life issues that adults with autism face. We explain what life can be like for autistic individuals after high school, we explore some ways people with autism can prepare for romantic adult relationships, and we help prepare the autistic adult and his or her caregivers for the financial aspects of independence, whether it's full or partial.

Part V: The Part of Tens

Of course, lists are what many readers can't resist looking at first. We don't mind; feel free to skip to the back of the book, where you can find lists full of helpful hints and tips. We present some answers for the challenging and sometimes uncomfortable questions people with autism (and their loved ones) are bound to hear. We also give you ten important things to do after you receive the autism diagnosis.

But wait — there's more! We include an Appendix at the end of the book that lists places you can go for treatment and associations and organizations that deal with research, treatment, advocacy, and parental issues. These organizations can help you build upon the information you find in this book.

Icons Used in This Book

The icons in this book help you find particular kinds of information that may be of use to you:

This icon gives tried and true time- and hassle-saving strategies that help you implement our suggestions and recommendations.

This icon denotes a take-home message that you should keep with you for the future. What you read here is the bottom line.

This icon presents information that you can read for further understanding; however, the info isn't necessary for grasping the concept.

This icon warns about potential traps that can derail you in your quest to live with and understand autism.

This icon draws your attention to ideas or methods that require further research to see if they fit your unique situation.

Where to Go from Here

Autism isn't a simple subject you can master in an afternoon, like, say, square dancing. (Please, no letters from angry square dancers!) As such, we didn't design the book to be a front-to-back page-turner that prepares you for a test or project. You can jump in at any point, depending on what you're looking for. For example, if you or someone you know has just been diagnosed with autism, you may want to read Chapters 1, 2, and 18 first to better understand autism and what you should do after a diagnosis. If you're a healthcare professional or caregiver dealing with autism, you may want to skip ahead to Part II, which covers health care for people with autism. If you're an educator, Part III is for you, as it deals with learning. And if you or someone you love is living with autism as an adult, Part IV includes chapters that discuss relationships, work, and money managing for adults with autism.

If you don't have an agenda and just want to begin building your knowledge of the subject, start on any page and see what you find. Also, stay alert for news in the media and in other books.

Part I

Understanding Autism

The 5th Wave

By Rich Tennant

"Which approach to autism were you looking for?
Educational, medicinal, health & fitness, fashion
and accessories, automotive, vacation spots,
investing, barbecue recipes,...?"

In this part . . .

*T*he main thing people lack when they first come into contact with people who have autism or first discover signs of the disorder in a loved one is knowledge. Knowledge is the key to understanding, acceptance, treatment, and happiness. Allow us to help bring you that knowledge!

In Part I, you get the big picture about autism and autism spectrum disorders, including Asperger Syndrome. We explain why autism isn't simple to diagnose or to treat; you find out what common symptoms many (but hardly all) people with autism share; and you review current theories about what causes autism and how Asperger Syndrome fits into the picture. You also review the different types of autism. As you begin to understand what autism is and what it isn't, you start to see how you can make good decisions about treatment and education for people with autism.

Chapter 1

Autism: The Big Picture

With Lauren Underwood, PhD

In This Chapter

▶ Consuming the known facts about autism

▶ Reviewing the diagnostic process and symptoms of autism

▶ Coping with the impact of an autism diagnosis

▶ Implementing interventions to help your child's condition

▶ Taking steps if you think you have (or know of someone with) undiagnosed autism

*P*arents *never* want to hear that their child has been diagnosed with autism — and, at least initially, they certainly find it very difficult to accept the fact that autism has no known cure. However, if you observe characteristics in your child that you can't explain or alleviate, and if you can associate some of these characteristics with autism, you need to discuss your concerns with your doctor immediately. And if your child already has an autism diagnosis, you need to take action as soon as possible. Educate yourself about treatment options, and work with your doctor to formulate a treatment plan that meets your child's needs.

With emerging science, autistic children *are* getting better. Through treatment plans, the care of extraordinary physicians, and the support of family members and caregivers, autistic children are looking healthier, behaving more appropriately, making friends, having conversations, having play dates, and being mainstreamed at school. Your child can significantly improve and go on to maximize his or her potential abilities.

But before you reap the benefits of and make decisions about your child's healthcare, you need to empower yourself with knowledge. This chapter is a great starting point, because it provides a big-picture look at autism: what it is, how doctors diagnose it, and how you can manage the symptoms to make a difference in your child's life and yours — and you can!

What We Know — and Don't Know — about Autism

If your child has a developmental disability, such as an autism spectrum disorder, it's very unlikely that anything you did, or any specific event, caused his or her condition. Autism is a complex and not very well understood condition. Researchers are working on finding answers, but the questions themselves still aren't clear. As a result, the research is fragmented, and many theories are in the testing stage. Researchers are rapidly gathering data, but in the meantime, they disagree about how to interpret it. For example, researchers may observe malfunctions in different processes in the body of an autistic individual, but they can't agree on whether a particular problem is a symptom or a cause of autism. So, debates are ongoing in the medical community about what causes autism and how to treat it. (See Chapter 3 for a detailed discussion on the causes of autism.)

Here are the facts that all professionals and caregivers *can* agree on:

- Developmental disabilities such as autism are brain-based, neurological conditions that have more to do with biology than with psychology.

- Autism is the most common member of a family called *autism spectrum disorders* (ASDs), also known as Pervasive Developmental Disorders (PDDs).

- Autism is usually diagnosed by the time a child is 3 years old.

- Autism is found in every country, every ethnic group, and every socio-economic class.

- Autism affects as many as one and a half million people in the United States alone, with 24,000 children being diagnosed every year. This figure is comparable to other Western countries.

- Autism is diagnosed four times as often in boys than in girls.

- One in 166 children are being diagnosed with autism in the United States. That figure has skyrocketed in the last 30 years.

- Children who are diagnosed with an autism spectrum disorder need early intervention as soon as possible.

And here are the topics that professionals and caregivers are still debating:

- Autism is thought to be biologically based, although researchers are still trying to understand its exact causes. In other words, a child's genetic makeup must be predisposed to allow autism to develop, but genes are *not* the same as causes. A genetic predisposition provides fertile soil for a trigger, but researchers haven't been able to pinpoint the exact triggers (see Chapter 3 for more on the topic of causation). Each diagnosed case of autism appears to have its own pattern, like a fingerprint.

✔ Some experts believe autism has one overriding cause, and others insist that it has multiple causes. Some research divides autism into different subtypes based on the supposed trigger.

✔ Biomedical treatments can improve autism symptoms, but the debate rages on about whether biomedical treatments deal with the root causes of the disorder or simply help children who were "not really autistic" in the first place. The medical community doesn't widely accept many biomedical treatments; however, some doctors practice the techniques and experience great success with their patients.

Despite what the medical community still doesn't know about autism, we have reason for hope. New techniques for studying the human brain may lead to cures, new treatments, and interventions for autism and other puzzling neurological riddles such as Alzheimer's and Attention Deficit/Hyperactivity Disorder (see Chapter 2 for more on disorders that doctors may associate with autism). In addition, advocates are proposing more funding and legislation that will expand knowledge of autism as of press time.

Making the Diagnosis: Learning Your ASDs

The typical diagnosis of autism is a trickle-down process:

1. **You notice some atypical characteristics for your child at his or her particular age.**

2. **You schedule an appointment with your pediatrician, and if she suspects a developmental disorder, she refers you to a specialist (such as a neurologist).**

3. **The specialist tests your child to see whether any of the autism spectrum disorder categories apply and makes the diagnosis.**

Sometimes, a child can go undiagnosed until school age. With mild autism, a child may never be diagnosed. The pages that follow prepare you for the process at hand. See Chapter 2 for info on the different types of autism, Chapter 4 for more on receiving a medical diagnosis, and Chapter 18 to find out what to do after you receive a diagnosis of autism.

Looks can be deceiving

Because many people with autism seem physically healthy, some people — even parents of autistic children — believe the milder forms of autism aren't real disabilities at all. Outsiders may believe the diagnosis doesn't excuse poor behavior, and they blame the parents or the child himself for his lack of control. This blame game is unfortunate, because a neurological disability left untreated can have a far-reaching impact on a person's well-being and ability to achieve potential in life. For a list of responses to this reaction and other unfortunate beliefs, head to Chapter 17.

Understanding the diagnostic criteria

Autistic disorder is classified in the *Diagnostic and Statistical Manual,* a reference published by the American Psychiatric Association, as having 6 or more symptoms from a list of 12 possible symptoms, which the manual groups into three areas: social interaction, communication, and behavior. The DSM is revised regularly, and so are the categories.

Your child must have at least six symptoms, with at least two symptoms indicating social-interaction deficits and one symptom in each of the communication and stereotyped-patterns-of-behavior categories. A child who has most of the symptoms — up to 12, according to the American Psychiatric Association — will usually be diagnosed as *autistic,* or sometimes as having *classic autism.* Others who have only a few symptoms may be classified as *developmentally disabled, with autistic-like features.* If you're thinking this sounds imprecise, you're right. Researchers are still debating which disorders belong on the autism spectrum. Chapter 2 goes into more detail about autistic subtypes and related disorders.

Asperger Syndrome is also listed as one of the Pervasive Developmental Disorders. Diagnosticians focus on the social and behavioral categories for this part of the spectrum, due to the *lack* of significant clinical delay in verbal communication in people with Asperger Syndrome. (See Chapter 5 for more about Asperger Syndrome.)

Here are the 12 symptoms listed within their respective categories:

✓ **Social interaction:**

- Marked impairment in the use of multiple nonverbal behaviors

- Failure to develop age-appropriate peer relationships

- Lack of spontaneous seeking to share interests and achievements with others

- Lack of social or emotional reciprocity

✔ **Communication:**

- Delay in or lack of spoken language development (with no compensation through alternative modes of communication) in verbal persons

- Marked impairment in conversational skills

- Stereotyped and repetitive use of language

- Lack of spontaneous age-appropriate make-believe or social-imitative play

✔ **Behavior:**

- Preoccupation with at least one stereotyped and restricted pattern of interest to an abnormal degree

- Inflexible adherence to nonfunctional routines or rituals

- Repetitive motor mannerisms and preoccupation with parts of objects

- Persistent preoccupation with parts of objects

Besides showing at least six of these symptoms, your child also needs to show a delay in social interaction, social communication, or symbolic or imaginative play. The DSM and diagnosticians agree that these symptoms generally must occur before the child is 3 years old. A diagnosis of autism can occur later (even up to old age) if it's clear that the symptoms began before the age of 3.

After looking at the symptoms, criteria, and the vague labels attached, you may begin to think that autism isn't a very informative label. However, the diagnosis is a starting point for getting treatment. Although the Food and Drug Administration (FDA) hasn't approved any medical treatments for autism itself, it has approved treatments for related problems that may occur, such as irritable bowel syndrome, anxiety, vitamin deficiencies, and other physical conditions from which autistic people frequently suffer. When you treat those health issues, you can reduce or even eliminate many symptoms.

Seeing the signs: Autism symptoms

Professionals diagnose autism based upon symptoms shown in the categories of social interaction, communication, and behavior (see the previous section). We take the following sections to explain the categories of symptoms in greater detail.

Early diagnosis and intervention — before the age of 3 — are very important, because research shows that many features of autism respond better when you deal with them early. Sadly, some children don't receive an official diagnosis until years after their parents first suspect that something is wrong, which means they lose valuable time. Even some doctors don't have the necessary facts to provide an accurate diagnosis. You know your child better than any doctor, so if you disagree with a doctor's assessment, you should get a second opinion. Trust your instincts if you think your child isn't developing normally. (See Chapters 4 and 6 for more on finding the right doctors and choosing the best medication plans.)

Social development

People with autism — partly because of the problems they have with communication — have difficulty developing friendships and playing cooperatively with others. Often, kids with autism don't imitate others' behaviors, as children usually do, and they don't share their thoughts and observations. They also don't spontaneously try to connect with others, as other children will.

Despite the challenges children with autism face regarding social interaction, they still have the desire to interact. Children with autism may just need direct instruction to learn what others pick up by mere observation.

Even mildly autistic children who have normal language development (a diagnosis known as *Asperger Syndrome,* to which we devote Chapter 5) find it difficult to form peer relationships because of their problems in understanding social protocols and others' motivations. This social awkwardness can happen even if a child's IQ is off the charts. Children on this end of the autism spectrum display little understanding of appropriate behaviors, and they may be criticized for being "brutally honest," but many people note that they commonly lack pretension, dishonesty, flattery, and guile. However, they can also be quite hurt by their inability to connect socially, although they may not be able to express these emotions. Most people on this part of the spectrum lack the emotional vocabulary.

If you're a caregiver who wants to aid in your child's social development, the chapters in Part III can be of great help. If you're an autistic adult, head to Part IV to discover some tips on socialization.

Communication

Autistic individuals have trouble with language development, sometimes losing speech at 18-24 months (known as *regressive autism*), talking only late in development, or not talking at all. Children may repeat words and phrases like television commercials (a condition known as *echolalia*), having no apparent understanding of their meaning. The children may hear words but not be able to make sense of what they mean.

Non-verbal communication is also impaired in children with autism. Commonly, autistic individuals may not understand what gestures mean. They won't point to objects. They may not make eye contact or smile when smiled at. Their responses or lack of responses can be isolating, resulting in communication barriers rising between them and other people.

The chapters of Part III can take you from possible interventions to tips on how to improve your child's ability to communicate.

Behavior (activities and interests)

Autistic children often have obsessions or preoccupations with objects or with fantasy worlds (they may have trouble distinguishing fantasy from reality) that go beyond the normal interests of a developing child. For example, a child may play exclusively with string or believe she's an animal. She may have trouble transitioning from one activity to the next and insist on sticking to a ritual or routine — even one that seems to have no meaning. Repeated mannerisms such as hand flapping, rocking, or walking on one's toes may become habits.

Doctors are certain that autism affects the way the brain functions (and autopsies of autistic brains show abnormalities in different areas), causing a sometimes distinctive set of behavioral symptoms. Each behavioral symptom can range from mild to severe. To complicate things further, not all children diagnosed as autistic display all the behavioral symptoms. The behavioral symptoms govern the diagnosis, making treatment problematic.

Coexisting issues

Other conditions often coexist with autism, further complicating the diagnostic and treatment picture (and researchers are still debating whether the conditions are causes of autism; see Chapter 3). Some of the more common coexisting conditions include the following:

- Mental retardation
- Hyperlexia
- Obsessive compulsive disorder (OCD)
- Attention Deficit/Hyperactivity Disorder (AD/HD)
- Dyslexia

Conditions are considered *comorbid* if they occur at the same time as the autistic symptoms and are deemed to have roughly equal "weight" by the diagnostician. Other associative conditions such as depression are often secondary to the autism — in other words, a person's difficulties in interacting with the environment and connecting with others result in a depressive disorder.

Understanding the Far-Reaching Impact of Autism

An autism diagnosis has a far-reaching impact in your personal community. It affects not only the immediate family of the autistic person, but also extended family members, schoolmates, friends, medical providers, and many others with whom the person comes into contact. If you're a person with autism or the caregiver of a person with autism, you have to bear the brunt of the emotional impact of the diagnosis. But don't worry! With a positive attitude, you can weather the storm and enjoy the calmer waters that result from greater understanding and acceptance of how autism makes you the valued person you are. The following sections explain how the disorder can affect different people and how you can cope and help others cope.

How autism can affect the diagnosed individual

An autistic child faces large obstacles. He most likely needs (or will need) academic support in school; interventions for behavior before entering school; and help in communicating and socially interacting with others. Autistic children don't pick up social cues and nonverbal language and behavior, so they need a great deal of social support in order to make friends, interact successfully in social situations, and eventually become adults who can hold jobs, relationships, and financial security. This support, combined with physical symptoms that can be debilitating if left untreated, can make the autistic person feel like an outsider, as if he were literally "born on the wrong planet."

Understanding your autistic child is half the battle. The sooner he's diagnosed, the better the prognosis. If you're an autistic adult, you may have gone through most of your life undiagnosed and feeling different or odd, but you never quite knew why that was the case. We hope to help you understand yourself better with the information and advice in this book. People who are diagnosed today face a better future than ever before. Knowledge about treatment options and educational interventions is expanding rapidly, and a body of evidence on what works and what doesn't is accumulating.

How autism can affect families, schools, and communities

The ripples of a child's autism diagnosis can be felt throughout the child's family, the school system he attends, and the community of which he is a part. Within the family structure, parents may have to shift many resources — time as well as money — to focus on helping the autistic person, which may put strains on their marriage, on work, and on their relationships with siblings. Autism can tear families apart, as evidenced by the high divorce rate among parents of autistic children. (We talk about relationships between autistic children and their siblings, extended family members, and peers in Chapter 13.)

The rapid rise in diagnoses of autism in the United States (see Chapter 3) has created an enormous challenge for schools and teachers, many of whom aren't trained to deal with this once-rare condition. Community services are available in many places to help parents of autistic children, but the rise in spending hasn't kept up with the rise in numbers. Autistic people often require special-education services and have special health-care needs that schools and hospitals are just learning how to manage. But, as with the diagnostic process, awareness is getting better. You can help by becoming an advocate for autism. Find doctors and plans that work for your child, help your child's teachers learn how to give proper care and treatment, and know your rights under the law. Parts II and III will help you greatly in these areas.

 An enormous, educational consciousness-raising project on the subject of autism is underway, and we hope to be part of it. For example, April is Autism Awareness Month, where autism-related organizations pay special attention to increasing awareness of the condition through conferences, articles, rallies, and other means of publicity. Get involved!

How autism can affect caregivers

If you're the parent or caregiver of a child diagnosed with autism, you have a new job to add to your résumé. You now have to spend large amounts of time trying to help your child. And if you have other children and a spouse, you have to focus on your autistic child while making sure you don't neglect those relationships.

You'll likely have to redefine what your child's success in school and life will look like. You should continue to have high standards for your child, but be aware that progress will likely come in small steps and require hard work. The success of many autistic people wasn't easily achieved; success is hard-won for both the autistic person and the parents.

And unless money is no object, the disorder can put a strain on your financial resources, which means you may be faced with some hard decisions about your lifestyle and priorities. You may need to put off some of your plans or be creative with your assets until your expenses stabilize. (Head to Chapter 16 for more on money matters.)

What does all this extra work and burden mean for a parent or caregiver? It means stress, and plenty of it. Dealing with the stress, grief, guilt, anxiety, and pressure of caring for your autistic child and continuing to try to carry on with day-to-day life is a challenge for all caregivers of children with autism. For instance, the caregiver is responsible (with the help of some exceptional physicians/healthcare providers) for

- ✔ Personal education about ASDs and other subjects that may be quite foreign
- ✔ Deciding which interventions to try among the myriad options
- ✔ Picking caregivers and any therapists who work with your child outside of school
- ✔ Choosing schools and behavioral programs

✔ Being the case manager for your child's healthcare

✔ Implementing all the choices into one treatment and education program

Meanwhile, you hope that you make the right choices. Not only do you have the stress of many options and choices, but also you live in fear — fear that if your child gets lost or runs away, he won't be able to say who he is or where he lives, for instance. And within the chaos of all these challenges, you must try to keep a house, a family, and perhaps even a boss happy. Your marriage may be strained like never before, and many marriages don't make it. On the other hand, if you work at it, you can strengthen your bond with your partner, with your family, and with the child with autism. You can pull together like you never could've imagined. It's crucial that you "keep it together" and don't let the strain become overwhelming.

You can get a major boost and some much-needed empathy by joining a face-to-face or an Internet-based support group, where you can meet other parents of autistic children and share your experiences (see the Appendix for more). When you have support, you realize that you're not alone in your feelings and that you *can* cope.

Navigating the Sea of Interventions

After a professional (or multiple professionals) makes the autism diagnosis, the real work begins. Autistic people need much help. And because they're so varied in their symptoms and medical issues, they need individualized programs. Parents and others involved with their treatment and education need to realize that an integrated approach works best to ferret out the exact issues and work toward achieving the highest potential of each affected individual.

You'll probably be working with more than one doctor and specialist, so you have to act as your child's case manager, coordinating everything that goes on. This responsibility can be daunting, so we devote Chapter 4 to explaining the process of medical treatment to guide caregivers through it.

Many parents elect to pay out of pocket for more experimental or cutting-edge treatments in hopes of hitting a results gold mine. We don't discourage this way of thinking, but we firmly believe in fully investigating all your options before proceeding with what can be expensive, unpredictable procedures. You want to avoid jumping on every trend that comes along and bankrupting yourself in the process.

Whatever treatment options you decide to explore, be cautious about believing everything you hear and read — even from other parents, whose situations may be different from yours. Unfortunately, unscrupulous people will try to make a buck on people like you. People will attempt to exploit your concern for your child by selling you a program or remedy that probably won't work. Be on the defensive. Just because some treatment brokered over the Internet was the answer for one child doesn't mean it will work for yours. The effectiveness of the treatments you implement should be scientifically proven and, at the very least, safe.

The following sections go into more detail about the intervention options available to you. Be sure to find out which are covered by insurance or government mandates (many of them are).

One problem with using more than one intervention at a time is separating the effects of different treatments. If a child is undergoing biomedical treatments while working with educational/behavioral therapy, keeping the effects of the treatments straight shouldn't be a problem, because the effects of behavioral therapies are usually slower. We suggest that if you use more than one intervention at a time (which you probably will), make sure you make only *one* change at a time. For example, avoid beginning a new diet at the same time as starting a new educational/behavioral approach. Start with one to determine its effect and then layer on the next.

Using behavioral, developmental, and other educationally based interventions

Behavioral, developmental, and other educationally based interventions aim to change a child's behaviors by working on his communicative, cognitive, and social skills. Existing interventions don't cure "autism," per se, but they do improve its symptoms.

The following list outlines many of the intervention options available to you today (for a complete look at these interventions, head to Chapter 9):

- ✔ **Applied Behavioral Analysis (ABA).** ABA — sometimes called the *Lovaas method* after its inventor, Dr. Ivar Lovaas — is the most common behavioral intervention. It focuses on modifying behavior itself through a system of rewards and (much less commonly) punishments. The process is most often performed by trained therapists, who create a highly structured, individualized, and systematic learning environment for the children. ABA requires a large amount of time — at least four hours a day — to be effective. (Dr. Lovaas states that five to ten hours a week of behavioral therapy isn't enough to show a significant difference.)

- ✔ **Floortime.** This therapy is gaining wider acceptance today. Created by Stanley Greenspan, Floortime, also known as DIR therapy (Developmental Individual Difference Relation-Based Intervention), stresses emotional bonding with the child and requires the parents or guardians to do most of the therapy. Floortime concentrates on developing affection in the child with autism and looks toward closing the developmental gaps between where a child is and where he's expected to be. This program is also structured, individualized, and systematic and requires a large amount of time to be effective (at least four hours a day).

- ✔ **Miller Method.** The Miller Method focuses more on cognitive development and aims to close the developmental gaps between where a child is and where she's expected to be. Practitioners of the Miller Method strive to understand the world from the child's point of view. They believe that every child, no matter how confused she seems, is just trying to make sense of a confusing environment — and that it's the practitioner's job to help the child. Another goal of the Miller Method is to enable the child to make choices about her interactions with the environment instead of being constrained by routines and rituals.

- ✔ **Verbal Behavior.** This is a more recent, updated version of ABA. It stresses techniques to obtain verbalization from the child.

- ✔ **TEACCH.** Developed at the University of North Carolina at Chapel Hill, the TEACCH (Treatment and Education of Autistic and Communication Handicapped Children) approach focuses on employing other approaches as needed to provide an environment that enables the person with autism to be successful at using her strengths.

- ✔ **Daily Life Therapy.** This program, initially developed in Japan and now also residing in Massachusetts, focuses on balancing the physical, emotional, and intellectual components of a child. The program strives to teach children with autism to successfully interact in groups and, later on, in society.

- ✔ **Relationship Development Intervention.** This intervention concentrates on helping children with autism enjoy the pleasures of sharing experiences with others. Practitioners teach the children to be flexible in their interactions with others and to develop emotional connectedness.

When choosing a program for your child, you must realize that many approaches can be helpful — if you and the program's practitioners implement the therapy with the needs of your child in mind, and if the practitioners are skilled and caring individuals. Those are two BIG ifs.

The quality of the practitioners may be the single most important variable in your child's progress, whether you choose ABA, TEACCH, DIR, or some program you get off the back of a cereal box. You can find good and poor practitioners of all methods, and in many cases, the methods aren't really that dramatically different from each other in practice.

So, you should choose a program you feel comfortable with, but make sure to pay the most attention to *who* is working with your child and how the program is tailored (or not) to him. Is the teacher flexible and sensitive to your child's needs, yet disciplined in approach, for example?

Implementing occupational and speech-language therapies

People with autism are known to have difficulties in the areas of speech, motor skills, and sensory processing. If your child has trouble with speech and/or motor skills, you can ask for recommendations to speech-language pathologists and occupational therapists to help your child communicate better and improve her physical skills, including motor-coordination difficulties such as trouble with balance, clapping, or holding a pen steady to write legibly. (For more on these types of therapies, check out Chapter 10.)

Most people with autism have sensory issues they deal with. Usually, these sensory difficulties aren't due to any physical problems with the eyes, ears, mouth, or nose; they occur at the level where the brain processes input. So, the body may collect sensory information properly, but the brain doesn't interpret the information correctly. For instance, an autistic person may have trouble hearing and seeing at the same time. Autistic people also can have hypersensitive nervous systems, with senses that are so highly acute that fire sirens or scratchy clothes are physically painful. An autistic person may seem to withstand pain or fear better than the norm and do risky things such as walk on high ledges because he has no fear of falling.

If your child has sensory issues, you can employ *sensory integration therapy* to treat the sensory confusion that happens when some people with autism can't process sensory information correctly. The therapy is designed to reduce the sensory overload by bringing your child's sensory inputs in line. (For more information on sensory issues, look to Chapter 10.)

Practitioners often perform sensory integration, or SI, as part of occupational therapy or as one component of a behavioral intervention program (see the previous section). SI includes different types of *listening therapies,* which view autism as primarily stemming from a fundamental communication disorder. Doctors today use listening therapies to treat problems such as learning disabilities and AD/HD.

Medicating symptoms that can accompany autism

After you receive a diagnosis of autism for your child, you'll implement a treatment program that lasts until the child can function without support from that intervention. At that point, your doctor may prescribe medications to treat symptoms that accompany the autism disorder if needed, such as aggression, self-injury, anxiety, OCD-like characteristics, and depression. (Medicating children with autism is often controversial, as Chapter 6 explains.) Medication treatment should focus on symptoms that put the person at risk of harming himself or others or that inhibit the person's ability to gain from other treatment programming.

Medications commonly prescribed for adults and older children with autism include the following:

- Antipsychotics, such as Risperdal
- Stimulants to treat hyperactivity, such as Ritalin
- Antidepressants, such as Prozac and Zoloft
- Antianxiety medications, such as Xanax

Although no medications can cure the underlying neurobiology of autism, researchers are working to isolate the mechanisms in the brain that create the difficulties experienced by autistic individuals.

Applying biomedical and natural interventions

A growing school of thought considers autism a biomedical disorder that can be helped or even cured by changing the person's diet or removing toxins from his system and his environment. As of this writing, much anecdotal evidence — but little clinical evidence (the kind that doctors look for to make judgments, and the kind the FDA uses to make regulations) — is available that demonstrates results with some, but not all, autistic children. Clinical evidence is minimal because researchers find it tricky — ethically as well as logistically — to do a controlled study with autistic individuals. A *controlled study* occurs when researchers test a treatment variable against a control group that receives no treatment. Although the science has been moving forward, parents don't have the time to wait and have tried many things in efforts to expand their options before it becomes too late for their children.

Some conventional practitioners claim that if a cure results from biomedical interventions, the person didn't really have autism in the first place. Because doctors don't have enough evidence to definitively answer the question "what is autism" in the first place, and because we believe many people just want to know what interventions are available for their children, we include information on biomedical treatments in Chapter 7 and on improving your child's diet in Chapter 8. Many of the interventions we provide, such as supplementation or special diets, have little or no risk when implemented under the supervision of a physician.

Educating and advocating

When you picked up this book, you started to learn about autism and what it means — an important first step. You have a great deal of information available, and you can work to educate yourself. It may be the most rewarding and personal learning experience you'll ever have.

When you know enough yourself to begin helping others, you'll find that you have an important role. You'll be teaching others about autism spectrum disorders and advocating for disabled people all over the world. We're not saying that you need to speak at conferences or lobby your local and state representatives (although many parents and autistic people do). However, we're confident that you'll care so much about increasing awareness and services that you'll find yourself explaining autism to others who don't understand it. Even a task that seems as small as making the special-education program at your local school more responsive to autistic needs makes you an effective advocate for your child and for others with autism. You'll also find that no task is "small" in the world of autism.

You'll run into many people who don't get it. You may feel the need to defend your parenting abilities or your decisions. People may give you funny or disapproving looks or make comments if you go out in public with an autistic child who does something to attract attention. You can try to explain to others about your child, or you can decide not to let others' erroneous assumptions affect your peace of mind. (For some clever responses to absurd questions, check out Chapter 17.)

Some parents and people with autism carry informational cards with them. These cards often give brief explanations of autism and list hints for interacting with autistic individuals. Handing a card to someone (unless the person thinks you're selling something!) usually helps the person to stop and reconsider his or her thinking. For a ready-to-go version of this card, check out the Cheat Sheet in the front of this book.

Here are some examples of biomedical interventions, which you can combine with behavioral interventions in an integrative approach:

- ✔ Vitamin therapy, such as B12
- ✔ Omega 3 supplementation
- ✔ Wheat-free/dairy-free (GF/CF) diet
- ✔ Chelation (removing metals, such as aluminum, from the body)

If You Think You (Or People You Care for) Have Undiagnosed Autism . . .

Perhaps you're reading this book because you've been diagnosed with an ASD (or you think you may have one), and you want to get a better idea of what to expect. Maybe your child has been diagnosed recently. Perhaps somebody close to you has a diagnosis, and you think you may have a touch of it also. You may even be unsure that the diagnosis fits. We're here to help you sort all this out, no matter your situation.

Autism, as you'll find out in this book, isn't a terrible fate. People on the autism spectrum have a great chance to lead fulfilling and productive lives. With all the interventions now available, autistic people who lead successful lives can become the rule rather than the exception. Consider the achievements of the following folks with autism: Temple Grandin (animal science professor, cattle processing consultant), Liane Holliday Willey (presenter, communications consultant, author), Dena Gassner (recipient of a Masters in social work, educational advocate), Kassiane Sibley (nationally renowned gymnast), Valerie Paradiz (author, presenter, executive director of a school for Asperger students), Jason "J-Mac" McElwain (unexpected basketball star), Johnny Seitz (mime, body mechanics expert), William Stillman (author, educational consultant), Jerry Newport (author, presenter), Jerod Poore (Webmaster), and David Hamrick (recipient of a Masters in meteorology).

If you think you have autism, or know a person who does, you have a number of options (in addition to reading this masterpiece, of course):

✔ You can read more about the autism spectrum on Web sites we list in the Appendix to get more help.

✔ You can become familiar with autism literature.

✔ You can take the self-scoring Autism Spectrum Quotient (ASQ) test, created by Simon Baron-Cohen, at www.wired.com/wired/archive/9.12/aqtest.html.

The ASQ is only a screening instrument that tests for the possibility of Asperger Syndrome in older children and adults (see Chapter 5 for more on Asperger's). Scoring over the threshold merely means the possibility of an autism spectrum condition exists. For a true diagnosis and for help, see a qualified professional (start by checking out Chapter 4).

✔ If your concern is for a younger child whom you fear is more severely affected by autism, consider filling out the Miller Diagnostic Survey at www.millermethod.org/mds. Although you must pay a $100 fee for obtaining a report written by the senior staff at the Language and Cognitive Development Center, the results can provide useful insights on how to understand and help your child.

You should think of this assessment as a preliminary informative tool, not as a substitute for a direct, personal evaluation of a child by a qualified professional.

Chapter 2

From Classification to Treatment: Scanning the Autism Spectrum

In This Chapter

▶ Reviewing an overview of the autism subtypes

▶ Separating conditions that resemble autism from the diagnosis

▶ Identifying the disorder early in childhood and treating it promptly

▶ Giving an autistic child the best medical care and learning assistance

***

*A*utistic? You can't believe your child is autistic. Yes, he spends hours lining up his trucks in formations, but so did you when you were 4 years old, right? If you've heard of the disorder, you think of autistic children as closed off to others, angry, nonverbal, and in possession of some kind of special talent, like the ability to do lightning-fast calculations in his head. Your child doesn't fit this mental image. He seems very calm and expressive.

Even if your child doesn't point to objects, look at you the way his sister did at his age, or initiate conversations unless he wants something, you chalk it up to self-sufficiency and shyness, and you consider his fascination with light switches and toilet handles to be signs of a budding engineering talent. So why is your doctor talking this nonsense about Pervasive Developmental Disorders and autism spectrum disorders? And why would you put your child in some kind of training program when he should be out playing with his friends? Well, come to think of it, he doesn't seem inclined to play with other kids at all. He doesn't seem to have any friends.

Autism is a set, or "bucket" of behavioral symptoms that fall along a continuum from normal to abnormal with few dividing lines. Because science offers no brain scan or medical test that clearly identifies specific neurological disorders, diagnosis is still controversial and imprecise. Doctors base diagnosis on behavioral symptoms, which are subject to misinterpretation and may change over time. Symptoms can range from mild to severe.

The group of developmental disabilities we cover in this chapter is often called the *autism spectrum,* and the phrase *autism spectrum disorders* (ASD) may replace the term (Pervasive Developmental Disorders) PDD in the medical lexicon because people who support those with autism consider it more useful. In this chapter, we outline the subtypes of the autism spectrum and other conditions that people confuse with or that frequently occur along with autism. We also explore the benefits of early detection and treatment.

Every child with developmental problems, no matter the terminology that accompanies the problems — whether PDD, autistic, or autistic-like — still needs an individualized program designed to address his or her strengths and weaknesses. The same child may receive different diagnoses from different doctors, although — and this is what you need to keep in mind — the educational prescription is likely to be similar.

Surveying the Colors of Autism

Some people classify autism spectrum disorders into subtypes by their presumed causes, but because science hasn't yet resolved the causes, this practice is controversial and not widely accepted. (More discussion about causes appears in Chapter 3.)

You can also look at autism as a spectrum ranging from severe to light (see Figure 2-1). Leo Kanner observed the severe end of autism when he first wrote about the disorder in 1943, discussing children with severe challenges in communication and socialization. There is a perceived homogeneity of people at the severe end of the spectrum as depicted by the circles within the autism spectrum severity wedge in Figure 2-1. People with high-functioning autism (HFA) and Asperger Syndrome may be less severely affected, blending into general society. (In this book, Asperger's is considered part of the autism spectrum, although its precise relationship to autism remains unestablished.) Additionally, the notion of greater diversity of persons at the less severely affected end of the spectrum is depicted with the largest number of different shapes in Figure 2-1, as the condition fades into subclinical characteristics of autism and typical society. Persons with autistic tendencies that impact their daily lives but aren't strong or numerous enough to warrant diagnoses are often referred to as *autistic cousins,* a term reportedly developed by Kathy Grant when talking about people with a limited number of autistic tendencies at an Autism Network International event run by Jim Sinclair. John Ratey, MD, author of *Shadow Syndromes* (Bantam) and numerous other books, considers such people to have "shadow autism."

For the purposes of this book, we distinguish between Asperger's and HFA. Some researchers include Attention Deficit/Hyperactivity Disorder (AD/HD) on a broader autism spectrum because of its similarities to Asperger's, including the challenge of attention; others claim AD/HD is a clinically distinct disorder that may occur simultaneously with autism. We don't consider AD/HD a part of the autism spectrum in this book.

On the other hand, some researchers don't consider Asperger Syndrome to be autism at all; others consider it the same as high-functioning autism.

Figure 2-1:
The autism spectrum severity wedge — as viewed by Dan Rosenn, MD — depicts how autism ranges from severe to light.

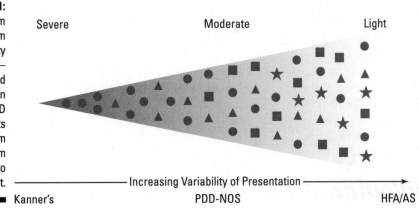

Severe   Moderate   Light

———————————— Increasing Variability of Presentation ————————→

Kanner's   PDD-NOS   HFA/AS

Child researchers Hans Asperger and Leo Kanner both (independently) described autism as a disorder in the 1940s, and speculation has continued on whether they were explaining variations of autism or separate conditions entirely.

Severe (or "classic") autism

Sometimes referred to as Kanner's Syndrome, severe autism is the classic type of autism that books and films often portray to great dramatic effect. You may also hear it called infantile autism, childhood autism, or simply autism disorder. Individuals with the classic type of autism may have more, and are more heavily affected by, symptoms within the areas of communication, social development, and activities and interests that we list in Chapter 1, or they may have only a few obvious ones. Some of the symptoms can be so debilitating — like a lack of functional communication — and the sensory issues so severe that the afflicted can barely stand to remain in their own skin. Other symptoms may be mild; a person may have good verbal communication skills but is unable to understand pragmatics, or the meaning "between the words".

People who are less-severely impaired by their autism are said to have high-functioning autism (HFA) or Asperger Syndrome (see the section "Asperger Syndrome" for more on, well, Asperger Syndrome).

Language develops late or not at all in people with Kanner's Syndrome, which is the main distinction between classic autism and Asperger's, as of this writing. Dr. Temple Grandin, a professor of animal science at Colorado State University who lectures and writes frequently on autism, and Kathy Grant, a political science graduate and autism advocate who has chronicled her sensory sensitivities, are some famous examples of high-functioning people with classic autism.

More than a misunderstood memo

As an instructor of autism spectrum disorders at Antioch College and in special education courses, much of my (author Stephen Shore's) understanding of social situations and office politics remains academic.

In my book *Beyond the Wall: My Experiences with Autism and Asperger Syndrome* (Autism Asperger Publishing Company), I write of sending a memo to a dean, quoting a department chairman word for word, with an innocent intent to lay everything about a situation on the table without considering others' reactions. The memo was passed on and misconstrued as disparaging toward the man, who I describe as an admired mentor.

It had never occurred to me that whatever I wrote to my dean would be repeated verbatim to somebody else and misinterpreted. The lesson for me is that I must write all memos as if anyone in the entire college may read them, and if I see a possibility that someone may look bad, I need to take special pains to prevent it.

What's the big deal, you ask? Anybody could make such a mistake — sending a memo that others misinterpret. But I think it goes further than being the stereotypical bookish, absent-minded professor. I have significant trouble remembering my students' faces, yet my senses are so sharp that I find shaving painful and threadbare socks — even when worn by others — profoundly upsetting.

Though I was initially diagnosed as a toddler as having "atypical development with strong autistic tendencies," my parents disregarded professional advice for institutionalization. With much support from my parents, teachers, and others, I was able to transcend others' low expectations, which is what I encourage others with autism to achieve. At one time considered classically autistic, I'm now thought of as an individual with Asperger Syndrome, or mild autism. I attribute many successful interpersonal situations I encounter to the assistance of outside interpretation from my wife and others, enabling me to have what I feel is a productive and fulfilling career.

PDD and PDD-NOS

Pervasive Developmental Disorder (PDD) is the category containing autism, Asperger Syndrome, Pervasive Developmental Disorder-Not Otherwise Specified (PDD-NOS), Childhood Disintegrative Disorder, and Rett Syndrome. PDD-NOS is a catchall diagnosis for people having most but not all the characteristics of autism (see Chapter 1 for more on symptoms). People with these disorders are often described as "autistic-like" or developmentally delayed with autism symptoms; recently, experts have put them on the autism spectrum.

Although classified under the Pervasive Developmental Disorders, Rett Syndrome has identifiable physical differences such as reduced muscle tone (causing the child to seem "floppy") and stereotyped hand movements such as wringing or waving. Additionally, Rett Syndrome produces an identifiable chromosomal difference.

People with PDD-NOS need some special services but don't fit the behavioral criteria for any of the other categories of autism. Maybe the person lacks meaningful speech or has stereotypical movements such as hand flapping or rocking, but he or she doesn't have enough of the symptoms to fill the symptom bucket and be considered autistic. This lack of a label may make it tougher to get services, because the autism label — although considered stigmatizing by some people — does generally get you educational services in most places (see Part III for more on autism and education).

Because autism is a spectrum disorder without a clear dividing line, some people fall just on the other side of the line — they don't qualify for autism disorder because of late onset of symptoms, or they don't have enough behavioral symptoms. However, their disorder significantly impacts daily functioning on a regular basis.

Asperger Syndrome

Individuals with *Asperger Syndrome* range from people who may be considered a little eccentric to people who have serious difficulties socially, educationally, and professionally because they lack basic understanding of human interactions. People in the latter group often have to learn by rote things that other people consider common sense, such as how to read facial expressions, tones of voice (like sarcasm), and verbal expressions (such as "raining cats and dogs").

Many people with Asperger's have brilliant intellects yet are naïve and easily taken advantage of by others because they interpret situations at face value and miss social cues. Generally, "Aspies" lack common emotional responses and must learn appropriate social skills to function within society, but they're typically considered high functioning and may never be diagnosed at all. No obvious language delay comes with Asperger Syndrome; however, language tends to develop in a unique manner. Professionals dispute whether Asperger's should even be considered a disorder. People affected don't show the same delays in cognitive development or curiosity about their environment that people with classic autism do in childhood.

One well-known person with Asperger Syndrome is Liane Holliday Willey — a doctor of education, a writer, and a researcher — who realized she had the syndrome only after her daughter received a diagnosis. In her book, *Pretending to be Normal: Living with Asperger's Syndrome* (Jessica Kingsley Publishers), Willey explains how an undiagnosed individual often feels different from others but doesn't know why. The person doesn't seek a cure, only acceptance. "No matter what the hardships," Willey writes, "I do not wish for a cure to Asperger Syndrome. What I wish for is a cure for the common ill that pervades too many lives; the ill that makes people compare themselves to a normal that is measured in terms of perfect and absolute standards, most of which are impossible for anyone to reach."

Co-author Stephen Shore was once considered uneducable, but he has written poignantly about his struggles to understand social protocols that others take for granted (see the sidebar "More than a misunderstood memo" earlier in this chapter). Now considered to have Asperger Syndrome, Shore has written two other books and numerous articles, and he consults and presents internationally in addition to his work on this book.

You must understand that people with Asperger's don't lack feelings; their brains just function in such a way that they have trouble accessing and expressing feelings to others in a traditional manner. Chapter 5 describes how Asperger's relates to the autism spectrum.

Considering Conditions That Resemble Autism

Because doctors can't definitively, precisely diagnose autism, they encounter several other conditions and symptoms that tend to enter the diagnostic mix. This mixture makes awareness of conditions with related or similar symptoms important. The following sections outline such conditions and symptoms.

If a doctor diagnoses a child with some variant of autism spectrum disorder, such as PDD-NOS (see the previous section), the need for immediate intervention is the same. Such a diagnosis means that the child doesn't fit the clinical criteria for an autism diagnosis, and it doesn't address the severity of the symptoms that are present. You know whether or not your child needs help. Find out what help is available, get what your child needs, and don't sweat the diagnosis.

Childhood Disintegrative Disorder

Although not much is known about *Childhood Disintegrative Disorder,* children with this condition develop normally until they reach 3 to 4 years of age (rarely do children show change later than this, although some children develop this disorder as late as 10 years). At that point, they undergo a quick regression (faster than children with regressive-onset autism), usually losing all language ability and in some cases losing bowel and bladder control. In a show of other symptoms, the children can have epileptic seizures (Temple Grandin, a professor and writer living with autism, calls the children *regressive epileptics*), for which anticonvulsive drugs are often helpful, and motor disorders, probably caused by acute sensory processing problems.

The National Institute of Health considers Childhood Disintegrative Disorder part of the grouping of Pervasive Developmental Disorders (www.nimh.nih.gov/publicat/autism.cfm), but the federal Centers for Disease Control and Prevention disagrees. At any rate, Childhood Disintegrative Disorder is quite rare, and because they experience such a late onset of symptoms, these children require a very thorough medical workup. However, the individual treatment for these kids can be almost identical to treatment of autism.

Attention Deficit/Hyperactivity Disorder

Many children who exhibit more severe cases of Attention Deficit/Hyperactivity Disorder, or AD/HD, often share many of the characteristics and features with children at the high-functioning/Asperger's end of the autism spectrum — particularly in the areas of communication, social integration, and behavior. Some children get diagnosed with one of the disorders and then receive the other diagnosis at a later time.

Symptoms for both autism and AD/HD include problems with organization, sensory issues, attention, and social skills. However, the delay in acquiring language that occurs with more severe autism isn't consistent with AD/HD.

Diane Kennedy has three sons who have disabilities — one of whom was misdiagnosed with AD/HD rather than Asperger Syndrome — and she writes about how this happened in her book, *The ADHD-Autism Connection: A Step Toward More Accurate Diagnoses and Effective Treatments* (WaterBrook Press). If you think your child may be misdiagnosed, we recommend this book highly.

The lesson you (and doctors) should keep in mind is that the two disorders are frequently confused because of their overlapping behavioral symptoms. Also, hyperactivity doesn't always equal AD/HD. It can be part of many other childhood developmental problems.

The implication for parents is to know your child well and to make sure you get a second opinion with your child's diagnosis. AD/HD in schools is treated differently than autism: Although the disorder is considered a disability under the Americans with Disabilities Act, schools usually offer a different set of accommodations than they do for children on the autism spectrum.

Other possible diagnoses

Science has come a long way from the time when autism was confused with deafness or mental retardation, but not that far. Don't misunderstand: Some of the alternative diagnoses may be correct; that is, they may be present in addition to autism. However, a diagnosis of autism may better explain a person's symptoms than any of the psychological categories he or she can fall into when autism isn't a suspect.

If a child has "autistic tendencies" . . .

Jake was diagnosed as "developmentally disabled with autistic tendencies" at the age of 3, but his parents weren't satisfied with the diagnosis. His mother said she "ran from the autism label like the plague." Jake could recite videos and music lyrics, but he never expressed any of his own thoughts to his parents. (Many autistic children repeat phrases or words they hear often, such as television commercials, but they don't necessarily understand what they're saying. They can hear and repeat the words, but they can't process them. This is called *echolalia*.) And although he could identify letters of the alphabet at age 2 and work the microwave oven and computer at 3, Jake never initiated conversations or used language in a functional way — to express a meaningful request, for instance.

Jake's parents consulted with experts and decided to treat his condition as mainly *sensory integration disorder,* which means his brain has trouble organizing and making sense of sensory input from his environment. He was provided with auditory stimulation and sensory integration therapies (which we discuss in Chapter 10). After the first two weeks, his language began to blossom, and two years later, Jacob was speaking fluently and asking questions of his parents.

Every child won't respond to such treatment in the same way, but many parents are trying alternative therapies, with mixed success. The point is that doctors are applying a range of different diagnoses to the growing population of developmentally disabled kids, and a diagnosis of autistic tendencies may be given to a child who could just as easily receive an autism diagnosis. Jake's parents admit that they would've qualified for more financial assistance from their state had they accepted the autism diagnosis, yet they chose not to.

Sometimes people who are aggressive or seem resistant to authority are given a psychological diagnosis such as oppositional defiant disorder, conduct disorder, or borderline personality disorder. Bipolar disorder and depression are other diagnoses sometimes given to people who should be diagnosed with autism, which does lend itself to mood disorders. Obsessive compulsive disorder is also easily diagnosed in autistic children. A child may have any of these disorders in addition to autism, but autism should be considered the primary problem. You should press your doctors to investigate further if you aren't satisfied with the diagnosis or if your child doesn't improve after some rounds of medication.

Other syndromes that may look a bit like autism, but definitely aren't autism, include the following (**Note:** Some of these syndromes may occur *with* autism or be mistaken for autism; people can have more than one disorder at a time):

- Cornelia DeLange Syndrome
- Tourette's Syndrome
- Fragile X Syndrome
- William's Syndrome

✔ Down's Syndrome

✔ Landau-Kleffner Syndrome

Understanding Why Early Treatment Matters More than Classification

What an alphabet soup of diagnostic labels boils down to is that you need to worry more about actually understanding and treating a child's condition than about the clinical labels he or she gets stuck with. The previous sections in this chapter spend time outlining the subtypes and related disorders because the labels can be useful in some ways, but we don't want to focus solely on labels. The following sections stress the importance of early identification of problems, getting the best medical care available to you, and finding programs that can help children prosper with their conditions.

Despite the need to get past labels, you should recognize that a label is still very important for two reasons:

✔ The label is often the ticket to school, community, and medical services.

✔ Accepting the label given to the person you care for means that you've achieved an important milestone: You recognize that help is needed — and is on the way.

Attempting early identification and intervention

Researchers are able to identify symptoms of autism at younger ages, such as at 18 months, than ever before, a development that leads toward more emphasis on early treatment, simply because that time frame is where children can usually make the greatest gains. Pediatricians are now looking for potential markers, such as a larger head, and giving screening questionnaires to parents to identify early symptoms such as unusual eye contact and ability to follow a point. Also, autism experts are pressing pediatricians to use more direct observation to detect possible social clues, such as atypical vocalizations, including echolalia (the repetition of sounds and words from the environment; see the sidebar "'If a child has "autistic tendencies' . . ."). Other differences experts are pressing pediatricians to look for include

✔ A lack of joint attention

✔ A resistance to being held

✔ An appearance of deafness to words

The best thing you can do for your child — whether you think he or she's autistic or not — is to start an educational/behavioral program early to help with his or her communication deficits (for more on programs, see Chapter 9). And make sure your child gets medical help for any physical symptoms, such as digestive problems, he or she may experience. That's the bottom line.

According to Peter Mundy, a professor of psychology at the University of Miami, a social marker known as *joint attention* or *gaze following,* which neurotypical babies begin doing in the first 15 months of life, is impaired in autistic babies. Autistic babies don't follow or initiate eye contact in order to share an experience with a caregiver; they initiate eye contact for "instrumental purposes," which means to get something they need, such as food. Impaired joint attention can be a lifelong trait in autistic people, but Mundy says that if experts train doctors and parents to notice the trait earlier, caregivers may be able to identify and help children at risk as early as infancy.

Many professionals share a widespread agreement that social disengagement is what separates autism from other disorders. Children diagnosed with developmental disabilities share a common problem: They need help in communicating and developing social skills. Parents and other caregivers can teach these skills, and the sooner the better, because children's brains develop rapidly. So, whether your child is autistic or not, he or she still needs help, and you can focus on that.

We don't mean to imply that a diagnosis is unimportant, because it influences treatment, but in many cases where children are diagnosed as being on the autism spectrum, treatment is similar. And treatments that work for some children won't have any effect with others who have identical medical diagnoses.

Diagnoses and prognoses based on behavioral symptoms can and do change, as the stories of people such as Temple Grandin — an accomplished professor — and co-author Shore surely prove. Many people with autism have been misdiagnosed as having mental retardation, schizophrenia, AD/HD, and other conditions (see the section "Considering Conditions that Resemble Autism" for more).

Getting good medical care

People with autism require good medical care, both in diagnosis and in treatment. The proper medical care can help your child fulfill his or her potential and live a full and healthy life. But how do you know which doctor to trust? Credentials, although important, don't guarantee skill or insight in a professional. You need to have your child evaluated by more than one doctor. Experts in one particular disorder are likely to see every child through that diagnostic lens.

Although many treatments are changing as doctors diagnose many new cases of autism, and the medical profession and the public are more aware today, keep in mind that most parents of autistic children see the disorder before the pediatrician does. In fact, in many cases, parents see something years before doctors formally diagnose it. You know your child's behavior and history better than anyone. You need to communicate to professionals what problems you think she's having that impair her the most. You want your child to be helped, not just diagnosed. Don't allow anyone to dismiss your concerns arbitrarily. The sooner you get help, the better.

We know of one set of parents who found out about the diagnosis for their son, Jeffrey, by receiving a booklet and being told in hushed tones, "I'm sorry." That's a sorry way to deal with the issue. Jeff, now 7, can read at a higher level than grade level. He's exceeding everybody's expectations, and his parents have become active advocates in the autism community, partly because of the disappointing treatment they received from their first doctor.

If you think your doctor isn't taking your concerns seriously enough, you need to find a specialist and get more input. Many pediatricians don't have the training to screen for autism because they perceive it as rare and don't have experience with it. (You can find additional medical information in Chapter 4.)

Enrolling in effective early programs

Experts recommend enrolling children who show symptoms of autism in educational/behavioral programs as soon as parents and professionals identify the symptoms. Sometimes the school system is the first in line to refer the child for diagnosis, but you must remember that autism is a medical diagnosis, not an educational one.

Teaching credentials don't qualify a person to diagnose autism or other medical conditions. However, given that teachers are professionals familiar with many children, they can be very helpful in recommending an evaluation for children who they think may have trouble learning in traditional classrooms. So, if a teacher or school psychologist tells you that he or she believes your child may be autistic, you need to see a qualified professional.

A school psychologist, depending on the state and the individual's credentials or license, can diagnose a child (known as an *educational diagnosis*). A school can identify and label a child with autism for purposes of providing special services within the school setting. This label may or may not qualify an individual for community-based special services outside the school setting. The opposite is also true: If a doctor diagnoses a child with autism outside the school setting, the school is required to conduct an evaluation to determine what services are required by that individual child. The school isn't required, however, to provide a blanket set of services that the child may not even need.

Educational/behavioral interventions, which we discuss in detail in Chapter 9, are intensive, structured programs where a parent or a trained therapist works with a child to systematically teach behavior and communication skills. Most programs are based on behavior modification principles; some programs teach parents to work with their autistic children; and other programs are held in preschools that target play and communicative skills.

Some things to look for in a program include the following:

- ✔ Individualized attention paid to each child
- ✔ Broad-based curriculum that supports social interaction, play, and communication
- ✔ Systematic teaching that emphasizes outcomes (what the child should know and do)
- ✔ Family participation being encouraged by the facilitators
- ✔ A focus on functional skills (learning that has a purpose in the world)

Preschool-aged children can benefit greatly from a good early intervention program, and many states cover the costs under federal guidelines. Chapter 12 includes the educational rights of autistic individuals under federal legislation. With increasing diagnoses and knowledge, laws (and the funding for implementing them) are changing rapidly.

Chapter 3

Causes, Clusters, and Clues: Where Does Autism Come From?

In This Chapter

▶ Observing the rise of recent autism diagnoses

▶ Identifying genetic predisposition as a possible cause

▶ Rooting out environmental factors

▶ Resisting the urge to find a cure

*M*any things about autism remain unknown — including what every parent wants to know upon hearing a diagnosis: the causes of the disorder. We say "causes" rather than "cause" because it's possible — although not definite — that autism has several triggers. Research is still in the early stages, and the complexity of the condition means that scientists can draw very few definite conclusions. As of this writing, researchers have data that suggests correlations — or factors that are related to having autism — rather than data that suggests causation — or factors that would cause autism. The good news is that the U.S. government has increased funding substantially in recent times. The National Institute of Health now spends close to a billion dollars annually on autism research, up from $22 million as recently as 1997.

Because researchers have identified different types of autism, with different symptoms, they don't believe one theory on the causes will fit all types. Some autistic disorders may be environmental, and some may be entirely genetic. We just don't know. In the absence of any categorical answer for the question of autism's causes, researchers are proposing and debunking theories while they continue to study genetic and environmental factors that may help fill in pieces of the puzzle. In this chapter, we talk about what theories researchers have advanced and why. We also discuss the rising number of diagnoses of autism and what a cure would mean to people who have autism.

Although researchers will find a major cause for autism at some point — and many people think they've already found causes — that cause may not apply to everyone who has autism. So, bear this in mind: It isn't your fault. Your child was born with the genetic predisposition. It has become clear that autism is a neurobiological disorder with genetic roots — parenting has nothing to do with it. The best thing a wise parent can do is to keep current with interventions (see Chapter 9) and be cautious about where you put your money (see Chapter 16 for more on money matters).

Considering the Rise in Diagnoses

When the medical profession first diagnosed autism in the 1940s, the rate was considered to be between 1 and 4 out of 10,000 people. Since then — especially since the 1980s — science has seen a dramatic increase in the number of people with autism. According to the Centers for Disease Control in Atlanta, the incidence of autism spectrum disorders is 1 in 166 American children. (Autism appears in every industrialized country at roughly the same frequency. Researchers don't have good data on its incidence in developing countries, because the reporting and medical systems in these countries aren't fully functioning in many cases. However, many epidemiologists believe that the rates in these countries are likely similar.)

Some people contend that the population of autism has seen no real increase; they believe the numbers only indicate more accuracy in diagnosis. For instance, they say people who would've been diagnosed with mental retardation in the past now receive a proper diagnosis of autism. Also, they make the point that increased awareness of autism has led to more diagnoses in people considered borderline cases, such as those with Asperger Syndrome (see Chapter 5).

It appears from research, however, that even after professionals began controlling for better diagnoses and awareness of autism, they've seen an increase in cases of autism — not Asperger Syndrome — that they can't explain. This increase has led to great debate regarding the possible triggers.

The reality of the increased incidence is probably somewhere between greater awareness and better diagnostic tools, with some of the increase resulting from inappropriate autism labeling in pursuit of better educational services.

Exploring the Genetic Link

Researchers believe that a genetic component or predisposition is present in the majority of people who develop autism spectrum disorders. They point to irregular segments of genetic code as the culprits for some autism cases.

A genetic predisposition, however, doesn't dictate what may develop. A predisposition isn't the same as a cause. A person can have a genetic predisposition to heart disease or cancer but avoid it by living a careful lifestyle. Genetics doesn't equal destiny. Unfortunately, a person can have a genetic predisposition, lead a healthy lifestyle, and still develop a disorder. The following sections explore the connections between genetics and autism.

Familial patterns

Research has found that autism clusters in families. The federal Centers for Disease Control and Prevention (www.cdc.gov) has data showing the following diagnosis rates among family members:

- Identical twins, who have the same genetic makeup, have about a 75-percent concordance rate (meaning that both twins have autism).
- Fraternal (nonidentical) twins have a 3-percent concordance rate.
- The risk of autism in normal siblings ranges from 2 to 8 percent.
- Among families that contain diagnoses of autism, research shows a 10- to 40-percent increase in the diagnoses of other developmental disabilities, such as language delays and learning disabilities.

Researchers have concluded that families that carry autism genes also carry other conditions in members who don't necessarily have autism. The inheritance pattern for autism spectrum disorders is complex and suggests that mutations in a number of different genes (at least 10) may be involved, according to some research. That explains what Temple Grandin, an author and professor who has autism, calls the "highly variable nature" of autism. Craig Newschaffer at the Johns Hopkins School of Medicine estimates that 60 to 90 percent of all autism cases are genetically based. However, because of the complex nature of autism genetics, scientists don't have a test parents can order to see if their children are at an increased risk of developing the disorder.

Autism also tends to occur more frequently among individuals who have certain inherited medical conditions, including Fragile X syndrome, tuberous sclerosis, congenital rubella syndrome, and untreated phenylketonuria (PKU). (See Chapter 4 for more on diagnosing related medical conditions.)

Brain size and structure

Little is known about the etiology, or origins, of autism. Science has no test for it. But brain scans and other types of research have identified differences in the shape and structure of the brains — particularly in the frontal lobes — of autistic people, including those with Asperger Syndrome. Researchers are scanning DNA to try to put the genetic puzzle together and develop treatments, diagnostic screening tools, and tests that will help identify autism earlier.

Researchers haven't ruled out problems in pregnancy and delivery. Maybe the child gets exposed to neurotoxins (brain cell–destroying substances) such as mercury from contaminated fish, for instance, or experiences damage during the delivery process. These so-called environmental insults, or traumas, can interact with genetics to result in autism (see the section "Examining Biomedical Theories" later in this chapter for more on environmental factors).

For a picture of the human brain and the areas we mention in the following sections, check out Figure 3-1.

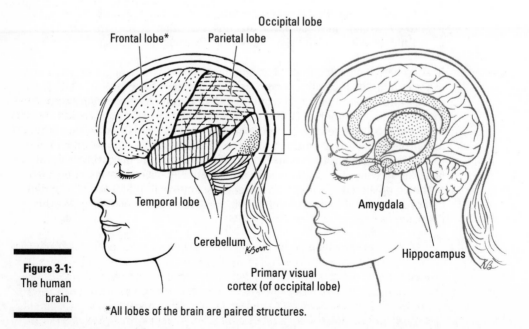

Figure 3-1:
The human
brain.

*All lobes of the brain are paired structures.

Initial clues about the brain

An abnormality in brain size and structure (along with functioning) is the general consensus for what causes autism, yet researchers don't know exactly which kinds of abnormalities they can attribute to genetics. Researchers at the Autism Tissue Program in Princeton, N.J. (www.brainbank.org), which studies donated brain tissue to understand autistic behaviors, say the cause of spectrum disorders could be innate genetic anomalies or environmental insults, or trauma. Research has found abnormalities in the brains of autistic individuals, namely in several neurotransmitter systems (neurotransmitters are the chemical messengers of the brain).

Researchers have found a larger overall brain size (or volume) in autistic children 12 and younger, although the parietal lobes — associated with movement, orientation, recognition, and perception of stimuli — are smaller than normal. The brain is actually often heavier in young children with autism. Also, the amygdala and the hippocampus, the memory center, are larger in autistic children but are the same size or smaller in adolescents and adults. It seems, however, that the connections are missing or not working correctly when the brain tries to process information between different local systems. Imagine that you can call your aunt in the next county, but when you try to call long distance, you can't get a line. This gives you a small taste of what autistic people must deal with.

An overgrowth of nerve connections in the brain, according to one theory, may cause the brain to become overwhelmed with neurotransmitter signals. This theory is consistent with research studies that have found that autistic babies' heads may grow faster than normal at various points. Why would this overgrowth occur? The normal cell "pruning" process of the fetus doesn't occur, and too many neurons exist.

How does autism develop?

Why would genetic abnormalities of the brain lead to autism? This isn't well understood, and researchers have different theories. Some researchers think of autism as a disorder of brain-circuit dysfunction. Researcher Eric Courchesne from the University of California found abnormal growth in the frontal cortexes of autistic brains; he deduced that the only normally functioning parts of the autistic brain are the visual cortex and the areas in the back of the brain that store memories. The frontal cortex is involved with sensory interpretation, which may explain why the visual cortex (responsible for visual perception) functions normally, yet autistic people seem to have visual processing (understanding what they see) issues.

Dr. Margaret Bauman, a pediatric neurologist and director of the LADDERS Clinic at Massachusetts General Hospital (www.ladders.org), believes that the structural problems of the autistic brain are primarily in the limbic system, which includes the amygdala (the emotion center) and the cerebellum, which is associated with the regulation and coordination of movement, posture, and balance. The cerebellum's involvement with a person's motor function could also explain the poor motor skills that individuals on the autism spectrum often display.

John Ratey, MD, author of *The User's Guide to the Brain* (Vintage Books) and professor of psychiatry at Harvard Medical School, writes that many autistic persons have eye-movement and hearing difficulties and facial-nerve palsy consistent with brainstem injury during their mothers' first trimester of pregnancy.

Other studies show increased cerebellum size, but increased by the same proportion as the brain as a whole. One study, conducted by Aylward, Minshew, and others found that the cerebrum (and other specific structures) was abnormally large in relation to the size of the brain as a whole.

Some parts of the brain work really well in certain autistic individuals, however. Temple Grandin, an author and professor who has autism, is one example. She has something akin to a videocamera in her head, allowing her to replay images and examine their details. Yet, she feels that other parts of her brain are underdeveloped. For example, she was never able to learn algebra because she couldn't visualize the concepts.

The brain-gut connection

Some researchers have focused on what they call the "second brain": the gut. The nervous system of the upper gastrointestinal, or GI, tract is extremely complex, and not much is known about how it interacts with the brain. This brain/gut connection is the focus of neurogastroenterology.

Dr. Jill James, a professor of pediatrics at the University of Arkansas, and Dr. Richard Deth, a Northeastern University neuropharmacologist, have conducted a preliminary study that found autistic children have great difficulty with what scientists call the methylation process.

Methylation is a metabolic process of making a molecule longer by adding a carbon. It's necessary for regulating DNA synthesis and enzymes, building neurotransmitters, synchronizing neurons, and to make cellular energy (see Chapter 7 for more on the process).

James's and Deth's work has been interpreted as follows: The faulty methylation process means that autistic people can't eliminate heavy metals such as aluminum, cadmium, lead, and mercury from their systems. Some researchers believe these metals lead to the symptoms of autism (you can get more detail on the heavy metals in the section "Heavy-metal poisoning hypotheses" later in this chapter).

Problems with methylation may be genetic or environmentally induced (see the section "Examining Biomedical Theories" for more on this), or they may occur through an interaction between genetics and the environment. Such findings are preliminary and require further research.

The testosterone link

A theory proposed by a British researcher, Simon Baron-Cohen, explains autism as the result of right-brain dominance, a pattern typically seen in males. He theorizes that too much testosterone in utero leads to the symptoms of autism. Autism, in this theory, is simply being "too male."

Baron-Cohen's research shows that fetuses producing high levels of testosterone may have a higher chance of developing autism. And it seems to be consistent with the fact that autistic boys outnumber autistic girls.

Baron-Cohen believes that the human brain specializes either in empathy (being able to appreciate and understand the emotions of others) or in understanding systems (being able to manipulate data). The former is an E-type brain, and the latter is an S-type brain, and he says that most boys have the S-type brain.

When studying the relationship between empathy and autism, Baron-Cohen found that children who experienced high-prenatal testosterone levels make less eye contact as toddlers and have lower communication skills at age 4, although he concedes that the necessary evidence to prove his theory isn't available. Other researchers have also criticized his work as playing upon stereotypes of girls as good with people and boys as good with objects. Those stereotypes may have some biological basis, but many exceptions to this generalization exist. Another problem with this research is that Baron-Cohen's paradigm doesn't explain all the symptoms of autism.

Examining Biomedical Theories

Researchers suggest that several distinct autistic subtypes exist that differ not necessarily in their symptoms and presentation, but in their causes. Some scientists believe that environmental factors (sometimes coupled with genetic factors) may explain what causes autism and the increase in autism diagnoses. They say that genetic factors alone can't be sufficient for the number of cases seen today; thus, a search for environmental triggers that cause autism in genetically susceptible individuals is underway.

Keeping elephants away: A correlation study

Here's an elephant joke I (co-author Stephen Shore) like to tell my statistics students while we're studying correlation:

I've been riding the 66 bus for the past five years. On most of my trips, I like to throw small pieces of tissue out the window along the way. Finally, another fellow who regularly rides the same bus asked with great curiosity, "Why do you keep throwing paper out the window?" I told him that I have a great fear of elephants. He looked at me strangely and commented that little pieces of paper wouldn't keep them away. "They sure do," I said. "I haven't seen an elephant in any of my five years of travel on this bus!" The correlation between my littering the street with paper and the lack of elephants in downtown Boston doesn't illustrate, however, whether my actions cause the elephants to stay away. Autism researchers face a similar correlation problem. Do the conditions autistic people have cause the autism, or are they simply results of the autism?

In this section, we discuss theories involving allergies or food intolerances, heavy-metal poisoning, and autoimmune responses and triggers. Researchers are currently investigating all the theories, which means that none of them have enough supporting evidence to say they've been proven correct as of this writing. The problem (which we explain in the upcoming sidebar) is establishing that causation is taking place, not simply correlation. None of the previously conducted research has been able to determine if the brain differences, the poor elimination of toxins, the poor processing of proteins, and any of the other issues are causes or simply results of the autism.

What do allergies have to do with it?

The type of allergy that plays a role in autism is different than the allergies most people are aware of, such as reactions to bee stings. The kind of allergy associated with autism doesn't show up immediately; thus, you can more accurately refer to these allergies as intolerances to substances (as we discuss in Chapter 8). Many autistic individuals are intolerant of dairy products or other common foods such as eggs. Some people believe that these intolerances wreak such havoc with the brain that they actually cause autism. Others argue that anyone who's cured of autistic symptoms by reduced exposure to allergens was never autistic in the first place. Researchers have the proverbial chicken and egg problem here.

One theory, the *cerebral allergy theory,* points to how some intolerances are common across most of the autism spectrum. The theory states that the stomachs of some autistic people lack the enzymes needed to digest some proteins, and that these proteins cause harm to their brains by migrating into their bloodstreams (via leaky guts; see Chapter 7); the proteins may also cause the diarrhea or constipation common in autistic children. According to the Autism Society of America's "Statement on Dietary Interventions," research has found "elevated levels of certain peptides" in the urine of autistic children. The ASA also says the following:

> "The incomplete breakdown and the excessive absorption of peptides may cause disruption in biochemical and neuroregulatory processes in the brain, affecting brain functions. Until there is more information as to why these proteins are not broken down, the removal of proteins from the diet is the only way to prevent further neurological and gastrointestinal damage."

Some parents who remove dairy products (containing casein) or wheat products (containing gluten), which are structurally similar proteins, report improvements in digestion, mood, and sleep. (For more on diet and what you can do to help, see Chapter 8.) Some parents have claimed cures for their children through dietary and other interventions.

The maldigestion of dietary proteins theory also carries the label *opioid peptide theory,* because it seems that these proteins can act like opiates, or painkillers, in the systems of people who can't digest them.

Heavy-metal poisoning hypotheses

If a child has too much metal in his or her system, it may be genetic or environmentally induced, or it may occur through an interaction between genetics and the environment. The problem is significant because high levels of these metals can disrupt the brain and the nervous system, resulting in autistic symptoms. Research done by neuropharmacologist Dr. Richard Deth, of Northeastern University, among others, is consistent with a heavy-metal theory of autism (not the title of a bad hair band from the 1980s, we promise). With this hypothesis, researchers state that a metal such as mercury or lead can cause neurodevelopmental disorders in a subset of susceptible children who lack the genetic ability to excrete heavy metals from their systems.

Some potential sources of mercury or other metals harmful to the body include the following:

- ✔ Dental amalgams or fillings
- ✔ Fish, such as tuna
- ✔ Power-plant emissions
- ✔ Lead-based paint

✔ Cigarette smoke

✔ Well or tap water

✔ Vaccines

✔ Swimming pools and hot tubs treated with copper sulfate

Some autistic children have been shown to have, when tested, excessively high levels of metals in their systems, although research has not yet established this as fact. Most healthy bodies excrete metals, but researchers have theorized that autistic children have great difficulty excreting them because of lower rates of glutathione and other proteins that work to eliminate metals such as aluminum, cadmium, lead, and mercury. (See Chapter 7 for a discussion of *chelation,* or the removal of heavy metals, a controversial step that some parents are taking to protect their children.)

The vaccination controversy

Research has provided two theories about vaccines and their role in autism. The first relates to the role of thimerosal, a mercury-based preservative that used to come in a number of vaccines as well as contact-lens solutions. The second theory deals with a possible bad-interaction effect between the components of the Measles, Mumps, Rubella (MMR) vaccination, which is a live vaccination that doesn't contain thimerosal, and the presence of residual measles in the digestive tract (see the section "Autoimmune or virus-induced theories of causation").

These theories have been advanced to attempt to explain the regressive form of autism. Between 18 to 24 months is when most children with regressive autism begin showing symptoms, which is the same period of time when children receive many vaccinations, resulting in a high correlation between that period of time and the onset of autistic tendencies. However, correlation isn't causation (as we explain in the sidebar "Keeping elephants away: A correlation study").

The debate about thimerosal is ongoing, although the National Academies' Institute of Medicine in Washington, D.C., has stated that it has found no conclusive evidence to implicate thimerosal in vaccines. Yet, some researchers, many parents, and the Autism Society of America (ASA) don't believe that professionals have done enough research to completely rule out damage. The ASA issued a statement saying that "Large-scale, epidemiological studies, which do not prove cause and effect, cannot appropriately answer the question at hand." The epidemiological studies used to disprove the theory, the society argues, didn't take into account that only a small subset of a population may be genetically susceptible to developing autism.

In any case, you may want to reconsider your child's vaccination schedule. According to Stephanie Cave, who wrote *What Your Doctor May Not Tell You About Children's Vaccinations* (Warner Books), a child in the United States now receives up to 33 shots by the age of 5. In some cases, a 15-month-old child may get as many as half a dozen shots in a single medical visit. Cave doesn't advocate eliminating the vaccination of children. Rather, she makes recommendations for safer vaccinations by adjusting the administration schedule to allow the children's immunological systems, and other systems, to accommodate the materials injected into their bodies. (See Chapter 6 for more on inoculations.)

One subset of the heavy-metal theory proposes that pregnant women who ingest contaminated fish or have fillings containing mercury can pass the metals on to a developing fetus. However, it may not even be necessary for a child to gain exposure to higher-than-normal levels of a toxin — if he can't excrete metals from his system, even normal exposure may be problematic. Therefore, if a child has a heavy metal problem, doctors can't say for sure whether it's primarily an exposure problem or an excretion problem.

The heavy-metal pattern isn't identical in all cases. Many symptoms of autism are similar to the symptoms of heavy-metal poisoning. Although the symptoms of mercury poisoning and autism overlap by about 90 percent, some researchers have pointed out that the pattern of mercury poisoning is quite different from that of autism.

Autoimmune or virus-induced theories of causation

Anywhere from 30 to 70 percent of autistic children have subtle immune system abnormalities. Some doctors believe that autism may be triggered during pregnancy, due to environmental influences to the developing baby. Natural stress hormones from the mother, or any trauma such as chemical exposures, may disrupt normal early development.

Immune-system problems in a pregnant woman or developing child may also contribute to the symptoms, and maternal viral infections may be one of the noninherited causes. For example, epidemiological studies show a risk of autism in the offspring of mothers exposed to the rubella virus, or German measles, early in their pregnancies.

Many autistic individuals have family members with autoimmune diseases such as diabetes or rheumatoid arthritis, suggesting a link between autism and autoimmune problems. Certain research has suggested that a disruption in the balance of cytokines (protein molecules that carry messages between B, T, and other immune cells and that affect sleep and fever responses) is a possible cause of autism.

As you can see, some research suggests evidence for autoimmune theories, but other research is inconclusive. Autopsies of people with autism have revealed unusually low numbers of critical immune system signaling components, called *Purkinje cells*. However, research hasn't yet turned up a correlation between autoantibodies in the blood and brain abnormalities.

Research such as Andrew Wakefield's initial study in 1998, which found traces of measles in the stomachs of some autistic children, has implications unrelated to the thimerosal controversy (see the previous sidebar). Some theorists have used these findings to speculate that faulty immune system reactions to the measles virus itself, not the mercury-laden preservative thimerosal found in some other vaccines, cause autism symptoms. In other words, the autistic children's systems couldn't eliminate the virus the way that normal children do after vaccination, so the virus stayed in their bodies.

We give you more discussion on safe inoculation scheduling in Chapter 6.

The Backlash Against the Cure

One day we will have a better understanding of autism and its causes. Until then, some autistic people say they want to have relief from some of the unpleasant symptoms of autism, but they don't necessarily want to be "cured." Being "neurotypical," they say, isn't for them. In other words, they don't want to give up any of their unique attributes.

A number of autistic individuals have spoken out, suggesting that they don't need or want to be cured and expressing the opinion that intolerance of people who are different from the norm is the greater problem. Many people argue that autism, particularly Asperger Syndrome, isn't a disease or a disorder in need of treatment or cure; they believe autism is simply a different type of brain wiring.

These advocates warn that trying to eliminate autism from the population will result in the loss of great talents and diversity for future generations. They find the idea of developing a genetic test to detect autism in a fetus especially disturbing and alarming. Society benefits from the talents of autistic people, they say.

Autistic or supposed-autistic historical figures have made great contributions to society, and their unconventional thinking generates innovative solutions to problems. Society may lose these abilities forever if we eradicate all traces of autism. Even founding father Thomas Jefferson, in the book *Diagnosing Jefferson* (Future Horizons), by Norm Ledgin, is theorized to have had Asperger's.

This strain of thinking points to the delights, growth, and greater perspective that a child with any level of autism brings to a family. Some siblings of autistic children may have greater burdens, but through their challenges, they grow up to be leaders for tolerance and understanding. (For more on familial relationships dealing with autism, see Chapter 13.)

Some individuals with ASD, on the other hand, say that autism has caused enough pain in their lives that they wish for a cure.

The gift of a special perspective

Chris Collins is the father of an autistic child, Nikki. He believes that autism isn't a disorder, but a gift. "People often react to Nikki's autism by saying, 'I'm so sorry,'" Collins says, but he considers himself lucky to have such a special daughter. Collins lives with his wife, Eileen, and their three children in New Jersey, where Nikki attends school (half the time with a classroom aide, half without). Here's how he describes life with Nikki:

"Our daughter, Nikki, is the second of three children. Born in 1995, Nikki is a strikingly beautiful little girl with a very charismatic personality. We call her the 'air that we breathe' as a family. We learned about seven years ago she is autistic. Shortly after that day, my wife and I made a decision in very casual fashion: We were going to pursue the same path of happiness that we planned on our wedding day. We were going to treat Nikki exactly as planned. We were going to continue to enjoy all the things in life that we promised ourselves that we would enjoy, and Nikki would be part of every minute of it. We have learned more about love, appreciation and the things that really matter in life than we could have ever imagined. Nikki is an amazing human being who teaches very strong lessons each and every day. One very significant characteristic of autism is that she only sees the world in a literal sense. There is no sarcasm, exaggeration, substitution, or lies. Everything is what it is, and what a wonderful influence and lesson that has been for our family. One recent day, while on vacation, my wife and I were casually talking about the possibility of ever finding a cure for autism. My 12-year-old son, Christopher, quickly interrupted and with tremendous conviction and emotion said, 'I hope not. I want Nikki to stay exactly the way she is.'"

"We as a family have no illusions and do not labor in the belief of a miracle cure. Nikki will most likely live with us for the rest of our lives. She will never have close friends or ever be interested in the fun things that are so important to little girls. We know that the stares and the embarrassment over her peculiar behavior in public places will be there forever. We know that every public venture or event could have the potential for unknown adventure. We also know that having Nikki has been a gift that far exceeds anything that we could have ever hoped for in life. Although a major characteristic of autism is the need for sameness, a day does not go by that Nikki does not do or say something new that makes us stop and think about how special her perspective on her surroundings is. She's a little girl who loves Christmas but couldn't care less about gifts. It's the lights, the decorations, and the warmth that she feels in the house that make her so happy. One year it took until June for her to open the last of her Christmas presents. As a family, we have chosen to appreciate that gift and live our lives, thankful every day for an autistic child to be part of our lives. We have made the conscious decision that we would not let autism slow us down, but rather allow it to make the ride of life more rewarding."

For more perspectives on how autism affects familial relationships, check out Chapter 13.

Most people believe that it remains our moral and ethical obligation to people with autism, as well as to society as a whole, to continue developing interventions aimed at helping people with autism use their strengths in order to build fulfilling and productive lives.

On the subject of a cure

Here are the words some autistic people offer up about cures:

- **Temple Grandin:** "If I could press a button and not have autism, I wouldn't do it."

- **Donna Williams:** "Some people seek 'cures' as though there is a 'normal' person within an 'autistic' shell just waiting, like sleeping beauty, for the spell to be broken. Some look only for causes, forgetting the 'now' that people with 'autism' and those who support them have to tackle today and again tomorrow." (*Autism: An Inside-Out Approach* [Jessica Kingsley Publishers])

- **Unknown author:** "Sometimes I feel angry when I read about attempts being made to 'cure' autism. I do not wish to be 'cured' from my autism, and many autistic persons who are able to communicate their feelings say the same thing. Autism is not something that I have, it is something that I am. Autism is in every emotion I experience, in every thought I think . . . Everything! Autism is not a cage, with us as the prisoners. You cannot talk about a person 'emerging' from autism. If it were possible to remove autism from a person, you would get a different person. A person who, perhaps, fits in better with his surroundings. Maybe a person who abides by the rules of society more. A person who does not stick out. That person will look identical to the previous one, but will be a different person nonetheless." Taken from within.autistics.org/ nocure.html.

- **Co-author Stephen Shore:** "Fortunately, I am able to successfully use my set of characteristics, which we refer to as autism, and do not wish to be 'cured' out of a fulfilling and productive life. However, we are duty-bound to help persons more severely affected with autism to lead fruitful lives to their greatest potential by using their strengths."

Chapter 4

Getting a Diagnosis

With Lauren Underwood, PhD

*P*erhaps your child has become withdrawn from the world or lost his abilities of speech. Maybe he enjoys spinning objects hours on end, and you're concerned. Maybe a preschool or elementary school teacher recently capped her comments on your child's difficult time with a suggestion for an evaluation just to make sure everything is okay. You even took your child to his pediatrician recently, and the doctor looked quizzical after the examination and recommended that you see a specialist. These are just some of the common pathways to an autism spectrum diagnosis.

Hearing a doctor associate the word *autism* with your child can be a terrifying experience for a parent. Acceptance is especially tough when the child's early development seemed normal. Any regressive changes the child experiences can be scary for the family and for the child himself. Your best course of action is to arm yourself with information. Ingesting as much info as you can helps you confront the fear, get a diagnosis, and set up a treatment plan that works for you and your child as quickly as possible (head to Parts II and III of this book for more info on treatment plans).

In this chapter, we help you track your child's symptoms so you can get a proper diagnosis; we point you in the right direction to find qualified professionals who can assess and help your child; and we begin to help you come to terms with this difficult situation so you can take the necessary action to ensure a full life for your family.

Tracking Your Child's Medical History

Many new parents keep a medical history or diary of some sort for their children (whether motivated by doctors, family history, or their own record-keeping instincts). A medical history is a helpful tool in any investigation of medical conditions that arise at any point in a child's life. The history is especially helpful in diagnosing autism because you've kept track of when the child reached milestones and you've possibly found patterns in medical symptoms.

You can keep a medical history for your child in a number of ways — in a computerized spreadsheet or in an unspectacular loose-leaf notebook, for example. Whatever method you choose, make sure your system is organized and makes it easy to pull out needed information about your child.

Here are some important bits of information to keep track of in your child's medical history:

- ✔ Location and date of the child's birth
- ✔ Any changes in feeding patterns or schedules
- ✔ Infections, including ear infections
- ✔ Antibiotics and other medications taken
- ✔ Vaccinations received
- ✔ Developmental milestones, including age of rolling over, smiling, sitting, crawling, talking, and walking
- ✔ Changes in the child's life, such as the following:
  - • Moving to a new home
  - • Change in family structure, such as marriage, divorce, death, siblings, grandparent moving in, change in health status of a close family member, and so on
  - • Starting or changing schools
  - • Making or losing friends or other social milestones
- ✔ Medical procedures and events, including
  - • Illnesses
  - • Treatments
  - • Surgeries
- ✔ Behaviors of concern, including
  - • Changes in verbal and other communicative ability
  - • Frustration

- Strained interaction with others
- Repetitive motions
- Perseveration

Make sure you keep records of the mother's pregnancy. The records may contain information such as medications taken or illnesses experienced during the pregnancy; the doctor can use this information to help make his or her diagnosis and recommendations for treatment.

If you haven't kept a history and you're now noticing behaviors that are out of the ordinary, you should start noting when you first began to see these behaviors and ask others close to your child if they've observed any differences. (For a review of common symptoms and warning signs, check out Chapter 1.)

Broaching the Possibility of Autism with a Doctor

For many parents, the search for a diagnosis begins when they sense a difference in their children (see Chapter 1). When they bring this "difference" to the attention of doctors, many parents come unarmed. They don't have all the helpful information, and they don't know what to expect. Don't worry; we're here to help you prepare.

You have three main steps to follow to get a diagnosis for autism and other conditions:

1. **Bring your concerns to your child's pediatrician or primary-care doctor during a routine appointment, phone conversation, or even during a special meeting you arrange to discuss concerns about your child.**

2. **Have a specific discussion with your doctor to get a referral to a specialist (such as a developmental pediatrician or neurologist) who's familiar with the autism spectrum.**

   Your aim isn't to determine a diagnosis during this meeting; you want to find an expert who can help you further.

3. **Meet with the specialist so he or she can administer the proper assessments to see if your child has autism.**

   This step deserves a full section of its own, so we provide it! See the section "Consulting a Specialist" later in this chapter to cover this step in detail.

Preparing for the consultation

These days, most doctors' pay is based on the number of patients they see over a given time, so they tend to give appointments a rushed feeling. Sometimes the doctor is out the door before the parents have a chance to voice their concerns. Recently, many doctors have been encouraged to improve their "bedside manner" — to take the time to be polite and properly explain their patients' medical conditions. Although it may be hard when frustration builds and emotions run high, do your best to remain polite and keep a good relationship with your doctor. It benefits you and your child in the long run to keep emotions on an even keel.

Proper preparation on your part can help keep your emotions in check and keep the meeting moving in a swift manner. Your goal is to prompt the doctor to schedule a consultation appointment or refer you to a professional who has knowledge of autism and can help you.

Here's a list of helpful items and mental reminders to have at the ready for the appointment:

✔ **Notes.** Notes can take the form of a diary detailing the child's behaviors of concern. For example, you may want to take note if your child is lining up blocks, having difficulty with transitions, feeling challenged by communication, displaying awkward social interaction, or exhibiting other autistic tendencies. (For help identifying autistic tendencies, take a look at Chapters 1 and 2.) In addition to specifics, you can jot down a general list of observations you're concerned about. Having a written record of your concerns makes it more likely that you'll get answers to your questions.

If possible, try to identify a correlation between foods and/or activities and the child's behavior. For example, a child with allergies may develop red ears after eating certain foods. Another child may throw a tantrum every time you turn the dishwasher on, due to a hearing oversensitivity.

✔ **Your child's medical history.** (For an explanation of the importance of this info, see the previous section.)

✔ **A short verbal summary of your concerns.** Decide ahead of time what you plan to say to the doctor so you can determine how much time it will take to get your message across. Most checkups last only 15 to 20 minutes these days, so you don't have much time.

Consider timing yourself for a five-minute explanation about the concerns you have about your child. Of course, five minutes isn't nearly enough time to properly express all your concerns. Remember, your only goal is to raise enough concern in the doctor to warrant a consultation appointment or a referral to a professional who's knowledgeable about autism. You should also consider leaving a bit of time for the doctor to ask questions of you.

> ✔ **Another person who's familiar with your child.** A supportive person can mention something you may forget or help take notes about what your doctor says.

Requesting a referral

The initial appointment you have with your primary caregiver should be focused on sharing your concerns about your child in order to merit a referral to a specialist. Come prepared (see the section "Preparing for the consultation" for tips) and feel free to request a referral if the doctor doesn't offer one. Tell your doctor that, if nothing else, you'd like to see a specialist to rule out the possibility of autism.

Some doctors, due to lack of knowledge about autism or other reasons, may be reluctant to make referrals. If you still feel a referral is warranted after she presents some concerns, we recommend the following approaches to help influence the physician's decision:

> ✔ **If your physician claims ignorance, educate her.** A claim of ignorance is actually an opportunity in wolf's clothing. Although you may feel discouraged by your physician's lack of knowledge, realize that she's being honest with herself and you. Grab this chance to suggest that she do further research. One very helpful source is the Web site First Signs at www.firstsigns.org. (Check out the Appendix in this book for others.)
>
> Make your physician's job even easier by providing some or all of the research material so she doesn't have to spend time looking for it.

> ✔ **Take a missed-milestone approach.** Bring up a milestone that children should pass within the next few months. Try to get the physician to agree to a referral if your child doesn't achieve that milestone by that time.

> ✔ **If your child is a toddler, consider breaking out a copy of the Checklist of Autism in Toddlers (CHAT).** Ask your physician to administer the simple exam. The parent or caretaker answers less than a dozen "yes" or "no" questions, and the physician answers five more. The CHAT is a screening, not a diagnostic instrument, meaning that a positive result strongly suggests the need for further diagnostics. You can find a copy of the CHAT on a number of Web sites, including www.depts.washington.edu/dataproj/chat.html.

> ✔ **Ask for a referral to a developmental pediatrician.** A developmental pediatrician specializes in pervasive developmental delays, so he or she can become your ally in the effort to convince your physician why an assessment is appropriate if your concerns are valid. Also, because seeing a developmental pediatrician is less expensive for the parent or caretaker than a full-blown diagnostic procedure, your doctor may be more willing to make this referral.

An added bonus: A developmental pediatrician may be helpful in locating resources to help your child, such as books and articles, Web sites, therapists, support groups, and other helpful organizations (for a thorough listing of resources, see the Appendix of this book).

- ✔ **Write a letter of appeal.** All managed-care groups have a board or other organization that patients can turn to for an appeal of a decision. Read the literature of the group carefully to make sure you don't miss deadlines or overlook other critical matters.

  Some applicable information about appeals and other aspects of filing for insurance reimbursement can be found at the Talk About Curing Autism (TACAnow) Web site (`www.tacanow.com/health_ins_reimbursement_tips.htm`) and at HealthSymphony.com. Sample letters cost $10 as of this writing, but that investment may represent many hours saved in drafting your own letter of appeal.

- ✔ **Get the physician's refusal in writing.** Many doctors don't want to commit to a refusal, so they may back down.

- ✔ **Find a specialist on your own.** You always have the option of obtaining an evaluation on your own from a qualified diagnostic professional or facility.

However, without a referral from a physician, it's much harder (or even impossible) to get reimbursement from your health plan. But don't panic. If the assessment results in an autism spectrum or other developmental delay diagnosis, you should send a letter to the doctor, with a copy to the insurance company, explaining why you overruled his or her objection. (If you saw a developmental pediatrician, you can also ask that specialist to write a letter to your doctor to help convince your primary care physician that an autism spectrum diagnosis is warranted.) Doing so can help you make a claim for an improper refusal and eventual reimbursement (plus make it easier to obtain referrals for additional services such as speech, occupational therapy, and other needed services in the future). This procedure is risky, however, because you may not receive a cent of reimbursement. You have to decide if the risk to a child with undiagnosed autism is far greater.

Consulting a Specialist

The specialist, or team of specialists, conducts the assessment of your child's condition and issues the appropriate diagnosis or diagnoses (in many cases, a child may have more than one diagnosis in addition to autism, such as dyspraxia, depression, Tourette's Syndrome, and so on).

In the pages that follow, we run you through the list of qualified specialists, give you questions to ask when you meet the specialist(s), prepare you to share all the necessary information, familiarize you with the assessment process, and outline the related conditions that complicate the autism diagnosis.

Contacting a qualified specialist

Only certain doctors are qualified to make an official diagnosis, and that qualification varies somewhat from state to state. In general, the medical and psychiatric community considers the following types of doctors (or doctorates) qualified to diagnose a child with an autism spectrum disorder:

- Medical doctor (for medical diagnoses)

    Note: Your child's primary-care doctor may be qualified to make an autism diagnosis, in the literal sense, but she may not feel qualified (or really *be* qualified).

- Psychiatrist (for autism spectrum disorders and conditions found in the *Diagnostic and Statistical Manual of Mental Disorders*)

    Commonly referred to as the DSM, the manual is published by the American Psychiatric Association and is used to diagnose mental disorders.

- Child and adolescent psychiatrist

- Psychologist who has a PhD

- Child neurologist or psychologist

- Developmental pediatrician

Which specialist you're referred to depends on, in part, who's doing the referring and on your needs. For example, a child with many medical issues may be better off seeing a developmental pediatrician. A neurologist, on the other hand, is more helpful in diagnosing and treating accompanying conditions such as epilepsy.

Often, people are nervous or anxious before going into the doctor's office. If you go in with a list of questions, you won't forget to ask the important questions due to anxiety — and you certainly don't want any hidden surprises regarding topics such as costs. Here are some good questions to prepare for the specialist for when you first meet:

- **What training have you had in developmental disabilities?** Ideally, the doctor has specialized in developmental disabilities and will mention his or her continuing education in this area over a number of years.

- **How many children in your practice have developmental disabilities?** You want a number that gives you confidence that he sees children with developmental disabilities on a regular basis.

✔ **What made you decide to work in the developmental disabilities area?** You want to hear a passionate response. Perhaps a person in the specialist's family or a friend has a developmental disability, or maybe she has an unexplainable attraction. Passion here is key.

✔ **Do you treat autistic patients?** If the specialist doesn't know (or believe) that treatment options are available for autism, "pooh-pooh" on him. Also, if the specialist isn't an advocate because some treatments are difficult or too time consuming, he probably isn't the doctor for you and your family.

✔ **How much do you charge?** This question is very important to ask! Be wary of exceedingly high office-visit charges. Unfortunately, because no standard medical treatments or labs are generally accepted for autism, insurance companies often don't accept submitted claims if the diagnosis of the patient is somewhere on the autism spectrum. This denial can significantly affect what a healthcare provider charges.

✔ **Do you take insurance?** Unfortunately, many times the answer to this question is no. Insurance companies don't customarily cover services for autistic children, and rather than trying to get reimbursed for their costs, many healthcare providers choose to directly charge their patients. It's up to you to file with your insurance company to try to get compensated.

When filing claims, make sure you list the specific diagnosis the conducted test is for — such as chronic diarrhea for a stool test rather than just "autism." Being specific can help you get insurance coverage more often.

✔ **How long is an office visit?** A typical visit can range from 15 minutes to 2 hours; it varies among healthcare providers. Usually, initial office visits are longer than follow-up visits.

✔ **Do we have time to talk after the examination is over?** Some healthcare providers offer time to follow up and some don't. If so, the specialist generally allows for a short conversation time (maybe 10 or 15 minutes), after an initial office visit, to review everything she has observed. If not, ask if the specialist holds phone consultations — this could be another way to follow up on questions you don't think of during the allotted time or ask about something you've thought of since your last appointment.

✔ **How many lab tests do you usually order? And how much do you charge for these tests?** The specialist may suggest additional laboratory testing beyond the standard medical laboratory testing. After all, if you don't look for the problem, you won't find it. Make sure you ask what forms of testing a standard lab can perform and what forms require a specialized lab. Occasionally, a healthcare provider will take advantage of the need for additional testing and overcharge. Find out about the available testing and related costs so you can be an educated consumer.

✔ **Do you check for food allergies?** Many autistic children tend to be prone to food allergies/intolerances. (See Chapter 8 for more diet info.) Their immune systems react improperly to the foods they eat. When these foods are eliminated, autistic symptoms are reduced. If the specialist says yes to this question, you know that she considers that there may be underlying biological conditions that affect autistic patients.

✔ **Do you check for celiac disease?** Parallels have been drawn between autistic children and patients with celiac disease (a digestive disease that damages the small intestine and interferes with the absorption of nutrients from food), so doctors need to rule out this condition and other gastrointestinal disorders.

✔ **Do you think candida (yeast) plays a role in autism?** Many children with autism have frequent ear infections when they're young and are treated with repeated doses of antibiotics. A yeast overgrowth is possible if the child has a faulty immune system. Many doctors believe that an overgrowth of candida in the GI tract can lead to both leaky-gut syndrome (take a look at Chapter 7 for more information on this condition) and a worsening of autistic symptoms. In many cases, treatment of yeast results in a reduction of autistic symptoms.

✔ **Are you willing to consider or explore medical treatments associated with biological symptoms of autism?** If the specialist is hesitant, speculative, or questioning, provide her with a copy of the paper mentioned in the sidebar in this section. You can find this paper in your public or college library as well as online at `http://aappolicy. aappublications.org/cgi/content/full/pediatrics;107/5/ 1221`.

The specialist you choose (through recommendations and trial-and-error) should

✔ Deal fairly, honestly, and respectfully. In other words, she should be upfront and realistic about expectations of improvement and recovery.

✔ Be reasonably priced.

✔ Communicate truthfully, providing you with informed consent — especially when considering alternative medical treatments.

✔ Work cooperatively with you. She should be available to answer your questions and discuss options with you.

✔ Act responsibly yet compassionately. She should consider alternative treatments in a systematic, sensible, and thoughtful way.

✔ Engage in continuous education, keeping abreast of any new developments in treatment as they arise.

✔ Support and respect your choices. She should allow you to be a contributor and listen to your concerns, never forcing you to do something against your better judgment.

It's okay to try stuff

The paper titled "The pediatrician's role in the diagnosis and management of autistic spectrum disorder in children" [*Pediatrics.* 2001 May; 107(5):E85] lists alternative treatments such as nutritional supplements, elimination diets, IVIG, secretin, and chelation to combat the effects of autism. The paper states that "Pediatricians should approach alternative therapies openly and compassionately, be willing to support a trial of therapy in select situations — in such that there are clear treatment objectives and pre-testing & post-testing." For more information on these treatments, take a look at Chapters 7, 8, and 9.

Sharing information

Through the years, you may have accumulated useful records about your child from other physicians, school departments, and people in regular contact with your child that will be helpful to the specialist. If not, you can be sure that most professionals and organizations have kept records of your child that you can access upon request. You can start by calling your doctor's support staff for a referral on where to find this information.

Make sure that you sign any necessary release forms and leave plenty of time for the transfer of information to occur. Try to plan it so that the information reaches the specialist about a week before your first appointment. *Note:* In many cases, the transfer of information can take up to a month or more.

Photocopying all records pertaining to your child along the way allows you to give this important information directly to the specialist without being at the mercy of other people's timetables. If you haven't started this practice yet, there's no better time than now. Although you need to be as prepared as possible, we realize that sometimes reality rears its ugly head, and you may need to go into your meetings without as much preparation as you'd like. Just be as prepared as possible from this point on!

Embarking on the assessment process

A specialist bases his or her diagnosis on several aspects. The assessment process usually takes more than one session and should include the elements we describe in the following sections, as the specialist seeks to find characteristics consistent with what's outlined in the *Diagnostic and Statistical Manual of Mental Disorders, 4th edition, Text Revised* (DSM IV-TR), a tool for diagnosing autism or other conditions. The DSM lists characteristics of hundreds of conditions with the coding numbers being used by providers for insurance reimbursement purposes.

Some practitioners may use the International Classification of Diseases (ICD) rather than or in addition to the DSM. The ICD is a detailed description of all known diseases and injuries and is published by the World Health Organization.

The main parts of the assessment process are the *structured interview* and *formal assessments,* steps that the specialist uses to diagnose your child and to get a picture of the child's particular needs. In the structured interview phase, the child and parent or other significant caretaker answer questions to give the examiner an idea of how the child functions as the specialist looks for clues of autism and tries to determine the child's specific need areas. Later that day or in another session, the doctor makes formal assessments by observing the child as he or she has free time to explore the office, engages with the examiner or assistant in game-like activities, and completes certain tasks upon request. The specialist uses information from these information-gathering sessions to diagnose your child and plan for appropriate intervention. The following sections dive into greater detail about the steps.

Structured interview

The structured interview process gives the specialist time to obtain a thorough review of the patient's developmental history. The notes and records you painstakingly prepared (hopefully) or painstakingly requested from doctors and schools (a good fallback plan) up to this point are invaluable.

Specialists have many assessment methods at their disposal to examine your child during the structured interview. Two of the best known and most reliable of the assessment instruments are the following:

- **Autism Diagnostic Interview-Revised (ADI-R):** During this assessment, the examiner asks probing questions in the areas of language, communication, social developmental, and play.

- **Diagnostic Interview for Social and Communication Disorders (DISCO):** This assessment profiles an individual's pattern of development and behavior for the diagnosis of autism and related conditions (as well as a determination of needs).

Other, less common possible interview assessments include the following:

- **Gilliam Autism Rating Scale (GARS):** A checklist for parents. This questionnaire, which takes only 5 to 10 minutes, focuses on four categories: stereotyped behaviors, communication, social interaction, and developmental disturbances.

- **Parent Interview for Autism (PIA):** This tool is a structured interview measuring the severity of autism over a number of behavioral domains and is helpful for supporting general recommendations. The PIA is more commonly used outside the United States.

Formal assessments

Formal assessments of your child include structured observations where the examiner observes as your child plays by him or herself or with you. At other times, the examiner plays games with the child to assess those interactions and test for specific skills. Here are some of the more well-known formal assessments:

- ✔ **Autism Diagnostic Observation Schedule (ADOS):** Focusing on communication and social behavior, the examiner uses this method to rate the child's attempts to accomplish a set of eight tasks on a scale ranging from "normal" to definitely "abnormal." A pre-linguistic version of this assessment is available as well.

- ✔ **Child Autism Rating Scale (CARS):** The CARS method is a rating scale for children with autism that includes 15 items the observer/scorer rates on a 4-point scale.

- ✔ **Autism Screening Instrument for Educational Planning, Revised (ASIEP-2):** By focusing on the behavioral domains of sensory input, relating, body concept, language, and social self-help, the ASIEP-2 aids in the evaluation of people on the autism spectrum.

During the formal interview, the specialist often tests for specific skills sets, and she may use some of the following additional assessment tools, according to the child's needs. (*Note:* Specialists use these tools and others like them to hone in on the child's needs rather than to give a diagnosis.)

- ✔ **Bayley Scales of Infant Development, Revised:** Designed to identify and suggest interventions for cognitive and motor delays, this assessment focuses on mental development and motor control.

- ✔ **Stanford-Binet Intelligence Scale:** This assessment focuses on verbal reasoning, abstract and visual reasoning, quantitative reasoning, and short-term memory, for comparisons with typical or average functioning.

- ✔ **Vineland Adaptive Behavior Scales:** For this approach, the examiner interviews the child's parents, teachers, or care providers in order to specifically assess adaptability and evaluate the areas of communication, daily living skills, socialization, motor skills, and maladaptive behaviors.

The three previous tests we mention were constructed for typically developing children. Comparing scores achieved by children with autism against "normal expected score" is difficult at best. The true power in these tests is in determining a child's characteristics as compared to diagnostic criteria.

The assessment follow-up

Shortly after the assessment process, the person (or persons) conducting the process makes an appointment to discuss her findings. Here are some of the more common diagnoses you may hear (in many cases, people receive two or more diagnoses; you can find much more about diagnoses and the different flavors of autism and related conditions in Chapter 2):

- ✔ Classic autism
- ✔ Asperger Syndrome (AS; see Chapter 5 for a thorough investigation)
- ✔ Pervasive Development Disorder — Not Otherwise Specified (PDD-NOS)
- ✔ Rett Syndrome
- ✔ Nonverbal learning disorder
- ✔ AD/HD
- ✔ Tourette's Syndrome
- ✔ Dyspraxia of speech

Finding out why she chose a diagnosis or diagnoses, as well as why she ruled others out, helps you gain a better understanding of the situation as she puts it into context. If you don't feel as if the specialist covers these topics in an adequate manner, feel free to ask the examiner the following questions, as suited to your situation:

- ✔ "What are the reasons for your diagnosis?"
- ✔ "What other diagnoses may also apply here and why?" (We cover other possible diagnoses in the section "Diagnosing related conditions.")
- ✔ "Can you name any other reasons for the onset of his or her symptoms?"

If you're happy with the specialist and the assessment process, you can move forward with her in the stages that follow. If you feel like the advice or service a specialist provides is inappropriate or unsatisfactory, you can ask for another referral from your primary care physician (if you feel comfortable, you can ask for names from the specialist to bring to your primary care physician) or make an appeal with your insurance company (we discuss appeals in the section "Requesting a referral").

Diagnosing related conditions

Professionals primarily diagnose autism spectrum disorders through the guidance of the *Diagnostic and Statistical Manual of Mental Disorders* (DSM), published by the American Psychiatric Association. As a result, doctors and other professionals qualified to give a diagnosis (see the section "Contacting a qualified specialist") determine whether a child has autism through behavioral characteristics. In fact, *no* medical test in existence at this time can reliably identify autism. So, why talk about medical issues in people with autism, period?

Because many people with autism often have accompanying medical conditions that deserve a diagnosis in their own right. The following list outlines some of these medical conditions:

- Bipolar disorder
- Anxiety
- Epilepsy
- Celiac disease (a digestive disorder related to a gluten intolerance)
- Post-traumatic stress disorder
- Attention Deficit/Hyperactivity Disorder (AD/HD)

  John Ratey, MD, believes that disorder of attention is a component of autism in general.
- Food allergies or sensitivities
- Drug allergies or sensitivities
- Specific phobias
- Immune system dysfunctions
- Low levels of metallothionein (a protein that helps your body metabolize and regulate metals)
- Sensory integration dysfunction (affects the way a person processes sensory information, like sounds, sights, and tastes)
- Dyspraxia (an impairment in the organization of movement)

The term for two or more diagnoses existing at the same time is *co-morbid*. It may be a horrible sounding word, but if you or someone close to you has autism, you're likely to hear it, so get used to it!

Doctors need to administer tests to rule out these medical disorders or to identify a co-morbid medical condition, which helps to pinpoint the proper diagnosis. These tests can be expensive, so be sure to find out if your insurance company covers them. Asking your doctor to verify the medical need for these types of tests increases the chance that your insurance company will cover them. For example, it's entirely reasonable for a doctor to order an electroencephalogram (EEG) for a child who's having seizures.

The following list outlines some medical tests your child may undergo, along with a brief explanation of why they may be helpful to you:

- **Hearing tests.** Due to sensory differences, many children with autism are initially thought to be deaf. An *audiogram* (a test that measures your body's ability to sense sounds at increasing and decreasing levels) or *tympanogram* (a test that measures your body's response to sound and pressure changes in the ear) will likely rule out a hearing impairment — or, in rare instances, prove that one exists.

✔ **Genetic testing.** Blood tests can rule out *Fragile X Syndrome* (a chromo-somal difference linked to autism in some patients) or other chromoso-mal differences that result in characteristic physical features and autistic-like behaviors. (For more information on the link between autism and Fragile X Syndrome, check out www.fragilex.org/html/autism.htm.)

✔ **Metabolic screening.** Blood, urine, and stool lab tests can determine how a person metabolizes food. The tests can also reveal allergies and other intolerances that you can treat with medication and dietary changes.

✔ **Brain assessments.** *Non-invasive* (meaning that a technician evaluates the body from the outside) brain tests look for possible differences in brain structure and activity. Some procedures include the following:

- **Electroencephalogram (EEG):** This test measures brain waves to look for seizures, tumors, and other differences. Because you need to obtain measurements when a seizure or other abnormality occurs, you may have to extend the EEG from an overnight test or day trip to as long as a week.

- **Magnetic Resonance Imaging (MRI):** Using a very powerful magnet, doctors get a high-resolution picture of the brain in order to look for physical differences.

- **Computer Assisted Axial Tomography (commonly known as a CAT Scan):** An X-ray tube rotates around the patient, providing a high-resolution picture of the brain structure (as well as other parts of the body, if needed) in a search for abnormalities.

With the possible exception of an EEG, medical tests don't indicate what spe-cific treatments or services will be effective; instead, they help identify or rule out some of the root causes of medical and (possibly) behavioral concerns.

Dealing with the Impact of the Diagnosis

Finding out your child has an autism spectrum disorder is very difficult. We're not going to tell you that the road ahead will be easy. You may have to rewrite the script of your child's life (and your own). You have a whole new set of issues, pressures, and decisions to deal with now. And people around you may not understand or appreciate the depth of what you're going through.

Important first steps include allowing yourself to process the diagnosis and then motivating yourself to take action. Early intervention is vital because the brain has its greatest plasticity during the early stages of the disorder's development (Chapter 18 provides a list of additional steps you should take immediately after receiving a diagnosis).

Coming to terms emotionally

In some ways, parents describe receiving the diagnosis of autism as a kind of death. "It felt like a death sentence — all our hopes and dreams about his future changed in a day," remembers one mother (who has since been named "Autism Parent of the Year").

And although a verdict of death for your child, yourself, or anyone's education is a big stretch, a diagnosis of autism does change your family's life. It requires a period of bereavement and the acknowledgement that life will never be the same. Finding out you have a disability or that you have to parent a child with one is a life-changing, momentous event, and you need to work through it.

You're not weak if you seek out help to deal with the emotional impact, nor should you feel guilty about the various negative emotions you experience during the process. It's normal to feel angry, sad, or hopeless at first. However, you don't want to allow this to paralyze you. If your emotions interfere with your ability to function or to help your child, you need more support. You shouldn't try to go it alone.

Parent support groups are godsends for the people who belong to them. Your peers in the group may not have answers for your child's situation, but they're going through similar struggles, and they'll listen and offer feedback. You may not consider yourself a "joiner," but going to only one meeting may convince you that a support group is a worthwhile investment of your time. (Joining a listserve may also be what you need to feel connected; see the Appendix for more info.)

Taking action

We have no known cure for autism, but an approach or collection of approaches can lessen the more severe effects of the disorder, allowing a person on the autism spectrum and his or her family to lead a fulfilling and productive life.

Because of the great diversity in the autism spectrum, each child has different needs. You need to take steps immediately to determine which intervention(s) works best for your child and locate persons who can provide that intervention such as an allergist, an immunologist, a gastroenterologist, or a nutritionist. (We discuss many of the more popular and successful interventions available to meet your child's needs in Parts II and III.) And because your child's needs tend to change over time, you need to constantly monitor his or her progress and work closely with your doctors.

Avoiding scams

After an autism spectrum disorder diagnosis, parents and other family members are often in shock and denial about their child's condition. This mindset puts you in an extremely vulnerable position. You may want to escape into some fantasy world and believe that you can find a "magic bullet" to make you child's autism . . . *disappear.* In this state, you very well may be willing to do whatever it takes to "cure" your child's autism. You're frantically looking for help, which means you're susceptible to accept it from people who claim that they have the "miracle cure."

Unfortunately, recovery of function from autism just doesn't happen like that. You need to be aware of hoaxes; false, deceptive, and/or misleading advertising; and promises that a particular treatment is "the cure." In the absence of any orthodox, widely accepted biomedical intervention that has substantial, totally proven benefits for treating autism, parents naturally want to explore all the possibilities. But you need to protect yourself. If a treatment seems too good to be true, it probably is. If a treatment seems too far out, it probably is. If a doctor seems too expensive, she probably is.

Here are some helpful hints to avoid the scam artists and avoid being taken advantage of:

- ✔ **Don't just spend whatever it takes.** Just because you're willing to spend the money doesn't mean your child will get better. Don't put a second mortgage on your house or take out loans you can't afford to pay back. Be prepared to spend money, but spend wisely. Bankrupting your family won't help your child.

  This advice goes for seeking medical help as well. Paying exorbitant charges or fees for services isn't the norm among respectable healthcare professionals' practices. Stay away from providers who double or even triple charge for what an office visit or test would cost!

- ✔ **Doctor shop.** Look around for medical professionals; you don't have to go with the first one you meet. Ask your primary care physician for multiple referrals or recommendations during the diagnostic process. Interviewing healthcare providers is an excellent way to get a feel about how they run their practices.

- ✔ **Seriously consider the ramifications of uprooting your family just to get the desired professional help in another city or state.** Some treatments require travel, but try to find comparable treatment close to home whenever possible.

- ✔ **Don't let anyone guilt you into a treatment.** No one should make you feel like no matter what you do, it isn't good enough, or that you can't spend enough, time, money, or effort trying to "fix" your child's autism.

✔ **Don't be humiliated or shamed into thinking that you owe a particular treatment to your child.** With help and feedback from doctors and your child, it's up to you to know what's best for his or her treatment. You should be battling the autism disorder, not any people butting in to lend their two cents.

Watch out for anyone who claims to be "an expert in the biology of autism"; anyone who charges exorbitant fees and/or misrepresents his or her personality; and anyone who says that he or she has the cure for autism. To date, there is no known absolute cure. You must rely on treatments that can lead to the reduction of autistic behaviors and toward recovery.

Chapter 5

Asperger Syndrome and Autism

· ·

· ·

Asperger Syndrome is classified as one of the Pervasive Developmental Disorders in the *Diagnostic and Statistical Manual of Mental Disorders* (see Chapters 2 and 4 for more on this manual). Although Asperger's is sometimes considered just a "dash of autism," people who are familiar with the condition know that kids (and adults) with the disorder face many significant challenges. A 5-year-old child spouting off about her passion for space exploration may be cute, but it may not be so cute to see the same behavior in an adult. One of the many challenges she faces is harnessing the motivating power behind her interest as she transitions to adulthood. Additionally, persons with Asperger Syndrome often go undiagnosed or get misdiagnosed, due to the often considerable verbal and mental strengths they may have to compensate for their weaknesses.

We've chosen to dedicate a chapter to Asperger Syndrome because of the wide variation between the strengths persons with the condition have and the challenges they face. In many situations, people with Asperger's function at typical or above typical levels. This high level of functioning in some areas often blinds parents, caretakers, teachers, and other professionals to some of the real challenges people with Asperger's face, making the need for advocation even greater.

In this chapter, we show you how Asperger Syndrome fits into the autism story. We identify the traits of a typical individual with Asperger Syndrome. To benefit the person with Asperger's and her family and friends, we look at strategies designed to help people with Asperger's cope with the social pressures, emotions, and stresses that affect them daily. Finally, we look at ways to ease the transition from school age to adulthood for those with Asperger Syndrome.

Discovering Where Asperger Syndrome Sits on the Autism Spectrum

People with Asperger Syndrome tend to be exceptional. Their ability to communicate, rote memory, and visual and other strengths often blind teachers, doctors, family members, and others of some real challenges in socialization, pragmatics, and in others areas. As a result, children and adults with Asperger Syndrome often don't get correct diagnoses or receive the proper treatment and support until later in life (compared to those who are more severely affected with autism and are more noticeable). Professionals sometimes refer to Asperger Syndrome as the "new kid on the block" because the diagnosis didn't even appear in the *Diagnostics and Statistical Manual of Mental Disorders* until 1994 (the DSM is published by the American Psychiatric Association and is used to diagnose mental disorders).

In order to become more familiar with Asperger's, which leads to more accurate diagnoses and better educational and social settings, you (along with doctors and teachers) need to become more familiar with the characteristics of the disorder. The following sections show you where the condition fits on the autism spectrum (see Chapters 1 and 2 for more information on the spectrum and the types of autism).

Examining common characteristics of Asperger's

Individuals with Asperger Syndrome often exhibit some of the following characteristics:

- ✔ **Average to above average IQ.** Not everyone with Asperger Syndrome is a genius; however, many people with this condition have significant intellectual gifts. People elsewhere on the autism spectrum tend to have lower *measurable* IQs (although this is a big generalization, and every case is unique).

- ✔ **Concrete "black-and-white" thinking.** Many people with Asperger Syndrome don't understand unspoken rules, due to difficulties with interpreting figures of speech and nonverbal communication. They tend to rely solely on the words themselves. Difficulty with perceiving nonverbal communication causes significant challenges during social interaction. The same characteristic holds true for people with more classic autism. However, this trait tends to be more startling in those with Asperger Syndrome, due to their often superior verbal skills.

As President Emeritus of the Asperger's Association of New England, author Stephen Shore sees dozens of people with Asperger Syndrome who have high IQs. However, due to challenges in understanding the unspoken rules of employment, they're greatly challenged in finding and being successful at any sort of typical job (see Chapters 14 and 15 for more on life after high school and Chapter 16 for more on money matters).

✔ **No significant clinical delay in verbal communication.** However, the verbal communication of people with Asperger's is often characterized by differences in melody, rhythm, tempo, and pitch of speech — otherwise known as *vocal prosody.* Individuals with Asperger Syndrome can often utter complete, grammatically correct sentences without knowing what they actually mean. This contrasts with people who are more severely affected with autism. People on this end of the spectrum may be nonverbal, meaning they communicate through means such as sign language and graphics.

✔ **Desire to have friends without knowing how to make and keep them.** This social conflict can result in loneliness and sometimes leads to the person using unusual ways to attract friends and, when entering adulthood, significant others. For example, a person with Asperger Syndrome may monologue about a personal passion without perceiving the nonverbal cues that the listener is getting bored and needs to have a chance to talk — or to change the subject. Co-author Stephen Shore defines a good time as spending a whole afternoon examining parked airplanes on a frozen lake in Alaska with a friend that he hasn't seen in four years who also has Asperger tendencies.

✔ **Sensitivities to sight, touch, hearing, taste, and smell.** Input to one or more of these senses often overwhelms people on the autism spectrum. (See Chapter 10 for more on sensory issues.)

Diagnosing Asperger Syndrome

The primary goal of diagnosis is to provide a shorthand summary of a person's characteristics, which lay the groundwork for developing accommodations for the person's needs. Like "Autistic Disorder," the *Diagnostics and Statistical Manual of Mental Disorders* (DSM) categorizes Asperger Syndrome as one of the Pervasive Developmental Disorders (PDD). Just as it does with classic autism (see Chapter 2), the DSM divides the diagnostic criteria for Asperger's into two categories in the following sections.

The manual stipulates that a person needs a total of six characteristics to receive an autism diagnosis; however, a person needs only two characteristics from Category 1 and one from Category 2 to receive a diagnosis of Asperger Syndrome. And tossing the categories aside, experts require a person to possess four additional characteristics to warrant an Asperger's diagnosis. Read on to survey the scene.

Looking at a typical person with Asperger Syndrome

Ten-year-old Sam is fascinated with airplanes and talks about them at every opportunity. In fact, he once held his own in a discussion about vector thrust steering with an Air Force pilot for an hour — until the gentleman tired! Sam almost always finds a way to bring airplanes into his interactions, which interferes with his education, life at home, and relationships.

In school, Sam exhibits difficulties in reading comprehension, but when an aide properly organizes his work, he performs above grade level in mathematics. Sam has difficulties in fine and gross motor control, and he's often the last picked for team sports in gym; most of the children in his inclusion class also shun him during lunch and recess. Sam's teacher indicates that right before gym, Sam's repetition of questions increases dramatically, and he rocks so much in his chair that it squeaks, disturbing the class.

One day, Sam's repetitive question for the day was "What time is math scheduled for today?" Math class had been cancelled for a general school assembly. Instead of telling Sam about the change in plans and risking a tantrum, the teacher responded with "Math will meet later today," figuring that she could help Sam deal with the schedule change after gym class. Sam's teacher answered his repeated requests with "later today". Each time the teacher rebuffed Sam's question, Sam would talk louder and rock harder in his chair. He also started flapping as he usually does when under stress.

Finally, the school called Sam's mother to remove him from school because he had bitten a teacher and was having a major meltdown on the classroom floor. Sam briefly apologized to his mother and fell asleep in the car on the way home.

What's going on with Sam? Sam has difficulties with transitions — especially unexpected ones. He needs help with organization and recognizing when he's getting upset, though he's very intelligent. In short, Sam has Asperger Syndrome.

Category 1

The first diagnostic category is qualitative impairment in social interaction, as manifested by at least two of the following:

- ✔ Marked impairment in the use of multiple nonverbal behaviors, such as eye-to-eye gaze, facial expression, body postures, and gestures to regulate social interaction. Simply put, the person has difficulty interpreting and expressing body language.

- ✔ Failure to develop peer relationships appropriate to developmental level. This often shows up with having friends and acquaintances that are older, younger, from other cultures, or who have other differences.

- ✔ Lack of spontaneous seeking to share enjoyment, achievements, and interests with other people (in other words, the individual doesn't show, bring, or point out objects of interest to other people).

- ✔ Lack of social or emotional empathy. The person may have difficulties in matching another person's emotion while interacting.

Category 2

The second diagnostic category is restricted, repetitive, and stereotyped patterns of behavior, interests, and activities, as manifested by at least one of the following:

- ✔ Encompassing preoccupation with one or more stereotyped and restricted patterns of interest that are abnormal either in intensity or focus
- ✔ Apparently inflexible adherence to specific, nonfunctional routines or rituals
- ✔ Stereotyped and repetitive motor mannerisms (like hand or finger flapping or twisting or complex whole-body movements)
- ✔ Persistent preoccupation with parts of objects

Final four Asperger necessities

A person must also meet the four criteria that follow in order to warrant a diagnosis of Asperger Syndrome:

- ✔ The behaviors and tendencies of the person cause clinically significant impairment in social, occupational, or other important areas of functioning.
- ✔ The person experiences no significant clinical delay in language (in other words, the person uses single words by the age of 2 years and communicative phrases by age of 3 years).

  Many diagnosticians use the criteria of "no significant clinical delay" as a major differentiating factor between autism and Asperger Syndrome.
- ✔ The person experiences no significant clinical delay in cognitive development or in the development of age-appropriate self-help skills, adaptive behavior (other than in social interaction), and curiosity about the environment.
- ✔ The person must not meet the diagnostic criteria for another specific Pervasive Developmental Disorder or schizophrenia.

Does your child have Asperger Syndrome?

If you believe your child meets or comes close to meeting the diagnostic criteria for Asperger Syndrome after reading through the previous sections, or if a caretaker or teacher expresses concerns, you may want to prompt a discussion with your child's pediatrician or other healthcare provider.

See Chapter 4 for more information on getting a diagnosis, developing a treatment plan, and finding the right doctor.

Feeling comfortable in your skin (and label)

Here are some words on diagnosis from co-author Stephen Shore:

"I'm often asked this question: 'Do you have autism or Asperger Syndrome?' Based on my childhood and current experiences, I consider myself to have Asperger Syndrome. However, I began to exhibit autistic tendencies at the age of 18 months, when I lost functional communication. My speech didn't begin to return until age 4, classifying me as autistic. My interests and other characteristics seem more Asperger-like. Finally, I realized that just considering myself as being on the autism spectrum is good enough for me."

The primary goal of diagnosis isn't to obtain a label, but to gain understanding of what's going on. A diagnosis helps to provide a shorthand summary of a person's characteristics.

Examining typical nondiagnostic personality traits of Asperger Syndrome

What the DSM fails to note is that although people with Asperger Syndrome don't often experience a significant clinical delay in language, the use of language, as well as vocal rhythm and melodies, tends to be quite unique in these people. What can you take from this? A number of additional common characteristics exist beyond what the DSM captures.

In the following list, we include common characteristics that make up the personality of someone with Asperger Syndrome:

- ✔ **Exhibits literal, rather than figurative, thought.** People with Asperger's find it difficult to accurately decode nonverbal communication (tone of voice, body language, facial expressions), so they often rely on words.

  For example, one time I (co-author Stephen Shore) was giving a presentation, and lunchtime was approaching. The conference organizer was concerned that I was going to run over on time. He asked me, "What time does your watch say?" My immediate response was, "My watch doesn't say anything because it can't talk." After the laughter died down, I realized that he really wanted me to be aware of the time, and I quickly wrapped up the presentation. (The section "Handling idioms and figures of speech" later in this chapter suggests ways you can help your child deal with overly literal thought.)

- ✔ **Experiences excess of emotions.** One common myth is that people with Asperger Syndrome don't feel emotions or empathize with other people. In fact, many report that they feel *too much* emotion but have difficulty recognizing what the emotions are and how to express them in a manner nonspectrum people can understand. Often, people with Asperger Syndrome seem to fly into a rage without notice. However, you can strive to teach people with Asperger's and those who support them to recognize behaviors and other clues that signal impending meltdowns and resulting behavioral outbursts. (For more on controlling emotions, see the section "Dealing with the Emotions Triggered by Asperger Syndrome" later in this chapter.)

✔ **Has trouble with socialization.** Communication experts suggest that body language and other nonverbal interactions make up as much as 70 percent of a person's total communication package, and most people with Asperger's have trouble recognizing these nonverbal cues. Some people with Asperger Syndrome seem shy — painfully aware that they lack the proper knowledge for successful social interaction. Others may be social responders of sorts, where they commit multiple social blunders in their eagerness to interact with others. However, people with Asperger Syndrome can learn important components of socialization with direct instruction. (For more on the topic of socialization, see the section "Helping People with Asperger Syndrome Socialize".)

✔ **Excels at academics (with appropriate intervention).** People with Asperger's seem to have average or greater IQs and are capable of grade-level work and higher, but they're often challenged by extremes in learning styles. Although a person's rote memory skills may be good, he may have a concrete and literal thinking style causing difficulties; he may also show rigidity, have problems with organizing material and efficiently organizing his time. However, you can make accommodations to meet his challenges by taking advantage of his intelligence.

Many people refer to children with Asperger Syndrome as "little professors" because, for example, they may engage their highly developed rote abilities using advanced vocabulary, all while maintaining adult tones of voice to discuss topics of special interest, such as vector thrusting in fighter planes. However, it may be difficult for them to generalize the use of specialized terms, such as "vector," in other areas such as mathematics or "thrusting" a fork into a piece of meat. They seem more mature than they are because of the way they talk, but don't be fooled — they often have very real challenges in cognitive flexibility, generalization, and organization of academic material.

✔ **Experiences sensory overload.** As with other forms of autism, people with Asperger's have some of their senses turned up "too high," whereas other senses don't register enough information. Environmental data received by a person with Asperger's has greater distortion than for people not on the autism spectrum. And some research indicates that people with Asperger's have a greater tendency to have a more negative response to sensory overload than persons with other forms of autism. (See Chapter 10 for tips on dealing with sensory overload.)

People with Asperger's tend to be visually based learners, yet they may favor aural, kinesthetic, or another sensory mode for learning. The problem is that whereas most people can learn through a non-favorite sense, people with Asperger's may find it impossible. This is why multi-modal (more than one sense) teaching is so important (see Part III for more on the educational issues that come with autism).

A social responder makes a gaffe

A *social responder* is a person with Asperger's who may commit multiple social blunders in an eagerness to interact with others. Sometimes such a person is aware of the need for working on her social skills and can misread a situation as she's trying to improve it. The following paragraphs illustrate one example of how this can happen.

Upon arriving to a church dinner, Dena Gassner, a person with Asperger Syndrome, noticed that a few people were putting silverware and plates on empty tables. Thinking that she should be polite and helpful, she quickly prepared the places at all the tables with eating utensils. "How rude of them to prepare only a few place settings" she thought, but she was determined

to demonstrate good social skills by keeping quiet about it.

Suddenly, a great commotion arose as the organizers frantically started preparing even more tables and food for what they thought were at least 100 more people than expected.

She soon realized that her eagerness to respond in what she thought was a socially appropriate way, had caused the chaos. Her behavior was completely against the unwritten rule that everyone was responsible for their own place settings and that placing utensils and a plate on the table, in fact, nonverbally communicated, "I have reserved this place for myself and family."

✔ **Exhibits poor motor skills.** The tendency toward poor motor skills, balance, and coordination often creates problems in myriad situations, from penmanship and art to games, physical education, and other social situations. As a result, tasks like writing by hand take a lot longer for children with Asperger's than for typical children.

However, it's important not to let your child get discouraged. You can do a lot with occupational therapists to help with poor motor skills. Additionally, enrolling a child with Asperger Syndrome in a movement-oriented class, such as one in the martial arts, can help with coordination and self-esteem. Interventions such as sensory integration or hippotherapy (which we describe in Chapter 10) can also be of great help.

Helping People with Asperger Syndrome Socialize

If you've ever experienced difficulty learning the customs of a culture when traveling to a foreign country, you have a small inkling of what it can be like to live with Asperger Syndrome on a daily basis. Professionals have developed numerous solutions to make life easier for people with Asperger's, both in school and socially. Many of these solutions have been adapted from other interventions for classic autism or created anew especially for Asperger's. We outline some of these unique strategies in this section.

It's vital that caregivers, educators, and doctors customize the program developed for people with Asperger Syndrome for the individual child's needs. It may be helpful to view the available solutions as part of a shopping list where you choose what you need and leave the rest in the store. (You can find additional sources for help on finding more solutions that you can customize for your situation in the Appendix.)

Finding the hidden curriculum

Because social interaction is one of the more striking impairments of people with Asperger Syndrome, many socialization solutions are based on what Brenda Smith Myles, a professor of special education and an Asperger Syndrome researcher at Kansas State University, refers to as the hidden curriculum. The *hidden curriculum* is the set of unwritten rules that nobody directly learns but that everyone knows. Myles's book, *The Hidden Curriculum: Practical Solutions for Understanding Unstated Rules in Social Situations* (Autism Asperger Publishing Company), written along with Melissa L. Trautman and Ronda L. Schelvan, shows how violations of these rules can make an individual a social outcast in school, in his or her community, and other locations.

Table 5-1 describes some of the places to find the hidden curriculum.

Table 5-1	Examples of Hidden Curriculum	
Location	*Sample Rule*	*Possible Consequence for Breaking the Rule*
Home	Everyone has a set place at the table	Arguments with family members
In relationships	Give the other person a chance to talk about what he or she is interested in	Lose friends
School	No swearing	Get in trouble with teachers
In the community	Give up your seat to an elderly person or person with a physical disability	Societal disapproval
With law enforcement officers	Get permission or signal intention before reaching into your pocket	The policeman may think you're hiding a weapon
Place of employment	Follow your supervisor's directions, even if you think you have a better way of accomplishing the task	Lose your job

You can tell social stories or role-play to handle many situations created by problems with hidden curriculum. When role-playing it can be helpful to act out the "wrong" and the "right" way of doing things. Here are some examples of hidden curriculum, corresponding with the entries in Table 5-1:

✔ Discuss and act out seating at the dinner table (if you have a specific order in your home).

✔ Engage in interactive conversation.

✔ Go over the appropriate times and places to swear, and discuss the swearing that often goes on among classmates.

✔ Practice giving up a seat to an elderly person or a person with a physical disability.

✔ Review appropriate behavior when approached by a police officer or first responder. Stress that the results of making a mistake can be pretty severe.

✔ Brainstorm suggestions to propose to a supervisor of a better way to do a task.

Handling idioms and figures of speech

Idioms are expressions where the intent or meaning differs from the literal depiction or face value of the words. For example, the common expression "just wait a second" usually entails waiting a good deal longer than a second, which can be hard if one interprets spoken language literally (as people with Asperger's do)!

Here are some more examples of idioms that can be confusing to people with Asperger's:

✔ Do you have the time? (Possible response: How can you *have* time?)

✔ Get off my back! (Possible response: I'm not on it!)

✔ Put a lid on it! (Possible response: Put a lid on what? What lid?)

✔ Don't hold your breath! (Possible response: Why would I?)

You can teach idioms and figures of speech through strategies such as cartooning, as suggested by comic-strip conversations that use stick figures and other simple symbols, along with conversation and thought bubbles. See Figure 5-1 for an example.

Solutions such as this work best with a visually based, concrete sequential learning style — a common characteristic of people with Asperger Syndrome.

Hidden curriculum: Not just for autistic people

Hidden curriculum is everywhere, and it trips up many people who don't reside on the autism spectrum. For example, a salesperson coming into a home for the first time who mistakenly sits in the owner's favorite chair probably loses the sale. The salesperson can sidestep this problem by simply asking where he or she should sit.

Likewise, a job applicant who sits down before the interviewer reduces his chance of landing the job. Apparently, the culture of sitting is a big deal!

A great resource for people with and without Asperger's to learn the hidden curriculum of body language is *The Definitive Book of Body Language* (Orion), by Allan and Barbara Pease.

Here are a few more ways you can teach idioms and figures of speech:

- ✔ Discuss possible explanations for idioms, followed by role-playing. Go through a situation where you take the idiom seriously, and follow it by doing what you should've done when such phases come up.

- ✔ Go on "idiom hunts." Watch a short sitcom or other television excerpt, and point out whenever you "sight" an idiom. When you spot one, have a discussion about its meaning (you can then role play, which I discuss in the previous bullet).

- ✔ Introduce interventions such as social stories and Power Cards, which we describe in Chapter 13.

Figure 5-1: A comic strip that shows how to explain the expression "Hold the door, please" to someone with Asperger Syndrome.

Asperger Syndrome isn't a fancy excuse for misbehavior

Sharon has a 15-year-old son with Asperger Syndrome named John. "Growing up, John said the strangest things at the strangest times. When riding in the cart at the grocery store, he'd say everything on his mind to passersby. He'd shout, 'Cancer will kill you, mister,' at 3 years old!'"

On another occasion, John told a man standing near them in a store that he had "a sassy face." The man looked at Sharon and said, "What did you do to this kid? You brainwashed him." Turning to John, he commented, "You should get a spanking for that attitude."

Even some of Sharon's friends and family thought the diagnosis of Asperger Syndrome was just a fancy excuse for John's misbehavior. They'd say, "He wouldn't act that way at my house. Don't believe everything those psychologists tell you."

Because most people with Asperger Syndrome have an average to above-average IQ, people tend to get blinded by their strengths. They wonder why people with Asperger's have such difficulty in areas such as making friends, being socially appropriate, or with certain subjects in school. People with Asperger Syndrome have strengths and challenges just like everyone else — just to a greater extreme.

Because Sharon's son has Asperger Syndrome, it's very likely that he needs direct instruction for proper social interaction. Two good interventions for teaching appropriate social interaction are social stories, by Carol Gray, and Power Cards, developed by Elisa Gagnon, which we discuss in this chapter.

Dealing with the Emotions Triggered by Asperger Syndrome

People with Asperger Syndrome feel emotions just as keenly as others, with two major differences:

- ✔ They tend to express emotions differently from typical expectations.
- ✔ They may not recognize the buildup of strong emotions such as anger — especially after a period of frustration.

The second difference often leads to the first — namely, the buildup of emotion can spill out in ways that people may see as unreasonable. At times, outbursts may be unavoidable, but caregivers do have some strategies at their disposal to help minimize episodes as much as possible.

In the following sections, we show you how to recognize each step of the rage cycle and how to plan and react so you can shorten or reduce the intensity of what can seem to rival a volcanic explosion. We also give you some tips to combat bullying, a common problem among children that can further impact your child's unstable emotional state.

Avoiding the rage cycle

Authors Brenda Smith Myles and Jack Southwick, who wrote *Asperger Syndrome and Difficult Moments: Practical Solutions for Tantrums, Rage and Meltdowns* (Autism Asperger Publishing Company), use the term *rage cycle* to refer to three things that happen when a person with Asperger Syndrome, as well as any supporters around him, misses the cues of what may seem like a volcano erupting.

The three stages of the rage cycle are *rumbling, rage,* and *recovery:*

1. **Rumbling:** The precursor of the impending human volcanic explosion. You can figuratively feel the ground shake, and you know that something bad is going to happen soon.

2. **Rage:** When the volcano blows. The child loses control of his emotional and physical being, and like with a volcano, you may experience a lot of noise and destruction.

3. **Recovery:** The aftermath of the eruption. Just as the community on the mountainside has to rebuild after the volcano erupts, the child and those around him need time to put themselves back together.

Check out Table 5-2 for common behaviors that occur during each of these stages, adapted from Myles's and Southwick's book.

Table 5-2	Common Rumbling, Rage, and Recovery Behaviors		
Rumbling	Increased verbal behaviors such as swearing, nonsense noises, unusual changes in vocal volume, or making threats	Increased stereotypical behavior such as grimacing, fidgeting, rocking, flapping, tearing paper, or tapping foot	Increased movement, including pacing, walking in circles, or leaving the room
Rage	Verbal behaviors such as screaming	Emotional expressions such as explosive impulsiveness and rage at self	Physical behaviors such as destroying property, biting, hitting, kicking, and self-injury
Recovery	Sleeping	Denial of rage behaviors and withdrawal into fantasy	Apologizing

Now that you have the background on emotional outbursts, you can move forward to take steps to curtail them. The following sections provide you with possible interventions for the rumbling stage, a survival guide for the rage stage, and tips for getting through the recovery stage when an episode takes place.

Interventions for the rumbling stage

It may seem like people with Asperger Syndrome fly into a rage without warning, but that isn't necessarily the case. By keeping the rage cycle in mind, people who support children or adults with Asperger Syndrome can learn to read the cues that indicate that the "volcano" is about to erupt.

Fortunately, you have a number of interventions (originally devised by Myles and Southwick) you can employ to help your child circumvent a rage episode during the rumbling stage. The following list presents some of these interventions:

- ✔ **Nonjudgmental removal.** Remove the child from a situation in a positive manner. For example, if a child is getting anxious from activity occurring in the kitchen, you could encourage him to take a box of tissue paper to another parent or sibling in the living room.

    In classroom situations, children with Asperger's often get fidgety. You can instruct the teacher to ask your child to bring an envelope to the office. The envelope is empty, and the child will most certainly take a detour or two on his trip. However, the 5 to 10 minutes of lost classroom time is a bargain in return for avoiding a meltdown and having the child's attention for the remaining class time.

    The point is to distract the child and interrupt the rumble-rage-recovery pattern. You need to make sure that these interruptions don't become a routine that enables the child to avoid work or other tasks at hand.

- ✔ **Support from routine.** Having a chart or visual schedule of the day's events at the ready can help the person with Asperger Syndrome feel more secure. The person can reassure himself as to what's coming next or prepare for what would otherwise be an unexpected change.

    Forewarned is forearmed. People with autism function much better if they can enjoy predictability. One way you can build more predictability is by making sure your child is aware of his schedule on a daily basis — especially if he must deviate from his usual routine. In fact, most people do better when their schedules are planned out.

- ✔ **Interest boosting.** Showing an interest in a person's passion shows that you value that person, and your actions can often disrupt rumbling. This intervention is also known as *redirecting*.

    A few minutes talking about or otherwise engaging in a child's passion may buy you several more minutes of getting through a difficult situation, such as waiting in the cashier's line at the supermarket.

It may seem like you're rewarding a child's misbehavior by allowing her to avoid a situation or do something more pleasant. However, if the child's ability to pay attention or control herself hasn't already reached zero during the rumbling stage, it soon will if she flies into a rage. Also, going into a rage is emotionally and physically exhausting, as well as embarrassing; it isn't something any child wants to do.

- ✔ **Acknowledging difficulties.** As with any person, acknowledging the difficulty of a task helps validate a child's feelings. For example, if your child talks out of turn during a conversation, you can state, "I know this is hard, Veronica, but the family rule is that everyone waits for the speaker to finish before making a comment."

- ✔ **Cool zone.** Designate a room with low sensory stimulation where a child can take his work or thoughts when the rumbling stage occurs. This will reduce the stress involved. Expecting the child to complete his work while in this room prevents the cool zone from becoming a way to avoid work, too.

- ✔ **Walk — don't talk.** Let the person with Asperger Syndrome walk to cool off. Make sure a safe person accompanies her. Unless the person with Asperger Syndrome tends to run away, the safe person should just walk along to calm the child down. The rule here is that the child can say anything or nothing, and the safe person remains quiet. Anything said "Can and will be used against you."

Surviving the rage stage

The rage stage can be scary and seem everlasting, especially because you want it to end so badly. The best advice we can give you is that during the rage cycle, the adult should remain calm, talk quietly, breath deeply, avoid power struggles, and be flexible at a time when the child is unable to. The following list gives you some more tips on getting through the period of rage with you, your surroundings, and, most importantly, your child in one piece:

- ✔ **Safety first.** A person in a rage stage has no control over herself and must be kept safe. Try to remove delicate and dangerous objects from the area. A rage state isn't a spectator sport. Everyone, except for the one or two people supporting the person with Asperger Syndrome, should leave the area.

  In a school situation, a teacher may ask an aide or other person to take the other students out of the classroom or at least away from the child in a rage state.

- ✔ **Stay low and slow.** Yelling back, making threats, and towering over someone in a rage state merely prolongs the situation and makes it worse. Breathe deeply, try to relax, and keep talking to a minimum — you can even try to say nothing at all.

> ✔ **Disengage emotionally.** The rage is about a situation — not you personally. The words the child may say and the behaviors he exhibits aren't under his control. Try to disengage and think about something else, such as planning a shopping list or dinner.

It can be helpful to graph the child's rage behaviors so that you can plan your responses to her actions. You'll quickly find out what works and what doesn't, based on our suggestions here.

If your child seems to experience the rage cycle frequently or engages in behaviors that are dangerous, you should consult a professional who's knowledgeable about Asperger Syndrome, such as a psychiatrist (see Chapter 4). Dramatic changes in the frequency of rage cycles may also warrant getting additional professional help.

Getting through recovery

After the "volcano" blows, the "mountain" becomes very tired. A child in recovery may apologize for her actions and then seem very tired, often going right to sleep. Give her all the sleeping time she needs, and take that time to recharge your batteries and go into damage control mode. If your child doesn't fall asleep, you can use relaxation techniques to help her calm down or redirect her to a low demand activity or passion of hers.

However, you must realize that your child is still very fragile at this stage, and you can trigger another eruption if you make too many demands of her. If your child is in the recovery stage, you should set aside any ideas of her being able to learn or interact with others. The recovery stage isn't a time for teaching new material or doing a "post mortem" on what just happened; that step can occur later.

At the time of recovery, referring to, reviewing, or trying to analyze the child's behavior during the rage state may turn her right back into a human volcano.

Do "timeouts" help?

A common punishment meted out to autistic children who exhibit challenging behaviors is to send them to timeout rooms, allowing them to think about what they did wrong and perhaps to calm down. In reality, a growing number of developmentally oriented practitioners question the validity of an imposed timeout. As one professional, Dr. Arnold Miller (who developed the Miller Method; see Chapter 9), says, "I question the practice of further isolating a child who already is challenged with socialization as being productive." Refer to the list in the section "Interventions for the rumbling stage" for more constructive ideas.

After the child has sufficiently recovered, consider gently reintegrating her into her routine, reviewing things she has already learned. This drives home the point that the day's work must still be done and that a bad incident in the morning need not spoil the whole day.

Working through frustration

Teaching others how to accurately decode the prelude of an emotional explosion is a bit like giving a hungry man a fish for dinner. The man is satisfied for a meal, but what happens when he's hungry again? It's much better to *teach* the man how to fish. Teaching a child with Asperger Syndrome to recognize his own emotional states and their intensities is much more powerful and is like teaching a man how to fish. Both the fisherman who knows how to fish and the child with Asperger Syndrome learn to get along in the world without constant aid.

However, the challenges of understanding the rules for social interaction make it difficult for people with Asperger Syndrome to plan and gauge their responses. Just as one may study and even carry a guidebook for getting along during a business trip to a foreign country, visual aids, such as Power Cards, can act as a resource for people with Asperger Syndrome (see Chapter 13).

For example, you can teach a child with Asperger Syndrome that when he feels frustrated, he can employ a number of tactics to calm himself down. The two major motivating factors behind Power Cards are employing a child's passion and involving a hero figure. For example, you can help a child with a special interest in space exploration cope with frustration by showing him a Power Card featuring a picture of Neil Armstrong, the first man to walk on the moon, and providing instruction on relaxation techniques.

For more information on Power Cards, take a look at the book *Power Cards: Using Special Interests to Motivate Children and Youth with Asperger Syndrome and Autism* (Autism Asperger Publishing Company), by Elisa Gagnon.

Using emotion thermometers to gauge emotional states

Making the most of the visual strengths of children and adults with Asperger Syndrome can be very helpful. To this end, you can help your loved one gauge his emotional state by making a thermometer that allows him to visualize the appropriate intensity of his emotional responses for a given situation. For example, in Figure 5-2, you see a thermometer with a 100-point scale. At the top, the point 100 indicates sublime happiness. You see 50 in the middle, which covers the neutral middle ground. And at the bottom, the frigid 0 point indicates a sad state. Working together with your child, you can draw a similar thermometer and write in some of the physiological signs indicating his different emotional states. For example, feeling cold, slow, and sleepy could indicate a sad state close to 0. When your child exhibits certain signs, you or another caretaker can refer the child to this thermometer to help him determine his emotional state when you see these behaviors and what he should do in order to take action. "Gee, I see that you're grimacing and pacing a lot. Let's check your emotional thermometer to see where your emotions are and what may help you calm down."

Along with the happy/sad thermometer, it helps to have a thermometer that determines the level of stress your loved one has. The thermometer in Figure 5-3 shows a 100-point scale, from high stress to completely content, complete with suggestions for visual clues and recommended interventions (for more on particular interventions, see the section "Interventions for the rumbling stage"). For example, if your child is pacing and grimacing, you may suggest that "we go check out the stress thermometer." When you both discover that your child's behaviors merit a 70 or higher stress level, you can work on techniques to bring that stress level down.

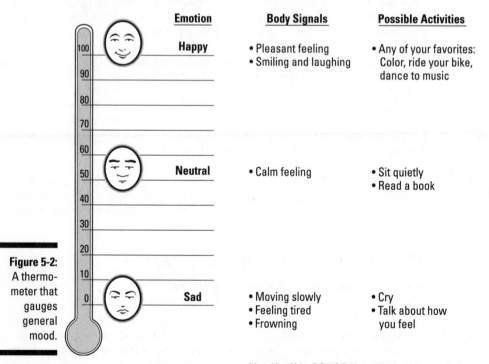

Figure 5-2:
A thermometer that gauges general mood.

	Emotion	Body Signals	Possible Activities
100 / 90	Happy	• Pleasant feeling • Smiling and laughing	• Any of your favorites: Color, ride your bike, dance to music
50	Neutral	• Calm feeling	• Sit quietly • Read a book
0	Sad	• Moving slowly • Feeling tired • Frowning	• Cry • Talk about how you feel

Adapted from Myles, B. [2005]. Children and Youth with Asperger Syndrome

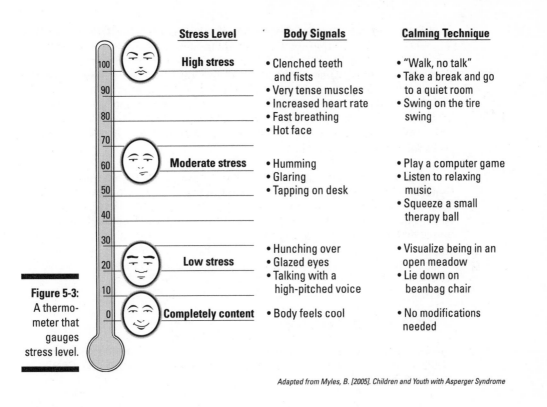

Stress Level	Body Signals	Calming Technique
High stress	• Clenched teeth and fists • Very tense muscles • Increased heart rate • Fast breathing • Hot face	• "Walk, no talk" • Take a break and go to a quiet room • Swing on the tire swing
Moderate stress	• Humming • Glaring • Tapping on desk	• Play a computer game • Listen to relaxing music • Squeeze a small therapy ball
Low stress	• Hunching over • Glazed eyes • Talking with a high-pitched voice	• Visualize being in an open meadow • Lie down on beanbag chair
Completely content	• Body feels cool	• No modifications needed

Figure 5-3: A thermometer that gauges stress level.

Adapted from Myles, B. [2005]. Children and Youth with Asperger Syndrome

Recognizing Bullying and Its Emotional Repercussions

Regrettably, bullying in school, on the playground, and beyond is a fact of life for people with differences. Most people on the autism spectrum report bullying experiences in school. Some research indicates that 94 percent of children with Asperger Syndrome are bullied in school.

Bullying is characterized by four key components:

✔ **A power imbalance.** The bully may be stronger, have better social awareness or social status, and have other physical or psychological advantages.

✔ **Intent to harm.** The bully takes negative actions with the intent to reduce the innocent person's standing in the community and to generally cause physical and emotional suffering or injury.

✔ **A distressed target.** A bully often focuses on a person who's different than most of the others in a group. A child with Asperger Syndrome often fits the bill.

✔ **Repeated negative actions.** Bullying isn't a simple, one-time event; it's a series of attacks that tend to escalate in nature.

Sometimes a teacher uses sarcasm to control students' behavior or to elicit particular results, often without malicious intent. This action is often referred to as *educational bullying.* If you suspect educational bullying, you may want to schedule an appointment with your child's principal to discuss your concerns. Make sure you address your concerns with the teaching style instead of blaming a teacher who likely means no harm.

Bullying can have significant negative impact for people with Asperger Syndrome. Some people report suffering from posttraumatic stress syndrome resulting from mistreatment by their peers. Other life-long effects range from poor self-esteem and depression to, for those with autism, an even greater reluctance to engage in social interaction for fear of reprisal. Intervention is important as soon as you detect signs of bullying. The following sections present the signs and give you tips for putting a stop to the bullying.

Signs of bullying

Difficulties in reading nonverbal social cues may be part of the reason why children with Asperger Syndrome have such a high rate of bullying. Consider the following example:

> Four students who are part of the "in crowd" walk up to Tommy and ask, "What's up?" Tommy thinks for a moment, lifts his eyes upward, and proceeds to report the number of lights in the ceiling and how the tiles are glued to the ceiling so that they remain "up." The other students laugh and say, "Great job, Tommy."

> Later, you ask Tommy about his classmates. Tommy says, "They are good friends of mine. They talk to me, ask me questions, and laugh a lot." You make up your mind to talk to Tommy's teacher about the situation.

If your child with Asperger's shows one or more of the following conditions or behaviors, chances are high that he or she is being bullied in school:

✔ **More scratches and bruises than usual.** Other school children may be pushing, punching, or otherwise excessively roughhousing your child.

✔ **School avoidance.** Your child may try to stay home, complaining of a stomachache or other illness. Sometimes school can be so stressful that the child becomes sick more often.

✔ **Changes in character.** The child may seem sad or depressed. Sometimes, the child being bullied acts out the events he or she experiences by becoming the bully to siblings or even pets.

Asperger Syndrome and violence

You may read news articles about people with, and suspected of having, Asperger Syndrome committing acts of violence. Some researchers blame the condition for a variety of heinous acts. However, you can reframe this issue with the realization that almost all these situations are preceded by a long history of bullying and ostracizing from society by classmates.

Most people with Asperger Syndrome and other disabilities report being bullied in grade school and beyond. Given the long-term negative effects of bullying on the person being bullied and on the bully, developing policies toward greater awareness of people with differences and enforcing zero tolerance for bullying in schools will go a long way in the fight to reduce acts of violence — acts that perhaps anyone is capable of when faced with consistent bullying.

Taming the bullies

Fortunately, a growing number of educators, parents, and others are realizing the life-long damaging effects on self-esteem that bullying can have. More and more schools are beginning to educate their faculty and students on detecting and preventing bullying, and more schools have adopted zero-tolerance policies for bullying.

The first step in stopping bullying is awareness. Due to the often covert nature of bullying, students report a teacher intervention rate of 25 percent, even though teachers report intervening almost 75 percent of the time during bullying incidents.

You can help increase awareness by gathering information from faculty, staff, students, and parents through anonymous surveys or small group discussions. It's important to bring together people who most likely have different definitions of bullying to some sort of consensus on detection and prevention.

One good resource for bullyproofing at the school, classroom, and individual levels is the book *Perfect Targets: Asperger Syndrome and Bullying,* by *Rebekah Heinrichs.* Another good resource for detecting and working out bullying issues for children is the Inventory of Wrongful Activities (I.O.W.A.), found at www. pathwayscourses.samhsa.gov/bully/bully_supplements.htm.

Transitioning to Adulthood

The interventions we describe in this chapter provide you with a template for dealing with challenges people with Asperger Syndrome face — challenges that remain in the transition to and during adulthood. Just as with other types of autism, children with Asperger Syndrome grow up to become adults with Asperger Syndrome. Some of the main challenges of adulthood for everyone on the autism spectrum include employment, interdependent living, continuing education, self-advocacy and disclosure, and relationships.

Most people spend 75 to 80 percent of their lives as adults. Asperger's doesn't go away when the child leaves school. Although it isn't possible to cure Asperger's, life tends to get better after graduation from high school as the person transitions into the adult worlds of community, work, and college.

Many people with Asperger Syndrome and high-functioning autism aren't attending secondary education or working to their potential because they haven't learned the skills needed for successful interdependent living. However, with just a little support, people at this end of the autism spectrum can lead fulfilling and productive lives. For example, a person challenged by organization can have someone help him keep his affairs in order a few times a week. The result may be a person who can now live independently, pay more taxes than service costs, and contribute to society.

One way to accomplish the goal of interdependence is to project into the future what accommodations the person may need to accomplish employment, living arrangements, and other goals, based on interests and current needs. For example, a person who needs assistance in transportation to school may want to investigate public and private transportation options for adults with disabilities.

For more information on transitioning to adulthood for all people on the autism spectrum, check out the chapters in Part IV.

Part II
Addressing Physical Needs

The 5th Wave
By Rich Tennant

"I know being with dogs and swimming with dolphins have proven therapeutic for ASDs, but when my doctor suggested Hippotherapy for our son I said there's no way he's getting in a mud hole with a giant pig."

In this part . . .

A growing population of parents with autistic children is knocking on the door of the medical profession, looking for answers and a cure. How does medical science meet this demand? Read on to find out. In Part II, we give you the current options for medical care for people with autism, ranging from medications that control secondary symptoms to biomedical treatments that have helped some people with autism live fuller, healthier lives. Some cures have been claimed, but doctors disagree on exactly what a cure looks like. As of now, we have no definitive cure for autism; no medically based assessments that tell you whether you have it; and no medical treatments that the FDA approves.

We also discuss what medications can and can't do for people with autism in this part, and we cover what new treatments promise and what they've been able to deliver (so far).

Chapter 6

Injecting Yourself with Knowledge about Autism Medication

. . . .

In This Chapter

▶ Reviewing the parameters of drug therapy

▶ Identifying the general challenges of medication

▶ Perusing the autism medicine cabinet

▶ Verifying vaccines

. . . .

To the date of this publication, no known medication can cure autism. However, medication *can* be incredibly useful in reducing conditions that often go along with having autism, such as debilitating anxiety, depression, seizures, aggressive behaviors, some sensory issues, insomnia, and digestive problems. With careful administration of medication from a qualified doctor (see Chapter 4), many people suffering from these conditions, autistic or not, can derive much more pleasure and enjoyment out of life.

In this chapter, we look at some of the more common medications and their effects, identify what side effects you need to watch out for, and highlight the particulars to be vigilant for when caring for people with autism.

Considering Drug Therapy

Taking medication, like almost everything people do, has its benefits and risks. For example, if you ride your bicycle to work, you have to balance the benefit of exercise, greater convenience, and saving money with the possibility of knee injury or getting hit by a car. Your most important job as a parent or caregiver is to be aware of *both* the benefits and risks so that you can make an informed decision when considering drug therapy for a child. We look at these factors in the following pages.

Looking at how medication can realistically help

Before you jump into a drug-therapy regimen for your child, you need to understand your motivations and what medications can and can't do. In particular, what are the goals for taking the medication? Do the potential gains outweigh the possible risks? How long do you need to wait to see if the medication achieves the desired effect? Make sure you do sufficient research, using the Internet, books, people who have taken the drugs, and, of course, medical doctors.

A medical doctor who can plainly explain the possibilities for both benefits and side effects of a medication is worth his or her weight in gold. For more information on finding and utilizing a good doctor, check out Chapter 4.

Here's the bottom line on what medications can and can't do:

✔ Medications *can*

- Address some of the symptoms that often occur with autism (like anxiety or depression; see the chapters in Part I for more info).

- Reduce some of the physical and mental causes of certain behaviors often associated with autism (like seizures, poor digestion, and some sensitivities).

- Help some people with autism begin to cope with their environments.

✔ Medications *can't*

- Cure autism.

- Make a person start talking.

- Make a person more intelligent.

- Make a person learn new skills.

Educating yourself and pursuing drug therapy

New medications and new information about existing drugs are constantly added to the mix of possible interventions, so the best way to proceed with the utmost care is by remaining current.

When you decide you have an interest in pursuing drug therapy, you should head to the following resources:

✔ **Start by making an appointment to discuss the pros and cons of some of the more common medications for children with autism with your doctor.** Never be afraid to discuss any questions or concerns you have with your doctor. That way, you can be prepared for potential problems such as side effects, which we discuss in the next section.

Bring another person with you to the appointment, if possible, to compare notes. You should also consider obtaining permission from the doctor to tape the conversation for your records.

✔ **Read up thoroughly on the medication, including its on- and off-label uses and its side effects.** Before you administer any medication, read up on the drug by using the latest version of the *Physician's Desk Reference* (Thomson PDR), available from a reference library for free or for purchase at a bookstore. You can also read up on literature from pharmaceutical company Web sites, as well as other trusted Web and written material.

The Pill Book (Bantam), by Harold Silverman, is an easy to read, accurate, and reliable introduction to many medications. You can find it in most large drugstores for under $10.

✔ **Look up what people have to say about a drug by using a search engine.** Just remember that you're often reading opinions from personal experiences, which can affect the reliability and validity of what's present.

Using medication wisely

Medicating an autistic person can be a catch-22 situation. An autistic person may need medication to function better within society, but the body of an autistic person does its best to reject medication. Medical tests have shown that autistic people are more prone to drug reactions and rare side effects that doctors don't often seem to worry about. People on the autism spectrum are more likely to have *paradoxical reactions,* which occur when a drug should function one way but does the opposite. And, generally speaking, the autistic population is more likely to experience *drug toxicity,* or toxic effects from a drug regardless of the amount taken. An autistic person's body doesn't always get rid of medications as fast as the average person's does. As a result, a person on the spectrum may need to start a medication at a much lower dose than normal and likely *remain* on that low dose. Careful monitoring by the person with autism, caretakers, and doctors is required.

The administration of medication changes the chemical function of any body, however, making it a very serious matter, so you need to follow a few simple rules before you alter your autistic child:

✔ **Start or stop medications only under the supervision of a qualified medical professional.** In other words, don't begin or end a program of medication on your own.

✔ **Follow instructions exactly.** Administer drugs at the recommended times and dosages, and follow all the directions.

✔ **Beware of mixing medications with certain substances, such as the following:**

- **Food:** For example, people shouldn't drink alcohol and grapefruit juice with certain medications. Discuss the food and drink effects of the medication you're administering with your child's doctor.

- **Other medications:** Inform the doctor (and the pharmacist for backup) of any other drugs you're administering, ranging from simple over-the-counter drugs (such as aspirin, cough medicine, or allergy pills) to the most tightly controlled substances. Dangerous interaction effects may exist between the medications.

- **Herbal, complementary, or other non-prescription supplements:** Inform your doctor about any therapies you may be pursuing because they may interact with the medications already being used — even if it means you must help provide the research by handing your doctor relevant articles. (See Chapter 7 for more info on supplements and the like.) For example, St. John's wort is so similar to a Selective Serotonin Reuptake Inhibitor (SSRI) that a person may experience a bad side effect if he or she is already taking Zoloft (an SSRI; see the following section for more on these drugs).

✔ **Identify any possible side effects related to the medication.** Common side effects can include

- Lethargy

- Insomnia

- Constipation

- Changes in appetite or weight

- Dry-mouth

- Nausea

If you're an autistic adult considering drug therapy, ask your doctor about any possible effects the medication may have on sperm counts and sexual function if you're a man and effects on fertility, pregnancy, and nursing if you're a woman. Also, find out if a family member has tried a drug you're considering. Given the genetic influence on drug tolerance, you may want to consider shying away from drugs that have caused blood relations to suffer from bad side effects.

✔ **Pay special attention to any black box warnings.** You find black box warnings, which may appear in all capital letters or surrounded by bold black boxes (hence the name), on antidepressants. The boxes warn parents about the increased risk of suicidal thoughts and behavior in children and adolescents being treated with these medications. Think of these warnings as a call for extra vigilance when administering such medications.

Wrong drugs happen

Kassiane Sibley, a person who has autism, writes about her experiences with anticonvulsants:

"The first anticonvulsant I tried was oxcarbamazepine (Trileptal). The doctor didn't believe me that autistic people have lazy livers, so I started on too high a dose. Because of this I was too tired to tell if it was working, and I fell down a lot. One day I was too stupid to remember how to write my name. These are not normal side effects. These are signs of wrong drug

syndrome. Yes I made that phrase up. I was switched immediately to another medication. A year and a half later I tried it again, on a much slower titration (dose raising) schedule. It brought me down from an elevated, manic mood, but it also triggered 2 kinds of seizures, including drop attacks. This might be why I fell so much the first time, but I wasn't aware I was epileptic then. Wrong drugs happen."

The good news is that the side effects associated with these drugs relate to full dosages. Medication prescribed for patients with autism tends to be at much lower doses, which often reduces the frequency and severity of negative side effects.

✔ **Be aware of possible errors.** Doctors and pharmacists *do* make mistakes, so if you suspect that the medication or dosage is wrong, contact the doctor or pharmacist.

✔ **If a drug or other intervention is working, think carefully before you change anything.** Even switching to or from generic versions of medication can be fraught with problems due to slight differences in manufacturing. However, if the child you care for is suffering from a strong side effect of a medication, you may want to consider switching despite the risk.

Identifying Helpful Medications

Medication doesn't cure autism, but it can help lessen some of the more debilitating effects. The medical field uses four major groupings of medication to help with the co-occurring characteristics of autism (see Chapters 2 and 3):

✔ Selective Serotonin Reuptake Inhibitors (SSRIs)

✔ Atypical antipsychotics

✔ Tricylic Drugs

✔ Antiepileptics

You can take a closer look at each category in the following sections. However, we start with information on beginning the medication search process with the right doctor, because the wrong doctor can send your child into a medical tailspin. We also discuss medications that deal with rage and other challenging behaviors in more severely affected people with autism at the end of this section.

Medications outside of these four groups can be helpful for people with autism as well. Make sure you consult with your doctor about all the available options if you aren't keen on any of the big four.

Beginning the process with a qualified doctor

You have many considerations when making decisions about medication, and a knowledgeable doctor can make the process so much smoother. A doctor who can help with medication decisions for your autistic child has the following characteristics (you can find more information about choosing the right doctor in Chapter 4):

- The doctor understands the implications autism spectrum disorders have in metabolizing medication based on experience.

- The doctor understands the concept of needing to start low and go slow with initial and continuing doses of medication.

- The doctor helps you understand the risks and benefits of medications to help you maintain perspectives on the possibility of side effects.

Like with all medications, you need to work closely with your prescribing physician when receiving autism meds for your child — especially if you observe no change in unwanted behaviors or symptoms, or you observe an unwanted change. Certainly, you should also keep your doctor aware of when things are going well.

The length of time your child takes a particular medication depends on factors such as the following:

- Has the effectiveness of the medication changed over the time of its use?

- Does a new medication your doctor introduces have a bad interaction with medication your child is currently taking?

- Can you get a generic drug available at a lower cost? Be aware, however, that even the slightest variation in chemical make-up between similar drugs from different manufacturers can have a large effect on the medically sensitive person with autism.

Drug reactions and autism

Shared by Kassiane Sibley, a person who has autism:

"In my case — and remember, everyone is different — if a med is processed by the liver, I will always be on a very low dose (sometimes below the normal start dose), but if it is processed by the kidneys, I will eventually end up on a rather high dose. Regardless of what organ deals with the medication, it takes me a long time to get to a final dose, assuming my body tolerates [the medication] at all. My doctor says he's never seen someone have so many drug allergies."

Selective Serotonin Reuptake Inhibitors (SSRIs)

SSRIs are types of antidepressants often used to reduce anxiety in people with autism. Your child may be debilitated with anxiety, which can severely reduce functioning. The application of SSRIs may enable him to interact more successfully with his environment. SSRI drugs can be expensive, and insurance companies tend to not cover autism-related medical expenses. However, you may have more success with coverage if your doctor codes the medication for "excess anxiety" in this case.

Chemical differences in people with autism may result in atypical reactions to medication. Often, people with autism are hypersensitive to antidepressants, and doctors should strongly consider beginning with one-third to one-half the normal starter dose. For many individuals, antidepressants continue to remain effective at the low does. Higher doses may cause agitation or insomnia. Be sure your doctor is aware of these potential dosage issues.

SSRIs promote the passing of information between neurons by inhibiting the reuptake of serotonin, a neurotransmitter that plays a role in mood, sleep, and appetite, to name a few. The additional time the serotonin remains between the cells increases the likelihood of the recipient cell recognizing the serotonin.

Common SSRIs

The current SSRIs available to you (generic name listed before the trade name) include the following (in order of when they came on the market):

> fluoxetine → Prozac, Fontex, Seromex, Seronil, Sarafem
>
> sertraline → Zoloft, Lustral
>
> paroxetine → Paxil, Seroxat, Aropax, Deroxat
>
> fluvoxamine → Luvox
>
> citalopram → Celexa, Cipramil, Emocal, Sepram
>
> escitalopram → Lexapro

The longer a drug has been on the market, the more doctors and users know about its usages and side effects.

As of press time, only Prozac and Zoloft are fully approved by the United States Food and Drug Administration (FDA) for people under 18 years of age.

Although not strictly considered addictive, SSRIs can cause withdrawal symptoms. Doctors associate withdrawal with anxiety, unusual body sensations, and dizziness. Withdrawal from an SSRI should occur only under the care of a competent professional.

Possible SSRI side effects

In 2004, researchers suggested a correlation between SSRIs and an increased risk of juvenile suicidal thinking (not actual suicide) in acutely depressed patients, measuring twice the rate of a placebo. It's important to note, however, that researchers saw no completed suicide in the SSRI group and one in the placebo group. As a result, all antidepressants (both SSRIs and tricyclics) carry the warning of increased suicide risk in children and adolescents.

Another concern is possible mental dullness associated with taking this class of drug. Some studies report reduced sexual function in as many as 41 to 83 percent of people taking SSRIs.

Atypical antipsychotic drugs

Atypical antipsychotic drugs are used to treat psychiatric conditions and are FDA-approved for treating schizophrenia. Doctors are using them more and more in place of what are known as *typical* or *first generation* antipsychotic drugs. In lower doses, these drugs serve to control anxiety, anger, and rage. For example, a doctor may prescribe 6 to 8 milligrams of Risperidal a day to a person with schizophrenia if needed, whereas a person on the autism spectrum may receive a dose of 0.5 to 1.0 milligram.

The term *atypical* refers to the fact that this class of drugs has a much lesser propensity to cause tardive dyskinesia (TD) and extrapyramidal symptoms (EPS) — both of which are movement disorders. TD is chronic and can be irreversible, and EPS is usually short term and disappears over time or with the discontinuation of the medication.

Not all is known about how atypical antipsychotic drugs function. Some researchers think that they work on both the serotonin and dopamine systems. What is known, we present in the following sections.

Common atypical antipsychotic drugs

Here's a list of some common atypical antipsychotics:

aripiprazole → Abilify

clozapine → Clozaril

olanzapine → Zyprexa

quetiapine → Seroquel

risperidone → Risperidal

ziprasidone → Geodon

Some research studies show that Risperidal is highly effective for reducing severe rage and aggression in children and adults with autism. Like with SSRIs (see the previous section), you need to strongly consider using a smaller than usual starting dose for people with autism. Consider taking up the dosage issue with a physician if drugs are being prescribed.

Possible atypical antipsychotic side effects

Atypical antipsychotic drugs tend to have more severe side effects than SSRIs and other autism medications.

In high doses, most of the atypical antipsychotic medications can cause sedation, (generally reversible) weight gain (as much as 30 pounds or more), tardive dyskinesia (TD), extrapyramidal symptoms (EPS), Type II diabetes, and hypotension. The atypicals, especially in antipsychotic doses, can also cause increases in cholesterol, blood sugar, and fatty acids in the blood. The risks of movement disorders increase with the length of time the drug is taken. Atypical antipsychotic drugs can also cause a life-threatening nervous-system problem called *neuroleptic malignant syndrome* (NMS) in very rare cases.

The good news is that people with autism usually don't require the higher antipsychotic doses, where the major side effects are much more likely.

Here are a few specific side effects associated with certain atypical antipsychotic drugs:

- ✔ **Abilify** can cause nausea, headache, insomnia, and minimal weight gain (but generally less EPS).

- ✔ **Clozaril** has less chance of causing EPS than some other atypical antipsychotic medications, and it can reduce TD from previous medications, but it causes increased salivation, dizziness, weight gain, hypotension, and *agranulocytosis* (a serious condition that requires frequent blood tests). However, this drug is rarely used for autism.

- ✔ **Geodon** users experience minimal weight gain but present no evidence of EPS or hypotension.

- ✔ **Risperidal** users have experienced weight gain and face a slightly higher risk of TD.

✔ **Seroquel** shows no evidence of EPS or minimal weight gain, but the drug is linked to some sedation and postural hypotension.

✔ **Zyprexa** clearly stimulates the appetite, causing obesity.

Tricyclic drugs

Tricyclic drugs used to be a doctor's first choice for treating depression, but doctors are now replacing them more and more with SSRIs and other drugs. However, because tricyclics are highly potent, their use continues, often when a patient experiences severe depression.

Research has shown that people with autism tend to have a greater incidence of depression than the general population. In some cases, the depression is *comorbid* (existing along with the primary disease or disorder). In other cases, people with autism may become depressed as they begin to realize their differences from the majority of the population. The condition becomes a barrier in developing relationships with others and hinders their ability to lead a fulfilling and productive life.

In either case, medication can help lift the dark cloud of depression and put the person with autism on the way to leading a fulfilling and productive life.

Author and Professor Temple Grandin, a person living with autism, reports that she still uses tricyclics, as she has for the past 25 years at the same low dose, because they work for her, and she's not going to change what works!

Common tricyclics

Here are a few common tricyclic drugs:

amitriptyline → Elavil, Endep, Tryptanol

amoxapine → Asendin

clomipramine → Anafranil

desipramine → Norpramin, Pertofrane

doxepin → Adapin, Sinequan

imipramine → Tofranil

nortriptyline → Pamelor

protriptyline → Vivactil

Possible tricyclic side effects

The serious side effects of taking tricyclics are relatively rare. However, they can include cardiac hazards, which may occur with all tricyclics. Make sure you find out if your child has any abnormalities in his or her EKG before you accept a prescription of tricyclics.

Tricyclics can be very dangerous, and possibly fatal, in overdose.

Bothersome, but common, side effects are more likely to occur. The following effects tend to lessen after about two weeks:

- ✔ Dry mouth
- ✔ Blurred vision
- ✔ Constipation due to slowed digestive processes

Other side effects may include

- ✔ Drowsiness
- ✔ Excess anxiety
- ✔ Difficulty with urination
- ✔ Cognition and memory difficulties
- ✔ Decrease in sexual libido
- ✔ Twitching of muscles
- ✔ Nausea
- ✔ Increased heart rate and heart rhythm irregularities

Antiepileptics (also known as anticonvulsants)

Many people with autism also have *epilepsy,* a disorder of the brain that results in recurrent, unprovoked seizures. The term *antiepileptics* refers to a class of drugs generally used to prevent epileptic seizures. What makes these drugs popular is that not only are they helpful to people on the autism spectrum with epilepsy, but they also have the ability to stabilize brain activity, which can assist in the control of aggressive outbursts, explosive behavior, self injurious behavior, and other challenging behaviors.

Common antiepileptics

Here are some names of different medications that doctors may prescribe for seizures:

carbamazapine → Tegretol

gabapentin → Neurontin

lamotrigine → Lamictal

leviteracetam → Keppra

valproate → Depakote

Possible antiepileptic side effects

One of the possible severe side effects of antiepileptics, especially with Depakote and Tegretol, is liver or bone marrow damage; these drugs require regular blood testing to make sure no harm is done to the liver and bones. Here are a few other specific risks and rewards commonly related to certain medications:

- ✓ **valproate:** In addition to anticonvulsant properties, this drug often helps reduce aggression and other explosive behaviors, but it also has a sedative effect and can cause an upset stomach and weight gain.

- ✓ **carbamazapine:** This drug has similar effects as valproate and could create a rash.

- ✓ **gabapentin and lamotrigine:** Both drugs appear to have the same effects as valproate, including the negative side effects. However, doctors have found insufficient information on how children tolerate the drugs. They do know, however, that lamotrigine can cause a severe rash.

As you can see from the previous list, some drugs have multiple uses within the autism spectrum. Sometimes doctors prescribe a drug for an *off-label use,* meaning that people take the drug for purposes other than the ones described on the label. For example, Nardil, an MAO inhibitor not often used anymore, was initially developed as an antidepressant. However, in the early 1970s, one doctor noticed that the drug also reduced the intensity of agoraphobia in patients, so he began prescribing Nardil for that use as well. Clonidine, another drug, is labeled for use as a high blood pressure treatment, but doctors also prescribe it to people with autism to deal with anxiety.

Medications for challenging behaviors in severely affected people with autism

Determining proper medication and other interventions for people more severely affected with autism can be a difficult task if they lack a form of functional communication to report how they feel. (For more information on communicating with someone who has autism, take a look at Chapter 10.) Making matters worse, people this severely affected experience rage due to their lack of functionality.

The following list provides some medications that may be helpful in reducing the rage caused by the inability to develop functional communication skills:

- ✓ **valproic acid:** Also known as Depakene, valproic acid can be helpful in controlling extreme rages that don't seem related to specific situations or persons. The medication also helps in reducing subclinical seizures, which may be a cause for some rage attacks.

You need to administer high doses of Depakene to achieve effectiveness. Therefore, you need to monitor for possible liver and blood damage — especially within the first six months.

✔ **risperidone:** Known by the brand name Risperidal, risperidone should be considered when you or doctors can determine the focus of the rage. Examples include when a person rages at specific people or situations.

Maximizing Safety When Vaccinating Your Child

Vaccines are dead or weakened cells of the toxic bacterium or virus of diseases that medical professionals have deemed worthy of elimination. Children are routinely vaccinated to eliminate diseases like polio, mumps, and measles. Some researchers believe that autism can be linked to these immunizations, or more specifically to *thimerosal,* a mercury-based preservative in some vaccines. The researchers believe this to be true for a certain set of children who are susceptible to the immunological stress from vaccinations. (For more on vaccinations as a cause for autism, check out Chapter 3.)

Whether thimerosal causes autism or not, it just doesn't seem like a good idea to inject mercury into anybody. Consider verifying that an injection is thimerosal-free before a doctor gives it to your child, whether he or she has autism or not, or to you.

Considering your child's medical history

Before vaccinating your child, consider his or her personal medical history with these questions:

✔ Has the child ever had any vaccine reactions?

✔ Does the child suffer from convulsions or neurological disorders?

✔ Has the child experienced severe allergies or intolerances to food, medications, or other substances?

✔ Does the child have any immune-system disorders?

✔ Is the child currently sick?

And, finally, you need to make sure you have the full information related to any medication your child takes, including vaccinations.

Ask yourself these questions:

- ✔ Do I have full information on the side effects?
- ✔ Do I know how to identify and report a vaccine reaction?
- ✔ Do I know the name of the manufacturer and lot number (or batch number) for researching whether vaccinations from this lot result in an unusually high number of adverse reactions?

Looking at an alternate vaccination schedule

Much of the research centered on reducing the burden that vaccines place on the immune and other systems of young children points toward adjusting the timing of the injections. Doing so allows a child's immune system to properly develop and safely metabolize the substances contained in the shots. You may want to consider modifying the vaccination schedule according to Stephanie Cave's book *What Your Doctor May Not Tell You About Children's Vaccinations* (Warner Books). Take a look at Table 6-1 for the details.

Table 6-1	Vaccination Schedule Proposed by Stephanie Cave		
Age in Months	*Vaccine*	*Age in Months*	*Vaccine*
Birth	Hepatitis B if Mom is Hep B positive; otherwise, wait until teenage years	18	DTaP
4	Haemophilus Influenzae, Type B Vaccine (Hib), Inactivated Polio Vaccine (IPV)	21	Rubella
5	Diptheria/Tetanus/acellular Pertussis Vaccine (DTaP)	24	Prevnar
7	Hib, IPV	30	Mumps
8	DTaP	48-60	Varicella (if not already immune)
9	DTaP	48-60	Hepatitis B series (at earliest)
15	Measles (at earliest)	48-60	Test titers for MMR (don't give unless not immune)
17	Hib, Oral Polio Vaccine (OPV)	48-60	DTaP, IPV boosters

Chapter 7

Improving Immunity and Boosting Biochemistry

By Jane M. El-Dahr, MD

- -

In This Chapter

▶ Discovering how the immune system works

▶ Understanding immune system abnormalities — blood, gut, and brain

▶ Boosting your (or your loved one's) immune system

▶ Benefiting from a biomedical approach

▶ Removing heavy metals from the body

- -

*A*lthough the medical profession long considered autism a disorder only of the brain, it has become increasingly clear over the last decade that many affected children have other medical problems in addition to brain issues. The immune system is out of whack in many autistic children, and the links between the immune, nervous, and gastrointestinal systems are becoming clearer. Medicine is also putting other symptoms into their proper places. For example, pain coming from the GI tract may cause some children on the spectrum to hurt themselves, so self-injurious behavior may have a biologic rather than behavioral cause. By understanding biochemical abnormalities and correcting them, doctors and caregivers can improve the level of functioning in an autistic child and marvel at the progress that occurs as the child becomes healthier.

In this chapter, you look at how the immune system may "go wrong" in some children, why their biochemistry may not be optimal, and why investigating heavy metals in their systems may be helpful. Armed with the information in this chapter, you should be able to ask your primary physician for some basic testing, and you'll be better prepared for the options offered by a physician who takes a more naturopathic approach. As much as traditional medicine has wanted to divide them, the brain and body *are* connected!

Much of what we cover in this chapter is still controversial in traditional medicine because few of these therapies have been proven effective in large clinical trials. However, parents (with the guidance of medical professionals) use many of these approaches regularly, in addition to conventional treatments. The goal for all children on the autism spectrum is maximizing their potential. Careful consideration of combining appropriate educational approaches (which we discuss in Part III) with suitable biomedical therapies is the best way to help them become healthy, happy, and as successful as they can be.

Taking a Look at the Balancing Act of the Immune System

What does the immune system have to do with a neuropsychiatric disorder like autism, where abnormal behavior is one of the defining components? The nervous and immune systems have many common features. Both systems store information in the form of memory and (hopefully!) recall the info when needed, and the two systems interact at cellular and biochemical levels, sharing many signals. It shouldn't be a surprise that immune responses can alter central nervous system (CNS) function, but traditional medicine has been slow to accept this.

The *immune system* is the body's Department of Defense. Its job is to figure out what's supposed to be in the body, sometimes called the *self,* and to try to get rid of any *non-self* invaders such as viruses, bacteria, or other foreign material. The key to a normal immune system is maintaining balance. A healthy immune system should

- Protect you from all foreign invaders by recognizing an infection in a rapid fashion and getting rid of it immediately.

- Get smarter over time, remembering that it fought the same infection in the past if it encounters the bug again.

- Respond to a "stop" signal when the battle should end instead of continuing to fight unnecessarily.

- Never cause any damage to you.

If an infection or disorder disrupts the balance, several things can go wrong with the immune system, including the following results:

- **Immune deficiency/dysfunction:** An ineffective or defective response, often leading to recurrent infections.

- **Hypersensitivity:** An overactive response of the immune system, disproportionate to the potential danger. The best-known example of hypersensitivity is an allergy, where the body reacts to a harmless stimuli (like tree pollen) by making antibodies with resulting histamine release.

Immunology 101

Here's a shortcut you can take to master some of the lingo that doctors and researchers use when talking about immunology. Although the alphabet soup language of immunity can be daunting, keep in mind that it can help you provide the best care for a child on the autism spectrum (and, hey, you don't have to go to medical school!). To make it easier, you can divide immunology into two main categories: *adaptive* and *innate*.

The adaptive part of the immune system recognizes pathogens and remembers them by using memory recognition molecules specific for each germ it has encountered. It "knows" whether a bacteria is strep (which can cause a sore throat) or staph (which can cause skin infections). Two components of the adaptive part of the immune system are the equivalent of heat-seeking computerized missiles aiming for a specific target: *immunoglobulins* and *lymphocytes*. Medical-types separate the adaptive immune system into the *immunoglobulin producing portion* (Th2) and the *cellular portion* (Th1).

Here's a list of the immunoglobulins and their functions:

- ✔ **IgA:** Present in tears, saliva, mucus, and in the gut lining; meant to stop bugs before they get past the surfaces of the body and cause infection

- ✔ **IgM:** The "rapid response" protein in the bloodstream, made rapidly but in small amounts

- ✔ **IgG:** The main bloodstream protection protein

- ✔ **IgE:** Fights parasites but also can cause allergies

Here are the two kinds of lymphocytes:

- ✔ **B cells:** Make antibodies

- ✔ **T cells:** Orchestrate the overall immune response

The adaptive system's goal is to keep the two sides appropriately functioning and balanced.

The innate part of the immune system is the older, more primitive and non-specific part that doesn't have "memory" for past infections. The innate side recognizes the surface of germs as "foreign," but it doesn't identify the specific bacteria it fights — it doesn't matter to the innate side whether the germ is strep or staph. You can think of the cells of the innate system functioning as though they're throwing hand grenades and setting land mines, hitting enemies without caring exactly who the victims are and sometimes causing collateral damage to healthy nearby tissue.

Other key components of the immune system are *cytokines* — the chemical messages that cells of the immune system use to communicate with each other. Just as the nervous system uses neurotransmitters for cellular communication and the endocrine system uses circulating hormones, the immune system uses cytokines to coordinate an "attack". Some cytokines "turn on" parts of the system, and others serve as "off" signals. Cytokine function in the GI tract is particularly important because the majority of the immune cells of the body reside there.

- ✔ **Autoimmunity:** An inappropriate reaction to self, mistakenly causing damage to the body. The immune system attacks its own tissues and cells. Lupus and rheumatoid arthritis are well-known examples of autoimmune disorders.

✔ **Inflammation:** Overactivity of the immune system, causing "bystander" damage to normal tissue while it tries to repair an injury or get rid of an infection. For example, when a splinter gets under your skin, the redness, swelling, tenderness, and warmth appear because of inflammation as your cells attack the piece of wood and repair the surrounding skin. If inflammation doesn't turn off when your body no longer needs it for healing, it becomes chronic and can cause damage to nearby healthy tissue.

Because autism is classified as a neuropsychiatric disorder, looking at how the immune system plays a role in a somewhat similar medical condition can be helpful. A well-characterized example of a neuropsychiatric disorder caused by an errant immune reaction is Pediatric Autoimmune Neuropsychiatric Disorder Associated with Streptococcus, or PANDAS. *PANDAS* is an autoimmune condition that occurs when previously healthy school-aged children suddenly develop obsessive compulsive disorder or Tourette's Syndrome (tics) following a bout of strep throat. The child's immune system gets rid of the strep bacteria by making antibodies to target the germ. However, by mistake, these antibodies also attack part of the brain, which leads to changes in behavior. By treating the strep infection with antibiotics and, if that isn't enough, the immune system with intravenous immunoglobulin, doctors can modulate the overreaction, diminishing the psychiatric symptoms. (For more on comorbid [or coexisting] conditions or conditions that resemble autism, check out Chapter 2.)

Exposing the Relationship between Autism and Immune Abnormalities

Although the relationship between autism and the immune system is complex and not yet fully understood, experts have found important clues based on studies of the blood, gut, and brain that may someday help pinpoint the origins of the disorder. *Cytokines,* the communication cells of the immune system, play a key role in the central nervous system, influencing mood, sleep, and appetite and in some cases acting as growth factors for nerves. Three bodily systems — the gut, the brain, and the immune system — "interpret" many of the same signals as they interface with the outside world, and fixing problems in one area may improve the functioning of all three systems. We should all hope to understand autism better in the future, but for now, treating immune problems that cause frequent infections or allergies may make a child feel better now and enable him to learn more during therapy or at school.

All four categories in the unfortunate game of "Immune System Gone Wrong" — deficiency, hypersensitivity, autoimmunity, and inflammation (see the previous section) — often appear in children on the autism spectrum. We explore these categories and other areas within the blood, gut, and brain in the following sections.

Analyzing immune measurements in the blood

In children with autism, more studies explore the immune measurements in blood than in the GI tract or brain (see the following sections "Exploring gut problems" and "Studying brain tissue"). Experts have found many types of immune abnormalities in autistic children by analyzing blood samples, such as

- Deficiencies causing increased infections
- Allergies
- Autoimmunity
- Overactivation

However, doctors have seen a great deal of individual variation when it comes to autism and the immune system. The following sections break down the most common findings in autistic children. (For a guide on how to take this information and use it to improve the health of your child, see the upcoming section "Improving Immunity".)

Infections

A significant number of autistic children have recurrent infections — especially ear infections — that start at an early age. The most common medical history given by parents is that the child was treated with multiple courses of antibiotics as an infant and toddler. More often than in typical children with a similar history, children with autism have immune deficiency with low immunoglobulin levels.

The most common finding is a low IgA level (measured in the blood but doing its work in tears, saliva, mucus, and in the gut lining), predisposing the child to respiratory and GI infections; some children have low IgG and/or IgM levels as well.

Immune cell numbers and function are also frequently low, making the children more prone to infections with viruses or yeast.

Allergies

Some people on the autism spectrum — especially those with eczema (or atopic dermatitis, a noncontagious skin condition), asthma, or a constant runny nose — have high levels of the immunoglobulin IgE and multiple allergies. Many allergies are caused by food or by indoor and outdoor allergens (like pet dander, dust mites, and pollen).

Autoimmunity

Several researchers have found that children with autism make autoantibodies to brain components (brain proteins, neurotransmitters or receptors, the myelin coating around nerve cells, and other things), but the significance of this connection remains uncertain. Researchers have found no clear evidence to date that the antibodies are directly attacking the brain or causing symptoms; however, they know that it isn't normal for the antibodies to be present in the bloodstream.

Additionally, doctors have observed an increased incidence of autoimmune diseases such as Hashimoto's (autoimmune) thyroiditis or rheumatoid arthritis in families of children on the autism spectrum when compared to families without affected children. Based both on these studies and on research dealing with immune function genes, there appears to be a genetic predisposition to autoimmunity in the families of children with autism.

Immune activation

Recent research has confirmed that signs of inflammation and activation, especially of the innate branch of the immune system (see the sidebar "Immunology 101"), are very common findings. One researcher, Dr. Jyonouchi, found that milk components (or wheat) cause the release of inflammatory cytokines (immune messages) from blood cells in many children with autism. Unfortunately, this research is only preliminary, and no test is available that detects every child on the autism spectrum with food sensitivity or predicts fully which child will benefit from a milk-free, wheat-free, or other type of diet. (For more information on addressing your child's dietary needs, check out Chapter 8.)

Exploring gut problems

Gastrointestinal (GI) symptoms of different types occur in many children with autism. Researchers have observed bloating, gas, abdominal pain, chronic diarrhea, chronic constipation, or a combination of problems in up to half of studied children with autism. Gastro-esophageal reflux (heartburn) is also common and may cause ulcers, leading to night awakenings from pain. Abnormal bowel movements — stools that have the texture of chocolate pudding instead of holding form like play dough or that contain visible undigested food — also occur in many cases.

The *intestinal lining* is the barrier between the contents of the gut and the bloodstream that filters nutrients into the blood. In a healthy gut, the cells in the lining are close together so that the spaces between are small, like a tea strainer rather than a colander. Damage to the intestinal lining (from an infection, allergy, or inflammation) can cause increased intestinal permeability, or *leaky gut,* so that incompletely digested proteins leak into the bloodstream where the immune system can "see" them and react to them. Increased gut permeability, first described in children with autism in 1996 but confirmed later by several researchers, is more common in autistic children than in the general population. It isn't clear what starts the process, but it's likely that trying to "calm down" the immune system in the gut would help stop the leakiness, which would further dampen the overstimulated immune system because fewer foreign proteins would get into the bloodstream.

Not every autistic child with gastrointestinal symptoms has immune reactivity to food, however, and not every autistic child with immune reactivity to food has gastrointestinal symptoms, so which children would benefit from dietary intervention remains very difficult to predict, but even the mainstream *Journal of Pediatrics* (May 2005) published an editorial featuring scientific findings "to support the rather 'gray' [rather than black and white] literature on unusual dietary responses in autism."

At the very least, children with frequent gastrointestinal symptoms or who seem to have frequent abdominal pain — doubling over unexpectedly, pressing their abdomens against furniture or the floor, crying with bowel movements, or waking up in the middle of the night crying — need an evaluation by a pediatric gastroenterologist. If your child has gastrointestinal symptoms, ask your primary care provider for a referral to a pediatric gastroenterologist. If that isn't possible, ask for a *comprehensive stool analysis test,* which can be of great help in determining if your child's digestion is normal, what (if any) pathogens are present, and what treatments may help. Ask your doctor for more information about this test (although traditional physicians may not be as familiar with it as alternative practitioners may be).

Dr. Andrew Wakefield described (and others have verified his research) the presence of *lympho-nodular hyperplasia* (LNH) in the GI tracts of a group of children with autism who had a history of regression. The glands (or lymph nodes) in the lining of the gut become swollen with the presence of abnormal populations of lymphocytes and inflammatory cytokines (immune system cells) like *TNF* (Tumor Necrosis Factor) in large amounts. The inflammation of the small and large bowel (enterocolitis) is similar to, but not the same as, what's seen in inflammatory bowel disease. The most controversial finding of all is the discovery of the measles virus present in the swollen nodes of the gut. Until researchers repeat Dr. Wakefield's study and confirm or deny his findings, the debate over the role of the measles virus and the MMR vaccine in autism will rage on.

Studying brain tissue

In 2005, researchers at Johns Hopkins University, using tissue samples taken during autopsy, observed immune changes in the brains of patients with autism. They found that cells that function as innate immune and support cells for neurons — called *microglia* and *astrocytes* — showed immune activation and inflammation (see the sidebar "Immunology 101" earlier in this chapter for more technical info).

Although researchers have found brain autoantibodies in the bloodstreams of autistic children in other studies (see the section "Analyzing immune measurements in the blood"), the Hopkins researchers didn't find any in the brains in their study. It's possible that when the Hopkins patients were younger, the adaptive parts of their immune systems may have been involved as well. However, the researchers haven't found any specific "markers" (which may be found if the adaptive part of the immune system was involved) to pinpoint what started the immune responses in the brains. The researchers think that a toxin, infection, or maternal infection during pregnancy may have initiated the processes. It remains unknown whether the immune activation starts in the brain or occurs in response to a stimulus from somewhere else, such as the gut.

Finding inflammation opens up the possibility of potential medical treatments at some point in the future and broadens researchers' thinking about the causes of autism (see Chapter 3). However, Hopkins researchers point out that no specific therapy can "undo" the brain findings at this time. The Johns Hopkins group has a technical but informative Web site on "FAQs regarding the meaning of neuroinflammatory findings in autism" at www.neuro.jhmi. edu/neuroimmunopath/autism_faqs.htm; hopefully they'll post more information as their research advances.

Other researchers have reported intriguing findings as well. One small study published in 2004 documented that autistic children who had previously shown the measles virus in their GI tracts also had the measles virus in their spinal fluid. Another research group found autoantibodies in the brain itself, present in the lining of brain blood vessels. Demonstrating specific immune abnormalities gives researchers clues to potential biomedical treatments that may be helpful to these children. Currently, studies have created far more questions than answers, but hopefully these answers are imminent and in turn will lead to the development of specific new therapies.

Improving Immunity

If a child with autism is sick and feels bad — especially if he's in pain from chronic constipation, gut inflammation, or ear infection — his behavior may worsen because he feels terrible and can't concentrate. The "double whammy" is that on top of all this, the child can't communicate what's wrong because of the autism itself, leading to even more frustration and negative behavior. Treating these immune-system symptoms can help the child's overall level of functioning and behavior. In this section, we look at first-line, second-line, and third-line strategies for treatment of immune system issues in autistic children.

Some of the things we discuss here are mainstream and apply to any child with similar symptoms. Other options have only anecdotal evidence in terms of helping children on the autism spectrum, but they may or may not be worth considering based on your child's symptoms and your pocketbook situation (in other words, many of the treatments can be expensive). Hopefully, you can find a sympathetic medical professional to help you sort through these potential therapies (see Chapters 4 and 6 for more on finding the right medical care).

Each child with autism is different, which means professionals must evaluate each child for his or her particular group of symptoms and laboratory abnormalities. Medicine can't give you a "one-size-fits-all" therapy, but it can give you many therapies and strategies that can improve your child's situation and help him achieve his optimal level of functioning. Some first-line therapies benefit most children and are fairly simple to implement, and other second- and third-line interventions require prescribed medication and close supervision by medical professionals.

Focusing on first-line fundamentals

You, the autistic child's caregiver (or the autistic adult, in the flesh), are the first line of defense when it comes to improving the immune system. Eating a well-balanced diet as "naturally" as possible (see Chapter 8) is a good start, but you have many tactics at your disposal. The following list shows first-line strategies you can consider implementing on your own. The strategies are generally safe and not terribly expensive, and (except for the dietary changes) they're proven to support and regulate the immune system in other similar disorders (no large trials have been conducted in autism).

You should discuss these strategies with your healthcare provider. Most physicians are at least a little familiar with them, but professionals who use a naturopathic approach (even if they've never treated children with autism) are the most knowledgeable options.

 ✔ **Deciding on a diet:** Although committing to a specific diet is daunting, and you have no perfect way to determine how your family will benefit, giving your loved one a healthy diet containing few additives or processed foods is a good step toward boosting his immune system. If a food stimulates your child's immune system, avoiding it can only improve his condition. At the very least, you should consider a trial of complete avoidance of milk, because it seems to be the most common culprit; however, you should strongly consider eliminating any other suspect food (see Chapter 8 for more on changing a diet). *Note:* A child avoiding milk should get 500 to 600 milligrams of calcium twice a day, either by calcium-fortified orange juice or with a supplement. Digestive enzymes, like EnZym-Complete/DPPIV/Isogest, may be beneficial, but they aren't substitutes for removing offending foods completely.

✔ **Protecting with probiotics:** The "good" bacteria in the gut are very important in regulating the gastrointestinal tract. Frequent antibiotic use (common for autistic children) kills these helpful bacteria, but you can replace them with over-the-counter supplements (look for Lactobacillus or Bifidobacterium listed as ingredients) or live-culture yogurt (found in health-food stores; this yogurt isn't for those avoiding milk). Such products, known as *probiotics,* have been widely used in combating inflammatory bowel disease and infectious diarrhea. Probiotics increase IgA levels in the gut and regulate immune signals, decreasing intestinal permeability and inflammation (see the sidebar "Immunology 101").

Try live rather than freeze-dried brands of probiotics in your local health-food store (found with the refrigerated supplements), or order brands like Pro-Bio Gold or Culturelle online from suppliers specializing in products for children with autism. Aim for at least 1 billion bacteria per day. Try casein-free supplements containing a single strain of bacteria or those with mixed strains — whichever works better for your child. Often, rotating brands can help, so just buy a one-month supply until you get gut symptoms under control.

✔ **Employing EFAs:** Essential fatty acids (EFAs), especially omega 3s, lower pro-inflammatory cytokine release, and they help to seal gut leaks. Fish oil is a good source of omega 3, but you need to be sure it's mercury-free (it should say on the packaging). Start with 1,000 to 2,000 milligrams per day of two common omega 3 fatty acids combined — eicosapentaenoic acid (EPA) and docosahexanoic acid (DHA).

✔ **Adding antioxidants:** Combating inflammation with antioxidant vitamins, such as A, C, and E, and using antioxidant supplements, like Co-Q10 (a coenzyme that has a similar structure to vitamin K and acts as a catalyst for energy production; give 10 to 25 mg daily), can help regulate the immune system and decrease inflammation.

Some naturopathic physicians have used a short "blast" of high-dose vitamin A with success, but you should attempt this only under supervision because vitamin A can be toxic at large doses; see the following sections for more complicated therapies.

Seeking out second-line strategies

Even if you see improvement with the first-line defenses you enact to improve your child's immune system (see the previous section), your child may require additional strategies to relieve pain or experience greater improvement. Here are a few second-line options that may be trickier to perform on your own or require a prescription, a referral to a specialist, or specialized testing:

✔ **Defeating dysbiosis:** *Dysbiosis* occurs when normally harmless bacteria and yeasts cause disease by altering the nutrition or immune responses of the host. Getting rid of pathogens in the gut calms down the immune system and helps GI symptoms. Appropriate antibiotics, used judiciously, have been shown to decrease autistic symptoms. However, the effects are not permanent, so you should use other means to keep abnormal bacteria from coming back after your child completes the course of antibiotics. Prescription antifungal medications, especially short courses, and antiyeast supplements, such as garlic derivatives or the "friendly" yeast (saccharomyces boulardii), can help if the situation doesn't improve after you try the first-line therapies.

✔ **Contemplating colostrum:** Children with low IgA levels (see the sidebar "Immunology 101") or those with more severe chronic diarrhea may need extra help in tackling gut issues. Hopefully, you can get a referral to a gastroenterologist, but if you can't or you want to improve the situation while you wait for an appointment with the specialist, other therapies may help. Colostrum, a supplement containing a concentrated derivative of cow's milk that features high levels of helpful antibodies, can help chronic gastrointestinal symptoms or dysbiosis if other approaches don't help, although it should be certified casein-free if your child is avoiding milk.

Another approach is to take intravenous immunoglobulin (IVIG), the same product used to treat immune deficiency, and put it in capsules for oral use so that it fights pathogens in the gut. A trial of a commercial product is currently underway (see the next section for more on IVIG).

✔ **Attacking allergies:** Nasal allergies have been shown to affect concentration and memory, two important issues for autistic children. Doctors should test children with chronic runny noses, asthma, eczema, or recurrent ear infections and sinusitis for traditional allergies with skin testing or with a blood radioallergosorbent test (RAST). If you choose, you can avoid allergens *and* try treatment with nonsedating antihistamines or antiinflammatory allergy medications (like Singulair).

✔ **Investigating infections:** Doctors should evaluate children on the autism spectrum who have recurrent infections just like typical children — by measuring immunoglobulin levels and conducting allergy testing.

✔ **Modifying metals:** If you've found that heavy metals influence your child's immune system, it makes sense to remove them. (Check out the section "Getting the Lead [and Mercury] Out" later in this chapter for more information.)

Tackling third-line therapies

Some aggressive therapies may become necessary when simpler, more controlled therapies (see the previous two sections) aren't working. Typically, such third-line-of-defense therapies are appropriate or accessible only for some children, as determined by a physician. Here's a list of aggressive therapies you and your doctor may discuss:

- ✔ **Colitis therapy:** For children who have severe gut inflammation (known as *colitis*), which is diagnosed by a gastroenterologist, your doctor may prescribe antiinflammatory medications normally used to combat inflammatory bowel disease.

- ✔ **Antiviral agents:** It isn't possible at the time of this book to fully define the significance of viruses in autism. The role of chronic viral infections and the efficacy of antiviral agents are still matters of dispute. However, you may consider a trial of an antiviral medication if your autistic child seems to lose skills at the time of a viral infection. Anecdotally antiviral drugs benefit some children, but many of these medications have side effects on neurotransmitters and on the brain, so how they work or for whom isn't clear.

Until doctors resolve the debate, children on the autism spectrum can get blood tests to see if they have adequate responses to their first MMR (the combined vaccine against measles, mumps, and rubella) to determine if they need boosters at age 4 or 5 years instead of getting it automatically.

- ✔ **IVIG:** *Intravenous immunoglobulin* (IVIG), a blood product containing antibodies pooled from many donors, is very helpful in combating infections in children whose own immunoglobulin levels are low. Even if it doesn't directly improve symptoms of autism, it should dramatically decrease the severity and frequency of infections in children with low IgG levels and help the children to feel much better. Doctors should give IVIG to immunodeficient children with autism just as they would to children with the same low immunoglobulin levels who don't have autism. Dr. Gupta from the University of California noted improvements in functioning in some autistic children who received replacement (low-dose) IVIG.

    Doctors also may use high-dose IVIG in autoimmune disorders (including PANDAS) to modulate the immune system; this treatment also has been reported to benefit some autistic children, especially those with high levels of brain autoantibodies, although researchers have only anecdotal evidence at this time.

    IVIG therapy is very, very expensive and is rarely covered by insurance. Also, an experienced physician should supervise this treatment because too high a dose can cause low white-blood counts and other adverse effects.

- ✔ **Other aggressive options:** Now that researchers have found some evidence of inflammation and immune activation in a number of the brains of autistic children, specific therapies proven useful in treating other neurologic disorders with similar findings are under investigation. Keep watching for new developments.

Biochemistry Begets Behavior: A New Way of Thinking

The traditional view is that autism is a group of behaviors caused by some defective gene or genes that enacted structural changes in the brain before the child was born. Traditional thinking dictates that because doctors can't repair structural brain abnormalities, they can do nothing to improve the child's level of functioning other than providing behavioral therapies.

The biomedical approach toward autism is based on a different idea — that autistic children have metabolic problems that doctors can diagnose and treat. Fixing broken biochemical pathways improves the immune system and helps to heal the gut, making the child feel better physically. Biomedical thinking insists that by paying attention to the medical (as opposed to only the psychiatric) issues of the children, along with the psychiatric and educational facets, caregivers and physicians can significantly improve the children's quality of life *and* their levels of functioning.

Because the idea of taking on biochemistry may seem even more daunting than tackling immunology, it helps to visualize biochemical pathways as roads taking a molecule from point A to point B to interact with another molecule. The body may provide three different possible paths or only one way to get there. Genetic variations contribute to how effectively molecules get from A to B — the average person's pathway may be the equivalent of having two lanes in each direction, and someone with "super" efficiency may represent an expressway. For many critical pathways, children with autism seem to have one-lane roads, so the metabolism isn't very efficient. On top of that, autistic kids experience environmental issues that reduce the efficiency even more by changing road conditions or blocking parts of the path, causing biochemical gridlock.

The following sections address the pathway issues autistic children face and how their metabolism functions as a result.

Shedding light on the broken pathways

Blocked biochemical pathways affect an autistic child in many ways — decreasing normal cellular energy production, for example, or decreasing the body's ability to get rid of toxic substances effectively. How much a block affects a child's body depends on how important the pathway is. If you're late getting to the barbershop, the consequence of letting your hair grow another day isn't the same as the consequence of not making it to the airport on time and missing a flight.

Research indicates that the two most-affected pathways in children with autism are methylation and sulfation:

- **Methylation** is the process of making a molecule longer by adding a carbon. This step is necessary for regulating DNA synthesis and enzymes, building neurotransmitters, synchronizing the firing of neurons, and creating cellular energy. Methylation is abnormal in the majority of children with autism.

- **Sulfation** is part of the biochemical pathway necessary for the removal of toxins from the body. It helps "pick up" waste molecules to dispose of them.

Another proven problem in children with autism is *oxidative stress,* equivalent to rust in the gears of metabolism. The stress is a chemical state resulting from inflammation, which keeps molecules "stuck" instead of easily bonding with each other.

Maximizing metabolism

It isn't easy to make neurotransmitters or any other molecules if the biochemical system is blocked and inefficient, so we know that biochemistry directly influences behavior. By measuring specific molecules and supplementing deficient components of the pathways, doctors can optimize metabolism so that behavior improves. For some children, metabolic deficiencies may be genetic. In others, a picky diet or poor absorption of nutrients through the gut is the problem.

Trying to normalize biochemical pathways can help improve overall functioning — you won't find a list of specific benefits for each supplement. You should discuss the approaches we present with your healthcare provider, but a practitioner with a naturopathic approach may be necessary to provide some of the options. Currently, studies are small, and available results are mostly anecdotal, but researchers like Jill James, Richard Deth, James Adams, and others are rapidly expanding the science behind the anecdotes.

Here are some things you can give to your child to improve metabolism and unblock the pathways causing problems:

- **Vitamins:** Vitamin levels are abnormal in many children with autism; it isn't unreasonable to consider supplementing, especially for children with poor diets, because many vitamins are necessary factors in multiple biochemical pathways. Such vitamins include

  - Antioxidant vitamins A, C, and E

  - The B vitamins to repair methylation, especially B6 (pyridoxine) or its active form P5P (pyridoxal 5-phosphate)

- B12 (cobalamin in the form methyl-cobalamin)

- Folic acid, or its active form, folinic acid

The simplest way to make sure your child has all these vitamins is by administering a multivitamin developed specifically for children on the spectrum, although methyl-B12 needs to be given by injection or nasal spray. An excellent resource for more information on doses for both vitamins and minerals (including appropriate multivitamins) is www.eas.asu.edu/~autism (go to the Advice link). You can also check out the Appendix in this book for more excellent resources.

✔ **Minerals:** Zinc and selenium levels are low in most autistic children, so you should ask your doctor about supplementing them while avoiding copper. Magnesium helps vitamin B6 function, and calcium supplementation is important for children on a milk-free diet.

✔ **Amino acids:** Measuring the child's blood amino-acid profile and supplementing as needed can help his body make proteins optimally, which improves metabolic functioning. Cysteine, the building block for glutathione, is frequently low in autistic children, but you can bolster it indirectly with the help of an experienced practitioner (it may not be well tolerated by itself).

✔ **Antioxidants:** Omega 3 fatty acids are frequently low in autistic children. (For more info on omega 3, see the section "Focusing on first-line fundamentals" earlier in this chapter.)

✔ **Glutathione:** Comprised of a string of three amino acids — cysteine, glycine, and glutamic acid — glutathione is the most important antioxidant inside cells of the body. Glutathione is critical for detoxification and energy production but is low in the majority of children on the autism spectrum (Jill James, 2005 and 2006). A naturopathic practitioner can discuss whether giving glutathione directly or boosting levels indirectly is the best approach for your child.

✔ **DMG/TMG (Dimethylglycine and Trimethylglycine):** Both of these supplements, which are available in health-food stores or through companies specializing in supplements for children with autism, help methylation, the most frequently "stuck" biochemical pathway. Consider starting with DMG, giving 125 mg once or twice daily.

✔ **Melatonin:** Melatonin is the body's sleep hormone and can help boost methylation. Start with 1 to 3 mg of melatonin (available in health-food stores) by mouth 30 minutes before bedtime. You can give it daily or intermittently, depending on how your child responds, particularly in children who have problems falling asleep.

Every child with autism is an individual, and most children are very sensitive to any changes in their systems, so you need to go "low and slow" when it comes to supplements or medications. Don't start everything at one time; wait at least two weeks before you add another supplement to the mix, and keep written records of your impressions of each supplement.

You may *not* want to tell your child's therapists or teachers about specific treatments you give, because their impressions of any improvements or setbacks in behavior or mood can be very helpful in deciding if the treatments have any benefit. Keep track of the observations made by people who are "blind" to any medical therapies in your written records. You should, however, keep your child's doctor in the loop for safety purposes.

Getting the Lead (and Mercury) Out

One of the most controversial topics in autism is the role of heavy metals in the disorder, with mercury being the most publicized and politicized. In addition to vaccines, exposure to mercury can come indirectly from the pregnant mother from fish eaten, dental fillings, or immunizations during the pregnancy — such as the flu shot or *rhogam,* given to mothers with Rh incompatability.

Other heavy metals also seem to be a problem for some children. Lead — found in the soil in many parts of the country from lead paint and leaded gasoline — and arsenic (a preservative in wood used on playgrounds) are particularly common.

Of note, exposure to heavy metals (with mercury being the best studied) causes far more abnormalities in animals with a genetic predisposition toward autoimmunity than in those without it (as is the case in children with autism). Additionally, animals and humans exposed to heavy metals often make anti-brain autoantibodies, especially with the right (or wrong, really) genetic background. Infections, either viral or bacterial, can also trigger autoimmunity in some disorders. Heavy metals can make viral infections more virulent and become chronic. The parallels between the immune system dysfunction in children on the autism spectrum and those seen in animals exposed to small doses of mercury are hard to ignore.

Why the autistic child?

The mercury-containing preservative *thimerosal* was used in routine childhood vaccines for decades, but the amount given increased in the early 1990s. But if all infants in the early 1990s received the same vaccines, why didn't every child get poisoned? Are children with autism "canaries in the coal mine" as the world becomes more toxic? Perhaps so. Several researchers have shown in the early 21st century that at least some children with autism have more heavy metals stored in their bodies, most likely because they have minimal ability to get rid of them through the body's detoxification system. Their biochemical and metabolic irregularities — such as low glutathione — interfere with the normal process of eliminating toxins and heavy metals, so without fixing the "broken" biochemistry, they continue to be more vulnerable to harm than other children, regardless of how they were exposed. (For more on biochemistry and metabolism, see the previous section.)

It's possible to give a medication to "pull out" heavy metals from the body, using medications called *chelators,* in order to measure whether unusual amounts of metals are present (see the final section of this chapter). Although it's still a highly controversial area, chelation is a potential option to explore for your child with autism.

Testing for toxicity

A *provocation test,* where doctors give your child a dose or several doses of an agent (called a *chelator*) that pulls metals out of the body — with urine collected before and after — is the most common way to demonstrate an abnormally high body burden of heavy metals. Not every child with a high level of metals or who ultimately benefits from removal of metals has a positive provocative test, and many children excrete other metals such as lead or arsenic before the test "pulls" any mercury out. As a result, this type of testing isn't well accepted by mainstream physicians; families who are interested need to find an experienced naturopathic practitioner to explore this option.

Traditional ways to test for heavy metals in the body include analyses of blood, hair, or urine. These tests turn up positive if the person is continually being exposed to a metal, such as with children who play in dirt contaminated by lead paint chips. But the tests aren't helpful if the exposure occurred in the past (because the metals have moved into the tissues instead of remaining in the bloodstream) or if the child has a fundamental problem in excreting the metal — both of which are likely true for children with autism. Metals stored in the body are notoriously difficult to detect because they're sequestered (or hidden). Measuring stored metals requires giving a "provoking" agent first.

Chelating

Chelation (pronounced *kee-lay-shun*) is the process of removing a heavy metal from the body via the bloodstream by using a medication that binds to the metal, allowing the body to excrete it through urine or stool. Many anecdotal reports from parents and clinicians indicate that the removal of toxic heavy metals has benefited a significant number of children with autism, although much controversy remains. Because no medication is specifically approved by the Food and Drug Administration (FDA) to remove mercury, naturopathic doctors currently use a number of agents, or chelators, by different routes — by mouth, intravenously, by suppository, or by a cream applied to the skin.

Examining the mercury hypothesis

A very important study supporting the "mercury hypothesis" of autism came from Columbia University in New York. Researchers took infant mice and mimicked the childhood vaccine schedule of the early 1990s, injecting baby mice with doses of the mercury preservative thimerosal — doses equivalent to those American infants received in the first six months of life. Results showed that animals with a genetic predisposition to autoimmunity had significant changes both in behavior and in brain structure; mice with a genetic resistance to autoimmunity had no abnormalities. Interestingly, both genetics *and* exposure to the metal were necessary. The fact that researchers observed these effects in mice *in the same brain areas* found to be abnormal in children with autism — even though they injected the mercury *after* the animals were born — is provocative.

Here's a list of the most common chelators:

- **DMSA (dimercaptosuccinnic acid, or Chemet):** FDA approved for removing lead in children with high lead levels and used for mercury poisoning in the United States. Published data supports its ability to pull mercury from autistic children. A great deal of anecdotal data currently indicates that DMSA also helps improve autistic symptoms, especially if given before adolescence. A controlled trial — where a treatment is compared in a head-to-head way with a "dummy" treatment, or *placebo,* to prove the treatment's effectiveness — is underway as of this writing.

- **DMPS (sodium dimercaptopropanesulfonate):** Not FDA approved for use in the United States, but doctors use it in Europe to treat mercury toxicity. DMPS may be better at removing mercury from the body than DMSA, but the safety profile isn't as well established. DMPS can be made to order by a compounding pharmacy (one where the pharmacist is licensed to specifically prepare individualized prescriptions instead of dispensing "ready-made" manufactured medications as a traditional pharmacy does) in the United States with a physician's order.

- **TTFD (thiamine tetrahydrofurfuryl disulfide, or Alithiamine):** A derivative of vitamin B1 (thiamine), TTFD isn't approved by the FDA except as an investigational drug for use in autism, but you may be able to obtain it from a compounding pharmacy if ordered by a physician. TTFD is most commonly applied to the skin, and a pharmacist can compound it with glutathione.

   This chelator is very safe, but many patients will have a skunky odor if they excrete metals bound to TTFD, so most people apply it at night and shower in the morning.

- **EDTA (ethylenediaminetetraacetic acid):** This chelator is particularly effective for removal of lead, but only a physician who's very familiar with how to give EDTA safely should administer it because mistakes can be life-threatening.

✔ **Sprays:** Several spray formulations for chelation are available on the market, but efficacy isn't as well documented with the sprays as with the other chelating agents.

It's wise to approach chelation knowing as much as possible. An excellent resource is www.autismwebsite.com/ARI/vaccine/heavymetals.pdf, which gives in-depth information.

First and foremost, to obtain a provocation challenge test (see the previous section) or to pursue chelating as ongoing treatment, you need to find an experienced healthcare practitioner to guide you through the process and individualize the treatment plan. Don't be afraid to ask around!

Before beginning chelation . . .

To make chelation safe and effective, complete these steps first before administering a chelating agent and after meeting with the practitioner who will guide you through the process (consult with your physician if you're already giving chelators and haven't taken these steps):

✔ Start vitamin and mineral supplements, because chelators will remove zinc and essential minerals in addition to the heavy metals.

✔ Clean out your child's gut as much as possible, especially alleviating constipation, if you will give the chelator by mouth.

✔ Boost antioxidant and glutathione levels (see the section "Maximizing metabolism").

✔ Make sure that your child has minimal ongoing exposure to toxins. For example, the child shouldn't eat large fish such as tuna. If the child needs to have a tooth filled during treatment, ask for porcelain or non-silver amalgams. And make sure that immunizations given to the child have trace or no thimerosal.

Although vaccines in the 1990s and before used thimerosal (mercury) as a preservative, routine childhood vaccines in the United States no longer contain more than trace mercury (with the exception of the flu vaccine, which is available with and without). Vaccination is important and saves lives, but you need to know what's being given to your child.

Understanding the chelation caveats

Although many children with autism excrete significant amounts of heavy metals during chelation and see the benefits, researchers have little evidence that any chelating agent can remove mercury from the brain. Because many of the chelating medications are also powerful antioxidants and help to restore sulfation chemistry, there may be more than one mode of action taking place.

Chelators have potential side effects, such as skin rashes or alterations of liver chemistries. Children should always be under medical supervision when undergoing chelation. They should be monitored with regular blood counts and liver-function tests, and doctors should check them to make sure that needed minerals like zinc are being replaced.

Chapter 8

Optimizing Nutrition

With Jane M. El-Dahr, MD, and Lauren Underwood, PhD

In This Chapter

▶ Keeping your dietary expectations in check

▶ Eliminating offending foods from your child's diet

▶ Considering going wheat and dairy free

▶ Introducing supplements to balance the diet

▶ Reviewing implementation strategies for your child's diet

*Y*ou are what you eat. How many times have you heard that expression? We're guessing a ton. People love to throw it around because what we eat has such a profound effect on how we feel and behave. And diet may just be able to help cure what ails us. What are we getting at? Well, we're here to talk about the role of nutrition in autism.

Parents of children with autism and adults with autism have noticed that dietary interventions — such as eliminating wheat and dairy products (common food allergens), adding supplements, or both — can go so far as to reduce autistic symptoms in some people. The autistic person's digestion can improve, and the diet can have positive effects on behavior, moods, and overall functioning.

In this chapter, we look at some of the dietary approaches that have worked for people and how you can implement them. We talk about changing a child's diet, but you can apply any of the advice we present to autistic adults, too. The approaches we introduce are safe — if you ensure that a medical doctor, nutritionist, or other qualified person supervises their use. You don't need prescriptions for any intervention we suggest. As a matter of fact, at times, the most difficult part of this journey may not be the actual diet itself, but handling your hopes and expectations, especially in a skeptical environment.

 The mounting evidence of the positive effect diet can have is leading to interesting new findings in the area of autism theories (see Chapters 2 and 3 for more information), but as of this writing, experts don't have a great deal of data regarding the interaction of diet and autism. An October 2005 editorial and study published in *The Journal of Pediatrics* noted that the GF/CF dietary intervention (which we explain in this chapter) appears to help some autistic individuals. Although you won't find any peer-reviewed research to support every recommendation we make in this chapter, *The Journal of Pediatrics* editorial explained that science backs up the parental reports and case studies that show that changing your diet makes a difference for many. Don't let the lack of evidence stop you. Improving diet and digestion is always a desirable goal.

Tempering Your Expectations

Changing the diet of an autistic person can go a long way to helping the person cope, but you need to remember that just because a treatment works for one person doesn't mean it will help your loved one. Each person with autism is unique in his symptoms and, hence, his treatment. After trying different dietary approaches, many parents report some benefits to their child's digestion and overall functioning. Some report enormous benefits, and other parents see no benefit at all.

Unless you observe a clear difference in your child after you change his diet, food sensitivities or diet may not play a role in his autism. But you also need to realize that some changes may occur immediately, and others take months.

Some of the tips we present in this chapter, such as avoiding refined sugars and artificial sweeteners, are common-sense behaviors that everyone should follow. Other actions are more complicated and difficult or may require you to suspend or ignore conventional wisdom you hold about what's healthy or nutritious for your child. For instance, cow's milk isn't essential for health in a dairy-intolerant individual — it interferes with health. You can get your child the nutrients that come in a glass of milk, such as calcium and vitamin D, through other sources that don't wreak havoc with his delicate system. But no matter the interventions you try, we recommend that you implement them slowly, one at a time, so that you can identify what exactly has an effect (see the section "Implementing Your Plan" for more tips on this topic).

Considering Your Dietary Intervention Options

When it comes to diets, as I'm sure you can glean from the myriad commercials that cross the television screen, you have options. When it comes to diets that an autistic person should consider, the options include nutritional supplementation, eliminating foods that may be causing digestive problems, and trying special diets. Parents have tried many of these options in conjunction with behavioral and other interventions (see Chapter 9), and you won't be alone if you try them. However, you should consult a doctor or qualified nutritionist for most of them.

Don't put all your faith in a radical approach, especially one that comes from the Internet, where pseudoscience constantly masquerades as news. A sound approach should be supported by more than one source. Be especially wary of companies that require you to use only their products or take only their advice. People will take advantage of a parent who appears desperate for help, and many parents of autistic children have spent thousands on "miracle cures" that were miraculous only in their ability to enrich their marketers.

Cleaning up your child's diet

It isn't uncommon to hear the parents of an autistic child say the *only things* that their child will eat are French fries, pizza, potato chips, and chicken nuggets! If your child begins to desire only junk food, warning sirens should start ringing — this isn't a healthy diet! Any food(s) that a person solely eats or eats in excess isn't healthy.

A good way to clean up your child's diet is to reduce junk food intake. Eliminating refined sugars and other processed foods can help improve his general well-being. Whether your child is autistic or not, he needs to eat healthily. And if he is autistic, eating healthy food is even more important because his immune and digestive systems need all the help they can get to function properly.

You must make sure that your child's school fully cooperates, as well as any caregivers, friends, and relatives. Many schools are becoming more nutrition-conscious, particularly with the rising obesity and diabetes levels in children. If your child's school focuses on special-needs children, it should ensure that your child isn't the only person on a special diet; the school should be used to accommodating such diets (see the section "Eating on the road" in this chapter for more eating tips for the road).

Do your best to involve your child in outdoor activities and sports if he's capable. His enjoyment and social interaction will keep the focus away from food.

Eliminating refined sugars and other processed foods

Cleaning up your child's diet by eliminating refined sugars and other processed foods may improve his functioning dramatically. Avoid foods and additives such as

- ✔ Commercial baked goods and candy
- ✔ Soft drinks and high sugar juices
- ✔ Nitrites/nitrates

✔ MSG (monosodium glutamate [also known as hydrolyzed proteins])

✔ Artificial colorings (such as red or blue dyes)

✔ Artificial sweeteners (such as saccharin or aspartame)

Concentrate on whole, organically grown foods like fresh fruits and vegetables that don't contain sugars and aren't processed. You want to know what's in the food you're feeding to your child, which is why reading food labels is important. Deciphering food labels (the listings of the ingredients in descending order of predominance) can be tricky. Generally, the longer the list, the more likely it is that you'll find an ingredient that you don't want your child to ingest. And if you can't pronounce the name of the ingredient, you probably shouldn't eat it!

Natural foods are what your child will do best with. Your child's diet doesn't have to be as varied as the typical American diet to be well-balanced. Many cultures around the world eat mainly the same foods with no adverse effects.

If you serve meat products or eggs, make sure they don't come from animals treated with hormones or antibiotics.

Considering food sensitivities

Many foods can trigger immune system reactions in a sensitive person's system. Some common food sensitivities for autistic individuals include the following:

✔ Wheat, whole wheat, oats, barley, corn

✔ Eggs, chicken, shellfish

✔ Peanuts

✔ Cow's milk, yogurt, ice cream, cheese, chocolate

✔ Refined sugar, aspartame and saccharine, and caffeine

✔ Chemical additives such as sulfur dioxide and MSG

✔ Citrus and nightshade vegetables (tomatoes, eggplant, potatoes)

✔ Yeast and alcohol

Soy, which people often use to replace other proteins in their diets, may not be the best choice for your child. Many people who don't tolerate foods such as dairy or wheat have intolerances to soy because the protein structure of soy is very similar to that of milk. If you find that this is the case with your child, consider potato or rice milk rather than soymilk. And because soy protein is similar to gluten and casein, some diet proponents recommend removing it as well. Besides gluten and casein, some parents report that removing corn or soy led to noticeable improvement in their children.

Allergies versus sensitivities

You may be curious about the difference between a food sensitivity and a food allergy. You often hear the two terms used interchangeably. Both can cause inflammation in your system, but food allergies usually provoke instant antibody reactions in your blood such as hives, nausea, headaches, or swelling. One common allergic symptom is eczema (also known as *atopic dermatitis*), an itchy red rash most common in the elbow creases or behind the knees (less frequently, allergic reactions may include difficulty breathing and/or anaphylactic shock).

Sensitivities, such as metabolic food disorders like lactose intolerance, don't affect the same part of your immune system and can be slower to act. Sensitivities can cause dizziness, fatigue, and headaches, which may not happen right after you eat the food, making them hard to detect. Many people have food sensitivities and don't know it. Some common symptoms of food sensitivities are headaches, flushing of the skin, red ears, red cheeks, hyperactivity/dizziness and/or fatigue, tantruming, acne, digestive problems, ear infections (especially if chronic), insomnia, and mental confusion.

Watch out for sweeteners as well. Don't take any chances if your child is hypersensitive. Stick to natural sweeteners that include maple syrup, honey, and stevia (a natural alternative to sugar or aspartame).

Going wheat and dairy free

Eliminating wheat and dairy from the diet is one of the first steps you should take after you get a diagnosis (see Chapter 18 for a list of more steps). Typically, doctors recommend a gluten-free (wheat, oats, rye and some other grains) and casein-free (milk and all byproducts of milk) regimen — the *GF/CF diet* — for autistic individuals. Why does this diet work? One school of thought says that gluten and casein are responsible for improperly broken-down dietary peptides — part of the opioid theory of autism — or that immune system dysregulation causes an abnormal immune response, whereby the body reacts to these substances by attacking itself. (See Chapter 3 for theories of autism related to this.)

"But bread and cheese are staples of the American diet!" We understand your frustration. To make your job tougher, autistic children can be notoriously picky eaters. Just remember that your child will feel better after you remove these products from his diet, so the hassle is well worth it. (See the section "Easing the transition" later in this chapter for tips.)

Sifting gluten and casein from everyday foods

You can find gluten and gluten-like proteins in wheat and other grains — including oats, rye, barley, bulgur, durum, kamut, and spelt — and in foods made from those grains. You can also find them in food starches, semolina, couscous, malt, some vinegars, soy sauce, flavorings, artificial colors, and hydrolyzed vegetable proteins. Gliadorphin (or gluteomorphin) is a peptide derived from the wheat protein gluten. Other related grains such as rye, barley, and oats also contain the sequence of amino acids found in gluten.

Casein is a protein present in milk and products containing milk, such as cheese, butter, yogurt, ice cream, whey, and even some brands of margarine. Manufacturers also may add it to non-milk products such as soy cheese, hot dogs, and tuna fish in the form of *caseinate*. Casomorphin (or caseomorhin) is a peptide derived from the milk protein casein.

"Hidden" milk and wheat can appear in ingredient lists, such as curds, caseinate, lactose, lactoglobulin, lactalbumin, bran, spices, or certain types of vinegar.

Some autistic patients have reported mild to dramatic improvements in speech and/or behavior after the removal of gluten and casein. Some have also reported fewer bouts of diarrhea and loose stools. No large clinical study exists yet to back up the GF/CF diet — such a study is expensive and difficult to do — and no foolproof test can determine who will be a responder. However, for any parent of a child caught in the vicious circle of autism, this is a treatment worth trying.

Beginning the GF/CF diet can seem difficult. Making up your mind to actually *do it* can also be difficult. Heck, finding out what products contain gluten and casein can be difficult (for some help, see the sidebar "Sifting gluten and casein from everyday foods"). But after you get the hang of it, like any diet, maintaining it is relatively easy. Just remember: Trying the diet and struggling through it to end up with a happier, healthier, higher functioning autistic child sounds much better than living with a poorly functioning child.

Be systematic in your approach, taking the following suggestions to heart:

1. **Try removing dairy first.**

   Doctors often suggest that you remove milk first because the body clears itself of milk/casein the quickest, and because dairy is the most problematic as far as the immune systems of autistic children go.

   Generally, if improvements occur, you'll observe them within the first few days to weeks, but it can be gradual.

2. **Try to keep your child dairy free for at least two weeks.**

   If you're not sure if your child is drawing any benefit, you can return a small amount of milk to the diet and see what happens. If the child's behavior deteriorates after you return the milk, you should return the child to a milk-free diet. If you see a clear worsening of behavior when you "challenge" your child with a food after at least a six- to eight-week period of "elimination", you know that the child is sensitive to that food. If however, after two months, you "challenge" the child, and observe no adverse reaction, then the reality is that this child most likely does not have this food sensitivity.

3. Try removing gluten/wheat.

Give this tactic at least three months and up to six to evaluate; it may take up to six months on a gluten-free diet for the body to rid itself of all gluten.

REMEMBER

A sensitive individual will feel the effects after ingesting even a very small amount of the protein, so make sure you remove all gluten and casein products from the diet entirely.

Trying other specialized diets

Some diets that nutritionists recommend for food-sensitive individuals have support in autism circles, although they have less experience with autism specifically (as opposed to GF/CF, which is widely practiced) and aren't discussed as often. For example, candida is a common yeast infection, and candida diets (used to treat *candidiasis*) eliminate yeast and sugar intake. An important reason to look at yeast as a contributor to autistic symptoms is that yeast is easily and safely treatable. If you suspect yeast may be a culprit in your child's condition, discuss this with your doctor. (*The Journal of Pediatrics* reported yeast overgrowth in the intestinal tract of some autistic children in May 2005. Consider the following sources for investigation: *The Yeast Connection: A Medical Breakthrough,* by William G. Crook, MD, [www.yeastconnection.com] and *Feast Without Yeast: 4 Stages to Better Health*, by Bruce Semon, MD, PhD, and Lori Kornblum.)

The Specific Carbohydrate Diet (SCD) — which removes specific carbohydrates, aptly enough — is a grain-free, lactose-free, and sucrose-free dietary regimen. The diet works by severely limiting the availability of carbohydrates to intestinal microbes, which require carbohydrates for energy. Researchers at Massachusetts General Hospital have found that children with autism frequently lack the enzymes in their gut that normally digest sugars, which is why this diet may particularly help those who continue to have GI symptoms despite other treatments. An alternative is to try a dietary enzyme product such as Carb-Digest (which specifically breaks down the problematic sugars) first before attempting this diet. Head to www. scdiet.org for more information.

Feingold's diet, commonly used among the AD/HD community, advocates eliminating all additives and chemicals from your child's diet; the diet may also call for the elimination of salicylates, which means you take out some fruits and vegetables and virtually all processed foods (check out www.feingold.org for more information). Feingold suggests that synthetic food additives can have serious learning, behavior, and/or health effects on sensitive people.

It's especially important when avoiding foods in the wheat and dairy categories to make sure your child eats well most of the time and that you supplement the things you take away when you extract gluten and casein from the
diet (see the following section for more).

Supplementing your child's diet

Dietary supplements promote the healing of the immune system, which is
compromised in many autistic individuals. They can also pick up the slack
when you eliminate parts of your child's previously unhealthy diet (see the
previous sections). We discuss many of these supplements in detail in
Chapter 7, so you should head there for more on the immune system and
why we recommend certain supplements.

Balancing essential fatty acids

Sometimes called "brain foods," essential fatty acids appear to be out of balance in the American diet (try watching some reality television for the evidence). You should have a balance of the fatty acids omega 3 and omega 6 in
your diet; yet, Americans typically eat much more omega 6, leading to an
omega 3 deficiency. See Table 8-1 for symptoms of fatty acid deficiencies
when it comes to omega 3 and omega 6.

Table 8-1	The Symptoms of Omega 3 and Omega 6 Deficiency
Omega 3	*Omega 6*
Dry skin	Excessive thirst and sweating
Tingling in arms and legs	Frequent urination
Immune dysfunction	Rough, dry skin
Sticky platelets	Poor wound healing

*(From Dr. Tapan Audhya, professor of endocrinology at New York University, who specializes in
nutritional biochemistry. Used with permission.)*

After 9 to 11 months of essential-fatty-acid supplementation, Dr. Audhya
(refer to Table 8-1) reports that you may see changes in blood pressure and
heart rate. Digestive and sleep patterns seem to improve after 6 to 9 months
in most cases, and abnormal bowel movements reduce by 80 percent. Social
withdrawal and repetitive movements may also lessen, allowing your autistic
child to interact with others more effectively.

You don't need a doctor's supervision to try to remedy a fatty-acid deficiency
because it's safe to do so on your own, and it's very common and easy to

remedy. The supplements help boost the immune system and increase over-all health. Some research shows that cod-liver oil, for example, has a positive effect in raising attention levels. Some people think cod-liver oil, which has omega 3 and natural forms of vitamins A and D, tastes bad. Not true! It should taste like salad oil; if it doesn't, it's rancid. You can purchase flavored chew-able forms of cod-liver oil if you still can't stand the taste. Cod-liver oil has omega 3 and natural forms of vitamin A and vitamin D. (See Chapter 7 for more information on fatty-acid supplementation.)

However, you should avoid very large doses of vitamins A and D because overdoses can be dangerous. And make sure the fish oils you use are high quality and that the manufacturer certifies them for low heavy-metal content. You don't want to create a metal-toxicity problem when you're trying to heal! Also, we don't recommend that you try to get all the oils from fish because of the high levels of mercury in many fish supplies.

Adding helpful vitamins and minerals

Autistic people often seem to have nutritional deficiencies, which is probably why you're waist-deep in this chapter. Researchers aren't sure which came first: the deficiencies or the autism. However, they do know that vitamins and minerals can help ease the strain of a testy system. In this section, we provide some supplements you should consider with your nutritionist's and doctor's input. (See Chapter 7 for an expanded version of this material, as well.)

Bernard Rimland, PhD, director of the Autism Research Institute (ARI) (www.autismwebsite.com/ari/index.htm) and a founder of the movement Defeat Autism Now! (DAN!), reports that vitamin B-6, given with magnesium, helps approximately 50 percent of people who try it, according to his studies. You can find more information on this research and other interventions at the Web site of ARI, which collects data on parents' experiences with drugs and nutritional supplementation. ARI has a database of more than 1,000 children who, according to Rimland, were "recovered" through biomedical means.

Nearly every study on the effects of large doses of vitamin B-6 shows positive results with no side effects. You include magnesium, a calming agent, to bal-ance the B-6 because they work together in the body. You should also include other B vitamins, such as folic acid, with the magnesium supplementation.

Your grandmother was right!

Epsom salt baths, a good source of magnesium (just ask your grandmother), really do work for calming some autistic kids. The active ingredi-ent, magnesium sulfate, relaxes, calms, and detoxifies the body. Sitting in a warm bath with about one cup of dissolved Epsom salts for 15 to 20 minutes can calm down a stressed, hyper-active child.

Other frequently recommended supplements include the following (this isn't a comprehensive list; you can find more complete information on these and other supplements in Chapter 7):

✔ DMG, or dimethylglycine, is a safe food that helps half of all autistic adults and children by improving speech and behavioral patterns. DMG is a naturally occurring substance taken by marathon runners to boost their immune systems. You can purchase it in health-food stores; the FDA even considers it a food.

✔ Pancreatic or digestive enzymes can help with digestive disturbances, such as constipation or chronic diarrhea, which are often seen with autism.

✔ Probiotic (good bacteria) supplementation focuses on *leaky gut* (see Chapter 7), which interferes with the absorption of nutrients into the body, and with abnormal bacteria overgrowth that results in a lack of "good" bacteria, which autistic people often experience.

✔ Buffered vitamin C boosts the immune system. We have high concentrations of vitamin C in the brain, and vitamin C helps the immune system.

✔ Calcium is helpful, especially if you're avoiding dairy products (see the section "Going wheat and dairy free"). You can find calcium in green vegetables such as spinach and broccoli, in nuts, and in seeds.

Implementing Your Plan

Sometimes food can have obvious bad effects, such as diarrhea or abdominal pain, but other times it takes some sleuthing and time to figure out what's really going on — like when your child's sleep patterns are off or she seems inattentive and you don't know why. So, you need a way to catalogue the food you give compared to the symptoms you see. This leads to — unfortunately — more paperwork. Keeping track of what your child eats and how she behaves for several weeks can tell you a great deal about potential allergies or intolerances. You can share your findings with your doctor and ask him to recommend a dietary intervention that may help your child.

Keeping a food and symptom diary

An effective way to figure out what foods distress your child's system before you take your concerns and suggestions to a doctor to begin your plan (see the next section) is to track what your child eats and how it affects her behavior for at least several weeks. The simplest kind of food and symptom diary works like this:

1. Take a sheet of paper and divide it into four columns.

2. **Label the columns in order from left to right as follows: Date, Time, Food, and Reaction.**

3. **Use the diary to chart any physical or behavioral symptoms, such as tantrums, irritability, drowsiness, stomach pain, sleep pattern, bowel function, including the approximate time of onset.**

   The more detail, the better, but don't be overzealous! At first you'll want to mark everything, but the novelty will wear off over time.

Table 8-2 provides an example diary entry you can use as a model.

Table 8-2		A Simple Food Diary		
Date	*Time*	*Food*	*Reaction*	*General Notes*
4/17	3 p.m.	Pretzels, grapes	Tantrum	Seemed to have stomachache; sleepy
4/17	6 p.m.	Chicken breast, rice, and carrots	No reaction	
4/18	1 p.m.	Peanut butter sandwich	Irritable for two hours	Poor sleep; diarrhea

Keeping a diary, among other things, can help you identify problems that don't stem from your child's autism. Aggression, for example, isn't part of the definition of autism, so if you see aggression after your child eats certain foods, the food is probably the culprit, not autism. Medical problems like intestinal disorders are treatable, and doctors should treat these symptoms, not dismiss them as autism-related.

The tricky part is that you may not see any pattern develop immediately. People tend to eat different foods together, not separately, so you may not be able to isolate the symptoms readily. If you have some trouble, you can begin to do some simple testing.

Say, for example, that you suspect eggs are causing your child some digestive distress. You start by keeping anything that contains eggs or has traces of eggs (food labels in the United States are required to give this information) from the child's diet for at least a week, and then you try giving her a little bit of the suspected allergen and closely monitoring the results. Now answer these questions:

- ✔ Did being away from the food reduce any of her symptoms?
- ✔ Did anything happen when you went back to the allergen that didn't happen during the previous week?
- ✔ Did your child become particularly withdrawn or particularly aggressive within hours of eating the food?

The answers to these questions tell you which foods to definitely avoid and which ones to keep an eye on. Retest the questionable items to be sure you see a connection before removing them entirely. Some of your child's behaviors may be triggered by other sensitivities she may have, such as temperature, noise, or bright lights.

You can take what you've found to your doctor or a nutritional expert (see the next section) to put your child on a specific diet aimed at improving her functioning (see the previous sections in this chapter for more on specific types of dietary interventions).

You can use your diary to track your child's progress with other interventions, too, so make sure you include which supplements you start and when you introduced them so you can monitor those as well.

Involving professionals

You take action on your dietary plan by finding an experienced professional to advise you on how to safely find a healthy diet for your child. Because dietary intervention isn't universally accepted, you need to find a doctor or nutritionist who's open to working with you, or else you'll get little support in your efforts. Some interventions, such as the GF/CF regime and essential fatty acid supplementation, are so safe you can do them on your own without risk. However, a qualified nutritionist can help enormously — especially one who has experience with food sensitivities.

Why specifically do you get your doctor or nutritionist involved? We don't consider it optional for most of the interventions we discuss here, and here's why: You need to ensure that you aren't depriving your child of essential nutrients when you alter his diet. Although he may be eating only pizza now, you don't want to cause or worsen any nutritional deficiencies.

Show your food diary (see the previous section) to your doctor or nutritionist and ask what dietary interventions he recommends.

Your doctor should continue to monitor your child's health during any nutritional intervention so he can recommend any necessary supplements to support the nutrients that may be temporarily lacking in the daily diet. Your doctor or nutritionist also should perform appropriate tests. Tests are needed to monitor your child if he's taking very high doses of a certain supplement, for instance.

You can't find an absolutely reliable test to determine who will be a responder to any kind of diet. However, lab testing may help you decide whether to consider trying a GF/CF diet or help convince other family members that it's worth a try. The following list mentions tests you may want to ask your healthcare professional about:

✔ The IgG food allergy test can provide clues regarding food intolerances. Most standard labs (like LabCorp or Quest) perform this test with a laboratory screening of a sample of blood drawn from the patient. Most insurance companies cover this testing.

✔ An IgE food allergy test, which also features a laboratory screening of a sample of blood, looks for Immunoglobulin E, a type of protein that's produced against a specific food — a food-specific antibody that circulates in the blood stream. The person must experience an exposure to the type of food before the body produces this type of response. Another way to test is by prick testing the skin to foods.

In the beginning of an intervention, we don't recommend telling others — teachers, relatives, friends, therapists — about any specific dietary interventions you're trying. That way, if anyone reports any changes in your child, no preconceived thoughts or feelings about the intervention influence what the others say. However, if you think that outsiders will compromise your efforts by giving your child foods you want to eliminate, you must consider informing them.

If your child is taking any medications during the dietary intervention, don't stop giving the meds without talking to your doctor. If you see improvements as a result of the supplements, you may want to taper off the medication to see what happens, but not without your doctor's supervision.

Easing the transition

It can be tough to change your eating habits, and even tougher to change somebody else's. This is especially true in the case of autistic children, who may refuse to try new foods in favor of sticking to foods they like.

Accepting change is easier when it's gradual and accompanied by pleasant substitutes. You should try to replace offending foods with new foods the child likes instead of eliminating entire categories that may be staples of the child's diet. Look for ways to make your child's favorite foods familiar without including offending ingredients. For example, you can make pizza without wheat flour, topped with casein-free cheese (see the section "Going wheat and dairy free"). You can also help your child discover new favorite foods. Experiment with new dishes and ethnic cuisines (under your doctor's permission, of course; see the previous section).

Be aware that food manufacturers are known to change their ingredients without warning. Some of their foods may still be included on Web lists, or ingredients may just change without you knowing it. We can't stress the importance of reading labels on all your food purchases enough! Also, beware of sugar-free claims on packaged foods. These foods may be high in other types of sugar, such as alcohol sugars, or they may contain artificial sweeteners. Read the labels carefully and don't buy anything that advertises a sweetener as the first or second ingredient listed.

It may be hard to create substitutes for the foods your child loved in the past, but be patient and persistent. The good news is that many people have stepped in to make it easier for the harried and overwhelmed parent. You can find cookbooks, Web sites, mail-order catalogs, and entire lines of products for special diets. As awareness of food allergies and intolerances continues to rise, companies that produce gluten-free bread, pasta, and dairy-free foods are proliferating.

Special Diets for Special Kids, by Lisa Lewis (Future Horizons), is a great resource for autistic kids. A mother of autistic children herself, Lewis explains both how and why to implement a dietary intervention strategy for children and adults with autism. Also, the Autism Network for Dietary Intervention, www.autismndi.com, founded by Lisa Lewis and Karyn Seroussi, is very helpful.

Natural foods stores, such as Trader Joe's, and Whole Foods stores are good places to find whole, unprocessed foods and organic fruits and vegetables. Some online and mail order companies include the following:

- ✔ Miss Roben's: www.missroben.com — 800-891-0083
- ✔ Kinnikinnick Foods: www.kinnikinnick.com — 877-503-4466
- ✔ Ener-G Foods: www.ener-g.com — 800-331-5222

Other Web sites, such as www.gfcfdiet.com, list foods that are gluten-free and casein-free and are commercially available at most standard groceries.

Experimenting with specialized diets

For children who have multiple food sensitivities, it may seem like everything they eat causes a reaction. For such a child, an *allergy elimination diet* may be the best course of action. In this diet, you start from scratch by providing bland foods, such as brown rice and steamed green vegetables, which sensitive individuals can tolerate. These foods stabilize your child's digestion. After you stick to this for a few days — with vitamin and mineral supplementation, of course (see the section "Supplementing your child's diet") — you start reintroducing other types of foods one at a time and watching what happens. For instance, the first week you may make eggs, the second week you add nuts and legumes, the third week brings meats and poultry, and so on. (As with all diets, you need a doctor or clinical nutritionist to help you implement this diet safely; see the section "Involving professionals".)

A *rotation diet* is another option that may be worth a try. With this diet, your child eats some foods for only a few days and then stops; these foods rotate in and out of the diet. This process helps your child handle foods that he's sensitive to by decreasing exposure to them.

If you do reintroduce a culprit food, and you see a reaction, it can take several days for the body to remove it again. And regardless of the interventions you try, you should implement them slowly, one at a time, so that you can try to identify what exactly has a positive or negative effect.

Eating the same or similar foods repeatedly aggravates people with food sensitivity. For instance, when you eat a wheat-based cereal with milk in the morning, pizza for lunch, and fettuccine alfredo for dinner, you're eating the same basic foods — dairy and wheat, just in different forms.

Eating on the road

Eating away from home on a special diet can be tricky, but times are changing. Even fast-food outlets are responding to parents' complaints about gluten in the fries (restaurants sometimes use small amounts of wheat flour when frying).

When traveling, you should bring along as much food as you can so that your child won't go hungry if you can't find appropriate meals. The good news is that many restaurants are becoming more proactive and knowledgeable about dietary restrictions, and many servers are happy to assist with your special requests. Some menus even have sections designated gluten-free or dairy-free. Bring the child's food with you to restaurants if you aren't sure that you'll find something acceptable. If your waiter or manager asks or comments on the food, explain that your child has food sensitivities; the staff should be happy to accommodate you. Don't be shy!

When your child is old enough, she can do her own screening, but for now, speak to all people who may be providing food to ensure that they adhere to whatever plan you're following. Send acceptable snacks to teachers to have on hand, and offer to make replacement foods for school/birthday parties. Initially, you may not want to explain the specifics of what you're doing, but you may want to ask outsiders not to give your child any foods without your permission. That way, you can control what she eats away from home.

Part III
Enhancing Learning and Social Skills

The 5th Wave
By Rich Tennant

"Your son's autism is still affecting his job, but we're learning to deal with some of his repetitive symptoms. For instance, he <u>always</u> shows up on time, <u>always</u> puts in a full day's work, and <u>always</u> lets me know when my toupee's not on straight."

In this part . . .

Educational/developmental/behavioral interventions or programs for children with autism can deliver inspiring results. The trick is in finding a program that's tailored to the unique needs of your child or student, without busting the bank. We're here to help you with this in Part III.

Teachers and parents have a great deal to do with the success of programs, and we give suggestions for what good teachers do and the responsibilities (and rights) of parents in the schools. Knowing the law is half the battle. We help you choose wisely among the many money-draining options, and we let you know what the federal government says you're entitled to, gratis, from your local school district. We include educational tips for understanding sensory issues and how they may affect how each child learns and experiences his or her world. Finally, we give you tips for improving your loved one's social skills so he or she can foster healthy relationships with friends and family members.

Chapter 9

Choosing an Appropriate Behavioral, Developmental, or Educational Intervention

● ●

In This Chapter

▶ Knowing what to look for in behavioral, developmental, and educational programs

▶ Evaluating state-of-the-art approaches, interventions and therapies, and philosophies

▶ Determining which intervention (or interventions) is best for your child

● ●

*A*lthough children with autism may have intelligence to spare, they often have trouble communicating. Meaningful, spontaneous communication doesn't occur naturally, as it does with neurotypical children. Most young children learn by imitating, watching, and interacting with others, but in the autistic brain, these abilities don't develop on schedule.

A child who has difficulty processing and responding to verbal requests — such as "What's your name?" — is unable to take part in social and academic settings without some help. Behavioral, developmental, and educational training can be a form of this help.

But one size absolutely does not fit all when it comes to autistic and developmentally disabled children. Some generalizations are true, however, such as the following: Early behavioral, developmental, and educational intervention gives autistic individuals a good chance of making strong progress toward obtaining the skills needed for academic and social success before they enter the school arena.

In this chapter, we explain how the more well-known training approaches work, what to look for in a good home-based or school program, how to decide which intervention is best for your child's needs, and — combined with the information in Chapters 4, 6, and 11 — how to evaluate therapists and teachers.

We explore other types of medical interventions in Part II of this book, as well as nonmedical interventions in Chapters 10 and 11 that can work in conjunction with the therapies we mention in this chapter. You should continuously evaluate and monitor your child to determine if the programs you implement are helping, or else why bother having them? If your child doesn't respond to a technically perfect, high-priced intervention backed by the best theories, you have a Rolls Royce with no wheels — expensive and impressive, perhaps, but useless for getting anywhere.

Understanding What to Look for in the Alphabet Soup of Approaches

The fruit of past research in autism includes myriad interventions, approaches, and techniques for working with children on the autism spectrum. Many parents and other caregivers that support people with autism often wonder which approaches and techniques are the best.

Unfortunately, deciding on the proper course of treatment can be difficult. The difficulty of choosing a methodology is compounded by the lack of evidence-based research across the different approaches. On one hand, plenty of research points to the significant health benefits of exercise — as emphasized by the Daily Life Therapy methodology we describe later in this chapter. However, evidence-based research for individual methods — much less comparing the approaches — remains lacking as a whole, possibly due to the difficulty in managing the many variables such as teacher competence, home life, hours spent in an intervention, medical issues, and so on.

Reframing the question "What's the best methodology?" to "Which methodology is best for this person at this time?" is a much more helpful approach. The most important thing to your child's improvement is that you choose a program that's individually tailored for your child's needs. But first, with the help of a knowledgeable professional, you must select a basic approach, or perhaps a combination of approaches. How do you choose a basic approach when 1) no single approach has consistently performed better than the others, and 2) some children benefit more from one approach than another? The key is to determine the approach that best fits the child's needs at the current time. Becoming familiar with the promising approaches we outline in this chapter will help you determine the best fit according to the child's challenges, personality, and family needs.

Actions and behaviors that lead to success in all interventions

Educational research on autism is exploding, and experts and families alike can now say many things with confidence about what works and what doesn't. Research has shown the following actions and behaviors to be aspects of a successful program for autistic children:

- ✔ At least 25 hours a week of systematic, planned, data-based instruction that actively focuses on engaging the child's mind, not just keeping him busy

- ✔ Teaching that stresses functional, meaningful, and spontaneous behaviors, such as asking for a glass of water, rather than isolated skills that don't have a purpose in real-life communication, such as touching one's nose

- ✔ Setting the kind of goals appropriate for any child, such as developing independence and social responsibility, which too much emphasis on a discrete-trials approach may lack

  Discrete-trials involve breaking down tasks into tiny components, which the child learns separately. This method can be helpful in teaching particular skills rather than in teaching social interaction.

- ✔ Predictability and routine on a daily basis, within a dynamic framework that evolves as the child progresses

- ✔ Ongoing assessment of outcomes

- ✔ Tools for students and teachers to communicate with each other

  You often see problem behaviors, such as head banging and pinching, in the brightest kids because they feel frustrated with being unable to communicate. You can eliminate problem behaviors by helping a child communicate simple messages, such as "I'm confused and need a break," even if the child needs to communicate by sign language or on a keyboard (see Chapter 10).

- ✔ Generalization of skills across multiple environments

  Does the child understand the dangers of touching a hot stove in other houses, not just his or her own, for example?

Keys to success in educational interventions

In a school setting, look for the following keys to a successful treatment program:

- Small teacher-to-child ratios
- Time spent in the presence of non-autistic peers so kids can see appropriate behavior modeled

    Intensive instruction with other disabled children is necessary, but too much time spent with others who have similar disabilities can be limiting.

    Some children may need to be in a separate environment for a period of time before being included in a regular education plan. For these situations, teachers must have a plan for gradual and meaningful inclusion of the children.

- Plans for a transition from the preschool classroom to grammar school.

    It's also important to plan for transitions to middle school and high school at the appropriate times. Older kids living with autism must also plan for life after K-12, which involves employment, appropriate interdependent living, community interaction, and relationships (see Chapters 14 and 15).

- Social instruction delivered throughout the day — for example, teaching proper interaction with peers, such as taking turns, and appropriate communication as well as learning to take another's perspective.

Research shows that individuals with autism tend to lack a function called the *Theory of Mind,* which aids you in imagining situations from other perspectives. In one study by Uta Frith, a professor of cognitive development in London, children were shown a box containing an object that was removed after another researcher left the room. When the researcher came back, the children made the assumption that the researcher knew the box was now empty, although the person couldn't have known this. The children couldn't grasp that the other person's experience had been different from their own. The Theory of Mind, which develops in non-autistic children at about age 3 or 4, makes dealing with other people much easier, and not having this ability causes difficulty for many autistic individuals. However, when groups of people with autism gather together at autism conferences, they seem to understand each other well. Perhaps what we are really looking at are challenges of autistic people understanding the non-autistic mind — and people not on the autism spectrum comprehending autistic thought patterns.

Exploring Popular Intervention Approaches

In this section, we explore some popular methods for teaching children on the autism spectrum vital skills such as communication, social interaction, academics, and appropriate behavior; these skills enable them to lead fulfilling and productive lives to the best of their potential. Specifically, we highlight seven approaches here: first, five methodologies/interventions/therapies (including Applied Behavioral Analysis, Daily Life Therapy, Developmental

Individual Difference Relation-Based Intervention, Miller Method, and Relationship Development Intervention) and then two philosophies (including Treatment and Education of Autistic and Communication Handicapped Children and Social Communication Emotional Regulation Transactional Support Model) that you can use to combine certain methods according to the needs of the child.

We hope that you find one or more of them suitable to you and your child's needs and outlook on life. Looking at the salient components of these methodologies, we attempt to outline where you can find each approach, who applies each method, and some of the unique contributions of each particular approach as you consider a program for your child.

The bad news? The cost of these approaches is dear. Many run from $30,000 to around $100,000 a year for implementation. Here's the question you must ask yourself and your family: How much more dear is the cost of *not* applying an intervention that your child needs — an intervention that may mean the difference between lifetime custodial care and living an interdependent, fulfilling, and productive life (see Part IV for more on these topics).

We realize that reality tends to rear its ugly head. It isn't easy for most people to come up with such resources. For some advice, see the end of this chapter and Chapters 16 and 18 for ideas on best utilizing the scarce dollars that you have to devote to caring for people with autism.

Applied Behavioral Analysis (ABA)

Applied Behavioral Analysis, or ABA, is a way of teaching and reinforcing appropriate behaviors. Psychologist Ivar Lovaas of the Lovaas Institute for Early Intervention at UCLA developed this technique. Professionals often use ABA techniques as a basis for designing behavioral interventions for autistic individuals.

Lovaas developed his applied behavior modification techniques to teach children to respond to requests and to communicate, and his methods have become one of the standards for the behavioral treatment of autism.

You can find Applied Behavioral Analysis in many public and private schools, where kids work with special-education teachers and some special-education school aides, and practiced by some private therapists who specialize in working with children on the autism spectrum. *Note:* ABA providers should be board certified.

Make sure that the practitioner employing the Applied Behavioral Analysis method takes into account the cognitive-developmental level of the child, as well as any possible neurological challenges, such as sub-clinical seizures, that may affect the child's behavior. (In contrast to drop and petit mal seizures, subclinical seizures show no outward manifestation, save for possible periods of "spacing out".)

Understanding how ABA works

Currently, the ABA method places more emphasis on engaging the child on his own terms, learning in natural settings, and using the child's own curiosity about a subject in which to build a lesson. In short, the ABA approach strives to be more like how children learn naturally and less like a classroom exercise or skills training.

The focus is on engaging the child continually and discouraging him from wandering off to activities such as repetitive play or self-stimulation (also known as stimming; see Chapter 10). ABA isn't meant to be unpleasant for the child; you should provide plenty of breaks, rewards, and opportunities for play.

Getting to the root of behavior

The concept of analyzing Antecedence, Behavior, Consequence may be one of the most valuable contributions of ABA. Analyzing the source of a behavior and what may be causing it is useful no matter what methodology or approach you use. The challenge of figuring out the meaning of behavior starts with examining possible *antecedents*. For example, suppose your child has a tantrum when you turn on the television. You want to analyze *what* causes this behavior. Maybe your child experiences sensory overload from the high pitch of the picture tube (that most people can't even hear), or maybe he perceives the screen-flicker rate the way most people see a strobe light. A rare possibility is that your child is seeking attention.

Consequence refers to the conditions maintaining the behavior. By acting out, your child motivates you to turn off the TV. With some experimentation, such as using an LCD screen rather than a picture tube to eliminate the possible sensory overload, you can work toward finding a solution to the challenging behavior. (You can find out more about analyzing behavior by using a Functional Behavioral Assessment in Chapter 11.)

Breaking actions into little steps

You may also hear the term *discrete trial* when exploring the ABA approach. The discrete trial approach was the original type of ABA. Using the idea of "task analysis," you break down a skill or routine into minute parts, and you teach each part separately and chained together as an entire procedure. Discrete trial training takes place in a one-on-one teaching situation and emphasizes rote skill building through very systematic and consistent approach by the practitioner. For instance, a child could spend hours practicing tying her shoes or buttering a piece of bread after breaking down the task into its separate components. Here are some example steps for the bread-buttering process:

1. **Open the cabinet.**

2. **Remove a small plate and put it on the counter.**

3. **Open the breadbox.**

4. **Remove a piece of bread and place it on the plate.**

5. **Open the refrigerator.**

6. **Take out the butter and place it on the counter.**

7. **Take the top off the butter dish and place it on the counter.**

8. **Open the silverware drawer.**

9. **Pick up a butter knife and hold it in your dominant hand.**

10. **Use the butter knife to slice off a small chunk of butter.**

11. **Hold the bread on the plate by the edges with your nondominant hand.**

12. **With the butter facing downward, wipe the knife across the surface of the bread, using long strokes and pressing lightly.**

13. **Take another small chunk of butter (see Step 10) if needed.**

14. **Continue Steps 10 through 12 until you cover the surface of the bread with butter.**

If the child does the task correctly, you reward her. You don't reinforce incorrect responses; you weed them out systematically by repetitive trials. Some children may be able to combine steps, and others may need one or more individual steps broken down further. Here's to hoping that the butter isn't too cold and spreads easily!

Forming ABA conclusions

Does the ABA approach work? Lovaas' 1987 landmark study showed that 40 hours a week leads to a significant increase in functioning. However, critics point out that he performed the study on a small number of selected high-functioning autistic children and not on a random sample.

Many have taken Lovaas' conclusions to mean that less than 40 hours weekly is useless, which isn't necessarily true. Research shows that children who receive targeted, intensive therapy — no matter which intervention — can be helped with as little as 25 hours a week.

Also, the type of structured routine provided by behavioral programs works well for many people with autism. Just as some neurotypical people, many people with autism don't react well to frequent changes and need help dealing with new situations. Some people on the autism spectrum need more structure than others, and ABA may be one way to achieve that.

Introducing the new kid on the block: Applied Verbal Behavior (AVB)

Applied Verbal Behavior (AVB) is an approach to ABA that stresses language development. AVB programs, based on behavioral psychologist B.F. Skinner's theories about the origin of verbal behavior, have become popular over the last decade. Skinner broke language down into the following categories:

- Requests
- Imitation
- Expressive labels
- Following instructions
- Responding to verbal behaviors

AVB teaches children to imitate, follow instruction, match, and what Skinner called *manding* — making requests by using vocalizations, signs, or a Picture Exchange Communication System (PECS). (See Chapter 10 for more on PECS.)

The rationale behind AVB is that language is supposed to be the foundation for many other skills; therefore, when you teach language first, you make other skills easier to acquire.

AVB differs from traditional ABA practices in that it's less formal and structured, and the process occurs more in the natural environment. Also, the approach tries to minimize errors through systematic prompting and fading. The approach has fewer studies available than discrete trial training, but the principles it's based on are similar.

Getting more information about ABA and AVB

You can find more information on ABA at the following sources:

> The Cambridge Center for Behavioral Studies Publication Office
> 336 Baker Ave.
> Concord, Massachusetts 01742-2107
> *Phone:* 978-369-2227
> *Web:* www.behavior.org/autism

For more information on board-certified practitioners, go to the Web site of the Behavior Analyst Certification Board at www.bacb.com.

You can find more information about AVB at www.behavior.org/vb/index.cfm?page=http%3A// www.behavior.org/vb/verbal_behavior_catania.cfm.

Daily Life Therapy (DLT)

The late Dr. Kiyo Kitahara of Tokyo developed Daily Life Therapy (DLT) in the 1960s. Originally a kindergarten teacher, Dr. Kitahara began forming her principles of DLT from working with one of her children who was on the autism spectrum. In addition to vigorous exercise and a fine-arts program, Daily Life Therapy mirrors Japanese philosophy by placing a heavy emphasis on group interaction rather than the intensive one-on-one teaching you find in other interventions. Instruction takes place in a classroom with a number of other children; practitioners provide supports to enable the autistic child to benefit from group-oriented teaching.

Although DLT is primarily a day school, residential options exist for a limited number of children, where the tenets of DLT are generalized to their living situations. Children ages 3 to 13 are accepted and may stay until they "age out" at 21 if needed. As of press time, there are no certified DLT practitioners, and the approach is available only in Tokyo, Japan, and in Boston, Massachusetts. However, schools in South Korea, Uruguay, and the United Kingdom are developing DLT programs with support from the Musashino (Japan) and Boston Higashi Schools.

Understanding how DLT works

Some experts, including the late Dr. Kitahara, feel that children learn more when exposed to the interaction of other students. Therefore, DLT emphasizes group dynamics rather than the individual instruction concentrated on in other approaches. DLT also focuses on physical education and emotional regulation through art, music, and academics — topics that form the core of the program. The program also emphasizes the acquisition and development of communication and daily living skills.

Physical conditioning

Practitioners of DLT believe regular and rigorous exercise builds a foundation for good health. Children attending the Higashi Schools (in Tokyo or Boston; see the section "Getting more information about DLT") start the day jogging or learning to ride a unicycle, walking on stilts, doing jumping jacks, and performing other gymnastics demonstrated regularly at school festivals. Educators at both the Boston and Tokyo schools find that regular exercise helps reduce excess stimming and aggressive behaviors, promotes better sleep habits, and paves the way to emotional stability and academic success. Plus, with the endorphins that regular exercise releases, the students (and the faculty as a result) feel much better. Figure 9-1 shows students competing in a road race, which they've been training for on a daily basis through jogging and other physical activities.

Figure 9-1:
Higashi students competing in a road race.

Emotional regulation

Mastery of self-care skills is believed to help with the development of self-esteem and contributes to emotional stability, which is vital to getting along with others and yourself. Higashi's programs in the fine arts and music take over where physical education leaves off. Each child learns how to play the recorder — not only for the musical aspects, but also for practicing vital skills in communication and working with others. Cooperating with others for a common goal is exemplified by the Higashi Schools' stunning *Jazz Band,* which regularly performs both on and off the Boston school campus. In addition to music, DLT's extensive art program enables the students' work to appear on book covers and other venues.

Academics

Education is the primary reason why most students attend school. Like with the other aspects of daily life at DLT schools, teachers educate in a group format. However, the schools provide plenty of support to students on the autism spectrum with a high teacher-to-student ratio. As much as possible, instructors at the schools strive to teach their students as close to grade level as possible.

Getting more information about DLT

Dr. Kitahara provided a three-volume set to fully describe the DLT program:

Daily Life Therapy: A Method of Educating Autistic Children (Nimrod Press)

The Boston Higashi School's address is as follows

Boston Higashi School
800 North Main St.
Randolph, MA 02368
Phone: 617-921-0800
Web: www.bostonhigashi.org

In Japan, the Musashino Higashi Gakuen is an elite private school for regular-education students. What's interesting is that in addition to the school being in high demand by parents of regular-education students, about one-third of the population (of around 600) is made up of children on the autism spectrum. With the autistic students included as much as possible, it's almost impossible for a casual observer to differentiate between the children with autism and those without. Here's the contact info for the school:

Musashino Higashi Gakuen
3-25-3 Nishikubo Musashino, Tokyo, Japan 180-0013
Phone: 0422-54-8611
Web: www.musashino-higashi.org

Developmental Individual Difference Relation-Based Intervention (DIR)

Practitioners of *Developmental Individual Difference Relation-Based Intervention* (DIR), developed by Stanley Greenspan and Serena Wieder, approach autism from a developmental point of view rather than as a behavioral issue. DIR is a less-structured model for behavioral intervention, focusing on strengthening and then building upon the emotional bond of the child with his or her caregiver. This method is often referred to as *Floortime;* however, the Floortime component is only part of the approach.

In a departure from the DSM descriptors of autism (see Chapter 2), Greenspan and Wieder recognize that children with autism tend to have biological challenges interfering with the processing of sensory input, and that they have difficulties with motor planning and sequencing tasks.

Understanding how DIR works

Like with TEACCH and SCERTS (discussed later in this chapter), DIR is centered on using existing therapies as well as developing new approaches to encourage children to pass through six hierarchal functional-developmental milestones. One of the unique contributions of DIR is that practitioners take into account the individuality of each child when bringing him or her into the world of human relatedness. Additionally, you place an emphasis on working with the entire family as opposed to just the child.

In their book *The Child With Special Needs* (Perseus Books), Greenspan and Wieder identify their six developmental milestones a child with autism needs to master in order to develop the necessary skills in communication, thinking, and coping with the world on an emotional level. Due to the developmental nature of the stages, a child must master each milestone before attempting to reach the next level.

The following list presents the six milestones that a qualified DIR practitioner helps guide a child through:

1. **Self-regulation and interest in the world.** Success in the first stage means the child can use his five outer senses of sight, touch, taste, smell, and hearing, as well as the two inner senses — the vestibular (for balance) and proprioception (for awareness of the body) — to gather information from the environment. At the same time, the child learns self-regulation, enabling successful interaction with the environment. The child begins to form threads of connectedness with the objects and people around him. (You can discover more about the senses in Chapter 10.)

   A child who hasn't mastered this stage becomes overwhelmed with sensory input, resulting in irritable behavior such as a whining or a tantrum. Other children may take little interest in their environment and seem detached. Most interaction with your child at this point should be sensory-motor related, such as swinging, tickling, and bouncing. You need to be aware of the child's regulatory state so you don't over-stimulate him.

   You can find more information on how to interact with your child and on carrying out the following stages at the Web site home.sprintmail.com/~janettevance/floor_time.htm#ToSixDevelopmental Milestones.

2. **Intimacy.** A child at the second stage seeks interaction with her peers and others in a warm, joyful, and loving manner. The child takes the thin Stage-1 threads for relating to objects and people and parlays them into enjoyment and pleasure. If the child doesn't reach this stage, she interprets her environment as a confusing, scary, and painful place, which often results in a desire to seek the company of adults, who generally have more patience than the child's peers.

3. **Two-way communication.** At the third stage, a child understands the impact of her interactions with others, which results in greater security when relating to people. The child displays two-way communication with gestures to both initiate interaction and to respond to communication from others. The child can now weave the threads of interaction with the environment into yarn for a stronger connectedness with her environment.

   A child who doesn't reach this level can be hard to engage, may seem oblivious, and may seem content to observe from the sidelines, as if she wants to get involved but doesn't know how. The child faces difficulties in reading nonverbal and pragmatic information and requires outside help to facilitate interaction and take initiative.

Practitioners of DIR refer to the initiation of communication as *opening,* and responding to another person's communication as *closing,* a circle of communication.

4. **Complex communication.** After the child masters the basics of communication, she can now string a series of gestures together in order to convey wishes and intentions, and she can read these gestures in others as well. The threads of connectedness, which she has now woven into yarn, become stronger as the child realizes the power of her communicative attempts.

   Issues of sensory integration may be the causes for failure to work through this stage. Not reaching this stage results in a child who becomes overwhelmed when the complexity of two-way communication increases.

5. **Emotional ideas.** A child who masters the fifth stage can engage in representational play. For example, she may use a toy car for pretend races, travel, accidents, and repairs instead of turning it upside-down to spin the wheels. A girl may feed her baby doll and tell her "night night" when it's time to sleep. The child also begins to narrate these activities. Her words now have meaning; they don't just symbolize objects, events, people, and ideas. The child can use words to explain thoughts and feelings and to create stories about particular objects, such as the car or the doll.

   A child who can't master this level may still show an interest in toys and keep calm, but she'll communicate only when motivated by a need. For example, the child may spend most of her time spinning the wheels of her toy car rather than using it as an object to drive to a location.

6. **Emotional thinking.** A child who masters this stage can connect patches of emotional expression and separate representative pretend-play events to form a quilt of emotional connectedness. For example, instead of playing with toy cars and dolls as separate events, the child connects the two activities. After the doll goes to sleep, mommy and daddy doll may put her into the car for a drive to the ice cream store or to play at a friend's house. The child develops a greater understanding of self and how her actions affect another person, and vice versa. The child can interact on higher levels of emotion as her verbal and spatial skills increase. For example, the child can now say, "I'm happy that you gave me cookies and milk."

   A child who can't master this stage remains unable to link the emotional patches to form a complete quilt. Although it may seem like the child has mastered the previous emotional milestones, at times the achievements fall apart under stress, and the child can't close circles of communication.

As both the DIR and ABA approaches (see the section "Applied Behavioral Analysis [ABA]") continue to evolve, some autism experts note that DIR is complementary with ABA, as they both borrow what works from one another. The discrete trial training component of ABA is often preferred for a child who lacks basic cognitive and interactive skills. However, critics of ABA contend that it focuses so much on rote learning that it limits children; they perform tasks without gaining understanding of what they're doing. Defenders of ABA say that as ABA continues to evolve, many of the criticisms no longer apply. For example, actions such as spraying water or vinegar on a child to discourage a behavior are no longer practiced.

Getting more information about DIR

Dr. Greenspan and Dr. Wieder still practice DIR; however, the needs of autistic children are so great that additional certified practitioners are required. You can find a list of certified DIR practitioners on the DIR Web site at www.ICDL.com.

The Interdisciplinary Council of Developmental and Learning Disorders (ICDL) holds a large annual conference in Bethesda, Maryland. The conference features many presentations on DIR and other topics related to autism. The mailing address is as follows:

> Interdisciplinary Council of Developmental and Learning Disorders
> Stanley I. Greenspan, MD
> 4938 Hampden Lane, Suite 229
> Bethesda, MD 20814
> *Phone:* 301-656-2667

You can find additional information about DIR in the book *The Child with Special Needs* (Perseus Books), written by Dr. Greenspan and Dr. Wieder.

Miller Method

Arnold Miller spearheads the *Miller Method* from the Language and Cognitive Development Center (LCDC) in Massachusetts. The Miller Method aims to close gaps in how a child perceives and thinks about the world and in the child's developmental progress by using a *systems concept* — in other words, using the desire to complete units of behavior as a jumping off point for learning new things. The vehicle for the learning is elevation on specially built structures about 2½ feet above the ground.

The developmental aspect of the Miller Method considers children with autism spectrum disorders as completely or partially stuck at earlier stages of development; therefore, the approach structures its interventions to spur on development. The cognitive aspect of the Miller Method promotes cognitive development by structuring the environment to be conducive to increased cognitive development. The emphasis on thought processes contrasts with other, more behaviorally oriented approaches, which devote most of their focus to stimuli and responses.

The Miller Method is based at the LCDC, located in Massachusetts. You can also find certified practitioners throughout the United States and Canada (see the section "Getting more information about the Miller Method"). Unique to the Miller Method is its Video Conferencing Oversight (VCO), where Arnold Miller and other senior staff members supervise sessions via cameras, television monitors, and ISDN lines or the Internet.

Understanding how the Miller Method works

Defined by Arnold Miller, founder of the Miller Method, as an organized unit of behavior around an object, person, or event, the *system concept* serves as the engine behind the power of the Miller Method. A *system* is a coherent organization (functional or nonfunctional) of behavior involving an object, event, or person. Systems may be quite small, such as opening and closing doors, or quite elaborate, such as sorting videos on the shelf in alphabetical order. The hallmark of a successfully formed system is a desire evident in the child to continue the activity after an interruption occurs.

The concept of the system plays a role in restoring normal development in the Miller Method in two ways:

✔ Building on the repetitive behaviors (systems) the children manage to achieve, such as lining up blocks.

✔ Teaching children certain behaviors that they haven't been able to spontaneously develop by introducing repetitive activities, such as teaching a child how to pour water from a cup.

Practitioners of the Miller Method use the power of an *interrupted system* to teach functional communication and general expansion of a child's awareness of the world around him. If you've ever left off the last word of a song, such as "Twinkle Twinkle Little Star," in anticipation of a child's response to end the song, you've disrupted the system of a musical phrase hoping that the child will fill in the last word.

For typical development to occur, practitioners of the Miller Method believe that the child must pass through the five stages indicated in the following list. The child experiences the first four stages prior to "repertoire" at the pre-executive functioning level. In other words, the child is driven to act by events in his or her environment without cognition:

1. **The first phase is *orienting*, where the child makes initial contact with a stimulus within her surroundings.**

   For instance, orienting in an infant can take place as she looks toward a rattle that an adult is shaking nearby.

2. **After orienting, the child engages with the stimulus by interacting with it.**

With the rattle example, engagement occurs as soon as the child reaches toward the rattle and makes contact with it. Arnold Miller believes that orienting and engagement are prerequisites for forming a system.

3. **A system forms when the child begins to act on the stimulus or develops another repetitive, predictable, organized unit of behavior around it.**

The child forms a system when she begins to shake the rattle after touching it or develops another repetitive, predictable behavior.

The child "owns" the system if both of the following two actions occur:

- The behavior continues on its own.

- The child makes a compensatory attempt to continue the behavior after the rattle is removed by shaking her hand as if she's still holding the rattle. You see compensatory actions if, for example, a song is played and the performer stops on the penultimate note. Audience members often react to complete this interrupted song (system) by singing the last note.

Referred to as a *system disruption,* removal of the rattle often elicits a functional communicative attempt to continue the shaking behavior, which commonly leads to a tantrum. However, before that tantrum occurs, there should be an attempt at functional communication, such as a vocalization geared to retrieving the rattle or perhaps sign language. When functional communication occurs, the practitioner should immediately return the rattle to the child. Should the session dissolve into a tantrum, the practitioners should return the rattle or make another attempt to reduce or eliminate the tantrum. The concept of employing system disruption is a central concept of the Miller Method.

4. **A *ritual* forms when salient sensory input from an aspect of the system activates the entire behavior.**

For example, just the sight, touch, or sound of the rattle causes the child to shake her hand as if she's actually holding the toy. If you put other toys in the room, the child will still be compelled to interact only with the rattle.

At this point, salient stimuli from the environment externally drive behaviors. The child who can form a system is dominated by that system; she lacks the ability to choose whether to engage in the system.

5. **The final phase, where practitioners of the Miller Method strive to bring all children, is *repertoire.* At this stage of development, the child has the element of choice.**

The child can choose to interact with the rattle or some other toy. Post-executive function develops gradually over time from when the drive to engage with salient stimuli arises from external events to this engagement driven by internal events, or *choice.*

Elevated structures are employed in the Miller Method with the idea of raising a child's awareness of the world around him. Just as you pay more attention to where your feet are if they're on a raised plank, children with autism can focus better when placed on elevated objects. The concepts implemented when working with the elevated structure are then generalized to the ground. (You can find plans for building elevated structures at www. cognitivedesigns.com.)

In addition to promoting enhanced focus, the raised structure limits the tendency of children on the autism spectrum to "spin off" into space. Finally, the structure improves what Arnold Miller refers to as "architecture", meaning that the child's face is now at about the same level as the faces of adults.

One of the most unique forms of the raised structures is the elevated square (see Figure 9-2). This device consists of four 18-inch-wide planks set 2½ feet above the ground on four large wooden boxes, and is painted in yellow with blue trim. Each of the four corners has stations where the child can work on concepts such as "open", "close", "pick-up", "give", and so on.

Multiple practitioners should be present to assure that the student doesn't fall off.

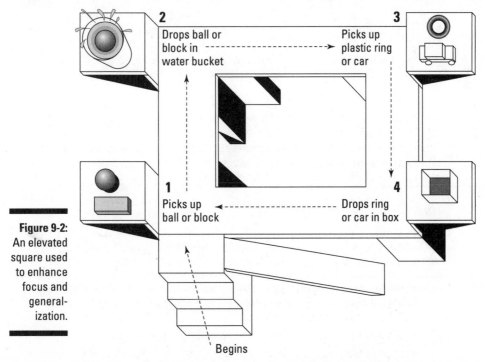

Figure 9-2:
An elevated square used to enhance focus and generalization.

Getting more information about the Miller Method

You can find more information about the Miller Method and its training programs from the following source:

> Language and Cognitive Development Center
> 154 Wells Ave., Suite 5
> Newton, MA 02459
> *Phone:* 800-218-5232
> *Web:* www.millermethod.org

You can also check out Arnold Miller's forthcoming book, *The Miller Method: Developing the Capacities of Children on the Autism Spectrum* (Jessica Kingsley Publishers) due out in 2007, which clearly describes the Miller Method approach and is full of ideas for helping people with autism.

Relationship Development Intervention (RDI)

Beginning in 1996, Steven Gutstein and Rachel Sheely constructed the treatment Relationship Development Intervention (RDI), based on concepts developed from prior autism interventions such as Applied Behavioral Analysis (ABA), the Miller Method (MM), and Developmental Individual Difference Relation-Based Intervention (DIR). Similar to the latter two methods, practitioners of RDI focus on remediating the delays and differences in cognition, emotion, communication, and social interaction that cause difficulties for autistic people.

Success with the RDI method requires heavy family involvement. Parents and other family members must help guide the child or relative toward more flexibility and thoughtfulness by presenting novel and increasingly unpredictable settings to challenge the child's growth. In addition to family members, the child's therapist, school staff, and other supporters must make a commitment to the child with autism for the method to achieve success.

Understanding how RDI works

Relationship Development Intervention emphasizes enabling people with autism to have a high quality of life. Practitioners achieve this goal by developing *dynamic intelligence* in their children that most people who don't reside on the spectrum seem to have. Practitioners attempt to create fun and enjoyable learning sessions for everyone involved to make the transition to dynamic intelligence easier for all affected participants.

Those of us who engage in spontaneous conversations and tell jokes may take dynamic intelligence for granted. Dynamic intelligence also creates the emotional connectedness of sharing a knowing glance, collaborating with others, drawing satisfaction with close friends and significant others, and living an appropriately interdependent life.

A stop-and-go experiment in co-regulation

Try the following experiment with a friend or coworker: As you walk down the hall or street, vary your pace while keeping up a conversation of your choice. Most likely, your friend will match your walking speed on a subconscious level. If you ask her if she noticed anything about your walking style, she may realize that you kept changing your speed. But, you had to bring the thought into her conscious mind with your question.

If your friend kept pace with your walking, she successfully co-regulated her behavior with you. Although we take co-regulation for granted as something that occurs naturally in most people, persons on the autism spectrum may lack this important social-interaction skill. However, people with autism can acquire the skill of co-regulation; this is one area that RDI focuses on.

The six areas of emotional intelligence

Practitioners of RDI strive to teach children with autism how to join in on the pleasures of life by developing six areas of emotional intelligence, as indicated on the RDI Web site (www.rdiconnect.com):

- ✔ **Emotional referencing** allows a person to understand how another person is feeling through verbal, nonverbal, and other communication pathways. For example, you can share the joy another person experiences or perceive a teacher's disapproving look before someone throws a spitball.

- ✔ **Social coordination** is what people use to match or complement others' emotions. For example, you may express sadness for a friend as he describes a lost opportunity or consciously put on a happy face to convince him that "it's not so bad after all". Social coordination also includes the ability to repair a breakdown or misunderstanding in communication.

- ✔ **Declarative language** allows you to make statements about the world by using words or nonverbal communication. This skill allows the person with autism to express and invite curiosity, participate in interactions, share perceptions and feelings, and coordinate actions with others. For example, you may say, "The sun is bright today!" or "You can do it."

- ✔ **Flexible thinking,** also known as cognitive shifting, enables you to go with the changing flow of events, even when they're unpredictable. You may say, "Although the 2 o'clock math class was cancelled due to a school assembly, I will remain calm and ask my teacher the math questions I have during lunchtime."

- ✔ **Relational information processing** means being able to adjust the volume of your voice to the environment. For example, a loud indoor voice is different from a loud outdoor voice. You employ relational information processing skill as you co-regulate your walking speed to match another person's speed. In this case, no single correct pace exists; the speed is based on external factors.

✔ **Foresight and hindsight** refers to a form of prediction and evaluation. For example, you may be able to predict the outcome of being polite and saying "Thank you". Hindsight enables a person to recall a time when a parent or friend got upset when she failed to give thanks for extra efforts.

The eight guiding principles of RDI

Educating children with autism on the six areas of competence (mentioned in the previous section) form an underpinning allowing an RDI practitioner to concentrate on eight guiding principals for enabling children with autism to more successfully interact with people and their environment.

An elementary woodshop teacher of mine used to frequently say, "The faster you go, the further behind you get." The same holds true with RDI. You need to take the amount of time necessary to achieve success, because you must give children time to properly master the earlier skills that serve as a foundation for later development.

1. **Building a strong foundation.**

    Practitioners develop systematic and measurable outcomes for the child's program. A sample outcome may be to have the child become flexible in choosing amongst a number of toys to play with.

2. **Developing a user-friendly environment.**

    Modifications and pacing are based on careful evaluation of a child's capability. In that way, a child has a safe environment in which to explore new ways of interacting. In other words, the pace of going through activities is often slowed at points where the child has to make a choice and when different choices are encouraged.

3. **Implementing guided participation through a "master" and "apprenticeship" relationship.**

    Usually fulfilled by the parents as they work side-by-side with the child to explore and develop new ways of understanding the child's environment. Sometimes, you may want another person who's significant in the child's life to serve as a "master." Initially, the master leads as the child takes on specific roles. As the child develops more ability to co-regulate, the master begins to serve more as a reference point for handling new and confusing situations. The final goal of this principle is for the child to become a "junior partner", engaging alongside the master as equals.

4. **Improving personal episodic memory.**

    People with autism often have very good procedural memories. Examples of procedural memory include arithmetic and factual descriptions of events. *Episodic memory,* on the other hand, engages the emotional aspects of interaction. By "freezing" the action at key points, you create a figurative spotlight that illuminates important emotional experiences. You then find ways to preserve that memory through regular review. Telling stories, with props as needed, as well as daily reflection are encouraged.

5. **Building motivation for dynamic systems.**

   You can motivate children by using the principle of episodic memory so they can remember the emotional content of activities. Children will then want to experience these emotions again, which serves as a powerful motivator to repeat the activities.

6. **Changing communication.**

   RDI practitioners encourage children with autism to use much more declarative rather than imperative statements. Declarative statements, such as "We're driving faster," "Oh oh," and "We can do it" focus on emotional states rather than questions or demands to modify an activity. Examples of imperative statements include "Put that toy away," "Look at me," or "Say please." Within the RDI model, declarative statements are used to predict, reflect, and regulate interaction and to demonstrate curiosity.

7. **Creating opportunities for practice.**

   Incidental learning makes teachable moments out of ordinary and unplanned events. For example, instead of just giving up your seat to a person in need on public transportation, you may explain *why* you're doing so.

   RDI practitioners take the concept of incidental learning one step further. They assist parents in adapting their schedules to increase the number of incidental learning events. For example, an activity as simple as walking around the block may be loaded with additional opportunities for practice. You can walk like cartoon characters, suddenly stop and start, pretend to walk on the moon, or pretend that a walking partner is blind and needs assistance from the child.

8. **Progressive generalization.**

   A child's successes in earlier systems form the foundation for engaging in more complex activities later. At this point, different people and settings should be employed. Before you may have removed potential distractions, but now you purposely introduce them into the child's environment with the goal of developing skills for focusing on what's important.

   For example, you may introduce the child to situations where communication frameworks break down and are impossible to repair. You may introduce increasing amounts of distraction and disorder from a television in another room, or you may "suddenly" run out of milk and have to determine what to do to correct the situation.

Throughout the RDI process, children are encouraged to engage in experience-sharing interactions; you don't restrict them to instrumental social interaction. Instrumental social interaction relies on rote scripts and is conducted to obtain a specific endpoint. In other words, people serve as "instruments," or the means to an end in order to obtain something we want (like information, money, food, or any other commodity). One such example is ordering a hamburger from a cashier.

Your challenge is to lead the child toward experience-sharing interactions, where people are related to as ends unto themselves in order to create common experiences. Experience-sharing interactions introduce novelty and variety into our lives. An example of such an experience is two friends deciding to take a walk in the woods for the sheer beauty of seeing the trees.

Getting more information about RDI

RDI is available from certified consultants throughout the United States, Canada, and Australia. Certified consultants have to participate in a rigorous training program and require recertification every 12 months. (You can find specific information on finding these consultants at the RDI Web site, www.rdiconnect.com.)

The amount of RDI a family involves is scaleable to its needs and other factors. By gleaning information from RDI Program books, DVDs, the program's two-day introductory workshop, and other sources, you can implement portions of the RDI Program as time and finances allow. Families who want to go "whole hog" can initiate the process of obtaining the RDI intervention with a phone call to the Connections Center at the number we list here. The program offers a four-day training for parents and caretakers engaging in full-time RDI intervention.

You can find additional information about RDI at the following source:

> Connections Center
> 4120 Bellaire Blvd.
> Houston, TX 77025
> *Phone:* 713-838-1362

Drs. Gutstein and Sheely published one book focused on RDI for young children and another for adolescents and adults:

> *Relationship Development Intervention with Young Children: Social and Emotional Development Activities for Asperger Syndrome, Autism, PDD and NLD* (Jessica Kingsley Publishers)

> *Relationship Development Intervention with Children, Adolescents and Adults: Social and Emotional Development Activities for Asperger Syndrome, Autism, PDD and NLD* (Jessica Kingsley Publishers)

Treatment and Education of Autistic and Communication Handicapped Children (TEACCH)

The TEACCH development began in the early 1970s as a reaction against the prevailing thought that autism is an emotional disorder. Centered at the University of North Carolina at Chapel Hill, TEACCH focuses on tailoring individualized programs, building on existing skills and interests, and respecting "the culture of autism." By emphasizing building on strengths more than remediating weaknesses, practitioners of TEACCH address a common criticism of many treatment programs.

Along with the SCERTS model (Social Communication, Emotional Regulation, and Transactional Support), TEACCH is more of a philosophy rather than an intervention — a philosophy based on assessing children with autism for their needs and using already existing approaches for helping people with autism lead fulfilling and productive lives.

Understanding how TEACCH works

Not quite a "method" in the strictest sense, TEACCH is actually a public health program of services for autistic people. Initially, the program was available only in North Carolina, but now you can find it in selected locations around the world. Because TEACCH is more of a philosophy of treatment rather than a specific method, practitioners of TEACCH make use of several techniques and methods — such as the highly structured learning environment of Applied Behavioral Analysis (ABA) and the person-centered approach of the Developmental Individual Difference, Relation-Based model (DIR) — in various combinations depending upon the individual's needs and emerging capabilities. TEACCH practitioners emphasize understanding the characteristics of people with autism as a basis for arranging their environments to maximize success.

You won't find any certified TEACCH therapists or consultants, per se. Although the TEACCH program offers a number of conferences, seminars, and workshops for learning the approach, no formal program prepares people as "official" or "certified" TEACCH practitioners at this time. However, educators from around the world attend the TEACCH-held training sessions and use the material to instruct children with autism — sometimes in a TEACCH-oriented classroom.

One primary example of the efforts of TEACCH practitioners to work with, rather than against, autism is in their structured-teaching approach. Grounded on understanding how people with autism think and function, the structured-teaching approach involves careful organization of the environment and predictable ordering of tasks and events. According to *The TEACCH Approach to Autism Spectrum Disorders,* by Gary B. Mesibov, Victoria Shea, and Eric Shopler

(Springer), practitioners employ the following elements to assure that the structured-teaching approach works with the characteristics of people on the autism spectrum:

✔ **Organization of physical environment:** TEACCH practitioners believe that children on the autistic spectrum don't always understand where they're supposed to be, and practitioners believe that clear physical boundaries can help.

Whether at school, home, the workplace, or in the community, boundaries are made wherever activities take place. The boundaries are made clear through placement of furniture and through visual cues, such as words for students who can read and pictorial reminders for kids who can't. For example, a young child may need areas delineated for play, schoolwork, eating, and the bathroom. An older child may have areas for work, leisure time, and practicing housekeeping skills.

✔ **Predictable sequence of events:** Predictability is important for reducing anxiety and helping people with autism become successful.

You can increase predictability for autistic (and other) people by implementing a daily schedule or a preplanned series of steps for activities such as work projects, therapy sessions, chores, and recreation. Students in a TEACCH setting have both a regular class schedule and an individual schedule for personal activities, which is very much like a "to-do" list used by many people.

✔ **Routines with flexibility:** Routines can help make sense of a confusing world by creating a sense of order and predictability. Prescribing healthy routines also helps prevent people with autism from developing nonfunctional routines, such as having to smell all the computers in a computer lab prior to starting work.

For a person with autism to be prepared for a world of continual changes, however, you have to build flexibility into the routines. For example, you can keep the routine structure for eating dinner essentially the same, but you can add in some variations in the food, the plates you use, your eating utensils, your placement at the table, and so on.

✔ **Visual schedules:** People with autism tend to be visually based rather than language-based. Therefore, providing a picture or written schedule for reference reduces the possibility of a person forgetting what you have previously communicated orally. A visual schedule can also help with getting through transitions such as getting on the bus to start the school day, moving from one location to another, and even getting ready for bed. Finally, and perhaps most importantly, visual schedules foster independence from adult support later in life, in addition to promoting feelings of security and competence.

Visual schedules can be text-based for persons able to read or picture-based for persons who haven't yet developed reading skills. You can use objects, such as a computer mouse to represent computer time, as symbols when creating the schedule. TEACCH practitioners stress the importance of making sure that each day's schedule varies from the previous day to some extent in order to keep kids from getting too attached to a routine (which is all too easy to do!).

✔ **Visually structured activities:** People with autism tend to have considerable visual strength combined with a need for concrete representation of tasks or activities. As a result, you can engage interest in a person with autism more successfully if you give him something to see, hold, or touch. Practitioners of TEACCH strive to make sure that they provide the following to a person with autism in a visual manner:

  • *Instruction:* One method of visual instruction includes providing a sample of the completed task, such as a pamphlet already folded into thirds with a stamp on it in preparation for mailing. You may also provide written instructions, as well as the use of a jig or silhouette to indicate exactly where the person should place an object — a plate silhouette for setting a table, for instance.

  • *Organization:* Many people with autism become overwhelmed when materials are in disarray. Perhaps you have some objects covering others so they can't be seen; you should organize these materials before the person begins working with them.

  • *Clarity:* Providing too many materials for a task can confuse people on the autistic spectrum. However, you can make an army of materials seem like a small militia if you categorize the components required for a task by using different shapes, colors, and textures to accentuate the differences. For example, if you provide two different pamphlets to prepare for mailing, you could use two contrasting colors such as blue and yellow to help differentiate between pamphlets.

✔ **Work/activity systems:** Work/activity systems provide a meaningful way for people with autism to approach tasks and situations, and they indicate the passage of time between the middle and end of an activity. In short, these systems approach the organization of a task with the following four elements in mind:

  • **What?** Practitioners should describe the task or tasks. For some, the task may be as simple as folding a piece of paper into thirds. For others, that single task may be one of the many tasks involved in stuffing, stamping, and placing envelopes into a bin for mailing.

  • **How much?** In a word, quantity. How many pieces of paper will the child fold, or how many envelopes will he prepare for mailing?

• **What progress have I made, and when am I finished?** Measuring progress is usually done visually. A practitioner can use a timer clearly showing the passage of time for time-oriented tasks. For folding pieces of paper or preparing envelopes, the increasing number of finished products or the decreasing amount of work left can serve as a visual status cue.

You can signify a finished task with a ringing bell or a timer at its end. A job is finished when all the work is done.

• **What happens next?** For the envelope-stuffing task, a practitioner can signify completion with a graphic on the table under the envelopes indicating the next step. Examples of "next steps" include going to see the teacher or going to the shelf in the room to restock the table. These instructions can also be a part of a pictorially based schedule board for persons who are nonverbal.

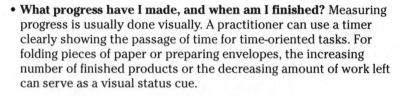

As with schedules, you can represent work/activity systems in a way the person can understand — be it with pictures, words, or objects that symbolize the events.

Getting more information about TEACCH

The American Psychiatric Association, the National Institute of Mental Health, and the American Psychological Association recognize TEACCH as an outstanding program. Along with these organizations, you can find more information about TEAACH from the following source:

Division TEACCH Administration and Research
CB# 7180, 310 Medical School Wing E
The University of North Carolina at Chapel Hill
Phone: 919-966-5156
Web: www.teacch.com

The TEACCH Approach to Autism Spectrum Disorders, by Gary B. Mesibov, Victoria Shea, and Eric Shopler (Springer), is very useful for explaining how TEACCH helps people with autism be more successful in their interactions with the environment and other people.

You can find more information for training with the TEACCH approach from the following source:

Roger Cox, PhD, TEACCH Training Director
CB# 7180, University of North Carolina at Chapel Hill
Chapel Hill, NC 27599-7180
Phone: (919) 966-6636
Web: www.teacch.com

Social Communication Emotional Regulation Transactional Support Model (SCERTS)

The Social Communication, Emotional Regulation, and Transactional Support Model (SCERTS) is a collaborative work between Barry Prizant, Amy Wetherby, Emily Rubin, Amy Laurent, and Patrick Rydell. Similar to the TEACCH method (which we review earlier in this chapter), one of the key characteristics of this model is to use whatever approaches exist to best match the child's needs, making it more of a philosophy than an intervention.

Realizing that no one approach fits all children on the autism spectrum, the collaborators, who are experts in the field of autism, strove to develop a model that would start by assessing the needs of children with autism. And rather than reinvent the wheel, they would make use of existing interventions, based on the assessments made.

Unlike some of the other approaches we outline in this chapter, SCERTS provides no certified practitioners. The developers of SCERTS offer this model in the form of an easy-to-read manual that provides structure and guidance for educators, therapists, family members, and others who support the needs of people on the autism spectrum.

The child is seen as an active participant in his learning rather than a bucket you need to fill with knowledge and skills in a rote manner. The SCERTS approach also places a heavy emphasis on the coordination of all persons involved to support the child with autism.

Understanding how SCERTS works

The SCERTS model is based on the following three components:

- ✔ Social communication
- ✔ Emotional regulation
- ✔ Transactional supports

According to the recently released book *The SCERTS Model: A Comprehensive Educational Approach for Children with Autism Spectrum Disorders* (Brookes), authored by the collaborators of the SCERTS approach, practitioners of SCERTS realize that most childhood growth and development takes place within a social environment of everyday routines and experiences rather than in isolation. The manual further indicates the importance of properly educating parents, caretakers, and others who help the child with autism.

Doing so enables them to assist the child with developing skills in communication and in regulating his emotional states in the social world. These skills are vital for achieving greater success through school, home, and in the community.

Practitioners of the SCERTS model begin with assessing a child's ability in the areas of social communication, emotional regulation, and transactional supports. Practitioners then employ, with frequent reassessment to accommodate changes in the child's needs, the approaches and therapies best matching the child's needs.

Social communication

Placing a heavy emphasis on communicative ability, the developers of SCERTS believe that a person's level of social communicative competence directly affects his or her success in relationships and satisfaction with the community he or she lives in, whether or not the person is on the autism spectrum. Therefore, teaching a child with autism skills in communication is considered a vital part of any program. Practitioners address two major areas of functioning as they construct a SCERTS program:

- ✔ **Joint attention:** Refers to the idea of sharing a reference point with another person. An example of joint attention is being able to follow where a partner is pointing or following a gaze to an object or another person.

  Practitioners may teach joint attention by using exaggerated facial and verbal responses to an unexpected or an anticipated event. You can teach following a point by pointing, turning your head, and gazing toward toys or other objects the child likes that are (in the beginning) partially hidden from view. Ideally, these objects should be close by and needed to accomplish a certain task. After the child is able to follow this nonverbal communication, you can try reducing the point and then the head turn, leaving only the eyes to indicate the direction of the object(s).

- ✔ **Symbol use:** Refers to how a person communicates. Some children who are more severely affected with autism may be at a pre-symbolic stage, using gestures or objects to communicate. For example, a child at the pre-symbolic stage may lift her arms if she wants Daddy to pick her up.

  The symbolic stage is signified by the use of signs, picture symbols such the Picture Exchange Communications System (PECS; see Chapter 10), and/or functional verbal communication. Ideally, a child will be able to switch communication modalities as needed so that when Daddy can't hear her request to be picked up because he's wearing headphones, she can revert to pointing at a PECS picture or even make the pre-symbolic gesture of lifting her arms.

Facility in both joint attention and symbol use results in a child successfully getting her needs met and reduces her reliance on unacceptable or challenging behaviors as a mode of communication.

Because SCERTS is a philosophy rather than an intervention, developing skills in the various aspects of SCERTS will be taught in different ways for each child. For example, one child may learn symbol use better through an Applied Behavioral Analysis–type discrete trial training approach, using PECS graphics. Yet another child may be better off using the Symbol Accentuation program developed as part of the Miller Method.

Emotional regulation

We all learn better when we're free of distracting thoughts and interferences from the environment, such as a jackhammer pounding down the street. However, most people can ignore this extraneous input from the environment. People with autism find it much harder to regulate internal emotional states or to ignore stimuli from the environment. The emphasis SCERTS places on emotional regulation is very helpful for people on the autism spectrum in allowing them to properly attend to the environment.

Emotional regulation focuses on finding and maintaining an optimum level of emotional arousal. This frees a child (or an adult) to be available for learning and having satisfactory interactions with the environment in general. The SCERTS program teaches kids how to seek and respond to support from adults in the following three areas of regulation:

- ✔ **Mutual regulation:** When experiencing an undue amount of stress, over-stimulation, or an emotionally destabilizing situation, a child with autism will be taught how to request or accept assistance from another person to help regain composure using whatever communication system works for her. For example, if a child with autism starts feeling overstimulated from a noisy birthday party, she will ask her mother to take her home.

- ✔ **Self-regulation:** Self-regulation refers to educating the child how to remain at an optimal level of arousal when confronted with a potentially stressful situation. For example, a person with autism may carry earplugs to the movies in preparation if the audio is too loud, or the person may be taught to point to an, "I am okay" graphic after falling down as a sort of reassuring self-talk.

- ✔ **Recovery from extreme dysregulation:** Recovery may be the hardest regulation to achieve because it involves what to do after a person with autism gets so overstimulated that he either has a tantrum or shuts down. A person will be taught how to pull himself out of a state of extreme dysregulation such as knowing to seek out the quiet of a prayer chapel in an airport when over stimulated by crowds and noise.

Transactional supports

The previous two Social Communication and Emotional Regulation components of SCERTS provide coping skills for the autistic child — useful for interaction with others and maintaining an optimal level of arousal. However, the third component of SCERTS, transactional supports, serves as a sort of glue that binds the first two parts together by instructing parents, teachers, therapists, and even other children how to best scaffold their support of those with autism. People can provide transactional support in four main areas:

✔ Interpersonally, or between people

✔ In both formal educational and incidental manners in all areas of life

✔ To families for seamless generalization between education, community, and home

✔ To professionals and other service providers

Getting more information about SCERTS

You can find more information about SCERTS at the following source:

Childhood Communication Services
Barry M. Prizant, PhD, CCC-SLPs
2024 Broad St.
Cranston, RI 02905
Phone: 401-467-7008
Web: www.barryprizant.com

Deciding Which Method Is Best for Your Child

The process of selecting the best intervention method for your child is error-less learning — there is no one right answer. Your main concern should be choosing the approach that seems to be the best fit.

Which of the approaches we outline in this chapter "speaks" to you and makes you want to investigate further? We hope many of them! For the best effect, the entire family should take part in the intervention process. Some lifestyles may fit better with a more prescriptive, rule-bound approach, such as one modeled on Applied Behavioral Analysis. Another family may be better off focusing on developmental levels and interactions based on the child's interests, through interventions such as the Miller Method or RDI.

Now that you're fortified with the basics of the most well-known approaches for helping persons on the autism spectrum, you can begin to narrow down your selection.

Word of mouth from other parents can be very helpful. Just remember that the suggestions of others are based upon how well their therapists and chosen approaches worked for the people with autism they support. The

needs of those people may be different from the needs of your child. The choice is between you, the person with autism that you care for, and others — such as family members, therapists, friends, and often your school system — who may be supporting this person. (Some school systems dictate what method or methods are used and some have more flexibility. You always have the option of exploring other schooling options if the public school in your community doesn't offer what you need; see Chapters 11 and 12.)

Financing the At-Home Program of Your Choice

Any at-home program you choose for your child is going to be costly. After all, you're hiring a person or group to work with your child, and you'll likely be legally required to provide health insurance and other benefits if the person or group works more than a certain number of hours per week.

Before you give up on at-home programs because of cost, consider your options. Many parents with an average or below-average income have found ways to fund their child's treatment by believing that the long-term benefit of having such a program outweighs the short-term financial stress. The choice to proceed is a judgment call, however, that only you can make for your family.

Exploring your at-home options

You have many options at your disposal — options that have worked for other families. They range from major life changes to small shortcuts. Here are some possibilities:

- Turn to relatives for cash, get extra jobs, or downsize to a smaller home.

  Don't be shy about borrowing money if that's what it takes. Consider the sacrifices you willingly make for your child's future. You can negotiate services such as medical care in some cases.

- Organize a charitable effort, such as a golf tournament, with all the proceeds going to fund a program.

- Train college students to work with your autistic child (shortages of therapists in some places make it difficult to find qualified people). Talk to other parents or ask around at your local support group for references. Note that many government financial sources expect that the parent or caregiver will be providing a majority of interventions and care. These sources view the service providers (professionals) as trainers for the family.

- Move to a state or county within your state that has more services for disabled students.

> We've even heard of families temporarily living apart in order to get services while maintaining employment for a spouse.
>
> ✔ Petition your school system to expand its services, and go to court if necessary.
>
> A growing number of attorneys specialize in special-needs law and are willing to take on such cases.

We don't recommend that you try to do the intervention yourself, at least for more than a few hours a week, because you already have enough on your plate. In some cases, health insurance covers at-home treatments. Autism is, after all, a medical problem. Be sure to check with your insurance provider.

Some insurers may try to avoid paying autism claims, so many healthcare providers are becoming more targeted in their prescriptions. In place of autism, they may list a more specific diagnosis, such as a gastrointestinal disorder, when submitting claims. The moral is: Know your policy.

Obtaining government assistance

For the entire United States, the federal Medicaid program administers the EPSDT, or Early Periodic Screening, Diagnosis, Treatment program, for children enrolled in Medicaid. Children up to age 21 can receive preventive healthcare services (the government considers behavioral programs to be preventive care in many cases).

The EPSDT program requires states to cover services that are medically necessary to improve or prevent a condition. It also requires states to actively arrange the treatments, through referrals or direct contact. The list of medically necessary services includes the following:

✔ Diagnostic evaluation and intervention

✔ Inpatient and outpatient hospital services and rural health clinic services

✔ Laboratory and X-ray services

✔ Home healthcare services

✔ Physical therapy and related services

✔ Community-supported living services

✔ Case management services

✔ Other medical services prescribed by a doctor or by another licensed healthcare provider

Do-it-yourself Medicaid

What can you do if you're unhappy with the lack of flexibility and service provided by your state's Medicaid agency? Consider this: Some parents in Maryland and Tennessee have gone so far as to allow people they know to act as Medicaid service providers. In some states, friends and family members (other than parents or spouses) of a disabled person are legally permitted to join forces and become part of a *microboard* — a self-directed support organization for one individual. People often organize a board when the person is very disabled and requires a great deal of care — sometimes 24-hour supervision. If the person's needs change, the provider can change services without going through waiting lists or over other hurdles. The microboard puts the complete focus on the person's needs and desires. Everyone in the disabled person's life will appreciate the personal, focused attention and resources that a group of caring and concerned individuals can provide.

Medicaid is usually means-tested for minors, which means that you can't participate if your family's assets are above a certain amount. Recognizing that this limitation causes many middle-class families to slip through the cracks, the federal government created what's known as the *Katie Beckett waiver* (or Medicaid waiver). Some families qualify for substantial financial support — even funding for a full-time program — by using this waiver, which makes exceptions for incomes that exceed normal Medicaid guidelines.

The Medicaid waiver, in which the state picks up half the cost of the treatment and the federal government picks up the rest, isn't available in every state, however. Within the broader federal guidelines, different states have various Medicaid programs and rules. You can find the law in your state from a local disability advocacy organization, or you can try the following government Web site: www.cms.hhs.gov/MedicaidStWaivProgDemoPGI. Don't overlook the economic impact of government benefits when choosing where to live or choosing a future guardian for your child. (For more on guardianship, see Chapter 16.)

In the states in which the Medicaid waiver does exist, there may be a waiting list of many years, so sign up as quickly as you can to get on the waiting list.

Chapter 10

Dealing with Learning and Sensory Differences

Close your eyes and imagine what a cat looks like. Do you envision a generic feline with two ears, four paws, and a tail? Most people do, but Temple Grandin, the best-selling author of *Thinking in Pictures* (Vintage) and a person living with autism, can't imagine a generic image of a cat, or of any other animal for that matter. She can remember what a cat looks like only by flipping through an imagery slideshow in her head of cats she's seen before. Learning sequential, nonvisual information is also challenging for Grandin and for others like her. Algebra is one concept she could never grasp, for instance, because she can't form pictures of what's happening; she can understand geometry, on the other hand.

Although all autistic individuals may not see the world in exacting photo-graphic detail, most autistic individuals experience the world differently. Their senses don't process information in the same way, so they experience seeing, hearing, smelling, tasting, and touching in a unique manner. In this chapter, we explain the unusual ways that people with autism experience their worlds, give you ways to handle their unique behavior, and introduce some interventions that can help them in educational and social settings so they can communicate and process sensory information. An *intervention* is a system, therapy, or tool that serves to help people with autism overcome challenges that exist with the condition. Here are the three basic categories of intervention we discuss in this chapter:

✔ **Communicative and social interaction systems:** Tools designed to aid people with autism in communicating their needs in ways non-spectrum people can understand.

> ✔ **Sensory integration aids:** Interventions tailored to help the brain orga-
> nize the information it receives from the senses.
>
> ✔ **Neurotherapy:** A therapy designed to retrain the brain so it can calm
> down and maximize the benefits from and/or lessen its dependence on
> medications.

Not all the ideas in this chapter apply to every person with autism. Autism is a
wide spectrum that includes people with mild to severe symptoms, and those
symptoms vary. Thus, we continually stress individualized attention to your
situation. We can't give you a one-size-fits-all formula that works for everybody.

Autistic Learning: Transferring Skills and Providing Structure

All children can learn, but each child learns in a different way. Understanding
the unique way that your child learns and using that knowledge to your
advantage can make the difference between frustrating failure and success.
And with the latter comes continued motivation in learning. The brain —
especially a young child's brain — is open to change, continually building
new connections based on stimulation from one's environment. The autistic
brain is no different in this respect. The newly formed connections occur
across the autism spectrum, from the least to the most affected individuals.

Not all autistic individuals think in pictures, but many have trouble
generalizing — something that comes naturally to a typical brain. When you
generalize, you formulate general principles from particulars. When ques-
tioned about something he likes, a person with autism may list all the types
of animals he knows instead of making a general statement, such as "I like
animals." The autistic mind focuses on concrete, specific examples, not on
the big picture. People with autism can exemplify the proverbial "losing the
forest for the trees."

In the following pages, you find out how to help an autistic child take hold of
the big picture, focusing on concepts and ideas, and you see how a structured routine can make a world of difference for the child's ability to learn.

Thinking conceptually and transferring concepts

You can help most autistic children think conceptually by guiding them to
put details together to form ideas — preferably with visual symbols. You can
demonstrate abstract concepts like "more" or "less" with objects instead of

explaining them in words. To teach a child fractions, for example, you can use a piece of paper or a piece of fruit that you can cut up to show quarters, thirds, and halves. And to teach the word "fraction," you show the word with the pictorial example so that the child can form an association between the two.

Check out the animal example we present in the introduction to this section. Say that you want to teach an autistic child the categories of dogs. Whenever you go for a ride or a walk, point out the different types of dogs when you see them. Identify the dog as a dog and mention what kind of dog it is (Bulldog, Dalmatian, and so on). State what makes it a dog and not a cat or a bird. Picture books that show many kinds of dogs may be helpful.

A person with autism functions best with literal, concrete terms, not abstractly. Explaining a concept with detailed descriptions isn't as effective as showing a picture or the object itself. "A picture is worth a thousand words" is quite true for a person with autism. And to complicate matters, an autistic person will take idiomatic expressions like the previous quote so literally that he may ask, "What are the thousand words?"

Severely autistic children (or children with classic autism; see Chapter 2) may need to use touch as their most reliable learning method. You can walk a child with severe autistic symptoms through a new task by taking his hand and prompting him to touch the objects involved, because he may not understand the shape by sight if his visual processing is impaired.

A child with autism may also have trouble transferring a freshly learned skill, such as tying his shoelaces, to a new task if you alter the situation at all. For example, if you give him another pair of shoes that have, say, brightly colored laces made of a different material, he may not be able to use the skills he recently learned to tie them. Although the two situations may seem identical to you, the autistic child doesn't realize that the laces are still shoelaces and that he can tie them in the same way, because they look different than the ones he's used to. You should also maintain touch consistency when teaching tasks such as lacing shoes to a severely autistic child. If you introduce new touches, you must take time to acclimate the severely autistic child to the change.

When introducing an autistic child to a new situation, even if only one or two details have changed, you must take care to familiarize him with new aspects that may cause confusion. If he's going to a new school, for instance, you can help by taking him there before the first day to do a walkthrough, where you explain what will happen and show him where different items are located and how to use them. Perhaps you can even arrange for him to meet his new teachers.

And always remember to be understanding and compassionate. The normal anxieties a child faces in a new situation, like the first day of school, are increased by his difficulties in transferring behaviors to new settings — settings that seem conceptually similar but *appear* to him to be different.

Incorporating routine into daily life

One of the hardest things to understand about an autism spectrum disorder is the great importance many people with autism place on structure and routine. Susie shrieks if she can't watch her favorite video all the way through each time, even though she's seen it countless times. Bobby insists on lining up his cars and trucks in order of size, and if another child "messes up" his order, he can't relax until he returns each toy to its place. Will has to put on his shoes after his socks, and if his parents can't locate the shoes he likes best immediately, he asks for them repeatedly, sounding like a broken record, and won't put on anything else or stop asking until he gets them.

Dealing with the symptoms of autism isn't easy, and dealing with others' negative reactions just adds to the struggle. A person with autism may be battling feelings of chaos and anxiety. His world may be a confusing jumble of unrelated events, loud and painful sounds, or overly bright lights, like being in a funhouse where the entire environment is distorted.

In such a situation, the person feels the need to impose an order on the world just to survive and have a feeling of security. Not understanding or processing information from his senses and brain the way that others do, the person creates his own security. Nobody wants the feeling of security ripped away — particularly if you don't know why it's happening. You may not understand such behavior (and you don't have to), but you can help by maintaining routines and helping the child deal with new and unfamiliar routines.

Advocates for autism believe that non-autistic people have caused much damage by arbitrarily imposing their judgments about what's logical and acceptable behavior on people with autism. For the person with autism, his behavior serves a need and seems right and logical to him — what he's doing isn't irrational. For this reason, when you implement an intervention (found in later sections of this chapter), you analyze the child's behavior from a functional standpoint. To redirect a person's behavior, you must first understand the motivation for the behavior and what rewards the person gleans from it. You must assume that the behavior makes sense to the autistic person, even if it doesn't to you.

Writer and artist Donna Williams, a person living with autism, points out that it's important to know the difference between an autistic person's involuntary responses and behaviors, and actions that are authentic reflections of who the person is. You want to help the person get past the former; you want to encourage the latter. Automatic behaviors may vary across the autism spectrum. High-functioning individuals may exhibit an intense need to organize or learn intricate detail about everyday items, whereas low-functioning individuals may be resistant to physical change around them, such as chairs being moved around rooms.

One global mantra you can keep to reduce the chance of sensory overload when you attempt to introduce different routines is to keep things simple. Slow down the pace of your instruction, and simplify the information you give. Your child may have trouble attaching meaning to words you say, so give him time to make connections, and don't ever raise your voice.

The following list gives you some more tips for different situations:

- People with autism may fixate on certain activities, words, songs, or objects. The fixation isn't a random, senseless act, but an attempt to compensate or adapt to their inability to effectively connect meaning to others' words or actions.

  You should attempt to channel these fixations constructively (we give you suggestions in the section "Working toward functional communication"), but above all, you should meet these constructions with an attempt at understanding, not shame and criticism.

- Try to introduce new things, people, or places gradually by talking about them first. For example, you can "walk through" a visit to the dentist before it happens to identify people and items or to "watch" another person's (mom, sibling) exam. You can also use pictures or other graphics to represent the new experience. Do the things you'd normally do to comfort a typical child, only do more of them. The familiar is comforting, and people with autism need more comfort for their jangled nerves.

- Be sure to repeat simple questions you pose and remain patient. Many people with autism have slowed processing speeds (as slow as 8 to 10 seconds from hearing a request to the beginning of a response), so you shouldn't expect immediate responses. Many people with autism also have trouble accessing their long-term memories; they can store the information they learn, but they can't recall facts in new situations when needed. Use simple, concrete, stripped-down language when giving directions without introducing extra information that can slow down the processing of a person with autism.

- Try to teach new information to your child — even social skills, which Asperger children need help with (see Chapter 5) — through scripts or "social stories" that break down a process into easily remembered steps. For example, you can break down the process of getting ready in the morning into a series of steps, beginning with brushing your teeth and washing your face and ending with putting on your coat. (See Chapter 13 for a detailed description of social stories.)

  The autistic person can learn steps much easier if he or she can see them in pictures. Books are available with illustrated scripts for many common activities, or you can create your own social stories at home.

Bridging the Communication Gap

Research conducted on families shows that language and communication deficits are the most serious and stressful aspects of autism. Communicating successfully is a major challenge people with autism face. Their ability to communicate dramatically affects how well they interact socially in a non-autistic world. Many people with autism lack the skill to even request a glass of water or to ask that the volume of a television set be turned down. Without the ability to communicate effectively, life becomes an exercise in frustration, tension, and anxiety.

Because most persons with autism tend to have strong visual skills, a number of tools have been developed to help with communication and social interaction. In the pages that follow, we explain how you can work toward meaningful communication, implement technologies that can help with communication, and use music as a tool for communicating.

Developing sign language as a communication bridge

For children on the autism spectrum with significantly delayed verbal skills, early introduction of sign language training can be important in developing functional communication skills. The development of signing skills can also, in some cases, be an effective bridge toward developing verbal skills. In low-functioning children, sign language can be the foundation of functional communication.

One common myth is that teaching sign language to a child with autism or encouraging the use of pictures will delay development in expressive verbal communication. However, many leading experts believe that introducing these modes of communication will, in fact, speed up the speech development for the children. At the very least, if a child can never gain verbal fluency, he or she will have *some* form of functional communication.

To determine the appropriateness of introducing sign language at an early age, consult with a speech and language therapist who's acquainted with training children on the spectrum.

Working toward functional communication

Autistic individuals can excel at data collection — gathering facts and figures like little computers. However, in an educational program, you want to include life-skill building that goes beyond data collection. The child should be able to *use* the data that he collects, and the life skills you build should be meaningful and have purpose in the real world. In other words, you want to practice *functional communication.* For example, a child should be able to do math, of course, but he also needs to apply the math he's learning to the world so that he knows how to use math to make change when shopping in a store, for instance. Often, even children on the lowest end of the autism spectrum have the potential to develop basic communication skills that allow them to communicate their most basic needs to others.

A mistake parents make too often with programmed instruction (which we discuss in Chapter 9) is to focus on academic gains; they miss out on meaningful, functional communication. This results in children who can shoot through all the exercises in their programs with flying colors but can't ask for what they want to eat.

Children who are allowed to play video games for hours or watch television endlessly will disengage from the real world because their brains don't get enough stimulation. This troublesome fact is true for neurotypical children and doubly true for autistic children. So, you should pack your child's day full of meaningful interactions that keep his mind engaged with the world, not stimming (see the section "Socially unacceptable stimming") or tuning out for long periods.

Here are some ways you can promote engagement and connection (in other words, functional communication):

- ✔ Turn off the TV after one video or program, and limit video games to one hour a day.

- ✔ Talk to your child often, even if he or she doesn't seem to respond. Many people with autism have delayed sensory processing, meaning they may not respond immediately or even be able to respond, but they can understand what's happening. Like anyone else, autistic individuals don't like being ignored.

- ✔ Encourage areas of talent, like drawing or computer programming. A common mistake is to focus on weaknesses to the exclusion of strengths.

- ✔ Try to channel your child's passions or fixations, such as a love for trains or collecting, into something constructive. Kathy Grant, a high-functioning person with autism, has turned her interest in maps (she collects maps, flags, and items with foreign writing) into a vocation of traveling and writing about her experiences. She has a degree in political science and has visited Australia and Portugal, among other places.

Using assistive communication technology

Assistive technology is any device used to increase, maintain, or otherwise improve the capabilities of a person — whether the person has autism or not. Experts have created assistive technologies such as interactive language boards, visual schedules, and computerized communication systems to help people with autism — particularly those undergoing speech therapy — to communicate more readily while they work on improving their speech capabilities.

Most people use assistive technology; you just don't usually call the tools by that name. Day planners, PDAs, and shopping lists are the primarily text-based equivalents of visual schedules. (People on the autism spectrum and otherwise who have difficulty processing text are usually helped by graphically based visual schedules using low, medium, or high technology to help remember routines, expected behaviors, and to organize their lives.) E-mail, text messages, and instant messengers are computerized communication systems. Restaurant menus are interactive language boards.

Not all assistive technology devices relate to communication; the communication devices just stand out. Other common types of assistive devices include eyeglasses and hearing aids. Many of the assistive devices used by people with challenges are commonly employed by the majority of society and shouldn't necessarily be considered "special". Assistive technology has provided many new tools for autistic individuals to communicate visually, which can be their strongest sense. Some parents fear that these methods may hinder children from using spoken language, but researchers have no evidence to support this. If anything, helping children build communication skills lays the groundwork for spoken language.

How does using a visual system help a child to learn language? Understanding and performing nonverbal communication, such as gesturing and pointing, is a first step toward understanding verbal language for all humans. Using a keyboard to communicate doesn't stand in the way of talking; it helps language concepts form and develop so that a child can speak later when he's ready.

Research suggests that assistive technology positively effects reading and language skills. Some students have demonstrated greater frequency of spontaneous verbal utterances when a computer produced synthetic speech during learning tasks. Nonverbal people with autism also showed a reduction of challenging behaviors as their expressive communication abilities increased.

In the following sections, we examine ways you can get assistive technology into the classroom for your child, and we look at the categories of assistive technology.

You often have many ways to skin the proverbial assistive-technology cat. For example, a person with fine motor control challenges may be helped by simply pointing to and moving Mayer Johnson pictures affixed to a piece of stiff cardboard. Others may find help in using magnetic cards that contain pre-recorded text with a Language Master. For another person, it may be easier to carry around a DynaVox or laptop with a touch screen to point at enlarged pictures that the machine verbalizes. It depends on the requirements of the person.

Furthermore, assistive technology isn't a cure-all answer. To have the greatest benefit for the child, proper training and support are necessary for integrating assistive technology into learning curriculum. Research suggests that teaching strategies for educators work best when they include a combination of workshops, modeling, practice in simulated and real settings, feedback about performance, and coaching during actual practice.

Getting technology assistance into the classroom

The best way to assure that your child's school provides the needed assistive technology is to write what your child requires into his Individualized Education Program (IEP; see Chapters 11 and 12). If you're lucky, your child goes to a forward-thinking school that already provides the equipment for student use. Other schools may have to purchase the equipment if parents demonstrate the need in IEPs.

Even though it may not seem right, some schools may just outright deny the need for such equipment by refusing to write it in the IEP. At that point you may want to consider whether it's worth appealing the IEP or whether you want to spend your own funds to acquire the necessary equipment instead. Keep in mind that low-tech equipment (see the following section) is less expensive than high-tech equipment. The good news is that, in many cases, low-tech equipment may be all that your child requires.

When becoming acquainted with assistive technology, you'll find that low-tech devices are the most adaptable. For example, you may use a single set of pictures for a number of applications, such as in developing schedules, shopping lists, calendars, and social narratives.

Low-technology assistance

Low technology refers to visual strategies that don't involve electronic devices and that tend to be easy to use. Some examples of low-tech equipment include dry erase boards, clipboards, three-ring binders, manila file folders, photo albums, laminated graphics (such as those from Picture Exchange Communication System [PECS]), photographs, and highlight tape.

Some uses for low-tech devices include the following:

- ✔ **Calendars** to assist with memory deficits and routines
- ✔ **Schedules** to assist with routines and changes in routines
- ✔ **Shopping lists** to assist with memory
- ✔ **Pictures** to assist with comparing, identification, or expressive communication

Building schedules can assist with expressive communication when the child has the opportunity to help put the schedule together. Working with a schedule can also help with receptive communication (when the time comes to change from one activity to another, for example).

Developed by Pyramid Educational Consultants, the Picture Exchange Communication System (PECS; see Figure 10-1) is a database of over 3,000 graphics that can help a nonverbal person with his or her receptive and expressive communication efforts. PECS works with children, adolescents, and adults who have communicative, cognitive, and physical difficulties. The PECS isn't just a visual support; it involves using a specific protocol (which is explained in the *PECS Training Manual*, 2nd Edition, written by Lori Frost, MS, CCC/SLP, and Andrew Bondy, PhD).

In the first phase of PECS, the person learns to initiate communication by requesting an item. Later phases involve making sentences and responding to questions. Although language isn't necessary in PECS, it often develops through the use of PECS.

For information on purchasing the PECS, you can go to Pyramid's Web site at www.pecs.com.

Figure 10-1:
A visual system, such as a Picture Exchange Communication System, makes communication easier for a visual learner.

Another program, Writing with Symbols 2000 (available at www.widgit.com/products/wws2000/index.htm), serves as a bridge between graphically based and text-based communication. Graphics from Mayer-Johnson and Widgit Rebus symbols appear together with words so that a person who understands only graphics can choose what he or she wants to communicate with the words appearing under the graphics. Text-based people can type out text, and the program will include the accompanying graphic.

Medium-technology assistance

Medium technology includes simple electronic devices such as tape recorders, overhead projectors, timers, calculators, and voice output machines. One such device, the Language Master, uses 3 x 8-inch cards with recordable magnetic strips for short verbal messages; you can place pictures and other cues on the cards. Another device, the Talk Pad, has four large buttons on which you can attach pictures, symbols, or other cues to represent the verbal message generated when the button is pushed. Other output devices such as the Voice in the Box and the Step by Step Communicator work in similar ways.

Unlike the low-tech devices, medium-tech items are often less adaptable and more cumbersome. However, they may be more effective in filling a specific need of the individual in a limited number of settings or situations.

Some uses for medium-tech devices include:

- Enhancing expressive vocal communication through Voice Output Communication Aids (VOCAs) that produce synthetic or digitized speech output when activated by individuals

- Attending (focusing on the task at hand) and organization

- Sequencing (putting things in order) and phonics

Boardmaker, a software program available for both Mac- and Windows-based computers, uses PECS (see the previous section) and other graphics for developing communication strips, schedules, calendars, and other materials for communication. You can use the graphics in conjunction with assistive communication devices such as DynaVox and the Language Master.

DynaVox is an electronic device that displays a series of graphics, which the machine verbalizes when the user points to them. One form of the Language Master, by Franklin, is available in office supply stores and is used primarily for word pronunciation and definitions. Another form by Drake uses cards with a magnetic strip to record and play back words and phrases and is designed to teach reading to children.

Boardmaker and other communication products are available from the Mayer-Johnson Company at www.mayerjohnson.com. DynaVox is available from www.dynavoxsys.com. You can find info on the Franklin Language Master at www.freedomscientific.com/fs_products/franklin.asp and the Drake system at www.btinternet.com/~drakegroup/drake02/lm_system.htm.

High-technology assistance

High-technology devices are more complicated but can be very powerful. High-tech devices include video cameras, computers, and Personal Digital Assistants (PDAs) that are available from most electronic vendors. You may need to acquire other high-tech devices from companies that specialize in selling products for people with special needs. Such devices include adaptive hardware and specialized and complex voice output devices. For instance, you may want to check out the Cyrano Communicator, from One Wright Company, which uses a modified Hewlett Packard Personal Digital Assistant. Look for more on the Cyrano Communicator at www.cyranocommunicator.com.

High-tech items can be nearly as adaptable as low-tech items and more specific in use than medium-tech items, but the adaptability or specificity can come with a large price.

Some uses for high-tech devices include working on improving the following skills:

- ✔ Receptive language skills such as naming objects and people as well as following routines such as getting dressed or eating breakfast

- ✔ Expressive language skills such as categorization (organizing objects or concepts into groups) and pragmatics (using language in the proper social context)

- ✔ Social skills such as identifying proper behavior, asking for assistance, maintaining topics, and reducing perseveration (uncontrollably repeating a gesture, sound, or phrase)

- ✔ Nonverbal communication such as body language and facial expressions

- ✔ Maintaining personal space and volume of speech

- ✔ Activities of daily living such as brushing your teeth, hygiene, and washing your hands

- ✔ Academics such as penmanship, drawing, and essays

Receptive communication refers to what communication a person can understand through listening, seeing, or other means. *Expressive communication* refers to making one's thoughts known to others verbally, through sign language, pictures, or other means. People with autism tend to have stronger receptive communication skills, but just because the receptive skills are stronger than the expressive skills doesn't mean that the receptive skills are perfect or even adequate. On the other side of the coin, good expressive skills can mask (or hide) receptive skill deficits.

People with autism tend to be attracted to high-tech devices such as computers because of their predictability and consistency, compared to the relatively unpredictable nature of human responses. Computers don't send confusing social messages, and they place the person in control, allowing for her to become an independent learner.

Computers can help autistic individuals who have motor problems to communicate. Even if a person can't hold a pencil, she still may be able to type. Many individuals with autism have trouble with their handwriting, also. Using keyboards can free them from the difficult task of holding a pen to paper, which makes communicating their thoughts easier.

Enjoying music therapy

Music therapy is the process of using music to address the physical, emotional, and social needs of an individual. In other words, it focuses on achieving non-musical goals, such as body and environmental awareness, motor control, social interaction, and communication, using music as the medium. Although autism affects neurological structures involved with speech, research shows that communication through music often remains intact. This strength, in some cases, allows music therapy to assist individuals on the spectrum to better express their feelings and improve their communication skills.

Music therapy may look like a therapist and child just "having fun" together. In actuality, the music therapist needs extensive education and training in order to become properly certified. Upon certification, the therapist is qualified to use music as a means to enhance social, communication, and physical skills. The therapist pays close to attention to cues from the participant as he or she reacts to music and attempts to channel the hopefully positive reactions into more meaningful social and emotional expression.

Music can benefit people who have autism in many ways. Check out the following benefits:

- ✔ Provides another (nonverbal) form of communication
- ✔ Gives kids the potential to do something they may be good at
- ✔ Provides an enjoyable forum in which to interact

Music communicates with a different part of the brain than language. Research suggests that involvement with music at an early age encourages neural connections in the brains of children during periods of critical development.

Music can be inclusive even for low-functioning autistic people who can't follow directions well. It provides an opportunity to connect with others without language and to have fun.

If we've sparked your interest in this therapy, you can contact the American Music Therapy Association (www.musictherapy.org) for more information about music therapy and to find a certified music therapist.

I (co-author Stephen Shore) teach autistic children how to play musical instruments. I focus on teaching instruments such as piano or recorder, depending upon the student's interest. Unlike the relationships created in a music therapy class, where the teacher puts the emphasis on using music to accomplish extra-musical goals, music lessons for autistic individuals provide a way for them to make friends and get involved in the community, perhaps as a member of a local band. Above all, you need to remember that music can be plain old fun.

Make sure you have music around the house. Whether you put on classical, jazz, or rock and roll, the person with autism is likely to have a response. If the response is negative, that type of music is probably not the person's favorite. To people with autism, as with all people, music allows them to tap into thoughts and feelings they may not consciously be aware of. People use music for entertainment, to relax, or as a reward for a job well done. People with autism are no different. My parents played mostly classical music for as long as I can remember. I feel that my intensive exposure to music played a key role in my leading a fulfilling and productive life, and it has led me to the role of teaching children with autism how to play musical instruments.

Other arts, such as drawing, painting, and writing, are similar. Some people with autism have exceptional visual memories and can reproduce scenes from memory that look like photographs in their detailed accuracy. Try your best to include the arts in your family's life.

"Retraining" the Brain through Neurotherapy

Neurotherapy (also called *neurofeedback*) is a noninvasive form of mental training, similar to the biofeedback athletes use to achieve better physical performance. Neurotherapy, however, trains not the body, but the brain itself. You can actually train your brain to be calmer through this technique, and many autistic individuals who use this intervention see some excellent results. (High-functioning individuals with more intact communication skills will more likely benefit from this therapy.) One of the best results? The therapy often reduces the need for medications. Keep reading to find out how the therapy works, how you can implement it, and for some research-based testimonials!

Neurotherapy isn't a medical treatment; it's an educational one that works to condition the brain to re-regulate itself. To get the best results, you should use neurotherapy in conjunction with a program that addresses other needs of the autistic individual within the family system. You need to manage other environmental stressors, in other words, for neurotherapy to have lasting and significant benefit. You may want to let your primary care physician know that your child is participating in neurotherapy in order to facilitate communication with the physician about the overall treatment plan of the child.

Examining and implementing neurotherapy

Why does neurotherapy work? At one time, scientists believed that your brain stayed the same throughout your lifetime. Neuroscientists today continue to discover that the brain is an amazingly flexible and adaptable organ (often described as *plasticity*), particularly when you're young. This makes it a prime candidate for transformation.

How does neurotherapy work? Neurotherapy uses *electroencephalography* (EEG) tracings that show electrical activity, or brain waves (which is why the therapy is also known as *EEG biofeedback*). Neurotherapy clinicians believe that autistic individuals have far too much delta and theta activity (greater than 50 percent of their total brain waves), so they look for this during examinations.

The slow delta and theta waves — usually displayed on a neurotypical person's EEG when he or she's asleep, not awake (see Figure 10-2) — create sleepiness. The individual with autism tries to cope by revving up his brain, which can cause him to get "stuck" with inappropriate levels, leading to hyperactivity and sleep problems. The focus of neurotherapy is to re-regulate these brain waves.

During a neurotherapy session, the neurotherapist attaches an electromagnetic sensor to the client's head at specific locations while the client observes a simple video game or series of images (see Figure 10-2). The sensor rewards the client's brain for achieving the desired state during the game with beeps and point scoring. By giving this reward, the therapy trains clients to calm their minds, ease their pain, or heal their trauma. The process is painless, safe, and has no side effects. And the intended effects of the treatment are involuntary — that is, the client doesn't need to understand what's being done to benefit from the treatment.

To find a competent neurotherapy practitioner, you can contact EEG Spectrum International, located in Canoga Park, California, on the Web at www.eegspectrum.com. If you want to know more about the emerging field of neurofeedback in general, we recommend that you check out *A Symphony in the Brain* (Grove Press), by Jim Robbins.

Figure 10-2:
Neurotherapy works to
stabilize the
delta and
theta brain
waves.

Reviewing a neurotherapy study

One pilot study conducted in 2000 compared a control group with groups
undergoing neurotherapy for an average of 36 sessions over 4½ months. The
study, which was published in the *Journal of Neurotherapy,* showed a 26-percent
reduction in autism symptom levels for people undergoing neurotherapy,
compared with 3 percent in the control group.

During the study, parents noticed significant improvements in socialization,
vocalization, sleep, and schoolwork, and they noticed less anxiety and
tantrums. The study conductors also tested children undergoing neurotherapy with the Autism Treatment Evaluation Checklist (you can access an Internet
scoring program for the checklist at www.autismeval.com/ari-atec).
The kids showed a 33-percent improvement in sociability, a 29-percent improvement in speech/language/communication, a 26-percent improvement in overall
health, and a 17-percent improvement in sensory/cognitive awareness.

For a scientific look at neurotherapy and autism, you can check out an
upcoming book that includes a chapter by the author of the controlled study,
Dr. B. Jarusiewicz. The book is *Neurofeedback: Dynamics and Clinical
Applications,* edited by J.R. Evans (Haworth Press, Inc.).

Sensory integration dysfunction as an autistic trait

I (co-author Stephen Shore) have yet to meet a single autistic person who doesn't have issues with sensory integration to some extent. One friend I have claims to have no sensory integration problems at all. However, I have to wonder why he draws the shades down in his home with the lights off, leaving him to live in the dark. Here are some other quirky tidbits:

✔ While in a library with another friend of mine one time, I suddenly noticed her eyes vibrating back and forth to the frequency of the fluorescent lights. She quickly asked to leave.

✔ I have to remove all the ticking clocks from anywhere I sleep.

Making Sense of Sensory Confusion

Imagine not knowing where your body ends and other objects begin. Imagine feeling pain when you hear high-pitched or loud noises (and yes, we're talking pain worse than hearing a loved one nag you). Imagine being able to use only one sense at a time — not smelling and tasting your pizza at the same time, for example. These are some of the descriptions autistic people have used to talk about their sensory worlds. In the pages that follow, we give you tips on managing the sensory challenges that your loved one may face, and we present some techniques and therapies at your disposal to help your loved one cope.

Observing sensory integration challenges

Occupational therapists practicing sensory-integration therapy divide the senses into inner and outer categories (see Figure 10-3). The outer senses are the five you learn in grade school: sight, touch, hearing, taste, and smell. The two important inner senses are the *vestibular* and the *proprioceptive*. The vestibular sense helps you keep your balance, and the proprioceptive sense tells you where your body parts are in space and how much force you need to use to accomplish a task. Therapists term anything that overwhelms one or more of the senses as a *sensory violator*. See Tables 10-1 and 10-2 for more on what differences in sensory input may feel like for autistic persons.

The inner and outer senses of people with autism aren't always reliable indicators of the world around them. The senses can be either insensitive or oversensitive to stimulation, and one sense can be highly acute while another is dull. How can a person learn in an educational setting in the typical way when the information she receives from her senses is often faulty or slow to arrive? Well, the person can't.

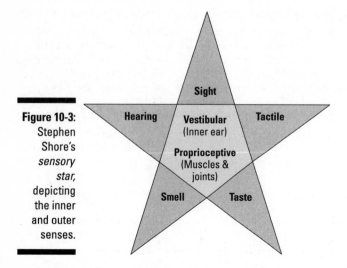

Figure 10-3:
Stephen
Shore's
*sensory
star,*
depicting
the inner
and outer
senses.

Table 10-1	Outer Senses for People with Autism		
Sense	*Possible Source*	*Seems Like . . .*	*Possible Reaction*
Sight	Fluorescent light	Strobe light	Escape or tantrum
Sound	Birds chirping	Bird's beak scraping the eardrum	Cover ears
Taste	Spicy food	Acid	Spit food out
Smell	Perfume	Bleach	Allergic-like response
Touch	Light contact	Electric shock, over-alerting	Strike out, violence

Table 10-2	Inner Senses for People with Autism		
Sense	*Function*	*What It Seems Like when Faulty*	*Possible Reaction*
Vestibular	Balance	Dizziness, falling	Clumsiness; avoid making feet leave the ground; spinning; thrill-seeking (such as bungee jumping, going on rollercoasters)
Proprioceptive	Movement	Moving through molasses	Excess fatigue; feeling like a bull in a china shop

Why do autistic individuals process sensory information so differently? Various scientific theories have attempted to explain what's going on. One explanation is that autistic brains have too many sensory connections and develop so rapidly that their "circuits" are easily overloaded with information coming in from their senses. Research has shown that children (under age 12) with autism have larger brains than average children; however, adult brains are normal in size, due to slower-than-average brain growth after age 12. One possible cause of this early brain growth is that a left-hemisphere defect may cause the right side of the brain to overcompensate by becoming larger. Another theory for the difference in sensory processing is that the presence of environmental toxins distorts neutral processing.

If you're interested in sensory therapy, you should find an occupational therapist who has experience administering assessments for sensory integration and providing the needed therapy. You'll enjoy the benefit of having a child who's more balanced and happy, and with activities such as swinging, rolling up in mats, pulling, and pushing, the therapy tends to be fun for the child and the therapist, too. You can find further information and qualified therapists by contacting the organization Sensory Integration International at www.sensoryint.com. In addition, your physician, hospital, and local autism support group or resource center can be fine sources.

Tomatis: From opera to occupational therapy

Auditory integration training, a currently controversial (but growing in popularity) form of sensory integration without much research backing, is designed to reduce hypersensitivity and improve clarity of hearing. When Dr. Alfred Tomatis first developed this training in France, people used the "Tomatis method" to train opera singers with a device called the *Electronic Ear.* This listening therapy uses sound stimulation through the electronic earphones to improve the attention, hearing, and sensory-processing capabilities of autistic people.

Listening therapies are just that — people listening to specially designed music through headphones, sometimes while doing other activities. The therapist adjusts the music periodically to filter different frequencies out, which is claimed to stimulate different parts of the ear or the brain.

Some practitioners use the training today, including Dr. Paul Madaule, who runs the Listening Centre (the first facility of its kind in North America) — a facility based on the Tomatis method in Toronto. Dr. Guy Berard applied Tomatis' ideas to develop the modern version of auditory integration training, or AIT, for people with autism and other neurological conditions. The Spectrum Center in Bethesda, Maryland, employs a combination of listening therapy and physical movement. Although the medical jury is still out, this whole-body approach claims to improve motor skills, coordination, and balance along with helping listening, memory, and attention skills.

The easy-to-administer and score Sensory Profile Assessments for different age groups, created by Dr. Winnie Dunn, are very helpful in determining the sensory needs of your loved one — whether or not he's on the autism spectrum. You can get copies of the assessments from Harcourt Assessment at www.sensoryprofile.com. A significant cost is associated with this assessment, and as such, we suggest that you consult with your physician or other members of your child's autism treatment team before you contract for an assessment.

Because sensory integration treatments are so new, much of the evidence for them is anecdotal. Research shows that children can benefit from several aspects of these treatments even if they don't show specific sensory gains. Children can benefit from the social engagement, focused attention, and use of toys in meaningful contexts that the therapy gives, for example.

Using hippotherapy

Like with sensory-integration therapy (see the previous section), *hippotherapy* focuses on organizing the inner and outer senses. However, with this unique modality, the child rides on the back of a horse! A therapist acquainted with hippotherapy and a specially trained horse conduct hippotherapy sessions. The child heightens her awareness by developing her vestibular and proprioceptive senses, which she accomplishes through using her trunk muscles to maintain balance on the horse. Additionally, the child benefits psychologically by learning how to communicate with and develop a relationship with the horse.

Another similarity to sensory-integration therapy is that the sessions are usually fun. You can find more information about hippotherapy, including where to find a certified therapist (and horse!), from the American Hippotherapy Association at www.americanhippotherapyassociation.org. Generally, therapists can adapt hippotherapy to assist children across the autism spectrum.

Working with speech-language pathologists

Speech-language pathologists work to improve speech and communication and can be part of school services (for more on education, see Chapters 11 and 12). When schools employ speech therapists, they're required to provide as many hours as is stipulated in your Individualized Education Program (IEP; see Chapters 11 and 12), but sometimes parents want more help and hire other therapists — either people working for the school or outside contractors — to work additional hours with their child. The American Speech and Hearing

Association, a trade group, accredits therapists and schools in its industry. You pay out of pocket for their services, and rates vary depending on where you live. In the New York City metropolitan area, therapists generally receive $75 to $90 an hour.

Before your child becomes a part of speech therapy, though, make sure the therapist involved understands how to work with people with autism.

Some speech-language pathologists are traditionally trained to focus on speech and language rather than communication. Therefore, you need to find a person who understands that communicating within a meaningful context, not just producing speech, is the goal of training a person with autism (see the section "Working toward functional communication" earlier in this chapter). Especially with children with Asperger's, who have no language delay, the focus needs to be on *pragmatics,* or learning conversational skills and how to read visual cues around language. If a therapist is inexperienced with autism, you may want to bring up the fact that people with autism need more visual aids.

Low-functioning children on the autism spectrum can also benefit from speech training. Speech training with children who are non-verbal involves getting them to vocalize, even if they just babble, and then rewarding that behavior until it becomes habitual.

Another type of therapy typically performed by speech-language pathologists is known as *feeding therapy,* which encourages children to eat new foods and helps them with any swallowing problems they may have. Many autistic children eat an extremely limited diet because they're averse to foods that have textures and smells they don't like. Feeding therapy can help them eat a more healthy, varied diet. (See Chapter 8 for more on optimizing nutrition for your child.) Pathologists with a background in feeding therapy often help autistic children by using integrative sensory techniques (see the section "Observing sensory integration challenges").

Seeing through Irlen-branded lenses

Helen Irlen, a former school psychologist and current Assistant Professor of Adult Learning Disabilities at California State University/Long Beach, estimates that almost 50 percent of people with autism have *scotopic sensitivity,* or unusual sensitivity to lights, glare, patterns, colors, and contrasts. Drawing on federal research from the early 1980s, Irlen developed what are now known as *Irlen lenses* to filter out colors of the infrared spectrum that interfere with visual perception in persons on the autism spectrum.

If you (or people you care for) have visual difficulties, Irlen lenses may help. Examples of difficulties include sensitivity to light intensity and glare, tunnel vision, troubles with reading because letters on the page seem to move, and trouble seeing contrasts.

If you have difficulties, you may want to consider going to a display that has sunglasses of different colors. Trying different glasses while reading a short passage may reveal that some colors are easier for you to read with than others. If so, you have unofficially screened yourself as a possible candidate for Irlen lenses. (You often hear suggestions for this exercise at Irlen lens presentations; we say "unofficially" because this isn't standard practice by those selling the lenses.)

As with all interventions, Irlen lenses help some persons with autism and not others. You can find more information about Irlen lenses, including locations for assessments for this intervention, at www.irlen.com.

Handling Your Child's Sensory Issues

If your autistic child is hypersensitive to noise or barely notices loud noises, you can tell he or she has unusual auditory processing. But what can you do about it? And how do you know if he or she has visual problems? Not to worry, we're here to help. This section gives you tips on how to discover and handle visual, hearing, and other sensory problems, and how to deal with socially unacceptable stimming.

For general purposes, though, here are some suggestions, proposed by Temple Grandin, PhD, to cope with your child's sensory issues:

- ✔ You can treat hyperactivity with a padded, weighted vest that calms the nervous system when worn for short periods. You should remove the vest after 20 minutes so the nervous system doesn't adapt to it.

- ✔ Don't always expect a person who can't hear and see at the same time to look at you while taking instructions. Some autistic people, such as Donna Williams, acclaimed author of *Somebody Somewhere: Breaking Free from the World of Autism* (Three Rivers Press), can process information from only one source at a time, such as vision or hearing.

- ✔ For older, nonverbal children and adults who have come to depend upon touch as their most reliable sense, give them a physical symbol of something to touch, like a spoon, to remind them of events such as mealtime.

The supermarket test

Public places, such as supermarkets or large department stores — with their loudspeakers, ringing bells, fluorescent lighting, crowds, strong smells, and other distractions — can be overwhelming sources of stimulation. If your child has tantrums and becomes unmanageable in such places, but you can take him to a place like the park and he remains calm, you can be pretty sure something is going on. Children who are *mono-channel* (only processing one sense at a time) or who are tired out are likely candidates for throwing tantrums in supermarkets.

If your child has a tantrum in a public place such as a supermarket and your attempts to soothe the child don't quickly quell the outburst, we suggest removing the child from the provoking environment. This removal will help limit the stress the child endures when in a panic-like state. We also suggest that you contact your child's physician, therapist, or other treatment providers to seek suggestions on behavior modification elements that can address tantruming behavior.

The eyes have it

One way you can tell if your child has visual processing problems is by observing how she handles uneven steps. If she responds with fear or tentativeness, she probably has trouble with depth perception. Some children with autism also have trouble making out bright, contrasting colors.

After you have your child's vision tested by an eye doctor, you should make an appointment with a developmental optometrist — a professional who specializes in testing how a person processes vision.

Here are some other signs that your child may have visual processing problems:

- ✔ She looks out of the corners of her eyes rather than straight ahead.
- ✔ She flicks her fingers around her eyes.
- ✔ She avoids checkerboard-tiled floors.
- ✔ She won't ride escalators.

Fluorescent lights are very distracting for many autistic people because they flicker, especially when the lights become older. Use incandescent bulbs around your home when possible. Even if fluorescents are present, a lamp with an old-fashioned bulb next to the child's work area helps. Similarly, flat-panel displays and laptops are less distracting than standard computer monitors.

Irlen-colored glasses (see the section "Seeing through Irlen-branded lenses") can also help with visual processing problems, as will black print on colored paper for reading. Don't ever use bright yellow, though!

The auditory-processing blues

Many autistic people are said to "hear in vowels." In other words, the individuals miss consonant sounds like the "c" in cat. When spoken aloud, such hard consonant sounds are actually shorter in duration than vowels, which makes them easier to miss and harder to process.

This type of auditory processing problem doesn't show up on a conventional hearing test because many autistic people have compensated for the problem. Sometimes people with autism even talk in vowels.

One way you can help is to speak slowly and enunciate your words clearly. Singing may also be easier than speaking for people with autism. You can sing to them and encourage them to sing back. Imagine the fun you can create! Don't sing too loud if the person is extremely sound-sensitive, though. A whisper may be enough volume.

People with autism not only feel pain from loud sounds, but also can be distracted or irritated by sounds most other people can't hear. For example, the flickering of fluorescent lights is accompanied by a hum or buzz that some people can hear. This buzz or hum can be as distracting or irritating as the flicker. Other people may be distracted by the scratching of a pencil on paper or a conversation occurring in the next room.

You can protect a child with autism from sounds that hurt his ears by recording the sounds on a tape recorder, allowing the child to imitate the sounds, and gradually increasing the volume to a tolerable level.

Socially unacceptable stimming

People with autism may insist on repeating certain behaviors, such as flapping their hands, rocking, spinning, flicking their fingers, or reciting the same songs or sentences for a few different reasons:

- ✔ To deal with overactive nervous systems
- ✔ To defend against situations they find anxiety provoking
- ✔ To reestablish awareness of their bodies in space (some autistic people have reported that they can't feel their bodies unless they move, which leads to disorientation)

This self-regulatory behavior is called *stimming*. The average brain isn't immune to such behavior; most people do it to up-regulate their brains in order to pay attention or to down-regulate when they feel too much anxiety. Think of the possible up- or down-regulatory movements you may make while sitting in class or a meeting:

- ✔ Jiggling your leg
- ✔ Biting the end of your pen or your nails
- ✔ Twirling your hair
- ✔ Doodling
- ✔ Slightly rocking back and forth

So, what's the difference between your movements and someone with autism? Most adults have mastered "socially acceptable" stimming behavior.

When stimming interferes with learning or social situations, the behaviors can cause problems for an autistic person. You should attempt to stop stimming behaviors when they present a danger to the individual or others around him. For example, you should cut off repetitive skin picking or head banging immediately. If the stimming prevents a child from participating effectively in therapies — such as when the child practices continuous hand flapping that prohibits the use of writing implements — you should stop the behavior if possible.

One way to interrupt the stimming is to distract the child from what he's doing with a prompt to do something else. Indirect redirection works best.

However, allowing the person with autism some time to "get it out of her system" may be the better approach. Stimming that doesn't present potential physical risks or take away from learning opportunities can generally be left alone.

In some instructional programs, children with autism are rewarded for finishing a task with a short period of stimming. Other instructional programs teach socially acceptable stimming, or they teach socially acceptable methods to excuse yourself so you can stim in private and then return.

Unless the individual is in immediate danger, don't physically restrain him from stimming, which may only lead to agitation and aggression. Also, you shouldn't make the child feel guilty or uncomfortable about his behavior — it fulfills a need the child is experiencing. Your job is not to let the child stim for long periods and disengage from others to an extreme. You want him to be free to be himself, but you also want him to be able to learn and respond to his environment when appropriate.

Dealing with the most severe behaviors

Parents need to pay attention to safety of their children first. Whether your child tantrums, stims, flees, or insists on other behaviors, you must provide safety first and foremost by addressing any behaviors that present acute threats to his individual safety directly. The greatest morbidity and mortality associated with a spectrum diagnosis is associated with accidents (falls, drowning, being hit by a car, and so on).

Whereas hands-on therapy modalities can contribute greatly to learning and growth for individuals on the spectrum, medications are often necessary to help address behaviors that present risk to a person on the spectrum. Potential medication benefits include reduced aggressiveness, self-injury, and extreme, repetitive behaviors.

When you address any severe behavior that your child exhibits, we suggest that you consult your child's physician for an assessment of medication appropriateness.

Chapter 11

Finding a Learning Environment That Fits Your Child's Needs

*P*eople with autism spectrum disorders display great diversity in learning styles and characteristics. Yet, you can focus on some generalities that can make a classroom an effective place for people with autism to learn. You can't stop at the classroom, though; the physical classroom is just one component of a quality education. You also need to rely on faculty, aides, and other personnel who understand (or at least comprehend) and can teach autistic children.

In this chapter, we take a look at what an effective classroom looks, sounds, feels, smells, and maybe even tastes like. We include important characteristics to look for in educators. We discuss some ways to approach the education of children with autism and show you how to develop accommodations and promote successful inclusion. Finally, we look at strategies for handling the inevitable challenging behaviors all autistic students exhibit from time to time. We hope that with the information we provide in this chapter, you can work with your child, his or her school system, other parents, and your child's peers to make the educational process as smooth, enriching, and enjoyable as possible.

Inclusion: To Be or Not to Be?

Inclusion is the strategy of including a special-needs student in a classroom with regular-education students. Successful inclusion occurs when, through proper support and planning, both the child with special needs and the regular-education students benefit from being in each other's presence. At its best, inclusion provides rich lessons about the positive aspects of the diversity of the human race. At its worst, inclusion places a child in an environment that fails to meet his or her special needs and that may be intimidating and uncomfortable. Successful inclusion in the school setting builds a foundation for the involvement of people with disabilities and other differences at home, the workplace, the community, and in society as a whole.

Although schools may give the impression that inclusion is an all-or-nothing proposition, the reality is that you can choose from many different scenarios. In fact, you can think of inclusion as a spectrum ranging from 0 to 100 percent. The following list presents ways to look at how the range of inclusion can work for students who have special needs (ranging from 100-percent inclusion to 0-percent inclusion):

- The student spends all his time in a regular-education classroom. Students at the 100-percent end need direct or indirect support from an aide or other school employee part or all of the time.

- The student spends most of his time in a regular-education setting, with or without support. He spends the rest of his education experience in a resource room or self-contained special-education room.

- The student divides his time equally between the regular-education room and a resource room or self-contained classroom.

- The student spends most of his time in a special-education setting, but he eats lunch with, has recess with, and participates in art, music, or physical-education classes with regular-education peers.

- The student spends all his time in a special-education setting within the public school.

High-functioning children on the spectrum may be able to spend more time in a regular classroom. In particular, individuals with Asperger Syndrome (see Chapter 5) who possess fluent language skills may be able to integrate into a regular classroom for the majority of the school day. When you consider that where a child falls on the spectrum influences inclusion planning, the importance of determining where a child falls on the spectrum becomes clear. The child's physician and other treatment team members should work in concert with school personnel to clarify where the child falls on the spectrum and where he should spend his time in the school setting. (Chapter 2 discusses the different classifications of autism, and Chapter 4 discusses receiving a diagnosis from medical professionals.)

A child's Individualized Education Program (IEP) should reference where the individual is on the spectrum and discuss what educational adaptations can best meet the needs of someone falling at that particular place on the spectrum (see Chapter 12 for a full discussion of IEPs). Parents and teachers should engage in consistent dialogue after diagnosis (see Chapter 18 for more actions to take immediately following a diagnosis). This dialogue should include discussions of how the school can best meet the educational needs of the child, given the impairments inherent in being at his particular level of the spectrum.

Recognizing an Effective Classroom

When you enter a classroom, whether it's a regular-needs room or a special-education room, you can sense when the teacher has suited the classroom for the education of students. For example, an effective classroom may feature the day's topics highlighted on the walls of the room in a concise and engaging manner. Such practices are signs of good teaching and should take place in every classroom.

In this section, we discuss important elements that you should look for in your child's learning environment.

You should visit your child's classroom often in order to understand what the teacher is currently emphasizing in class, which allows you to reinforce the classroom learning at home. For example, parents can make connections like, "That stop sign is red. Your teacher has a picture of red letters in your classroom." If the classroom doesn't seem to be conducive to your child's learning style, make some suggestions. For example, if the class is stark and devoid of engaging visual cues, you could gently suggest to the teacher that because your child is a visual learner, visual cues and points of emphasis placed on the classroom walls would be helpful to your child's ability to learn.

Maintaining routine and predictability

Routines are important to everyone. Most people can successfully work through changes, such as a change in class schedule because of a school assembly or a detour from the daily commute, with no more than some annoyance at the unexpected changes.

A person on the autism spectrum, however, may react to such changes with meltdowns or tantrums if they occur without warning. Educators used to insist on not making changes in the lives of people with autism. That insistence proved somewhat unrealistic, however — after all, life is full of changes. It all boils down to preparation. Providing proper notification of the changes can make life much easier for people with autism and for the people around them.

Blending special and regular needs

Take a moment to digest the following classroom descriptions and look for their defining characteristics:

You open the door of Susan's classroom to find a buzz of activity — like a beehive but not overwhelmingly loud. Today's schedule hangs on the wall near the blackboard, indicating that you're walking into science class and that today's topic is geography. The schedule then draws your eye to a highlighted announcement of a school assembly — highlighted because it's a change from the daily routine. Hearing laughter, you turn to see Susan laughing off a spill that occurred as she was helping a small group of students work on a project depicting erosion in a sandbox. The sandbox is painted to look like a tropical paradise. "I guess my sweater doesn't erode as quickly as the sand," you hear Susan say.

One of the two other adults helps a student select four pictures that represent the seasons from a bin to stick onto a piece of cardboard. The adult narrates his every move like an excited sportscaster at a hockey game. You also note similarly styled pictures stuck all over the room, depicting doors, windows, the teacher's desk, today's weather, and even a toilet — a sticker one child uses to gain permission to go to the bathroom.

The other adult divides her time between two separated groups. The first group is examining the smells and tastes attributed to a country in Northern Europe by sampling examples of local dishes. In the second group, one of the students is pointing to a map and reciting countries, their capitals, and their populations in a loud monotone voice, very much like a professor. "He must have swallowed an encyclopedia," you think to yourself. After a few minutes, a person, whom you later learn is a covert aide, walks over to that student, calmly places her hand on his desk, and the monologue stops.

After some time, Susan stands up from her place at the sandbox, walks to her desk, and holds up her hands as a nonverbal cue for the students to pack up their work and prepare for music class. In few minutes, the music teacher walks into the class to begin musical activities. The aides stay behind, and you talk with Susan about her teaching philosophy, all the while wondering if this is the right place for your autistic child.

From this description, you may be wondering, "Is this a special-education class or a regular-education class with autistic children?" We purposely leave that determination vague to emphasize that quality education is pretty similar when it comes to instruction for regular-education students and for those with special needs.

If your child is already enrolled in a class, ask your child's teacher to post the class schedule and call attention to any change before it happens — by highlighting it on the board, for example — to make the modification easier to handle. If you're looking for a satisfactory classroom for your child, make sure that the teacher clearly posts daily and even weekly expectations on the walls. It's also helpful to have the day's activities in order of occurrence posted in plain view. You may attempt to suggest to a prospective teacher that keeping the class on a regular routine would be helpful to your child.

Learning through all the senses

Just as you observe diversity in the learning styles of people in the general population, you see great diversity in the learning styles of people with autism. However, the two populations show a marked difference in one area: Although most people can learn by using their weaker senses, people with autism may find it impossible to educate themselves through their weaker senses. As a result, the more diverse a classroom can be when it comes to sensory teaching, the richer the experience for all children involved.

Your job is to advocate for your child to experience learning in many diverse ways. When you find a setting that seems to fit your child's needs, you can begin advocating for his sensory needs during discussion of his IEP (see Chapter 12), as this plan can direct your child to receive services presented in diverse ways to maximize the potential for learning. After you advocate for an IEP sensitive to sensory issues, you can continue to prompt your child's teacher to maintain the tenets of the IEP in her daily classroom activities. Finally, if you feel that the teacher isn't following the IEP in the classroom, you can appeal to members of the school's administration to ensure that the IEP is enforced.

The following list presents some approaches you can advocate for your child's teacher to use to create a *multi-sensory environment* in order to maximize her students' learning abilities (see Chapter 10 for more on dealing with sensory differences):

- ✔ **Visual:** Most people on the autism spectrum are visually oriented. A classroom can take advantage of this fact by including visual props to aid in learning. A posted schedule of the day's activities is one example of a visual prop. Having a student place pictures that depict the seasons on a piece of cardboard is another example.

- ✔ **Touch:** Teachers can encourage connections by asking children to describe how certain objects feel. For example, when working on letters or sounds, teachers can come up with examples with distinct "touches" to help children understand more about the topic under discussion. One tactic could be using a fuzzy piece of material when going over the spelling word of the word "fuzzy". Asking children to describe how "fuzzy" feels not only promotes language development, but also reinforces memory of the word.

- ✔ **Sound:** Sound can be an important cue for any child on the autism spectrum. As with touch, teachers can incorporate the use of certain sounds into the classroom to reinforce topics of discussion. Teachers can ask children to describe certain sounds and then use their descriptions as the jumping-off points for meaningful discussions among classmates.

  One technique to improve auditory learning is the *narration technique*. Developed by Arnold Miller, the narration technique replaces the often-heard "good job" uttered by people working with autistic children with an excited, emphatic description of what the child is doing, such as

Benefiting your child by violating his or her senses

Herman Fishbein, former executive director of the League School of Greater Boston for Children with Autism, had the unique opportunity to build a school for autistic kids from the ground up. One of his goals was to create a completely sensory-friendly environment. However, it soon became clear that the sensory oasis the League School provided didn't represent the world at large. As a result, Herman constructed a "sensory violation room" that's more characteristic of the environment the children will transition to after graduation. The sensory violation room is actually a simulated convenience store, complete with whirring refrigerator units, fluorescent lights, and a radio playing in the background.

Parents and educators learned three important lessons from this sensory violation room:

- ✔ Some autistic students had no problem with the convenience-store environment.

- ✔ Some students with sensory issues could accommodate for the noisier environment.

- ✔ Many students found out that they shouldn't even entertain the idea of working in an environment similar to that of a convenience store.

Be sure to stay in tune with your child's sensory needs, and do your best to make sure that his or her classroom complies with those needs.

"Billy is *walking up* the stairs!" As described in Dr. Miller's writings, one benefit of narration is that instead of uttering a "good job" to compliment achieved goals, people can help children learn to attach words to their actions.

Sound can also be distracting to children on the spectrum. Classroom objects that promote dissonant sound can include tile floors or fluorescent lighting. Incandescent lighting and the use of rugs can help reduce these distracting background noises.

- ✔ **Smell and taste:** If a child can smell or taste a particular object, his or her ability to maintain lasting memory of the object is increased. Teachers can use edible/fragrant objects such as fruits to reinforce memory of certain sounds or letters.

- ✔ **Kinesthetic:** A child with Asperger Syndrome who recites the names of countries, their capitals, and their populations as he points to them on a map uses his kinesthetic sense. Other students who observe these actions employ their visual and aural senses. The power of motion can also reinforce learning and the development of memory in many classroom scenarios. For example, asking a child to use his hands/body to imitate shapes can reinforce a day's lesson in geometry.

Evaluating the room itself

Think about your workspace or the workspaces you see on television or in retail stores/restaurants you go to. Does every item in the space have a place, and is every item in its place? If you work in an office, can you see your desk, or is it covered with papers? Are the tools of your job — a computer, pens, paper, and so on — organized for maximum efficiency? Have you included pictures of family, knickknacks, and other non-work items to give your space personality?

People organize workspaces to promote efficiency, and a classroom should be no different. Your child's classroom should be organized to create a warm, inviting place for students to learn and grow. The following list presents some aspects of a room well prepared for children with (and without) autism.

Make sure you work with your child's teacher to help create this environment. Don't be afraid to show her this list! If your child's teacher resists brightening up his room with inviting visual cues, for example, consider informing the school administration that your child and others in the classroom would benefit from positive visual classroom displays. Another option is to consider finding another educational situation, preferably within your child's current school, if you run into continued resistance from educators or administration.

- ✔ **Personal touch:** The room should reflect the personality of the teacher and his teaching style. For example, a teacher with an artistic flair may draw simple murals describing current classroom material. A teacher with an outgoing, happy personality may place positive statements around the room to encourage children to work hard.

- ✔ **Layout:** The geography of the room is very important. The layout should be logical and easy for both children and teachers to get around. For example, the room should provide sufficient space between the desks for people to walk around. However, all desks should have an easy line of sight between the students, teacher, blackboard, and other props the teacher uses for the class as a whole. Cramping children together increases the chance that a child on the spectrum would be easily distracted.

- ✔ **Good ventilation:** Studies have shown that people are more productive when they work in rooms with good air circulation and a comfortable temperature. Just think of how your production would decrease if you were sitting in the economy section of an airplane on a long flight! Children on the spectrum may notice poor ventilation and noxious odors more readily than others, thus increasing their classroom distraction level.

- ✔ **Appropriate noise level:** Active learning tends to be a bit noisy and may seem a little disorganized. However, if noise levels are so high that the teacher or children can't hear themselves think, the room is too loud. Because children on the spectrum often have keen and even hypersensitive hearing, distracting noises can greatly decrease their ability to focus on classroom work.

- ✔ **Comfortable lighting:** Studies show that people are more productive under nonfluorescent lighting. Natural lighting should be employed as much as possible. Many children on the spectrum are very sensitive to lighting that other children may be able to accept.

✔ **Appropriate furniture:** The furniture should fit the students and be in good condition. Clunky furniture can cause classroom accidents and injury, particularly for children on the spectrum with any motor skill delays.

✔ **Clean and tidy:** Tidy classrooms are more conducive to teaching and learning. A disorganized classroom presents children on the spectrum with confusion that decreases their ability to focus on classroom work.

✔ **Additional equipment and space to support routines:** For example, near the entrance of the room, you should find a space for students to leave and retrieve their outer clothes, knapsacks, and other possessions as they enter and leave. Depending on the developmental level of the children (and your child), you may see additional cubbyholes or other areas to retrieve or deposit schoolwork. Children on the spectrum can benefit greatly from classroom areas set aside to promote daily routines.

✔ **Rules and a code of conduct:** Sometimes, the school supplies the rules or develops them with student/parent input. Autistic children should follow the same classroom rules with regard to safety boundaries (no hitting, kicking, and so on), but the teacher may need to make some concessions if a child on the spectrum can't follow the classroom rules (for example, no moving in your seat for a child who exhibits automatic behaviors like repetitive movements).

Ask your child's teacher (or potential teacher) how she feels about the rules or code of conduct hanging in her classroom. The enthusiasm she expresses can tell you plenty about her teaching philosophy and approach.

✔ **Display of student work:** The room should feature a place or places for student work — be it math, art, or other projects — displayed for all students and visitors.

Check to see if the displays look new rather than old, faded, and tattered. A fresh display area is a good indication that the teacher cares for the students and their education.

✔ **Learning stations:** Ideally, the room should have areas dedicated to certain activities. Examples of different areas for work include the following:

- **Computer area:** An area with one or more computers dedicated to enhancing learning, improving break time, and serving as a reward for completing work.

- **Opening-circle, closing-circle, or story-time area:** Depending on the level of the students, engaging in these transition activities at a particular time can be helpful for transitioning in and out of school.

- **Quiet-time area:** A low sensory stimulation area that children can use to rest from sensory overload or to quietly read. The teacher should expect a child sitting in this area for a break from overstimulation to do his work there rather than at his desk. This expectation prevents the quite-time area from becoming a way to escape work. The break also helps the child begin to focus on his next task.

- **Other areas:** Depending on the size of the room and the objectives of the teacher, you may find additional areas for reading, writing, creative arts, and listening.

Observing a Good Teacher

The challenge of educating children with autism falls on both special-needs and regular educators, along with the various aides, therapists, and other school personnel that provide assistance. And you can't forget about the very important role of the parents. But when a child is away from his parents, the biggest burden falls on the teacher. Therefore, you need to make sure that this person can handle the burden and give your child the best education possible in the best setting possible.

In this section, we review the characteristics of teachers who promote strong learning environments for children on the autism spectrum, and we examine characteristics than can hinder a spectrum child's ability to learn. No matter the status of the children she oversees, a good teacher can be a real asset to her students' ability to maximize their school experience.

Characteristics to look for in an educator

When you observe a teacher's classroom (see the previous section, "Recognizing an Effective Classroom") and have discussions with your child's teacher or prospective teacher, keep the following list of words in mind. These words represent characteristics or behaviors that you should look for in an instructor, starting off with the all-important positive attitude — a must for the educator of a child on the spectrum:

- ✔ **Positive attitude.** The teacher should seem very happy with what she's doing, and you should see it in her interactions with the children and others in the classroom. A positive attitude goes a long way toward promoting a happy, engaging classroom environment and is the foundation for many other positive characteristics that promote a good classroom environment.

- ✔ **Creativity.** Does the teacher make the learning environment stimulating and fun while still catering to the needs of her students? Will your child be excited to attend class? Maybe your child's classroom or prospective classroom is the first place you've seen a sandbox painted like a tropical paradise.

- ✔ **Enthusiasm.** The teacher should seem eager and full of energy, both in class and during conversations with you.

- ✔ **Fairness.** Does the teacher's classroom provide for the needs of all students, giving them an equal chance for success? *Note:* Being fair doesn't necessarily mean giving the same kind of support for each child. An autistic child needs more support than other children in many cases, and a low-functioning child may need more (and different types of) support than a child with Asperger's.

✔ **Fallacy.** Hopefully you won't observe the teacher making any mistakes while teaching, but if you do observe mistakes, you hope that she promptly owns up to the errors and apologizes to her students.

✔ **Flexibility.** Does the teacher understand that the individual needs of all her children should dictate her lesson plans? Does she adapt her plans daily to meet these needs? From sensory to stimming needs, a teacher should be flexible enough to adapt her teaching style to all her kids, giving each child an equal opportunity to succeed.

✔ **Has high expectations.** Do most of the teacher's students strive to meet her high expectations? High-functioning children on the spectrum may be able to better understand the motivation behind trying to meet expectations.

In one well-known study, conductors gave a regular-education teacher a group of children who historically performed below grade level and told the teacher that these students were high achievers. As a result, the teacher had high expectations of the students and worked hard to enrich their curriculum, and the students strove to meet the teacher's high expectations.

✔ **Humorous.** You can find humor in unexpected places when it comes to autism, and the classroom is no exception. The teacher should take the high road of laughter rather than the angry option when harmless mishaps occur or students take creative projects in crazy directions.

✔ **Prepared.** Does the teacher project mastery over the material that she's teaching? Does she have a handle on how she can best teach the material to the comprehension level of her students?

✔ **Provides emotional safety and compassion.** Do all the students appear to belong to the classroom? Do the students go to the teacher with issues or concerns and feel safe doing so? You may also want to ask the teacher how she handles bullying, an unfortunate companion to autism in the school environment (see Chapter 5).

✔ **Respectful.** Does the teacher seem sensitive to the feelings of her students and work to reduce embarrassing situations? Does she respect all students, no matter their ability or function level, as the whole persons they are?

Warning flags to avoid in an educator

Certain personality traits you observe in prospective teachers for your child should cause great concern — concern enough that you should keep on looking (and wonder how they got into teaching in the first place). Parents should

engage in constant dialogue in anticipation of a negative classroom environment before they put their child in that classroom. If your child reports that
his once-happy learning environment is becoming a hostile classroom, you
should make an effort to advocate for change within the classroom before
you remove the child, because removal from the classroom often brings its
own transition stress that can inhibit a child's ability to learn.

Here are some behaviors that make your child's learning environment
unhealthy and harmful:

- ✔ **Negativity.** Just as a positive attitude should lead to teacher characteristics that promote learning (see the previous section), negativity can lead
  to characteristics that create a hostile classroom. Good educators focus
  on how they can facilitate their students' successes instead of concen-
  trating on their limitations.

  Parents of children on the spectrum need to find out if negative traits
  are developing in their child's teacher. If so, parents may need to report
  what they're noticing to the teacher's supervisor.

- ✔ **Lack of humility.** The best educators work for their students, realizing
  that no one has all the answers. The teacher should be willing to admit
  when she makes a mistake.

- ✔ **Yelling.** The only good reason to yell at a student is to avoid life-
  threatening danger (and even then, yelling may only increase panic). Of
  course, every good teacher is bound to have an "off day" and yell at a
  student. However, that should be an extremely rare occurrence.

Often, parents don't have a choice of teachers for their child. In such cases, it
makes sense for parents to try to be proactive with their child's assigned
teachers. Being proactive includes making suggestions without sounding like
you're passing negative judgment on the teachers. Suggestions for improvement often go over better than direct condemnation. If the proactive
approach doesn't work, you can react by talking with school administrators
about your concerns.

Developing Effective Accommodations

One of the biggest differences between the instruction of children with
autism or other special needs and regular-education students centers on the
degree of accommodations children with special needs must have in order to
have an equal chance of achieving success in the world of education.

Accommodations. A scary sounding word? Maybe, but only for teachers.
Accommodations are vital to an autistic child's education, so you should get
comfortable with the term. The Individuals with Disabilities Education Act
(IDEA) is a law that, among many things, requires all teachers to read a student's Individualized Education Program (IEP) and develop *accommodations,*

or changes in the methods of teaching and assessing a student that give the student an equal chance of success in his education as the regular-education students. Wow! That's a mouthful, and enough to scare off most teachers. Many teachers are terrified by the idea of having to make accommodations. (For more on the IDEA and IEPs, see Chapter 12.)

The fright comes from the changes in teaching style, the issue of fairness that may arise, and dealing with other students' reactions to the accommodations. Your job is to find a teacher who's up to the challenge (see the previous section for more info on finding the right teacher) and work with her to develop the proper accommodations, along with the child's IEP team. This section sets you down the road to development. Here, you see accommodations in action, you examine the issue of fairness, and you find techniques that promote inclusion in the learning environment.

Although teachers play a primary role in developing accommodations based upon the IEP, you know your child best, so you should work with teachers if you have suggestions for how your child can best learn material in the classroom.

Accommodations in action

To figure out how accommodations actually work in practice, consider the following common teaching strategies:

- ✔ Write an outline of today's class on the blackboard.

- ✔ Provide a handout that summarizes the Krebs Cycle in biology.

- ✔ Allow the kids to write out a test on paper or take it orally.

Now look at how these same strategies work when the teacher makes accommodations for specific students in the classroom:

- ✔ Write out an advance organizer for Sam, who has Asperger Syndrome, so he can follow the sequence of events in class. Sam could get a copy of the schedule in written form in addition to the outline on the board.

- ✔ Provide a handout that summarizes the Krebs Cycle in biology for Rebecca, who has Pervasive Development Disorder — Not Otherwise Specified. The teacher may decide to give handouts to all students because they can be helpful to students with and without autism spectrum disorders.

- ✔ Allow for an alternate assessment of learning through different output modalities for Aaron, who has been diagnosed with autism.

What's the difference in the educational intent between the first and second set of accommodations? *None!* The only difference is that what were originally common examples of good teaching practice have been written as accommodations in IEP-speak.

Accommodations, believe it or not, aren't that big a deal. They're generally just extensions of good teaching practice. Because of the great diversity of people on the autism spectrum, teachers can't provide a single set of accommodations that work for every student. Developing appropriate accommodations is a combination of understanding a student's learning style and knowing what educational (and other) adjustments a teacher can make. Sometimes, the development requires hatching some new techniques on your own.

Figure 11-1 is the beginning of what we call an enhanced laundry list of accommodations from co-author Stephen Shore's book, *Ask and Tell: Self-Advocacy and Disclosure for People on the Autism Spectrum* (Autism Asperger Publishing Company). The objective of this list is twofold:

> **Objective 1:** To consider which accommodation or accommodations are suitable. If educators and parents have previously used an accommodation, they can rate it on a scale of 1 to 5 for its effectiveness. A low score means the accommodation wasn't effective, and you may want to reconsider using it. A high score means you should strongly consider using that accommodation.

> **Objective 2:** To increase awareness of the different types of accommodations that exist, with an eye toward developing even more possibilities if no current accommodations are suitable.

Addressing the fairness of accommodations

The topic of fairness often comes up when teachers and parents discuss making accommodations for students with autism. Is it fair to give someone two hours to complete a test when the regular-education students have only one? Or what about letting a child with difficulty in penmanship answer her test verbally rather than in writing? Why should the teacher provide notes for one child but not the rest of the class? Is this fair?

Suppose you're dining with friends in a restaurant, and a piece of food gets stuck in your airway, preventing you from breathing. A waiter comes over and apologizes, saying that while he's trained to give the Heimlich maneuver to restore your breathing ability, he can't because he wouldn't have the time to serve all his other patrons.

Just as it is fair to provide you with the Heimlich in your time of need to equalize your chance at survival, it's fair to provide students what they need to have an equal chance of succeeding in their education. The other patrons aren't choking, so they don't need the same assistance, just as the regular-education students don't have your child's problems. It would be pretty hard for other parents to argue this fact. What position would they rather be in?

Student: _____ Date: _____

Teacher: _____ IEP Manager: _____

Used (Y/N)	Effectiveness (1-5)	Accommodation	Used (Y/N)	Effectiveness (1-5)	Accommodation
		Placement Preferential seating Small group			**Sensory** Lighting modifications Hat with visor Different-color paper Headphones Chewing gum Standing at desk Sitting on therapy ball Small therapy ball or other manipulative for hands Quiet (safe) room for dealing with sensory overload
		Assignments Reduced level of difficulty Shortened Assignments Reduced pencil/paper tasks Extended time Opportunity to respond orally			
		Instruction Shortened instruction Assignment notebook Frequent/immediate feedback Dictated information, answers on tape Taped lectures Reduced language level/reading style Incorporation of learning styles Peer tutoring/paired working assignments/tests Outline with due dates for assignments/tests Negotiates respites with teacher (medical) Restroom use (medical)			**Materials and technology** Taped text/material Highlighted text/materials Manipulatives Braille materials ESL materials Keyboard modifications Access to keyboard/word processor Large print Tape recorder in classroom Another student's notes Teacher's notes A note-taker in class

Figure 11-1:
A laundry list of attempted accommodations: Choose wisely!

		Behavior Positive reinforcement Frequent breaks Clearly defined limits/expectations Quiet time Behavior management plan			Extra set of books for home (physical) Electronic speller	
					Teacher supports Consultation Information Other	
		Testing Scheduling Setting Presentation Response Extended time Individual/small group testing Take test in quiet area Test read orally Take test orally Dictate answers to a test/quiz Use calculator on test/quiz Open-book exams			**Other** _____ _____ _____ _____	
				Notes _____ _____ _____ _____ _____ _____ _____ _____		

Figure 11-1:
Continued.

If or when fairness becomes an issue with your child's teacher or prospective teacher, other students, or other parents, be sure to reinforce with those questioning the accommodation that the changes afforded your child only attempt to put him on an even playing field — not to give him a leg up on the classroom. Parents who encounter questions of fairness should make it clear that their child suffers from a disorder that greatly impacts his ability to learn in standard ways. To treat all children in exactly the same way would put special-needs children at great disadvantages.

Issues of fairness tend to impact high-functioning kids more because more people believe high-functioning kids on the spectrum are getting an advantage, whereas low-function children may be more apt to receive "pity" because others feel they're markedly different and deserve accommodation. If you want to fight the battle head-on, attempt to advocate for your child by educating the ignorant about the issues that come with Asperger's and other forms of high-functioning autism.

Considering educational techniques for promoting inclusion

Successful inclusion (of special-needs kids into a classroom setting) can be very challenging for regular and special educators alike. In this section, we include nine ways to promote inclusion, adapted from the text *Adapting Curriculum and Instruction in Inclusive Classrooms: A Teacher's Desk Reference*, by Deschenes, Ebeling, and Sprague (The Center for School and Community Integration, Institute for the Study of Developmental Disabilities). The techniques use accommodations that aid in providing meaningful education to both the special- and regular-education students. Your child's teachers should look at these techniques and try to incorporate as many as possible into their accommodation planning. We also encourage parents to take this list to their IEP team meetings.

- **Amount of information.** Adapt the number of items that the teacher expects the student to learn or complete.

  Example: You can reduce the number words the student must learn for the weekly spelling test.

- **Time allotted.** Adapt the time allotted for learning, task completion, or testing.

  Example: Individualize a timeline for completing a task; increase or decrease the pace of learning.

- **Level of support.** Increase the amount of personal assistance with a specific student.

  Example: Assign peer buddies, teaching assistants, peer tutors, or cross-age tutors to work with the student.

- **Input of material.** Adapt the way you give instruction to the student.

  Example: Use different visual aids and as many senses as the child is able to learn with when teaching; plan more concrete examples; provide hands-on activities; place students in cooperative groups.

- **Difficulty of material.** Adapt the skill level of the work, the problem types, or the rules on how the student may approach the work.

  Example: Allow the use of a calculator to figure math problems; simplify task directions; change rules to accommodate learner needs.

- **Output of answers.** Adapt how the student can respond to instruction.

  Example: Instead of requiring the student to answer questions in writing, allow a verbal response. You can also use a communication book with some students or allow students to show knowledge with hands-on materials.

Geographical inclusion

While observing a music class some time ago, I (co-author Stephen Shore) noticed a child with Down's syndrome being kept very busy with some unrelated work in the back of the room. Although he seemed well behaved, he would occasionally make an inappropriate sound, causing the rest of the students to turn around, which distracted from the lesson. The music teacher then had to regain the attention of the class to continue. This happened four or five times during the class period.

What did all the children learn in class that day? I can be pretty sure the child with Down's syndrome learned whatever he was doing with the aide, but it certainly wasn't music. The regular-education children merely learned that people with disabilities really are different from everyone else. The inclusion of the child with Down's syndrome was limited to only his location, which is why I call it *geographical inclusion.* Geographical inclusion can lead to lasting stigmatization that can stay with a child on the autism spectrum for years to come. This method of inclusion only emphasizes differences, thus labeling a special-needs child as merely "different".

✔ **Participation requirements.** Adapt the extent to which the learner is involved in the task.

Example: In music, have the student hold a flag of the country the song is from. Or in geography, have the student hold up the map while others point out locations.

✔ **Alternate expectations.** Adapt the student's goals or your outcome expectations while allowing the student to use the same materials as other kids.

Example: In social studies, expect the student to locate only the states while others learn to locate the capitals as well.

✔ **Substitute curriculum.** Provide different instruction and materials to meet a student's individual goals while still aligning with the class curriculum.

Example: During a language test, the student can learn computer skills such as keyboarding in the computer lab, enabling the completion of writing assignments.

WARNING!

Take care to make sure that the curriculum substitution technique doesn't result in geographical inclusion. Check out the sidebar "Geographical inclusion" for details on the subject.

REMEMBER

The common goal behind these and other accommodations is the meaningful involvement of the person with a disability in school, as well as at home and in the community. This goal holds true for people across the autism spectrum. Low-functioning children may need more and different accommodations than individuals with Asperger's (see Chapter 5) or other forms of high-functioning autism, but the goal remains the same.

Weighing Your Options when the Public School System Falls Short

As students, parents, and society place more and more demands on educators, they have less time to properly understand and respond to the needs of students on the autism spectrum. Sometimes, the public school system as a whole is unable to provide for all the needs of a child — especially when these needs are unique. In these cases, the community is required to fund the student's education at a special school or residential program. Occasionally, students may need to (or parents may want them to) receive their education at home or even at a hospital.

With the cost of out-of-district placement often passing the six-figure mark, many schools systems are reluctant to go this route. However, if you truly feel that placement in another district is in the best interests of the person on the spectrum you're caring for, you may want to strongly consider engaging the services of a special-education advocate or lawyer. Problems with placement outside a given school system often occur with low-functioning children and others whose behaviors and needs at times render them impossible to accommodate within their assigned school districts.

Exploring the world of home schooling

The decision to home school is a very serious one. Some states are developing standards for students who are home schooled, making the process tougher. All students have the right to a free and appropriate education in a public school. You shouldn't feel the obligation to home school your child just because the school system can't accommodate him. Prior to settling on home schooling, you should be allowed to exhaust all means, including legal action, to try to get your local public school system to accommodate the needs of your child. A good question to ask yourself is, "Will my child be better off in a home-school situation that I can provide for him than where he is now, given what the school system will provide?" (For more on examining classrooms, teachers, and accommodations, see the previous sections in this chapter.)

The answer for each child varies. You must weigh the available resources in the community against the resources that you, the parents or guardians, can bring. Frequently, a family living in one community is better off home schooling their autistic child, while an autistic child just down the road in a neighboring town can obtain a better education in school. You should consider exhausting many options prior to home schooling — especially if you're not very comfortable home schooling your child.

Choosing to home school means that public education isn't a good fit for the child at *this* place and at *this* time. It doesn't necessarily reflect the quality of the educational institution, and it doesn't mean that your decision is permanent.

Here are a couple areas to consider when deciding how well the public school environment suits the needs of your child:

- **Academics.** Academics includes *what* and *how* the child learns. Is the required curriculum taught in a way that she can understand? Are educators and other personnel approachable? Do they seem to understand and respect your child? Are reasonable accommodations made?

- **Social.** Do school personnel and other classmates interact respectfully with your child, or is he a target for bullying?

Choosing to educate a child at home is a serious responsibility that involves a lot of time, money, patience, organization, and learning on your part. Here are some more aspects of home schooling to account for before you make the decision to teach a child at home (this list is intended to provide an idea of what's involved, not to cover all the issues):

- Both parents must agree.

- You have to have sufficient time to teach the child. Expect that teaching your child will amount to a full-time job. You'll most likely spend as much teaching time at home as teachers do in school.

- You need to understand the significant financial commitment involved. Expect that the costs of home schooling may approach the costs of schooling a child within the private school system; however, you have to pay costs of possibly $10,000 or more yourself depending upon how much outside help you hire. (See Chapter 9 for more info on financing at-home programs.)

- You should have a willingness to learn about teaching. Parent-teachers need to keep up with new and innovative education techniques just like classroom teachers. An Internet search on Home Schooling Autism will reveal many Web sites, such as `homeschooling.gomilpitas.com/weblinks/autism.htm`, and other resources for educating your child at home.

- You need to have a plan for supplementing the child's socialization. Parent-teachers must plan to integrate their child into some social setting with peers to promote effective social development.

- You need to determine if home schooling is right for you, the caregiver. If you have fears or misgivings about meeting the requirements for home schooling, this baseline stress may only worsen after you become responsible for your child's special-needs education.

A good start in making this decision is to contact other parents who have home schooling experience. You can also ask therapists and other professionals working with autistic children, and you can contact your local autism support organization (such as the Autism Society of America) to help you locate parents to talk to.

Considering other educational options

Other schooling options outside of public school, private school, and home schooling include educational opportunities at residential treatment facilities and special schools for individuals with developmental disabilities.

Although choosing to send your child to a residential facility is a difficult step, at times this may represent the safest and most appropriate option for a child on the autism spectrum. In particular, low-functioning children who exhibit intense maladaptive behaviors (aggression, self-injury, and so on) may need to learn within a controlled residential environment. If you think you need to consider this difficult decision, you should talk to a knowledge-able psychiatrist, psychologist, or other relevant professional.

You may worry that having your child live at a facility where education is pro-vided will weaken the bond between you and your child. What you need to understand is that above all other priorities, your child's safety must come first. If your child presents great risk to herself or to others by being in a home-schooled or classroom environment, residential treatment with associ-ated special-needs education may be the best and safest option available for learning.

Understanding and Reducing Challenging Behaviors

A child protests and drops to the floor when asked to work with other students in class or do his homework after school. Another child throws a tantrum with-out any definable reason (known to you; see Chapter 10). A student with Asperger Syndrome suddenly decides to eat her lunch outside of the lunch-room. These are just a few examples of what are known as *challenging behaviors,* or behaviors contrary to expectations that are difficult to deal with. It can be hard to get the child back on track after the behavior starts. Parents, educators, and other caregivers are challenged to figure out the causes of such actions.

Getting to the core of the behavior

Understanding the cause or causes of challenging behaviors, rather than just focusing on the actions, is the key to achieving meaningful success (in other words, reducing the challenging behaviors). You need to consider a few things that surround the behaviors to understand the behaviors. For autistic kids, more so than neurotypical kids, environmental factors often play a big part in behavior. Here are some surrounding events to check out:

- ✔ **The setting events:** The time of day, weather, food allergies, or any other factor that may be relevant

- ✔ **The antecedents:** What happened just before the incident

- ✔ **The consequences:** What consequences occurred as a result of the behavior

Performing a Functional Behavioral Assessment (FBA)

A Functional Behavioral Assessment (FBA) is a powerful key for addressing challenging behaviors. A clinician who has experience in assessing behavior in children and adolescents with autism spectrum disorders should conduct the assessment. The "clinician" position may be filled by a physician, psychologist, or social worker. You can consult your local educational laws to see if FBAs are a requirement if requested by a parent.

Some uses for the FBA include the following:

- ✔ Identifying the purposes of specific behaviors

- ✔ Selecting interventions for behavioral issues

- ✔ Integrating interventions through all stages of the Individualized Education Program (see Chapter 12)

One of the keys to the success of the FBA is that it looks beyond the specific behavior by identifying the social, affective, cognitive, and environmental factors associated with the occurrence of the behavior.

According to the Center for Effective Collaboration and Practice Web site, cecp.air.org, conducting an FBA requires you to follow six steps, which we outline in the following list:

1. Describe and verify the seriousness of the problem.

In other words, concretely define the challenging behavior and indicate just how serious the behavior is. Seriousness has to do with effect. Is the situation confined to just the student, or is the behavior affecting others or possibly endangering them? In other words, is the behavior frequent enough or serious enough that it interferes with the learning of the student or his peers?

Here's an example of stating the problem and making it concrete (see Figure 11-2):

- **Problem:** Alice displays out-of-seat behavior in math class.

- **Concrete:** After the teacher introduces the subject of the day's math class, Alice starts running around the room and shuts off the lights.

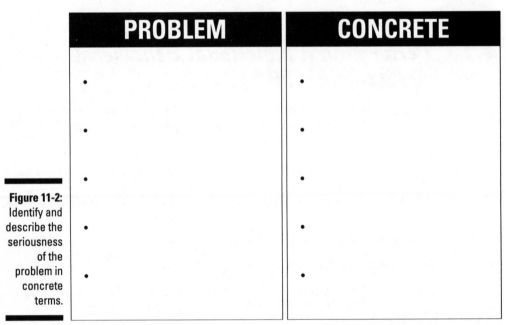

Figure 11-2:
Identify and describe the seriousness of the problem in concrete terms.

Courtesy of Center for Effective Collaboration and Practice

2. Refine the definition of the problem behavior.

Complete this step with both *direct assessment* (seeking the cause, identifying the behavior, and reinforcing consequences that maintain the action through actual observation) and *indirect assessment* (talking to others in the child's life about their observations on the behavior). An example for using the direct assessment form follows:

Direct Assessment (see Figure 11-3):

- **Antecedent:** Alice manages to stay in her seat for a few minutes and then begins to rock and vocalize before jumping out of her seat.

- **Behavior:** Alice runs around the room and often stops to look out the windows. She seems to flap less when she's near the windows. When she gets to the light switches, she turns the lights off. Usually, Alice returns to her seat after shutting off the lights.

- **Consequence:** Alice's teacher sends her to the time-out room. Is Alice being inadvertently reinforced to shut off the lights?

If Alice is inadvertently being reinforced to shut off the lights, you need to consider as many reasons as you can. One motivation for Alice may be that the lights are overwhelming her sensitive eyes.

Indirect Assessment (see Figure 11-4): Other people should write their observations on a child's challenging behaviors on this form.

3. **Collect information on the possible function of the problem behavior.** Every behavior serves a purpose for the autistic person (to communicate, to relieve anxiety, to self-stimulate, to exert control over his environment, to escape, to avoid, and so on). You have three general categories to keep in mind when determining behavioral function:

- **Behavior is communication.** People with autism may have no other way to communicate that they're experiencing sensory overload, having difficulty with transitions, or are unable to communicate needs or wants than with challenging behavior.

- **Social or tangible reinforcement.** This category is less common than many people think. However, if a child seems to be "seeking attention" from adults or peers, you should show that the child can receive attention in other, more positive ways.

- **Escape or avoidance.** Seek to determine what's perhaps difficult or boring about a situation. Why may a child be seeking to avoid interaction with a particular person?

4. **Analyze the information.** You have three ways to analyze behavioral information, which will hopefully result in a plan for resolving the challenging behavior:

- **Data triangulation.** This method is just a fancy way of determining if your observations jive with what others have seen. Use the form in Figure 11-5 to get started.

    For example, finding out that Alice behaves differently in, say, an art class that occurs before lunch may provide valuable insights for determining the cause of and finally modifying the behavior. Possible causes for her behavior may include food allergies and not understanding what's expected of her.

- **Problem pathway analysis.** You determine the sequence of events by writing down the setting event(s), antecedent event(s) that comes before, problem behavior(s), and the maintaining consequences (what keeps the behavior happening again and again). Check out Figure 11-6 for the pathway analysis form.

  From the material you've developed so far, you trace the behavior from what may be affecting Alice prior to school or your class all the way through what may be encouraging the situation to continue.

- **Competing problem pathway analysis.** This step adds to the material you write for the problem pathway analysis sheet (see Figure 11-6). By filling out this form, you include solutions (or accommodations) that can create new behaviors and new maintaining consequences for the child.

Student: _____ Observation date: _____

Observer: _____ Time: _____

Activity: _____ Class period: _____

Behavior: _____
_____
_____

ANTECEDENT	BEHAVIOR	CONSEQUENCE
•	•	•
•	•	•
•	•	•
•	•	•
•	•	•

Figure 11-3: Antecedent-Behavior-Consequence Observation Form A — Direct Assessment.

Courtesy of Center for Effective Collaboration and Practice

Student: _____	Observation date: _____
Observer: _____	Time: _____
Activity: _____	Class period: _____

Context of incident

Antecedent

Behavior

Consequence

Comments or other observations

Figure 11-4: Antecedent-Behavior-Consequence Observation Form B — Indirect Assessment.

Courtesy of Center for Effective Collaboration and Practice

For this analysis, you include competing events (what goes on that interferes with the inappropriate behavior), replacement behaviors (behaviors that a child can perform in place of the challenging behavior), and desired behavior (which you would like to see in place of the problem behavior). See Figure 11-7 for a form outline.

5. **Create a hypothesis statement regarding the probable function of the challenging behavior.** Based on the reason(s) you find through your research into the situation, you develop an educated guess as to the cause or causes of the behavior.

6. **Test the hypothesis.** See if the behavior repeats in similar situations. Find out if the behavior is extinguished when accommodations are made or if other, more positive behaviors are modeled to replace the challenging behavior.

The situation you observe needs continual monitoring. If the challenging behavior returns or another unsatisfactory situation develops, you need to find out what has changed in the child, both in and out of school. Also, as a child matures, he will experience different setting events, antecedents, and maintaining consequences surrounding behavior.

Student: _____ Date(s): _____		
	Source 1	**Source 2**	**Source 3**

Description

Interpretation

- Precipitating events:

- Maintaining consequences:

- Function(s):

Figure 11-5:
The Behavior Triangulation Form compares observations of the behavior.

Courtesy of Center for Effective Collaboration and Practice

Student: _____ Grade: _____ School: _____ Date: _____
Time: _____ Setting: _____

Setting event(s)		Triggering antecedent(s)		Problem behavior(s)		Maintaining consequences
•		•		•		•
•		•		•		•
•	→	•	→	•	→	•
•		•		•		•
•		•		•		•

Figure 11-6:
The Behavior Problem Pathway Form allows you to analyze the info you collect.

Courtesy of Center for Effective Collaboration and Practice

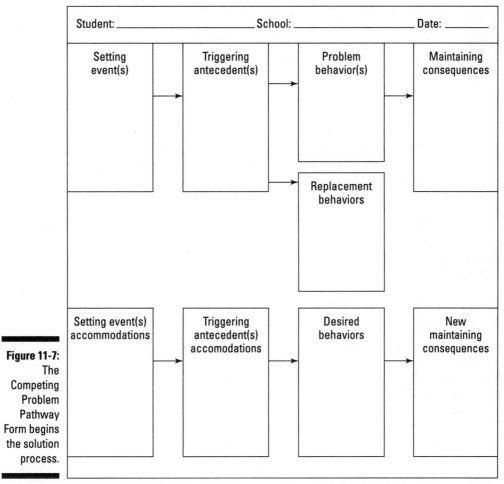

Student: _____ School: _____ Date: _____

| Setting event(s) | Triggering antecedent(s) | Problem behavior(s) | Maintaining consequences |

Replacement behaviors

| Setting event(s) accommodations | Triggering antecedent(s) accomodations | Desired behaviors | New maintaining consequences |

Figure 11-7: The Competing Problem Pathway Form begins the solution process.

Courtesy of Center for Effective Collaboration and Practice

Chapter 12

Legally Speaking: Making the Most of Your Child's Education

*T*he law says every child — regardless of disability — deserves an appropriate education. When you get down to brass tacks about what that education should entail, communication often breaks down. However, the process need not be nightmarish, adversarial, or confusing, and it won't be if you understand what public schools are legally bound to do for their special-needs kids and what your role is in making it happen.

In this chapter, we explain your child's rights under federal law and what you can expect your school system and other professionals to do to meet your child's educational needs. We also help you decipher some of that education-ese and show you how to ensure that your child gets the educational services to which he or she is entitled.

Navigating the Legal and Education Systems

Although it may seem like you're on your own at many times during your battle against the worldview of disability, you do have the law on your side when it comes to education. An autism diagnosis is considered a disability under federal law, and all children with disabilities — whose disability adversely affects their educational performance (remember this distinction) — are legally eligible for special services.

In the following pages, we outline some laws that aid you in your tug of war with the education system, and we help you keep track of the changes in legislation that affect your child's education. It helps to have people you trust on your side, so we also provide a few tips to lead in you the right direction.

Understanding what the law allows

Knowledge is your most powerful tool when working with your child's school district to ensure that he or she receives an education comparable with other children. And when it comes to knowledge concerning the law, you have to get used to some acronyms. Here comes the onslaught: Under the Individuals with Disabilities Education Act (IDEA); its reauthorization, the Individuals with Disabilities Education Improvement Act of 2004 (IDEA 2004); and other related federal laws, schools must provide a disabled child with the following:

- ✔ A *free appropriate public education* (FAPE), starting at age 3

- ✔ An *Individualized Education Program* (IEP) for children in school

- ✔ An *Individualized Family Service Plan* (IFSP) for preschoolers (ages 3–5) at risk, which takes into account the "strengths and needs" of parents

- ✔ A *least restrictive environment* (LRE), which keeps the child included in regular education as much as possible

   However, if the child receives more educational benefit by enrolling in a more restrictive program, the courts may favor that program.

- ✔ Active parental involvement in the process, including the right to attend every meeting about the child and examine all educational records

   The law that ensures access to records and confidentiality is called FERPA, or the Family Educational Rights and Privacy Act.

- ✔ *Extended school year* (ESY) *services* if a child needs help in the summer to maintain his or her progress or to keep from regressing

- ✔ Annual reviews of the IEP (see the section "Assessing Your Child's Progress" for a possible exception in the new law)

Armed with all the legal rights afforded by the law, you want to maximize your child's educational opportunities. After you make sure you understand what the law says, you can become actively involved in how your school system implements it in your child's education, with the IEP and other federal creations.

Keeping track of changes in the law

The legislation dealing with education for children with disabilities changes from time to time, and so does the way the courts interpret it. We don't have space to list most of the changes taking place of late, but we can give you some recent examples of what can change:

- ✔ The federal government now describes free appropriate public education (see the list in the previous section) as including preparation for "further education, employment, and independent living." The government added the part about "further education" in 2004.

- ✔ As of 2002, states are now required to ensure that disabled students meet appropriate "adequate yearly progress goals" that children under the No Child Left Behind Act (NCLBA) must meet.

- ✔ Teachers must be fully qualified to teach special education according to the Individuals with Disabilities Education Improvement Act (IDEA) of 2004.

- ✔ Diagnostic assessment measures, which are the foundation of IEP planning, must now be based upon sound methodology, according to the IDEA.

For more details on special education legislative changes, you can consult the U.S. Department of Education Web site (www.ed.gov, or more specifically www.ed.gov/parents/needs/speced/edpicks.jhtml?src=sm) and your own state department of education site for the latest information. At these sites, you can request publications put out by the Office of Special Education Programs (OSEP) so you can find out more about your legal rights. You can also find many helpful books on special education law that will explain how to advocate successfully, such as *Wrightslaw: From Emotions to Advocacy — The Special Education Survival Guide* (Harbor House Law Press, 2006) by Peter Wright and Pamela Darr Wright, two experts on the subject.

The bad news is that schools are becoming overwhelmed by a steep rise in special education students, and states are pushing to reduce paperwork by evaluating IEPs less often than once a year. Congress can reimburse states for up to 40 percent of the average per-pupil expenditure in public elementary schools and secondary schools in the United States, but the funding usually falls short, leaving states and schools to pick up most of the tab for the new legislation.

Often, under-funded federal mandates, on top of a shortage of special education teachers, mean that schools must balance the needs of children against their tight budgets.

What does this all mean for you? It means that your role in advocating for the child is critical. Try to develop strong relationships with educators, but know that even if schools want to do the best for their children (which they always assure you!), finances constrain them.

Staying Involved with Your Child's Education

Three situational factors can make or break your child's education:

- The quality of your child's teachers
- The match of your child's Individualized Education Program (IEP) with his or her needs
- Active parental involvement in the process

We concentrate on the last point here, because you have the most control over it. (The rest of this chapter covers IEPs, and Chapter 11 talks about how to evaluate classrooms.)

This may seem too obvious to state outright, but we hope you give us some slack: Parents who take an active role get better results. The law requires that all team meetings about a child's education be open to parents, so take advantage of this by showing up. Even if you don't say much, you hear what others say, and your mere presence there says something.

Memory often fails us in times of stress. Consider recording the meeting using an audiotape for review later when you're more relaxed. Make sure you're clear in your intent to tape the session.

Working within the system

Find an informal advocate in the school, such as a teacher or school psychologist whom you trust, to keep you informed and help you work within the system. And stay informed yourself, particularly about progress toward the goals in your child's IEP, which is so important that we devote most of this chapter to the subject.

Closer to home, you can attend board of education meetings and ask questions. Some questions you can ask about your school or district include the following:

- Does the administration provide support for special education? Is the administration spending available money for programs?
- Does the school system have a staff development program for special education professionals? Are the staffers keeping up with current theory, or are they stuck in outdated understandings of autism?

Educators may be experts in their fields, but you're the expert about your child. Don't be intimidated by any education-ese you may hear. People you deal with should always communicate clearly with you about what they're doing and why. If you don't understand a point, politely ask for an explanation in layman's terms. As educators, it's their job to educate you, too. However, taking an adversarial approach by, say, being accusatory or threatening early on is a good way to make enemies fast, not to get what we assume you really want: wholehearted cooperation and interest in your child's progress from people who can help.

Supporting your child at home

Within the three most important factors in your child's education — parental involvement, the IEP, and quality teaching — you have the most control over how you support your child at home. The IEP should spell out what your responsibilities are, as well as the school's.

A child's education isn't like ordering a meal in a restaurant; you can't order and then forget about it until the waiters bring your food out. You have to go into the kitchen and do some cooking yourself! Here are some informal steps you can take to help the process along:

- Find out what skills your child is working on in school, and spend some time at home reinforcing them.
- Share what you work on at home with your child's teachers, and ask if the school can reinforce those skills.
- Ask your child's teachers what you can do to help at home; they'll appreciate the question.
- Set high (but reasonable) expectations, but be emotionally supportive of all progress.

    Be willing to adjust your expectations (up or down). Just because you have to adjust expectations downward doesn't mean that you can raise your expectations again later. Sometimes, you need to address a hidden (masked) barrier before a child can reach your original expectation.

- Make sure that the timelines you set for reaching goals are reasonable, based on the student and the methods used.

    Outstanding individuals who exceed their supposed limitations usually do so because somebody working with them refuses to believe in those limits.

- Communicate well, and develop trusting relationships with teachers and other educational professionals who can help.

    Parents and educators need to be sure that they all speak the same language about what's expected and what's happening in the classroom.

- Join a parents' support group.

Don't base your judgments on rumors or solely on what you hear from other parents — their needs and circumstances may be quite different from yours. Talk directly to the people involved at the school.

Acting Early with an Individualized Family Service Plan (IFSP)

For a child with autism, early intervention is the single most important factor for quality of life, and the sooner the better. A child who receives intensive help before beginning kindergarten has a much better chance of not falling far behind.

American law requires that each state have early-intervention programs for babies and toddlers considered to be at risk of developmental disabilities, up to the age of 3. This law requires the states to have resources available; however, they don't have to pay for the programs.

Starting at age 3, though, local school districts *are* required to provide services to parents. These preschool programs, often called *Individualized Family Service Plans,* or IFSPs, are directed at helping parents, who need all the support they can get. Within 45 days of a child's evaluation and acceptance of eligibility for special-education services, an IFSP meeting must happen. This program, unlike the IEP, is targeted to helping the entire family, not just the child. When the child enters the public school system, the IFP no longer applies, and the child's needs are evaluated on an individual basis, not as part of a family unit.

An intervention at this stage may be able to reduce or even eliminate the need for more special education services for the rest of his or her school years. Such a development would be a good thing for everybody, and you should raise this point if the school district balks at your requests for special services. Not paying now may mean paying much more later.

Possible early interventions may include the following (Chapters 9 and 10 have more details on interventions):

✔ Educational/behavioral interventions, such as Applied Behavioral Analysis (ABA) and Floortime

✔ Complementary interventions, such as sensory integration; auditory or speech-language training; and other types of therapy that may improve speech, communication, listening skills, eye contact, comprehension, and emotional responsiveness

The interventions offered are based on what the school system thinks the individual family needs.

In general, autism specialists agree that the sooner a child gets some kind of therapy, the more progress he or she can make.

The National Research Council, a federal task force, recommends that children be put into an early intervention program immediately after diagnosis. For best results, preschool children should have intensive programming for at least 25 hours weekly. The 25 hours includes parental programming as well as professional programming. And teachers should work with no more than two children at a time, and parental training should be available.

Specifying Special: Entering the Public School System

When a child who may need special services enters the public school system at the age of 3 (the recommend age for such a step; see the section "Acting Early with an Individualized Family Service Plan [IFSP]"), a process begins that involves several steps. Your child has to receive an evaluation to establish his or her eligibility, and you have to undergo the process of implementing an Individualized Education Program (IEP). We show you the ropes in the pages that follow.

Always keep a paper trail, even if you don't foresee any problems. Write letters, tape record meetings, and keep up-to-date files. You also have the right to inspect and review all your child's educational records, according to the Family Educational Rights and Privacy Act (FERPA). The schools must keep records for a minimum of five years.

Some parents, on the other hand, may choose to take on a greater financial burden to avoid the "autism" label. See Chapter 2 if your child doesn't fit the criteria for autism but has similar difficulties.

Initiating an evaluation to establish eligibility

A child with special-services needs has to receive a special-education evaluation upon entering the public school system. The parents or the school district itself can initiate the evaluation, but parents must consent to it. If they disagree with the results of an evaluation, parents can legally take their child to an outside professional for an Independent Educational Evaluation (IEE), with the school district picking up the tab in some cases.

Only doctors and other qualified persons, not teachers, may diagnose autism. Schools are there to help with screening and referrals. For example, school psychologists can identify a child with autism for purposes of providing special services within the school setting. This label alone may or (more usually) may not qualify an individual for community-based special services outside the school setting (for example, Medicaid, SSI, and SSDI, which we discuss in Chapter 16). Also, if a child is diagnosed with autism outside the school setting, the school is required to evaluate to determine which services are required by that individual child, not to provide a blanket set of services that the child might not even need.

During the special-education evaluation, a team of specialists from different fields — usually called something like a *multi-disciplinary team* or a *child-study team* — assesses the child and decides, with parental input, if he's considered disabled under federal law. If he is, the team will decide whether his disability "adversely affects his educational performance" according to the statute, which makes him eligible for special-education services. (Again, parents may disagree and ask for a hearing with the state in order to appeal the school's decision.)

The evaluation will take into account the child's social and academic history, and the team will normally interview the parents to find out if there were any birth problems or prior educational issues. This is called a *social history.* According to law, the district may not use any one single measure to determine the child's eligibility, but must consider a range of factors, using commonly accepted assessment tools and strategies, and including parental input, to assess cognitive and behavioral factors, and the physical and developmental history of the child. Parents can help by providing accurate information on what the child knows and can do (a functional assessment).

The *Diagnostic and Statistical Manual,* a reference published by the American Psychiatric Association, classifies autistic disorder as having 6 or more symptoms from a list of 12 possible symptoms. The manual groups the symptoms into three areas: social interaction, communication, and behavior (Chapter 1 gives you the full lists). Because the law defines autism more broadly than the DSM does, some children with developmental disorders who wouldn't be diagnosed with autism under the DSM guidelines (for instance, if the kids don't have symptoms from all three groups) are classified as autistic so they can receive needed services.

Although this practice is often attacked as "diagnosis for services," supporters point out that it's only fair to help all children with disabilities, and that the criteria for developmental disabilities are in flux. In some states, children classified as developmentally disabled may not receive the services that children diagnosed with autism receive, although these children may need just as much help.

Implementing an Individualized Education Program (IEP)

The IEP is a very important process that you'll be taking part in for as long as your child is in special education. In this section, we take you through the steps, including forming an IEP team, developing a plan, and dealing with any problems that may come up along the way.

First things first, make sure the school's IEP process is up to speed. Here are some red flags to look out for:

- ✔ **The school is rushing the process.** It shouldn't take more than 90 days in most states, but it shouldn't take 2 weeks, either. The process needs to be thorough, which takes time. Did the school give you enough time to arrange to be at the initial meeting, and did it provide a time and place that worked well for you?

- ✔ **Poor communication.** Are any officials reluctant to explain situations to you or dismissive of your role? Are letters and memos about the child forwarded to you? The school should inform you of the time, location, participants, and the purpose for each IEP meeting, and it should allow you to bring your own expert(s) or friend(s) for moral support, if you desire.

  Bringing a trusted friend, even if the person isn't an expert, to an IEP meeting can help parents maintain a little objectivity.

- ✔ **The process isn't open.** You're legally entitled to attend every team meeting. You should also visit, observe classes, and talk to teachers. The law, don't forget, stresses parental involvement. You should also receive from the school a copy of your legal rights during the process.

  Parents have the right to have the meeting at a time and place they can attend. Being a no-show, however, reduces the school's willingness to accommodate those who are unable to meet during school hours.

Forming an IEP team

An IEP team conducts testing and classroom observations, meets with the child's parents or guardians, reviews data, and ultimately issues a report of recommendations. The school primarily forms the IEP team, and the team has, by federal law, a maximum of 60 days from when it receives parental consent for the evaluation to meet to begin developing the IEP.

Normally, IEP teams feature at least three occupations in addition to the parents. Examples of possible members include the following:

- ✔ Social worker
- ✔ Educational psychologist
- ✔ Special education teacher

✔ Speech or language pathologist

✔ Classroom teacher (if the student will be in regular classes)

✔ School administrator

✔ Occupational or physical therapist

✔ The child receiving services (see the sidebar "Involving your child in the IEP")

Of course, the makeup of the team isn't as casual as it may seem because of the possibilities. Here are some rules to consider:

✔ At least one classroom teacher must attend each meeting, unless the teacher submits a written report explaining why he or she should be excused (you need to consent to this).

✔ The parents and the child must attend each meeting, if the child is old enough and capable of participating (see the "Involving your child in the IEP" sidebar in this chapter).

✔ The team must include a representative of the school system.

✔ The team must include someone to interpret the evaluation results (see the section "Evaluating the IEP").

✔ The team must include, if applicable, a representative from the agency providing transition services to college or employment for your child when she graduates.

One person can fill multiple roles. Parents are also entitled to bring any person who has special knowledge about their child's disability, such as an advocate, specialist, or even a family friend. And parents who need a foreign language or sign language interpreter are entitled to request one.

Developing the IEP

The IEP isn't just a formality or mindless paperwork you need to get out of the way; it has a major role in a child's educational future. Not to overdramatize, but to you and the school, the IEP is what the Ten Commandments were to Moses, only with much more detail and, hopefully, written in a language you can understand.

The operative word in Individualized Education Program is *individualized*. Although each state (or even each school system) has its own forms for formatting the IEP document, the state should tailor the content of the document to each child's strengths and weaknesses; it shouldn't be standardized. You won't find a typical autistic child, so you shouldn't have typical IEPs. Every disabled child is unique, which the U.S. Department of Education acknowledges as the reason for developing a separate program for each student.

However, if the federal government is involved, you know that complete creative control is a thing of imagination. Some sections of the program are mandatory under federal law including:

✔ The child's "present level of academic achievement and functional performance" (in other words, how the child is performing in school now).

✔ Measurable annual goals, such as meeting state educational standards or other benchmarks.

✔ How progress toward annual goals will be measured and how often parents will hear of progress.

✔ Special education and related services to be provided, including extra help the child will get and professional training for educators to teach.

Federal law lists the related services in the following list as applicable to some children but not necessarily all. You don't get to choose whatever services look good. You and the school have to prove they fit the child's needs.

- Audiology services
- Counseling services
- Early identification and assessment of disabilities
- Medical services
- Occupational therapy
- Orientation and mobility services

- Parent counseling and training
- Physical therapy
- Recreation
- Rehabilitation counseling services
- School health services
- Social-work services
- Speech-language pathology services
- Transportation

✔ How much participation the child will have with regular classes and normal school activities.

✔ Which achievement tests the child can take, which the school will modify according to his or her needs, and how the school will modify the tests.

Some states' standardized achievement tests preclude modifications. For example, some achievement tests include a Reading Comprehension section. Because the creators of the test designed that section to be a comprehension of reading, a school official can't read that section to the individual taking the test. Such action would be considered "auditory comprehension."

✔ How often services will be provided after they begin, where they will take place, and for how long.

✔ For older children, anticipated transition services (beginning no later than age 14) for when they leave school.

Beyond these requirements, you should work with your child's school to make whatever other decisions are necessary for your child's situation using whatever process the school deems appropriate.

Involving your child in the IEP

You may want to consider involving your child in the development of his own IEP as appropriate to his ability. (A book edited by Stephen Shore, *Ask and Tell: Self-Advocacy and Disclosure for People on the Autism Spectrum* (Autism Asperger Publishing Company), has more ideas for child involvement.) The Individuals with Disabilities Education Act (IDEA) encourages the involvement of the child (and mandates it by the age of 14). Why is this? Because the more a child becomes involved in the development of his own education, the more success he will experience in advocating for his needs later in life. A nonverbal, hyperactive child may be able to interact with a few of the IEP team members for a couple minutes at the beginning of a meeting. Another child may be able to state what's difficult or easy in a class. Yet another child may be able to suggest accommodations and even lead parts of the IEP meeting under the watchful eye of the team leader. The possibilities for participation abound.

Evaluating the IEP

After you develop the IEP, you need to make sure that you're happy with it. In this section, we provide some guidelines for evaluating whether your IEP will be effective.

The law lists special factors that the IEP team must give strong consideration to, including the child's strengths, the parents' or guardians' ideas for enhancing the child's education, the results of recent evaluations, and state- and district-level test scores. Within these requirements, you can note the importance of parental input to the process. Here are some key ideas:

- **Don't assume that more is better where services are concerned.** Sometimes less is more, because some children are easily overstimulated. Use resources judiciously where you think they can make the biggest difference.

- **Focus on developing strengths as well as remediating weaknesses.** If the child has an interest in something, build on that interest. (You can find more on this topic in Chapter 10.)

- **Try to remain objective and rely on your common sense.** This tip is important. It's hard not to react emotionally if you feel professionals are misunderstanding or misdiagnosing your child, but try to hear people out before you reject their opinions. At that point, start your homework — research. Get a second opinion or evaluation.

- **Focus on your child's specific issues and how to help him reach his potential rather than diagnostic labels.** Unless you feel a label is hurting your child's opportunity to receive the kind of help she needs, you need to focus on remediating her difficulties instead of wasting tons of energy over whether to call it autism, Asperger's, or PDD.

When judging the IEP, look carefully at three parts:

✔ **The goals:** What the child should be able to do and when

✔ **The accommodations:** What the school will do to help the child reach those goals

✔ **The placement:** How your child will divide his or her time among regular and/or special-education classrooms (which is very important to the provision of accommodations)

The goals should be measurable and specific, and the accommodations — intended to ensure access to education — should match the goals. The child's placement is also a factor to which you want to give strong consideration. You should limit the goals to an annual cycle. Because the child doesn't have to meet short-term objectives (except for students who take alternative assessments), these goals are highly important. The more specific, the better.

Check out Table 12-1 for good and bad examples of goals to include in the IEP.

Table 12-1	Sample Goals for an IEP
The Good	Over the course of the year, the student will demonstrate mastery of geometric shapes, as indicated by a score at the 75th percentile on the Georgia Inventory of Geometric Proficiency. (***Note:*** No such test exists, but you get the idea that you should have a way to measure progress — not necessarily a test, but a benchmark.)
The Bad	By the second semester, the student will interact successfully with his peers. (What does it mean to "interact successfully"? How can success be determined and by whom? How can you measure it?)
The Ugly	The student will improve his mathematics skills and his attitude toward the subject. (By when will this happen? Which skills should the student concentrate on, exactly? How much should the skills improve? Will he know algebra or just his times tables? How will you measure his "attitude"?)

If the accommodations don't seem adequate to reach the goals, you need to ask why. For example, what good is a goal to double the child's spoken vocabulary by the end of the year if caregivers don't provide speech-language therapy to help meet that goal? Likewise, what good is having modifications, such as alternative assessments, but no goals to strive for? You don't want to be stuck holding a map without a destination. Make sure your IEP includes where the child is now, where she or he is going, and how he or she can get there.

The *placement* is where members of the IEP team carry out the program. Locations may include a regular classroom, a special-education classroom, or some combination of both. Placements should be in the *least restrictive environment,* by which the law dictates that the disabled child be included as much as possible with non-disabled children. The school should remove the child from the regular classroom only if he can't get the education he needs with supplemental aid and modifications.

Appealing if you're not satisfied with the IEP

The IEP team usually presents the IEP to parents during a team meeting, to which parents should always be invited. (Sometimes the meeting is held over videoconference or conference call.) If you would like additional time outside of the meeting to review the IEP (perhaps study it closely or ask other people to review it), you can ask to take it home. But be sure to make the whole team aware of your request because in many states the school will consider your not objecting to the terms at the meeting to be consent to go ahead and implement the IEP. Procedures vary around the country, but generally, if you don't actively object to the IEP, the school will begin providing services. If you're satisfied with the IEP, you can continue to the next section — if not, keep reading!

If you disagree with any part of the IEP, you don't have to consent to it. Make your concerns known either during the meeting or as soon as possible afterward and ask for changes. For example, if you don't agree with points in the IEP, such as the goals or the child's placement, you should first discuss your concerns with the IEP team and try to work out an agreement amicably. You don't have to take "no" for an answer. You can request more testing, an independent evaluation of the child, or mediation of the dispute. *Mediation* is a voluntary procedure, conducted by a trained, impartial mediator, for resolving a dispute between you and the school. (For more on disagreeing with the IEP team, see the sidebar "'How to disagree with the IEP team without starting World War III'".)

If mediation fails, you're entitled to a due-process hearing. The due-process hearing occurs before a hearing officer or an administrative law judge. To get a hearing, you must have a failed mediation proceeding, and you need to file a complaint by writing a letter directly to your state's education agency (this information is available from your school district), specifying which part of the Individuals with Disabilities Education Act (IDEA) you believe has been violated. The agency must resolve the complaint within 60 calendar days. An extension of that time limit is permitted only if exceptional circumstances exist with respect to the complaint. You can file a complaint on your own or by using an attorney. There are attorneys that specialize in special education law — try to find one of those or at least someone who is familiar with the process.

"How to disagree with the IEP team without starting World War III"

(Excerpted with permission from www.Wrightslaw.com, a Web site hosted by Peter and Pamela Wright, authors and experts on special education law.)

If you are presented with an IEP that is not appropriate for your child, you should advise the IEP team that you don't think the IEP is appropriate, and that it does not provide your child with enough help or the right kind of help. You should use facts to support your position (for example, facts from an evaluation of your child from a private sector evaluator or graphs of your child's test scores). Be polite but firm.

When the team asks you to sign consent to the IEP, write this statement on the IEP: "I consent to this IEP being implemented but I object to it for the reasons stated during the meeting." Sign your name.

Someone may get upset and claim you're not allowed to write on the IEP because it is a legal document. This is not true — you can write on your child's IEP.

You are a member of the team and a participant in the IEP process. The law requires you to make your objections clear. The IEP is the best document to use for this purpose. If someone tries to stop you, continue to write. If someone yanks the document away from you, continue to write as the IEP tears.

Stay calm. Take your copy of the IEP (whatever is left), stand, and say "Thank you. I guess this meeting is over." Extend your hand to shake theirs. Pick up your tape recorder and leave. (If you expect a dispute, you should tape record the meeting, openly.)

The IEP team now has a problem. You have advised (the team) in writing that its proposed program is not appropriate for your child. You also consented to implementing the program, so they should implement it.

Afterward, write a nice thank you letter to the head of the IEP team. Re-state your position: You consented to the school implementing the IEP because you believe an inadequate program is better than no program. However, you believe the proposed program is not appropriate.

You should assume that:

- ✔ A hearing will be necessary to resolve a problem.

- ✔ All school staff will testify against you.

- ✔ Staff's recollection of the facts will be completely different from yours.

- ✔ You cannot testify!

If you cannot testify, how can you tell your story? You tell your story with the tape, transcript of the meeting, your letter, and the IEP.

For instance, you may explain that your child isn't receiving the services stipulated in the IEP. The state has 60 days to resolve the complaint. The party requesting the hearing has the burden of proof. If the parent initiates the hearing, then the parent must prove that the school is not doing what is required to provide a "free appropriate public education." In some cases, the school district may request the hearing. The child's school should also provide information on low-cost legal or educational services you may need.

The due-process hearing is similar to a courtroom trial. You (or your lawyer if you hire one) can present evidence, have witnesses you choose attend the proceedings, and question and cross-examine all witnesses present.

The school must show you all evidence that it plans to present at least five working days before the hearing, and if it fails to comply, the school can't present it. Unlike on television, you have no surprise witnesses or evidence to worry about.

You may appeal a negative decision from the hearing officer to a reviewing officer, and if that fails, you can appeal once again to a higher court such as a U.S. District Court.

If you win your case, the school system is typically required to reimburse you for your legal fees and expenses. If you lose, or if the school offers to settle ten days before and the settlement offer is similar to what the hearing officer decides, you're on your own. You have to weigh the pros and cons of taking on this responsibility should you lose your case.

Whatever the outcome, you can get a transcript of the hearing. Keep a paper trail. Legal eagles like Peter Wright advise that keeping up-to-date and detailed records can be an invaluable tool for future planning or advocacy.

Assessing Your Child's Progress

You've just signed the IEP agreed upon by the entire IEP team. You walk out of the meeting with a copy of the document and knowledge that all the teachers and other professionals working with your child have access to that document and know their specific responsibilities under it.

Your focus should now turn to monitoring the progress being made toward the year-end goals of the IEP. The entire IEP team should review the IEP annually and revise it if necessary. For updates, you can contact the school and ask somebody you trust on the team what's happening. If the IEP is well-designed, you'll know what questions to ask! (See the previous section for more on developing and evaluating the IEP.)

Congress has approved a three-year IEP that may save you and the school some paperwork, but this plan is probably not a good idea for your child (or anyone else's!). None of the states as of this writing have actually initiated a three-year IEP. A great deal can happen in three years in a child's life. If you're asked to consent to it, just say no.

You can also have more than one IEP meeting a year, if necessary. More frequent reviews are called for if the child makes so much progress that she no longer needs services. Legally, you or your child's teachers can request additional meetings if, for example, any of the following apply:

✔ Observation of a lack of expected progress toward IEP goals

✔ New information that parents may have becomes available

  For example, your physician may have new findings to report about your child's diagnosis, or sudden changes in your child's home environment can create stress that may impact school behaviors.

✔ The results of any reevaluation necessitate an alteration

✔ The child's anticipated needs begin to change

Above all, strong and ongoing communication and cordial working relationships with school officials and employees will make your life easier.

Flexing Your Educational Rights When You Need To

You want to develop trusting relationships with teachers and other educational professionals who can help you and your child. Sometimes, however, you may feel strongly that your child isn't receiving what he needs and is entitled to in the legal sense. In that case, you shouldn't just roll over and agree with everything you're told.

If you're displeased with the situation in your school and have tried to resolve it peacefully to no avail, you must take a stand. (For an example of this, see the sidebar "Disagreeing with the IEP team without starting World War III".)

Your school or even your district may not have adequate services if your area doesn't have very many special-needs students. This inadequacy occurs because when the number of special education children in a given district goes up, so does the funding from the state and, thus, the services provided. For this reason, many people with special-needs children move to districts with large populations of special-needs kids, which in turn expands the programs in those districts and attracts more students.

Some of these options require financial outlay, whether for legal services or for educational services not provided by the school. For this reason, be sure that you are willing to pay for them before you reject the school's services.

✔ Working within the system by requesting *mediation* or a *due-process hearing* to get more services. Mediation is having a disinterested, trained mediator attempt to resolve your dispute. A due-process hearing is when you go before a judge or hearing officer to get a resolution to your complaint that your child's rights under IDEA have been violated.

  The losing party of the due-process hearing pays for the cost of the hearing. Mediation must take place before you can get a due-process hearing, which you should do only if all other resolution methods fail.

"We don't owe you a Cadillac"

Before he was 5, Daniel had spent two years in full-time behavioral therapy, setting his parents back about $33,000 per year. His parents jokingly referred to the money as "Daniel's Harvard education." When Mark, Daniel's father, went to the school district to talk about his son starting kindergarten in the public school, he — like any parent — wanted the best for Daniel, including everything the experts had recommended.

After hearing Mark out, the school psychologist responded apologetically that the district couldn't afford "the works" for every kid. "Look, our budget's on a shoestring. We care about helping Daniel, too, but we're required to prove that he's making measurable progress, not that he's reaching his full potential, as you're asking. We owe you a car, but you want a Cadillac. We don't owe you a Cadillac."

Mark says he knows the school's money is tight, but this is his child they're talking about. "We're going to put him in public school during the day, and supplement that with private behavioral therapy in the afternoons and on the weekends. It's a compromise, but we can't afford a Cadillac either."

Sadly, although educational services for autistic children are more necessary than any car, very few school systems can provide all the necessities at the level parents need. School systems are federally mandated to provide a free and appropriate public education (FAPE) — not one of maximal benefit. Be prepared to lobby the district for more services while shelling out more of your own resources to get your child the right services.

- ✔ Moving your child to another school or district that has more services, either for part of the day or full time.

- ✔ Enrolling your child in private school, or arranging other outside services, such as a home-based program, which the school may pick up under some circumstances.

  If you can show that your child isn't receiving appropriate services from the school, you may be entitled to reimbursement for private services. It is the parents' responsibility to prove that the school is not doing what is necessary. It is not the school's responsibility to prove that what it is doing is correct.

You must give the district a heads up before you pull your child from the school because of inadequate services either at an IEP meeting or by letter ten days before you remove the child. If you don't, you won't be eligible for reimbursement. Home-based programs can add up if you pay for professionals, but you can conduct them a bit more cheaply if you can train people yourself to work with your child. (One way to find potential helpers is by putting up signs in local college or university departments of education, special education, and psychology.) In addition to the financial strain, if you try to run a program all by yourself, you can quickly burn out.

Chapter 13

Fostering Healthy Relationships

· ·

· ·

*F*orming and maintaining social relationships are some of the toughest challenges faced by people with autism and those closest to them, because relationships depend upon effective communication. People with autism have trouble communicating with and understanding others, which can cause frequent misunderstandings with their non-autistic peers and siblings, which can lead to isolation and frustration for them. The unfortunate chain of events is very painful for parents and loved ones to watch and deal with.

The problem isn't that autistic children are antisocial or don't care about others. Your child may face sensory processing issues (see Chapter 10) or other challenges that make it difficult to keep up in conversation. Even children with Asperger's (discussed in Chapter 5), with excellent language skills, may misunderstand social cues and unwittingly come off as arrogant or self-centered because of their chattering. More likely, your child wants to connect but doesn't know how.

Autistic children aren't all that different from neurotypical kids when it comes to communication; they just need much more help and understanding. Their problems are more severe and require more patience. The worst thing a loved one can do is to give up helping the child to communicate. The best course of action is to go with gentle persistence. (For other tips on bridging the communication gap, check out Chapter 10.)

In this chapter, we help you recognize the social challenges your child faces, show you how to include the whole family to open up the lines of communication, and give you tips to help your child build and maintain relationships outside the family. *Note:* People with autism are all different, and they need individualized strategies to help them succeed with relationships. Take what you discover in this chapter and tailor it to your loved one to see what works best. (We deal with children here; you can find more information on adult relationships in Part IV.)

Recognizing the Social Challenges an Autistic Child Faces

You may observe a range of social behaviors on the autism spectrum. Some children with autism may be withdrawn and avoid other people completely; others may respond if people approach them first. Some children may even seem overeager to approach others, and in their excitement, they do so inappropriately. Children with the latter tendency may have good language skills and the desire to connect with others, but their lack of social understanding trips them up. In the following pages, we let you in on the myriad challenges autistic children face and how you can recognize the needs of your loved one.

Children with autism need simplicity to function at their best, which means you need to limit their social interactions to levels they feel comfortable with. You also need to realize that being social is much more tiring when you have to work harder to understand others. Autistic kids need rest after social interaction; don't try to force them to interact like typical children. Be sensitive to behavior that may indicate that he's had enough for the day. Tantrums and irritability, as with all children, can be signs of exhaustion.

Understanding social norms

Autistic people have trouble understanding *social norms,* which are unwritten behaviors that most children pick up naturally. Even mildly autistic people report a lifelong trouble with social norms. Often, when a typical child breaks a social rule, he or she knows better. The parent needs to remind the child, but then he will be aware of the rules he's breaking. People with autism, however, don't pick up social rules in the natural course of events.

Here are some social blunders autistic people may commit unwittingly:

- Blurting out embarrassing truths (you smell funny!)
- Talking about themselves without pausing to let other people talk
- Delivering one-sided monologues about their passions
- Taking things literally when a joke is being told

So, how can you help your loved one interact in social settings without offending anyone? With coaching, support, and understanding. In the beginning, you may have to teach by rote what seems to come instinctually for other children. The autistic child needs to learn with formal rules and rituals. For example, they need to practice social interactions by using techniques such as social stories (explained in this chapter). The process may feel strange and unnatural, but it works. Riding a bike probably seemed strange and unnatural the first time you tried it, too.

The instruction should also include how to read an environment. Different environments have different sets of behavioral expectations. The way one behaves at school is different than the way one behaves at a basketball game, which is different from the way one behaves at a formal banquet.

Without advance warning and coaching, many people with autism would have difficulty identifying, let's say, what behavior would be appropriate if a banquet was set up in a gymnasium in which they had previously played basketball. This type of behavior is not only related to being unable to pick up social cues, but to the need for structure and order. See Chapter 11 for more on the importance of structure and routine to autistic people.

It may seem like your child will never interact spontaneously and naturally in the beginning, but with practice and time, all the situations you practice will be likely to come more naturally to the child as she integrates social behaviors into her repertoire. But if a child is severely autistic, that may never happen.

People learn social skills, like any other set of skills; just because your child needs more support and may take longer doesn't mean she's incapable of learning and progressing. Most autistic children are capable of progress.

When your child is young, you may want to videotape her in social situations just to have a benchmark of progress in this area. You may be very pleasantly surprised later when you watch the tape. Also, you can get the process moving by having all family members encouraging the child and rewarding her with lavish praise for any communication attempts she makes.

Conversing and cooperating

Unless your family lives on a desert island (in which case you have other problems to worry about), you have to deal with other humans, and every child, regardless of his or her level of functioning, needs to communicate and cooperate with others. But just because a person can talk doesn't mean he or she can communicate. And just because someone can't talk, doesn't mean that they can't communicate.

A person on the autism spectrum might be able to speak very well and say what might be expected in a conversation, but that person still misses many vocal and body language cues unless she has been taught. Very good expressive communication skills can mask poor receptive communication and poor social skills. These terms are explained in the next section.

Communication barriers

Two of the communication terms you may hear from teachers or other professionals are *receptive language* and *expressive language*. Receptive refers to the ability to understand communication directed at you, whereas expressive concerns the ability to make others understand what you're communicating.

Autistic children don't often initiate conversations, but they do respond to others' initiations. In other words, their receptive language is stronger than their expressive language. However, given time and with help from behavioral programs, therapists, and immediate family members, autistic children can develop expressive language so they don't just repeat words back (known as *echolalia*) — they use language to express themselves.

For example, in the Miller Method, parents can narrate a child's actions, like an excited sportscaster might, to help them attach their activities to their words. See Chapters 9 and 10 for more language development tips.

Asperger communication

High-functioning people or folks with Asperger's face a cruel dilemma: The better they are at adjusting to school and work, the more social stigma they face when they inevitably run up against their biggest weaknesses — namely, not knowing what to do in social situations, even if the environment is the same. (For info on helping low-functioning people, see the following section.)

Autistic people can mistakenly assume that what they say makes sense to other people or that it's relevant, when neither may be true. The people on the other end of the conversations may be completely confused because they miss what the affected people think is obvious. Sometimes a person with Asperger's will try so hard to be understood by throwing out lots of words (what's called doing an *information dump*), that it will come across as aggressive or arrogant. In reality, the person is struggling to get the words out and make herself clear. She may give a lot of unnecessary detail to try to explain something that the other person doesn't seem to be getting.

As adults, autistic people may face rejection and the sad fact that few people are willing to take the time to help them understand how they may be misreading situations. At work, an affected person may have a hygiene problem, for example. Coworkers will avoid her, and she won't know why because nobody will say anything to her.

Many professionals working with high-functioning people with autism may forget about this disconnect between language and social skills and fail to address the social skill deficits. Autistic individuals need help while they're still in their formative years. As children, they need to be supported and coached by parents and professionals to take care of niceties such as personal hygiene, for example, even if they don't understand the need for all of them.

Supporting a child when verbal communication is minimal or nonexistent

A child at a more severe portion of the autism spectrum likely doesn't know how to cooperate and form friendships or associations with others. But make no mistake: Like any child, he wants to feel included, too. He may just take much longer and need a period of observing and working the communication through in his head before he's ready to try it himself.

For example, say you're taking your family out on a boat. Your autistic son may balk at wearing his lifejacket. You can solve this problem by having his siblings and adult family members put their jackets on first while he watches the entire process. After he observes, he may be ready to put his on in order to feel included. The child needs the extra time to fit in, as well as to understand what's expected of him.

You can support your child's social adjustment by following these tips (some of these tips may also apply to higher functioning children):

- ✔ **Get to know other parents at your child's school (not just the parents of the other students in the special-education class).** Arrange play dates while your children are young. Even if the children don't seem interested, get them together. Keep them practicing their social skills in real environments. (For more on interacting with other kids, see the section "Encouraging Your Child to Form Friendships".)

- ✔ **Encourage your child to play with other children.** Try to channel his interest in an isolated activity into activity with another person and broaden the scope of the activity. For example, if your child likes horses, take him horseback riding with other children.

- ✔ **After you demonstrate an activity or have your child watch other kids do it, give him a chance to absorb it and process it before he tries the activity himself.** It may take time — a day, a week, or more — for the information to sink in. Autistic kids like to observe new behaviors from a safe distance; later, they may be ready to try it. Also, don't give up on an activity too quickly. It may take some time for a feeling of safety and familiarity to develop, and, consequently, for enjoyment to build.

- ✔ **Speak slowly and clearly, and wait a period of time before repeating yourself.** Don't give too much information at once, and don't assume that if you don't get a response, your child didn't hear you. He may be processing what you said, and talking to him before he processes everything may cause him to need to reboot the entire thought sequence from the beginning. If he gives no response after a long time, do talk to him, but realize that he may have a slower processing speed. He probably understands more than you think. Encourage and reward any communication attempts he makes with smiles and praise, not candy.

- ✔ **Encourage participation in sporting activities.** Team sports are hard for autistic kids, but they can excel at individual sports such as swimming, jumping on a trampoline, tumbling, horseback riding, and so on. If other people are around, your child can indirectly take part with a group without having to directly interact with others.

- ✔ **Have your child's teacher support interaction by prompting her to pair children for activities or have your child tutor or be tutored by other children.** Sometimes, small groups work well; in other situations, children need to be one on one.

High functioning but still struggling

Kathy Grant, of Denver, is a high-functioning autistic woman who knew all her life that she was "different," but she didn't know why. Not until her junior year in college did she find out she's autistic. Today, Grant is a respite provider, working part-time for a family who has a young adult with autism. She received her political science degree from Maryville College in 1987. However, despite overcoming many obstacles, Kathy remembers having social struggles most of her life.

"As a child and teenager, I didn't have the skill of being interested in what other people were interested in and only talked about the stuff I was interested in. There were times at the dinner table, when the family would talk about things such as houses and real estate and I'd say "Lima, Peru!" or talk about Iranians, the hostages, and Ayatollah Khomeini while my Mom talked about getting Grandma a Christmas present. What I needed to be taught was how to listen and enter into conversation step by step, with patience and love." (Excerpted with permission from *Social Skills — My View*, an essay published in the Autism Society of America Colorado chapter's quarterly publication [1st quarter, 2003].)

> ✔ **Don't force eye contact.** It can be very difficult for a child with sensory processing difficulties to make consistent eye contact. (See Chapter 10 for more on sensory difficulties.)

What if your child just wants to play video games or stim out (see Chapter 10)? Don't let your child — even a child with sensory issues — tune out the world entirely. Be sensitive to sensory issues that may make some interactions that involve touching, loud noises, or flashing lights painful, but don't isolate your child. She needs to be around people for at least some of the day.

All in the Family

An autistic child's needs often complicate familial relationships, especially with siblings (never easy relationships in the first place). For example, siblings want a playmate, but the child with autism may not be inclined to play amicably with his or her sibling, or anyone else for that matter. This refusal causes frustration and confusion for the sibling, who, especially when very young, struggles to understand why her brother can't be "like other kids."

You can help your family by informing your kids about autism and the complications it introduces, understanding the challenges siblings face and helping them cope, and involving members of your extended family to create a network of help and understanding. We show you how in the next sections.

Talking about autism with your kids

How do you explain autism to your non-autistic children and to your autistic child? For the siblings, different levels of disclosure work at different ages:

✔ You can talk about the disorder when kids are young without calling it autism. For example, you can say, "We have to help your brother because he's different." You don't need to go into great detail in the beginning. Siblings are aware that something is different, especially when their brother is screaming or projectile vomiting.

✔ When kids get older, and for adults you want to bring in to your circle of trust, you can use the four-step method described later in this section.

You don't have to make up explanations for situations and behaviors you don't understand. Children will always ask "why," and sometimes you have no good answer. You can change the subject or, better yet, simply say, "We don't know yet."

Your child with autism needs to feel that his differences are okay. He isn't flawed, defective, or lacking any humanity. His brain is simply wired differently, and he has abilities that others may not share. He needs to hear that he's neither superior nor inferior — just differently abled.

I (co-author Stephen Shore) have developed a four-step method for telling children and adults that they're on the autism spectrum. Children and adults almost always know on some level that they're different from other people, and you need to validate their feelings. The process may take as little as 10 minutes or as long as several days, weeks, or months. The following list outlines the steps.

I like to use the word "strength" in place of "weakness" to avoid a negative connotation for a behavior or action where a child is experiencing difficulties.

1. **Building awareness of strengths.**

   This step is important because self-knowledge of one's strengths, and later challenges, is a precursor toward building self-determination.

2. **"Rack up" the child's strengths and challenges.**

   In other words, develop a list. If you can write the list down, you'll have a record for the child to refer to. Do your best to find a strength to accommodate for a challenge.

3. **Non-judgmentally compare the child's strengths with the strengths of other potential role models, friends, and family members.**

   Comparisons will help the child realize that different people all have different strengths and challenges.

A successful disclosure

Once, the parents of a music student asked me (co-author Stephen Shore) to disclose his Asperger Syndrome to him. After 15 minutes, we had gone through Step 4 of my process (see "Talking about autism with your kids") when he blurted, "Can we get back to the music lesson?"

Weeks later, I asked his father how his son handled the disclosure. The father beamed, saying, "My son loves having Asperger Syndrome! He spends much time online looking up information on his condition and is educating himself."

In fact, I didn't tell his son anything he didn't know; all I did was validate his experiences and inform him that his set of traits had a name. He's now empowered to find out more about his condition and has already begun to access the wealth of information available to help him.

This disclosure was a success!

---

4. **Introduce the label of autism or Asperger Syndrome as appropriate to summarize the child's condition.**

   Careful thinking through these four steps will increase the probability of success.

Usually, I precede mentioning the label with a statement like "There are scientists, educators, and others who study different characteristics of people. It so happens that your set of characteristics line up with what's called autism." (For more on autism and its forms, see Chapter 2.)

For kids who have Asperger's (see Chapter 5) and are undiagnosed, finding out the truth can be a big relief. They can replace their sense of difference and isolation with understanding and coping strategies. Knowledge lets them know that others are like them and that their difficulties have a name. The whole family discovers what they're dealing with, which makes life simpler.

It's important to note, however, that not all disclosures go well. For some, being labeled with a "syndrome" or "disorder" can be frightening. Some children may wonder why they've been labeled "different" than neurotypical kids. If your child has these feelings, you need to comfort him and assure him that he's still a special individual capable of living a very fulfilling life.

Considering the challenges siblings face

Siblings learn often-difficult lessons about how to deal with difference early on in life, and these lessons can lead to greater compassion, maturity, and social skills as adults. These lessons are even more important, and often more difficult, when autism is involved. The autistic sibling may be low functioning, and the other siblings have to learn to read his nonverbal signals. With a brother or sister who has Asperger's, siblings learn that not everybody thinks the way they do. The following sections explain how you can help non-autistic siblings adjust to their unique brother or sister, and how to get typical kids involved with an autistic child.

Non-autistic siblings can become overly responsible, or they may just withdraw and become depressed. Some children overcompensate to try to make their parents feel better or to gain attention that they may feel they're lacking, which can have a high emotional cost for the children. Don't let this behavior happen. Let each child know that he or she is a valuable family member just for being himself or herself, not for any accomplishments made. Every child needs to feel valued.

Helping brothers and sisters adjust

You have to devote quite a bit of your time and energy to your autistic child, of course, but you can't forget about the rest of your family. You can't avoid spending more time caring for the autistic child or children, of course, but you don't have to let the discrepancy be a source of disharmony.

Here are some general do's and don'ts for keeping the peace:

- ✔ Consider family therapy. Siblings may feel they need a forum to voice their concerns and negotiate.

- ✔ Structure play and interactions between the siblings. Help them play together by instructing the autistic child what he or she should do in a play situation. Model the behavior, or talk him or her through it. Pick structured games and activities that everyone can enjoy.

- ✔ Be fair. It may seem to siblings that a double standard applies — that you have a different set of rules for each child in the household. This may be true, but with good reason. You must explain this with honesty. Your children's special sibling has special needs and sometimes breaks rules unknowingly, which isn't willful misbehavior. Fairness means providing for each person's needs rather than treating everybody the same.

- ✔ Be open and communicate. Your neurotypical children may need to vent from time to time about the stresses they feel in a family with autism. Autism can be tough for your other kids, too, and it's normal that they may feel resentful or envious of all the attention the autistic sibling receives. Make it clear that having such feelings is okay, but hurting or mistreating the sibling isn't. Also let the siblings know that they can be proud of their brother or sister with autism.

- ✔ Don't protect the siblings and other family members from your emotions or the truth about what's happening with the autistic child. Children usually figure things out anyway, and it's better they hear it from you. If you don't openly communicate, they may think the disorder is contagious or that it's their fault.

- ✔ Help siblings take pride in the achievements of the autistic sibling. At times, they may be embarrassed or ashamed of having a "special" sister or brother — this is normal behavior, especially for teenagers. Help them to view the sibling in a positive light, and try to model patience and tolerance for them.

✔ Allow the siblings to set their own boundaries. They don't have to accept being hit or called names, having toys taken or broken, or having their space invaded. They maintain these rights, even with an autistic sibling.

Most amusement parks will give you a special pass that signifies you don't have to stand in line. All the kids will like that!

✔ Take siblings out for a meal or other special activity separately to make them feel special, too. They need to be the center of attention sometimes.

✔ Make life fun, and be a family. Turn activities into games, and don't ignore your autistic child, which can hurt. Give plenty of strokes and positive reinforcement to everyone. Also, don't try to do too much. Taking four kids and a child with autism, who isn't ready for crowds, to a baseball game, for example, is probably too much.

Some pieces of advice apply to younger siblings or older siblings exclusively. Follow these guidelines as closely as possible with respect to your situation:

✔ If you have young children, give them small bits of factual information when they're ready. Tailor the information to their age level, and don't expect them to understand autism itself — focus on observable behaviors and symptoms.

✔ Don't let older siblings become extra parents for the autistic child. Although you appreciate their help at times, and you must inform them of the dangers that their sibling can get into, you don't want to give them extra responsibilities. They need to be able to be children, and too much responsibility can get in the way of that. They may try to take emotional or financial responsibility from you. Let them know this isn't their job. Some siblings of disabled individuals feel they have to curtail their own dreams for the sake of the sibling; make it clear that you don't want this.

Siblings can become very upset about screaming or other behavior. They may resent being out in public when your autistic child causes a scene. Parents need to limit scenes the best way they can. Some ways to calm the autistic child include hand-held games, blankets, and weighted stuffed animals.

Getting siblings involved

Children find it difficult to be in a family where one person gets so much attention. The term "sibling rivalry" can take on new meaning if the sibling feels her autistic brother or sister gets all her parents' care and time. You can ease the pain of your non-autistic children by involving them in family activities and responsibilities and by making sure they have as much information about autism and autistic behavior as possible.

The following list gives you some ideas on how you can educate your children and how siblings can help:

✔ Make sure your kids know that life is harder in many ways for the autistic sister. Everyone should accept her the way she is. She may change, but maybe not in all the ways that the siblings want.

✔ Encourage the siblings to advocate for autistic people outside their home. Some kids can — only if they're comfortable, though — act as ambassadors for special-needs kids by giving talks to other classes at school or by informally explaining to their peers what autism means.

✔ Find activities that your autistic child and his siblings can enjoy together.

✔ Encourage siblings to allow their autistic sibling to take the role that he's good at. If he's a good navigator, for example, family members can let him call the shots so he feels competent, too.

✔ Let your kids know that just because their autistic sibling doesn't initiate contact, doesn't mean he doesn't want to play with them. Encourage them to get play started in a simple way. The child with autism may not respond right away, but that's okay. Encourage your kids to be patient and keep trying.

Your non-autistic kids can attend support-group meetings for siblings. The Autism Society of America (www.autism-society.org) or other autism support organizations have information about such meetings.

Including extended family

Not all extended family members need to know about the autism in the family. If they don't have much contact with your family, or if you don't think they'll be able to understand the condition or be supportive, it may be better not to tell them at all.

Your extended family can be helpful to the extent that they understand and accept the diagnosis of autism. Some families are competitive, and may not be supportive. Grandparents, aunts, or uncles may not accept your rules and may even try to undermine you by offering forbidden foods or "discipline" to the autistic child.

The autism diagnosis is a need to know situation. If you think the diagnosis significantly impacts the relationship your child and your family has with the extended family member, you need to disclose the condition.

If you decide on disclosure, start by talking about certain characteristics that the child has that may have attracted your attention. It may not be necessary to label the situation. You can say something like, "Johnny has trouble communicating or doesn't do well with crowds," without using the term "autism," if you think it will cause distress or confusion. Use your judgment.

"He's really sweet when he smiles" — A sister's wisdom

Meghan, a 7-year-old girl, loves Irish dancing, music class, and her golden retriever, Clancy. She also has a baby brother who was diagnosed with autism at the age of 2. Meghan offers her advice about life with (as of this writing) 5-year-old Collin:

"Collin loves when my friends come over. I tell my new friends: 'He has something called AW-tism. It's when your brain works different from everyone else, but that's okay. He's just like you and me but special and different.'"

"That's the word — special. He knows how to log on to the computer. When he grows up, I think he'll be a computer maker. He has a lot of talents — the computer, running."

"He's really sweet when he smiles and he's getting really good about sharing. He really likes the TV. Once, I was riding on the scooter and he kept saying 'my turn, my turn.' He gets really mad at me if I change the channel. He starts whining and running after me and he'll bite me. I get over it."

"Collin knows something that I don't know and I have to figure it out or he'll be taking over the whole world."

"One of my best moments was at the beach this summer. We sat on the beach together. That was one of the best moments of my life. We sat on the smooth rocky sand with the little baby clams. We sat under the seagulls. We kept on smiling as the waves crashed together."

"[When he bites] he's trying to tell me, 'your turn is up,' then 'you're gonna get it.' You have to learn to deal with it. If he bites, just say 'no.' You have to learn to be patient and say it again. If he does something wrong, give him other chances. Just remember to keep loving him no matter what. You'll find the answer when he's older and can talk to you."

Request that your relatives be sensitive to the child's individual needs, whatever they may be. For example, he may not wish to eat everything on his plate, or he may need to spend some time alone after being with the group. Family members shouldn't criticize or ridicule him for doing so.

Make your ground rules clear, even if extended family members don't agree with what you're doing. If anybody refuses to respect your judgment, you don't have to feel badly about limiting contact to holidays or when you can be around to supervise. You don't have to sacrifice your child for the rest of your family.

Encouraging Your Child to Form Friendships

You may think that your autistic child is uninterested in making friends. The more likely case is that he's eager to make friends, but his lack of social skills makes him the butt of jokes or teasing. With Asperger Syndrome particularly, a child's advanced vocabulary and arcane knowledge can set him apart. Asperger kids can seem arrogant or condescending to others who don't share their intellectual interests. (For more on Asperger's, see Chapter 5.) As for kids in other places on the autism spectrum, they often don't have the means to communicate their needs or reach out appropriately.

It can be hard for autistic kids to fit in. Yet, a few positive friendships may be all that a particular child needs or wants — he or she doesn't necessarily need a large group of friends to be happy. Many people prefer to have a few good relationships in which they feel understood and accepted rather than many superficial contacts. In this section, we discuss fostering friendships between autistic children with differing levels of communication and their peers.

 Encourage autistic kids to get to know other children like themselves and to spend time with safe adults. They may be more comfortable with kids like them and adults than with other children, although emotionally they're still very much children and need interaction with children their own age. Also, respect if your child has a frequent need for solitude, even if it isn't what you would choose for him.

Staging an emotional rescue

Autistic children have difficulty recognizing or being able to express emotion. The absence of visible emotion doesn't indicate emotional maturity or insensitivity, necessarily, although people can mistake the absence for these things in an older child. The emotional immaturity of autistic children shows in different ways. They may not be in touch with what they're feeling, and they may express their frustration and pain through tantrums, depression, or irritability. You need to help an autistic child learn to recognize and communicate feelings appropriately. Teach her the emotional vocabulary that she needs, even if it seems obvious to you. It isn't obvious to her.

An added challenge is that children with autism can be socially and emotionally inappropriate in their comments — not out of meanness, but simply because they don't know any better. From an early age, autistic children need a great deal of social coaching and communication support.

This list suggests ways to help a child's social and emotional adjustment:

✔ Walk him through social situations, such as going to a restaurant or going to the doctor, and demonstrate what social expectations and norms he must follow. Role-plays and social stories are also useful for modeling behavior. Asperger kids in particular enjoy the drama and can be gifted actors and mimics. "Social stories," a concept popularized by Carol Gray, provides many very helpful examples of this type of thing. See the next section for more on social stories.

If your child enjoys drama, consider signing him up for a drama class. Many adults with Asperger Syndrome report that enrolling in a drama course was incredibly helpful. Why? Because a drama class allows you to examine in minute detail many typical social interactions and practice them until you get them right. You can then generalize these skills to other situations (see Chapter 10 for more on transferring skills).

✔ Differentiate between social norms that she must follow (such as not talking during a movie) and those that are optional (such as making small talk). Explain that you perform certain behaviors out of social convention, and that if she breaks social conventions, she may make others uncomfortable, although the rule may have no apparent purpose.

✔ Take an activity your child enjoys doing alone, such as playing a video game, and have him do it with a parent, other child, or a sibling. Encourage him to start or join a club for others with similar interests.

✔ Provide your child with a quiet place to retreat when noise and commotion become overwhelming. Holidays and other group activities can be more stressful for an autistic child. It can be hard to filter out others' conversations when tons of noise pervades a room. Bring a CD player or iPod if the child likes music to help filter out the noise.

✔ Explain to relatives and others in contact with your child that touching her without warning can startle her or make her feel pain. They shouldn't take offense. It's a physical issue, not an emotional one.

✔ Your autistic child may have trouble empathizing or understanding why others feel the way they do. You need to stress that just as she wants respect for her own feelings and desires, others want this same respect, even if she doesn't think their feelings are "logical."

✔ Be sensitive to your child's possible sensitivities. Social situations involving meals mean that the child has the complicated task of attending to multiple stimuli: conversation, taste, smells, touch, and so on. Your child isn't being deliberately picky if she doesn't eat everything — she may have unpleasant reactions to certain foods. Many autistic children have to go on special diets — not because they're picky, but because they're sensitive to certain foods. (See Chapter 8 for more on diet.)

Creating social stories and calling on Power Cards

Developed by Carol Gray, *social stories* are vignettes designed to explain how social interactions work. As Gray explains in her book, *The New Social Story Book* (Future Horizons), the process of developing the story also increases social understanding for both the person with autism and persons supporting those with autism.

A social story contains directive, descriptive, and affirmative sentences. You use *directive sentences* to suggest appropriate actions and to instruct how to decode recognition. You use *affirmative sentences* to express commonly shared values or opinions of people in a given situation. *Descriptive* sentences are logical and accurate factual statements, summarizing the situation. For example, suppose a child blurts out answers in class without waiting to be picked by the teacher, and she gets frustrated when the teacher tells her that she should wait her turn. A caregiver could develop a social story that describes a student's perspectives, experiences, and interactions in a classroom.

Here's a sample social story with the type of sentences indicated:

> When the teacher asks a question, many students would like to provide an answer. *Descriptive*

> It's hard for a teacher to hear when several students try to answer at once. *Descriptive*

> Students in a classroom need to take turns talking. *Affirmative*

> When I want to answer a question that the teacher asks in class, I will try to sit quietly and raise my hand. *Directive*

> The teacher may call on me to answer or the teacher may give another student a turn at answering the question. *Descriptive*

Carol Gray recommends a ratio of 0 to 1 directive sentences to 2 to 5 descriptive and/or affirmative sentences to a social story.

Using *Power Cards* is another approach to improving social interaction. Power Cards employ a special interest or passion the child with autism has, along with a "hero" figure. As with social stories, a person supporting or teaching develops a vignette concerning a challenging area for the child. The helper goes over the story with the child and summarizes it on a small card, such as an index card.

Say you stick with the example of the child waiting to be chosen by the teacher. You can pair the behavior with the child's special interest in her favorite doll Sally, for example. Figure 13-1 shows an example of a Power Card featuring steps suggested by Sally for helping your child deal with the situation. Initially, the parent or other person supporting the person with autism provides reminders to use the Power Card as needed. The goal is to have the person on the autism spectrum independently know when and where to refer to these cards as appropriate.

Sally wants you to remember to choose one of the following ways to help calm yourself if you get frustrated when you wait for your teacher to call on you to answer a question. If one way doesn't work, try another. If the teacher doesn't call on you this time, he'll call on you later.

Figure 13-1:
Your child can learn to wait her turn in class with the use of a Power Card.

1. Take five deep breaths, exhaling slowly after each breath.
2. Close your eyes and slowly count backward from 10 to 1.
3. Quietly read a book at your desk.

Check out *Power Cards: Using Special Interests to Motivate Children and Youth with Asperger Syndrome and Autism,* by Elisa Gagnon (Autism Asperger Publishing Company), for more information on using Power Cards successfully.

Making conversation

Executive functioning is a term that describes the self-monitoring the brain enacts to take in information, process it, and respond to it. Autism interferes with executive functioning, meaning that autistic children can easily miss social cues and misread the facial expressions of others. For example, the child may notice that someone is crying, but not understand what that means and respond inappropriately by laughing or walking away. Autistic kids also aren't very aware of how they sound to others; thus, their speech can be too loud or have intonations or rhythms that seem off because they don't know how to modulate their voices. For these reasons, speech therapy can be very helpful — both professional and improvised, the latter of which is discussed in this section.

Autistic children take things literally in conversation and may have trouble understanding sarcasm, pretending, or when someone is lying or trying to con them. This naivete means that they may not understand the need to hold things back, making them easy prey for bullies or worse, child predators. Teach them early what constitutes appropriate conversation and behavior with strangers.

Here are some other suggestions for facilitating conversations:

✔ Explain that people sometimes say things they don't mean literally. This isn't necessarily lying, but it can be. Teach your child the difference between lying and joking. Tone of voice and facial expressions can be clues, but your child may have trouble decoding such subtleties. Encourage her to ask questions for clarification, such as "Are you kidding?" or "What do you mean?"

✔ Help your child prepare for new social events by talking about what will happen and what kinds of things you should say in those situations. The practice will ease anxiety for her and give her some tools.

✔ Clearly distinguish between honesty and rudeness. For example, he can say to Aunt Martha, "It hurts when you hug me like that." However, he should avoid saying "You look fatter every time I see you!"

✔ Help your child learn "give and take" in conversation. Sometimes Asperger children can alienate others by lecturing or monologuing about their own interests instead of listening or reciprocating in conversation. Teach her to bat the ball back by saying things like, "What do you think?" or "What about you?"

✔ Conversation between two people is infinitely easier than a conversation between three or more people. Some skills that work in a two-person conversation don't work in a larger conversation. The cues (such as when it is okay to talk) are much more subtle. (Many neurotypical people haven't mastered these skills.) For example, it's not uncommon for two or more people to begin talking at the same time. The person with autism will need coaching to learn to identify and handle situations such as this.

It helps to work out a discreet signal you can use with your child when he's in a group to indicate that he should yield the floor to someone else, lower his voice, or redirect his attention. The signal should be gentle and non-critical — something that won't make him feel worse about his social difficulties.

Any signal that the child knows to look for will work, but you don't want it to be obvious to others that you are communicating. We suggest something natural and inconspicuous such as tugging an earlobe, scratching your nose, or removing or cleaning eyeglasses.

Sparking interactive play

Initiating friendly play between typical people and a child who's more affected by autism may take time, but it is possible. Such interactions require scaffolding by a supportive person, such as an adult or older child who's knowledgeable about autism.

Often, playtime starts with parallel play, where the other person is playing alongside the child, allowing the child time to get comfortable with an outside presence. Here's a possible sequence of events for a child who loves to line up blocks in rows on the carpet:

1. **You get down next to the child and begin lining up your own row —
   next to his, but not so close that he becomes disturbed.**

2. **You try pushing one of his blocks out of alignment, slightly, after a
   few minutes, just to get his attention a little bit.**

   When he puts it back, you know he's aware of your presence.

3. **When you're sure that he's feeling safe, you can gradually prompt him
   to interact a little more by doing things such as turning your row side-
   ways toward his or building a bridge to his row.**

   Hopefully, he will meet you part of the way with his own blocks.

4. **You can try to get his attention by putting a block near your face so he
   has to make eye contact, however briefly.**

Any way you can get him to enter your world voluntarily is a step toward
mutual interaction. In this play, you build a bridge that's not only literal, but
also figurative. (These steps are from a cognitive-developmental method
known as the *Miller Method,* described more fully in Chapter 9.)

Respecting differences

A little acceptance and tolerance of your autistic child's differences goes a
long way — for your entire family. Family and friends of autistic children get
life lessons in understanding those who are different from them. Here are
some tips to keep the waves as smooth as possible:

- ✔ **Watch what expectations you place upon the child socially.** How many
  friends is enough? Is it for you or for her that you're doing something?
  Are you expecting behavior that she hasn't learned yet?

- ✔ **Be sensitive to overstimulation.** Social groups can be quite overwhelming and tiring for your child. When he gets home from school, let him
  be alone for a little while to decompress. At a party, while shopping, or
  at a theater, give him the opportunity to leave early, before he gets
  overstimulated.

- ✔ **Carefully tread the fine line between "fitting in" and "selling out."**
  You want your child to be accepted, but maybe the price of changing is
  too high. Maybe your child has no desire to pay that price. It may be
  better to change the child's classroom, school, or placement than to
  force something that isn't working out. Allow the child some input into
  what she wants from her life.

Part IV
Living with Autism as an Adult

The 5th Wave
By Rich Tennant

"Our daughter's been living independently with autism for years now, but that's because we provided her with skills. She knows how to cook, she knows how to shop, she knows how to find Prada on sale..."

In this part . . .

*A*dults with autism often get less attention than children with autism. We believe this needs to change, as evidenced by Part IV, and we're not the only ones. Adults with autism and Asperger's need help choosing careers, navigating the complexities of higher education, and understanding social relationships. In this part, we talk to both people on the autism spectrum and to those who support them about social skills, romantic relationships, and the worlds of work and college. Other facets of life that we cover include money issues, legal rights, and living options for adults.

Chapter 14

For Adults with Autism: Living Well after K-12

*L*ife after graduation from public school presents many opportunities and challenges for people both on and off the autism spectrum. You must manage your life by making some important decisions about seeking employment, furthering your education, choosing a living situation, and becoming involved in the community. Making big decisions can be especially challenging for people on the autism spectrum. Often, a person on the spectrum needs assistance in one or more of these areas.

In this chapter, we speak to you, a high-functioning adult on the autism spectrum who's looking to blaze a path in a new walk of life. We examine how you can handle all the inevitable decisions and stressors bound to come your way. We help you figure out when (and where) to pursue additional education. We give you tips for finding the right living situation. And we help you choose when and how to get involved in your community.

Finally, if you're a caregiver for someone on the autism spectrum, you know that caring for your child doesn't end when he turns 18 (whether he has autism or not). For the rest of your life, you'll be concerned and involved in the many choices and decisions he makes. If your child has autism, your level of involvement may be extensive. This chapter is here to assist you in helping your child succeed in life after high school. We devote separate "For caregivers" sections to help you make the most of your child's adult life.

Low-functioning autistic kids may have fewer opportunities than high-functioning kids after high school. Low-functioning kids can set goals that include finding a job, but the jobs they find may include work in supervised workshops or other areas of supported employment. However, all individuals on the autism spectrum should try to maximize their abilities, regardless of their functional capacity.

Discovering How to Live Interdependently

The majority of kids in high school want the same thing: independence. They achieve this by moving out of the house and getting a job or going to college. However, nobody is truly independent, and a person on the autism spectrum may never come close to independence. *Interdependent,* rather than independent, living is a more appropriate goal, because most people appropriately depend on others to get along. For example, a spouse may depend on his partner to keep the house clean or to take care of paying the bills, while he cooks and takes care of the laundry. Even a person on a deserted island depends on the weather, plants, and other animals to survive. The key to success — and this is especially important for someone on the autism spectrum — is finding *appropriate* interdependence.

Managing your daily life

Living interdependently begins with competency in regular living skills, such as the following:

- ✔ **Keeping your living area clean.** Cleaning and organizing can make your living space presentable to friends and family members who may visit you, and you save a great deal of time when you need to find something important.

- ✔ **Getting along with others, like roommates and neighbors.** You should try to get to know the people around you. People living with or close to you can be people who can potentially help and support you when you need it. Arguing with neighbors and roommates can cause stress and be both upsetting to you and the people you're upset with.

- ✔ **Managing your time, both free and structured.** You need to keep track of what you must do. You can get easily overwhelmed if you don't keep track of your time. Don't wait until the last possible moment to finish important tasks, like paying bills or signing up for class work.

✔ **Socializing with others, both professionally and personally.** Take the time to show that you're interested in the people around you. People appreciate when you ask how they're doing or even just say "hello." Consider looking into the Relationship Development Intervention, created by Steven Gutstein, which we describe in Chapter 9. This intervention gives you further work on developing skills in experience-sharing interactions.

✔ **Budgeting your money.** You must keep track of your money. If you can't keep a simple budget, you may get in financial trouble and not be able to pay for essential items like food and housing. You need to know how much of your money to allocate for life essentials (food, clothing, housing, and so on) versus how much money you can budget to spend on fun activities.

✔ **Preparing and eating nutritious meals.** A healthy diet contributes to a healthy body and mind. Eating regular nutritious meals gives you the energy to be able to do what you need to get done every day. (See Chapter 8 for more on optimizing your nutrition.)

✔ **Self-advocating and disclosing.** Self-advocacy becomes necessary when your condition significantly impacts a situation or relationship, and all parties need a better mutual understanding. And with self-advocacy comes disclosure; after all, you need to tell others *why* you're advocating.

For example, you may need to request that an employer use a certain type of lighting if you have visual sensitivities, or you may ask that directions be provided in written form if you have challenges with central auditory processing (in other words, your hearing gets scrambled). In these situations, you are advocating for yourself, and if the other parties want reasons, you may have to disclose.

If you're still in K-12, consult with your Individualized Education Program (IEP; see Chapter 12) team to begin learning the necessary skills to talk about your style of processing information and the helpful accommodations you need. Also, check out the "Practicing self-advocacy and disclosure" section later in this chapter.

Deciding where to live

Choosing a place to live is one of the most important decisions you'll make. Many considerations go into your decision on where to live. You need to consider the type of living situation you desire. For example, you may choose to live at home with your parents, or you may want to live by yourself or with roommates in a home, a condominium, or an apartment. You could also choose one of the many kinds of supported living situations, such as a group home or even an institution. You must decide which situation is suitable to your needs, desires, and financial situation.

Home/apartment living tends to rank the highest on the interdependence scale. However, you and those who support you can bring assistance into these living situations as needed. In the following list, we describe some of the more important characteristics of various living situations, along with some benefits and drawbacks of each:

- **Your parent's/caregivers' home:** Living at home often *seems* to be the easiest choice due to your familiarity with the surroundings and/or the people already living there. However, you need to think of how you'll manage when your parents or others can no longer help with managing the aspects of running a home. Living at home, though, is often the least expensive option.

- **Apartment/home:** Apartment/home living can involve having roommates or living alone, depending on your situation. You need a greater self-reliance because family members aren't present to help immediately if needed. Although living alone is often more expensive than living at home, you can reduce the cost by finding roommates. However, it's important that you find roommates you can get along with and who understand your needs.

- **Group home:** Group homes specialize in providing support to people with autism and other conditions. Given the additional support inherent in these living situations, group homes are likely to be more expensive than the first two options.

- **Institution:** You may choose to turn to an institution if you find that the other options can't meet or manage your needs. Although most people think of institutions as a last resort, they may be the answer for you.

We've just barely scratched the surface of what choices you have for your living arrangements. For further information, we suggest you contact your local Autism Society of America chapter (ASA; www.autism-society.org) or other organization devoted to helping the autism community.

For caregivers: Preparing your dependent to succeed from day one

It's never too early to start preparing your child for as much interdependent living as possible. You want your child to have competency in regular living skills to prepare him for a life of interdependence (see the previous section), so you can help by adhering to the suggestions in the following list:

- **Cleanliness:** Even young children can help keep their bedrooms and common areas of your home clean. For a person with Asperger Syndrome who just can't keep her room clean, you can at least insist on enlisting her help in keeping the rest of the house tidy. High-functioning children on the spectrum can begin learning the skills to keep their living areas clean after they develop the understanding of what unclean *is* when compared to cleanliness.

✔ **Getting along with others:** You should encourage a high-functioning child with verbal skills to try to interact with others as soon as she develops meaningful speech. Interventions such as social stories (created by Carol Grey), Power Cards (created by Elisa Gagnon), and other techniques can be very helpful in teaching people with Asperger Syndrome how to successfully get along with others. Look for more information about both systems in Chapter 13.

✔ **Time management:** You need to teach your child how to keep track of how much time she has to complete tasks. As soon as high-functioning children on the spectrum can tell time, you can begin to discuss with them the importance of being on time and keeping track of how long they have to get things done.

✔ **Budgeting money:** If your child is high-functioning and can appreciate the concept of money, you need to reinforce with your child that many items have a price and that monetary value is placed on objects and services in all aspects of the community.

✔ **Nutrition:** Teach your child to eat a healthy diet by providing her with healthy food options throughout her life. All caregivers of children on the spectrum should be models for nutritional eating.

✔ **Self-advocacy:** Self-advocacy is an important skill that should be directly taught to people on the autism spectrum. One of the best ways you can teach self-advocacy is to promote your child's involvement in her own Individualized Education Program (IEP) to the extent of her ability. (For more on IEPs, see Chapter 12.)

Even if your child isn't likely to be able to live as interdependently as you may have hoped for, you still can work on basic life skills like cleanliness and socialization to make life easier at home.

Out of the High-School Daze: Pursuing Higher Education

Higher education refers to education after high school. For people on or off the autism spectrum, higher education may involve further vocational education, a technical school, a two-year college, or a four-year university. Some people may choose to pursue higher education by attending and participating in classes or by taking correspondence or distance learning courses from home. You, a high-functioning individual on the autism spectrum, have just as many options as most people.

Like every neurotypical adult considering postsecondary education, your program should meet your needs. Unlike every neurotypical adult, however, you have some special considerations when choosing to pursue higher education. In this section, we cover these considerations to help prepare you for the road that lies ahead and get you out of your high-school daze!

Evaluating your educational options

When choosing the right place to continue your educational journey, you have to look at the characteristics, pros, and cons of the varied options available to you. The goal is to choose the option that's best for you instead of getting stuck on the type of institution providing the education. You need to consider your goals and find out what educational setting can best help you achieve those goals. If you want to be a carpenter, for instance, it makes sense to pursue vocational training at a local community college that focuses on carpentry instead of trying to get a bachelor's degree at a four-year college and then pursuing carpentry training.

Choosing face-to-face or distance learning

With the rise in technology, classes can now be held in a face-to-face format, which is the more traditional method, and through correspondence or distance learning. *Face-to-face education* takes place when a teacher, facilitator, or tutor provides instruction to learners in a group setting. *Distance learning* occurs when a student and a teacher are separated geographically (over some distance), and the learning and assessment takes place remotely, usually over the Internet. A teacher may post lectures and assignments on a Web site, and the student may submit papers via e-mail, for example.

As an adult living with autism, you must weigh the pros of each type of learning against the cons to decide what methods work best for your needs and goals. The following sections help you organize your thoughts.

The pros and cons of face-to-face learning

If you're looking for face-to-face educational opportunities, you should consult a guidance counselor at your school to discuss how to go about applying to such institutions. The application process for someone on the spectrum should generally be the same as the process for neurotypical kids. You may be able to get additional advice about how to apply by consulting your IEP team.

The benefits of face-to-face education for people with autism include

- Direct interaction with the instructor and other students, which can help with motivation
- A set time, which benefits people with autism who like to stick to routines

✔ Easy access to the resources of the educational institution

✔ Social opportunities for participating in study groups and making friends

The structured nature of face-to-face education often makes it easier for people with autism to interact with others because everyone is present for a common purpose.

Face-to-face education doesn't get all A's, though. Here are some of the drawbacks to this type of instruction for the autistic person:

✔ **Transportation requirements.** Transportation can be especially difficult if you don't drive or have access to public transportation or available acquaintances. You may be able to avoid this drawback if you address it ahead of time. Be sure to ask a potential school if it has transportation available to you after you arrive on campus. You can then use availability of transportation as a factor in your decision-making process.

✔ **Having to keep to a set schedule.** Usually, set, predictable schedules are agreeable to people with autism. However, this instruction method requires that you be available during class time on a consistent basis. Ask to see potential class schedules before picking a school. This way, you can try to find out ahead of time if class schedules will likely work out for you.

✔ **Environmental issues.** Some autistic students may experience a sensory assault from lighting, noise, and proximity to other students that may interfere with successful learning. Take the time to visit your school's rooms and buildings before enrolling. See if the setting appears conducive to your ability to learn. This way, you can test how things will be when you're in the same classroom as other students.

Although more stress may come with face-to-face learning, the potential gains from this learning style are often greater than in distance learning. Face-to-face learning can potentially improve your social skills, and the situations better mimic the "real world" of work where people directly interact throughout the day.

The pros and cons of distance learning

Distance learning involves interaction with your instructor through a communication channel such as a computer, telephone, or mailed correspondence. Many universities offer distance-learning programs. You can consult with your school guidance counselor or members of your IEP team for advice on finding distance learning opportunities.

Some of the benefits to distance education for an individual with autism include the following:

✔ **Easier access.** You can work with materials at home and anywhere you can find a computer, if a computer is necessary.

✔ **Scheduling flexibility.** Other than scheduled computer chat-room discussions, a common component of distance learning, you can usually do work according to your schedule.

✔ **Preferred environment.** Because you're in a familiar environment — most likely your home — you should have few, if any, problems with sensory issues.

However, distance learning isn't all "beer and skittles" for the autistic individual. You may find some significant drawbacks to distance education:

✔ **Motivation.** You must have strong internal motivation to get your work done because you don't have a face-to-face instructor to encourage you and peers to help you.

✔ **Setting aside study time.** You have to make sure you set aside time and space for studying and homework.

✔ **Less time to interact with others.** Distance learning doesn't expose you to daily social interaction. Individuals participating in distance learning need to make time for social activities during their free time and give the extra effort.

Considering the benefits of attending a community college

Transitioning to adulthood and higher education is a big challenge. Spending some time at a community college can ease that transition and may make sense for you for a number of practical reasons:

✔ **Greater awareness of student diversity:** I (co-author Stephen Shore) have noticed a greater number of people with learning differences at the community-college level than at four-year institutions. As a result, community colleges may have greater experience and expertise in working with students with disabilities.

Along with this diversity comes different levels of academic time commitment. At a community college, it may be just as acceptable to take one class as it is to take a full load in any given semester. At a four-year institution, you may find it more difficult to take a smaller course load.

And one of the best benefits of community college is that because you see a greater diversity of students, people with autism are more likely to be accepted.

✔ **A place to explore with less academic pressure and expense:** Many people come to a community college for educational exploration, not to feed the drive to complete a degree immediately. Many highly educated persons use community college as a sort of "graduate" program to explore other areas of interest.

Many students also use the community college experience as a transition to a four-year college or university. Several states have matriculation agreements with four-year colleges so that all the credits you earn in the first two years directly transfer to the state college or university — and at a great savings in tuition and fees for the student.

✔ **Practical education with master teachers:** Community-college faculty members tend to be closer to their areas of instruction than instructors at colleges and universities. Most instructors have master's degrees in their subject areas, which helps them focus more on the art of teaching and student service and less on research. An added bonus is that community-college instructors tend to have more time for providing extra help and advising students.

Here's a short list of the drawbacks that accompany a community-college education:

✔ **You may not be able to reach some of your lofty goals with a community-college education.** Individuals who want to pursue jobs that require four-year degrees won't be able to adequately prepare themselves for the work by attending a community-college two-year program.

✔ **The stigma.** Some people don't consider a community or two-year college to be a "real" place of higher education, even though it may be more real-world based than many four-year institutions.

Exploring the four-year university option

Here are a few good reasons to consider applying to a four-year institution for your higher education:

✔ **Diversity of topics.** A four-year college may have more classes and areas of focus to choose from.

✔ **Research orientation.** If you're interested in learning about and conducting research, a four-year university may be for you.

✔ **Stability.** It usually takes four years of full-time work to earn a bachelor's degree, and students may stay even longer for master's and doctoral courses if the institution provides them. Additionally, you tend to find more full-time and tenured faculty at these institutions. As a result, change usually comes more slowly (which may be a good thing, depending on your needs).

Community colleges tend to have open admissions, whereas four-year institutions lean toward competitive admissions. One method isn't necessarily better than the other; it all depends on your wants and needs.

As with your other higher-education options, the four-year institution comes with disadvantages that you need to consider before you send in your application letter:

- ✔ A four-year institution may have more options when it comes to classes and majors, but the majors provided may be general and not focused on job-specific abilities. If you want to be an accountant, for example, you may be able to take economics classes, but does the institution offer accounting-specific classes that prepare you for the real world?

- ✔ A four-year institution may not have comparable disability services, which provide you with needed accommodations. You may be in the vast minority when it comes to living on a college campus, so the institution may not cater to your needs as much.

- ✔ The expenses that come with a four-year institution are generally much greater than at community colleges.

- ✔ If you live on campus, you may have to share a room with other students. Living in a residence hall, with its noise and many other distractions, can be difficult for someone with sensory challenges and a high need for solitude and/or personal space. Consider whether this is optimal for you. On the other hand, living in close contact with other students allows you to make friends slowly, over the course of a year, by getting to know people and how they live up-close.

Getting the accommodations you need for higher education

In addition to making sure the higher-education program you're interested in is a good fit academically, socially, and otherwise, you have to make sure the disabilities office associated with the program (sometimes called the "office of student support" or "office of student success") can provide your needed accommodations.

After graduation from high school, protection under the Individuals with Disabilities Education Act (IDEA; see Chapter 12) ends, and the Americans with Disabilities Act (ADA) takes over. The major difference is this: The IDEA mandates that all public schools (K-12) find, assess, and provide accommodations in order to meet the legal tenets of "a free and appropriate" public education. The ADA merely requires institutes of higher education, on the other hand, to provide equal access to education. As a college student, you must meet with a disabilities counselor and advocate for these accommodations on your own (this applies to both distance and face-to-face learning programs).

Working with the disabilities office of the institution you affiliate with is important. Make an appointment with the disabilities office as part of a campus tour to find out what the office can provide along with its requirements for obtaining accommodations. You should find out answers to the following questions from the school's disabilities office before you decide to attend the school:

- ✔ **Can the school provide your needed accommodations?** A negative answer should motivate you to strongly reconsider applying to that school.

- ✔ **What documentation do you need to provide to obtain accommodations?** Many students lose out on accommodations for as long as a semester or more because they fail to provide appropriate documentation, such as medical documentation from their doctors describing their impairments.

- ✔ **How recent must your documentation be?** Many schools have a one- to three-year timeline. If you lack a recent key document, such as a recent neuropsychological examination, it can take as long as 18 months to get another test.

As a person with a disability, you have to advocate for your needs and disclose your condition on your own (see the following section). However, you can get help from a friend, family, or other person. You can bring this person with you to meetings with disabilities counselors, and this person can make sure you cover all the important details during your meetings.

Practicing self-advocacy and disclosure

There comes a time when every person with autism must make other people aware of their needs, followed by an explanation, in a way the other people can easily understand. For an autistic person attending an institution of higher learning, this time is inevitable and likely to happen often. For example, educators and other students may ask you why you receive certain accommodations from the institution. What you must decide is whether a full or a partial disclosure is necessary.

During disclosure, you should stick to the facts. For example, if a person asks you why you get to sit at your own table in the classroom, just say that you're easily distracted and suffer from autism, a disorder marked by communication delays and social skills impairment.

If you don't want to disclose any disabilities you have to other students, distance learning may be a better option for you, because you'd have to disclose only to those teaching you (see the section "Choosing face-to-face or distance learning" for more).

You can find more on the subject of self-advocacy and disclosure in co-author Stephen Shore's book, *Ask and Tell: Self-Advocacy and Disclosure for People on the Autism Spectrum* (Autism Asperger Publishing Company). People on the autism spectrum make all the contributions in the text.

Easing into higher education

If the commitment and socialization that come with higher education seem overwhelming, consider phasing in the different components of higher education one at a time. For example, instead of starting off as a full-time student at a residential college, you can begin with the following options and ease your way into full-time education:

- ✔ **Take fewer (or even just one) classes a semester.** Sure, cutting down on your course load may mean it will take longer to get through school, but extending your school days is much better than "crashing and burning" as a result of a full class load. *Note:* It may be difficult to take a very limited schedule at a residential college.

- ✔ **If you plan to live on campus, consider a single dorm room.** Some schools allow students to live in their own rooms, without roommates, if they can provide needed documentation (such as a letter from your doctor confirming your impairment and noting that you'll benefit from a single room). Inquire at the school's disability office for more information (see the section "Getting the accommodations you need for higher education").

- ✔ **Consider attending a local school and living at home.** Commuting from home (and possibly taking classes at home; see the section "Choosing face-to-face or distance learning") can ease the stress of going to a new school *and* having to move. You're most likely to find support for interdependent living at home.

- ✔ **Consider hiring a personal assistant.** You (or your caregiver) must arrange and pay for this service. Part-time help is much more inexpensive than hiring someone full time. Ask your institution's disabilities office if it can recommend anyone (even other students) to help you stay organized and on task while attending school.

If the idea of higher education seems too difficult at this time, you can postpone your continued education to a later time when you're more ready. In the meantime, spend a lot of time researching the many different aspects of higher education that we describe in this chapter. You can go through the strategies we recommend in this book to assess potential higher-education stressors and develop a plan to address each stressor before you go to school.

For caregivers: Helping your dependent realize his/her higher-education dreams

Parents and caregivers can provide a great deal of assistance during an individual's higher education decision-making process. You can help your spectrum child organize his search for higher-education opportunities by creating lists of potential educational stressors and of the strengths and weaknesses of how different educational opportunities can address these stressors.

After you and your dependent make a decision on higher education, consider helping the child set up a plan to structure the learning process. You can create a study schedule that motivates and keeps your loved one on track. Even if you need to include some flexibility, having a set time to work helps most people. (See the section "Discovering How to Live Interdependently" for more advice to this end.)

Time to Nurture Your Bank Account: Finding (and Keeping) Employment

After school, the next step of interdependent living is finding employment. Most people desire gainful employment in an area that they enjoy and that uses their strengths. The same holds true for people on the autism spectrum. (Maintaining employment while in a higher-education program may at times present overwhelming stress to someone on the spectrum.)

Levels of employment range from laboring in a *sheltered workshop* (a highly structured environment that offers considerable assistance), to supported noncompetitive employment, to fully competitive employment. This section focuses on helping you find the right position for your wants and needs, apply for and obtain the position, keep the position, and bow out gracefully when the time comes to move on. We also present the option of self-employment if that route seems more to your liking. Happy job hunting!

Before you accept a job, you need to determine what will happen after you get the job if you've been receiving government assistance for living and/or health insurance. Although being productive and earning a wage is preferable to receiving funding due to a disability, you need to be aware that most government programs have strict rules about how much money you can earn before they curtail or take away benefits.

If you determine that taking a job is too costly in terms of lost assistance or health insurance, you can still contribute to society on a volunteer basis. Leading a fulfilling and productive life while giving back to society doesn't depend on you earning money from traditional employment.

For more general info on the job-hunting process, check out *Job Hunting For Dummies,* 2nd Edition (Wiley), by Max Messmer. And you can find more info about obtaining fulfilling and productive employment in Temple Grandin and Kate Duffy's book, *Developing Talents* (Autism Asperger Publishing Company), and in Roger Meyer's *Asperger Syndrome Employment Handbook* (Jessica Kingsley Publishers).

Matching your skills and desires with job opportunities

As an autistic person, you have many factors to consider when beginning your job search, including the following:

- **Your skill set:** You should seek a position that involves a special interest or skill you have.

- **Issues unique to your condition:** You have to consider any sensory or distractibility issues you have when looking for a position. For example, if you have the aptitude and desire to work a cash register, but you have aural sensory issues, you may not be successful as a cashier in a busy fast-food restaurant. Instead, you may need to find employment in a position involving a slower, quieter pace.

- **Your social requirements:** Social requirements are important aspects of most jobs because most jobs involve interacting directly with coworkers or clients.

By matching available job opportunities with your characteristics and interests, you can experience employment success. Take a look at Table 14-1 to see some of the possibilities out there for you. And for a more detailed look into matching interests and careers, take a look at *A Guide for Successful Employment for Individuals with Autism* (Brookes), by Marcia Datlow Smith, Ronald G. Belcher, and Patricia Juhrs.

Table 14-1   Matching Your Needs to Possible Employment Positions

Personal Characteristics	Preferred Job Characteristics	Possible Positions
Deficit in verbal and nonverbal communication	Few communication requirements	Stocking shelves
Challenges in socialization	Limited contact with public, more solitary job duties	Filing, sorting, stapling, paper shredding, after-hours cleaning

Personal Characteristics	Preferred Job Characteristics	Possible Positions
Unusual response to sensory stimulation	Provider of preferred sensory input, ability to avoid noxious sensory stimulation	Hanging clothes, washing cars (for those who enjoy that type of tactile input)
Difficulty with change and transition	Few changes, stable work environment, little staff turnover, same work task all day	Small business, family business, assembly line
Strong visual-motor skills	Requires good visual-motor skills	Small-parts assembly, manufacturing, printing
Behavior problems	Few antecedents to challenging behaviors, with situations where possible problems don't endanger others	Situations where behavior doesn't cause dangerous situations; avoid factories or any jobs where heavy machinery is used
Savant skills	Responsibilities that capitalize on these strengths	Matching stock numbers to packing lists, mathematically oriented positions for those with math strengths
Rituals and compulsions	Attention to detail and exactness	Positions with repetitive tasks that must be done with high accuracy, such as counting items to be placed into packages or looking over products for defects

You can do your best to combat the issues you have if you really want a certain position. You can address any possible sound sensitivities, for example, by wearing headphones or earplugs.

Working with a job coach

Because of the great diversity of the autism spectrum, many characteristics of autism express themselves differently, to varying degrees, in different people. Often, a support person is helpful in providing support and training in areas that may be difficult for you. You can seek support from many different sources, and you can use any combination of support you see fit. Some of these sources include the following:

- ✔ **Job coach.** You can look for providers of vocational rehabilitation that will likely have job coaches as part of their services — coaches to assist you in the workplace. Job coaches can check on your work progress and help you to resolve conflicts if they develop on the job. As your advocate in the workplace, a job coach is able to "carve out" a position for you. In other words, he or she can take pieces from several jobs that you're able to complete well and that you like, which frees other employees to perform job duties that they do well and like. Sometimes, this may mean talking an employer into reworking your existing job descriptions.

- ✔ **Social worker.** A social worker can assist you in finding potential community resources that may support your employment, such as a job coach.

- ✔ **Mentor.** A mentor can be a model for how to conduct yourself at work. Try to find a mentor with a similar disability, because this person probably has already been through some of the same problems you're facing in the workplace.

Applying for and obtaining a position

You can apply for and obtain employment in several different ways: submitting a portfolio, pursuing networking opportunities, or sending a cover letter and résumé are a few. In some cases, you may use a combination of more than one method.

Whatever method you choose, one thing remains consistent: Employers focus on hiring dependable workers who can independently complete a job after training. Some characteristics that come with autism are advantageous to meeting these employer goals. Your job (or the job of your employment specialist or job coach) is to emphasize how the profile of a person with autism is beneficial to an employer — especially if the person hasn't hired people on the autism spectrum before. Here are some areas of benefit you can present to employers (that show how hiring people with autism can help a company):

- ✔ **Work skills.** Because people with autism commonly have strong visual-motor skills, they may enjoy exacting tasks where employers often experience high turnover rates.

- ✔ **Affinity for routine.** The preference for routine tends to drive employees with autism to be on time for work and to take only scheduled breaks and specified lunch times. Absenteeism due to illness is rare among people on the autism spectrum.

✔ **Less interest in socialization.** You can even reframe weaknesses in language and social interaction as positives because most people with autism don't take time from work to socialize.

Of course, these are only general examples within each category. You have a good grasp of your skill set, so make each point specific to your strengths. Now that you have an idea of what you can use to your advantage to get a job, you can apply this information when creating your portfolio or résumé and when attending your interview. The following sections show you the ropes.

Some employers may have concerns about training a person with autism; about you interfering with other people doing their jobs; about making accommodations; and about dealing with potential challenging behaviors. This is where a job coach or employment specialist can come in handy (see the section "Working with a job coach"). The job coach or employment specialist should assure the employer that he or she will provide support to handle these issues and, at least initially, serve as a bridge between you and your employer. The job coach needs to be able to provide the support needed in order for you to be successful on the job.

Creating a portfolio

You use a *portfolio,* or a collection of projects demonstrating your work capabilities, as an initial "calling card" when applying for a position. Submitting a portfolio places the focus on the work you can do rather than on the social aspects of an interview. The portfolio is probably the most powerful way for you to get your proverbial foot in the door to meet the person in charge of hiring. The goal is to have that person focus on the quality of your work rather than on any possible social challenges you may face due to autism.

A portfolio can include many different items, such as detailed drawings, technical reports, or any other work product you have previously created that speaks to your ability to understand and process information. If you want to get a mechanic position, for example, you may bring in pictures or scrapbooks of cars you've put together, for instance. If you have a specific interest or ability, you can highlight this ability in your portfolio.

Networking

Many people get jobs through personal leads by friends, acquaintances, or colleagues. Let others know you're looking for a job and that you'd appreciate them letting you know if they hear of possible opportunities. If you're not comfortable with the face-to-face networking associated with getting a job, you can use means other than face-to-face contact. Be sure to send your résumé out often and even post your résumé on the Internet at job-hunting Web sites.

Creating a cover letter and résumé

Most of the time, to get to the interview phase of the job-hunting process, you have to submit a cover letter and résumé to your potential employer. You should seek advice from your previous teachers or caregivers about how to craft straightforward, effective résumés and cover letters. You don't have to begin disclosure of your disability in your cover letter; just try to present your interest in the position clearly and have a well-organized résumé that supports your capability of doing the job. Be sure to include references of people you know well and who you think understand your disability and believe that your disability won't prevent you from being successful in the workplace. You should have at least one person you trust to proofread and possibly help you develop your cover letter and résumé.

When the company receives your cover letter and résumé, many people, like a human resources representative and hiring supervisor, will review it. Ultimately, the goal of your cover letter and résumé is to get the recruiters interested enough to call you in for an interview.

We could say a ton about writing a good cover letter and résumé, but you can find many books on the subject. You can check out books such as *Résumés For Dummies,* 4th Edition (Wiley), and *Cover Letters For Dummies,* 2nd Edition (Wiley), both by Joyce Lain Kennedy, along with the latest edition of Richard Bolles' *What Color Is Your Parachute* (Ten Speed Press) — a great guide for designing cover letters and résumés for employment and for finding employment suitable to your strengths.

Completing an interview

The interview can be the most challenging part of the job search for people with autism. This fact can be hard to swallow, because most employers agree that the most powerful variable in who they hire for positions isn't qualifications, but how well potential employees interview for the jobs.

If you have difficulties with social skills, you need to try hard to maintain appropriate social interactions, including using eye contact and appropriate nonverbal communication (nodding, smiling, and so on; see Chapter 10) to show appropriate interest in the conversation. You should also talk with your potential employer about whether your job coach can come along to your interview; this should be a joint decision between you and your coach. A job coach may be able to answer questions you can't answer, such as how the job coach can assist your potential employer in insuring your success in the workplace.

Maintaining your job

After an employer awards you with the position you've been seeking (congrats!), your work has just begun — no pun intended. Keeping a job depends on two requirements:

- ✔ **Doing the job to the satisfaction of your managing supervisor.** All employees are expected to meet the expectations of their employers. Make sure you understand what's involved in the job, how to do the job, and how to get help if you need it.

  Managing this requirement is usually pretty easy for an autistic person. If you run into any trouble, you can request/use any accommodations necessary to communicate questions you may have to your supervisor, support person, or job coach to make sure you can do the best job possible.

  If you have a job coach, it may be useful to have him approach your employer about accommodation. This tactic saves you from the initial stress of asking for accommodations. Over time, as you get more comfortable with your employers, you may become more willing to ask for accommodations on your own.

- ✔ **Meeting the social expectations of the job.** This requirement can be tougher for some people with autism. A large part of many jobs is maintaining good social relations with coworkers and supervisors. The subtly in workplace social dynamics can be very difficult for many people with autism to decode and respond to. If you have one, you can ask your job coach for advice on how to socialize appropriately with coworkers. You can also attempt to watch how your coworkers interact and then try to learn from these observations as you attempt to integrate yourself into the workplace social scene.

Gracefully exiting your position

Research shows that most people change jobs several times during their working lives. You may need to leave a job because of life circumstances, change of interests, or because you simply don't like your job or the people you work with.

Whatever your reasons for departing a position, you should thank the people you worked with for their assistance in helping you do a good job. In other words, you should leave gracefully. Doing so will preserve good relations and allow you to ask for a good recommendation in the future. It's also very possible that previous coworkers and supervisors will show up in future positions you'll be interested in pursuing. These people become part of your network, for better or for worse. Even if you feel you were let go for unfair reasons relating to your autism, it makes sense to leave your job on good terms, because this kind of parting can only work to help you in the future.

When you leave a job, you need to find out how being unemployed may impact the social-service (government) assistance you may be receiving. You may need to ask caregivers or others you trust to help you figure out how leaving a job will impact your financial situation.

Considering self-employment

Self-employment can be a viable option for many people on the autism spectrum. Some people like to work as consultants (computers, taxes, and so on) because they can go into situations, solve the problems, work on their own terms, and be out before office politics and socialization problems begin to take their toll. I (co-author Stephen Shore) have cobbled together a career by teaching college-level courses in autism and special education, working on worldwide consulting jobs, speaking on autism-related issues, writing, and teaching people with autism how to play music.

A self-employed individual still needs to look for work like someone employed at an outside business. In the case of self-employment, looking for work includes searching for buyers of your product or service. Tactics such as networking still come into play with self-employment, because you want to build a network of individuals who may be interested in buying your product or service.

Common characteristics of individuals who succeed in self-employment include an independent spirit and a strong work ethic. If you're going to be successful working on your own, you must be willing to expend a great deal of time and effort making your self-employment profitable. People who do well aren't people who always depend on positive feedback from others. You need to be somewhat independent-minded and willing to take some risks if you plan on being self-employed.

Most of the downsides of self-employment point to income, which can be unreliable. Self-employed individuals have to figure out how to pay their taxes and withhold taxes from their profits without the help of an employer. You also face additional organizational challenges, marketing needs, and other requirements that can be tough for people both on and off the autism spectrum.

For caregivers: Helping a dependent find employment

As a caregiver, you need to consider the challenges your loved one faces due to autism and the characteristics of autism he exhibits when looking into possible vocational choices and career paths for him. Examining the characteristics he exhibits (like a strong need for order and visual strength, for example) is actually just an extension of considering anybody's profile of strengths and challenges when determining the person's ability to hold a position. In other words, you want to conduct a mini-interview with your autistic loved one to find out what path best suits him. That path, of course, depends on where your loved one rests on the autism spectrum.

Helping a high-functioning individual find (and keep) employment

As a caregiver, you can assist the person in your life with high-functioning autism in his job search by committing to the following actions:

- ✔ Watch how he likes to spend most of his time, and suggest what type of work he may be happy with. (See the section "Matching your skills and desires with job opportunities".)

- ✔ Offer to develop, proofread, or even type résumés and cover letters he needs after he decides what type of employment he wants to pursue. If telephone communication is a challenge for him, offer to make calls. (See the section "Applying for and obtaining a position".)

- ✔ Help with networking by checking in with local social-service agencies. You can look to a vocational rehabilitation agency, special-education teachers, and community support groups, to name a few. You can also ask businesses in the area if they may have employee vacancies that require the skills your loved one possesses.

- ✔ Find a job coach or vocational rehabilitation counselor to assist in the job hunting. Supporting a person with autism is a complex and challenging task, so don't be afraid to enlist the help of a person with the proper background who can supply the needed assistance for obtaining and maintaining a job. (See the section "Working with a job coach".)

When the person under your care secures employment, your mission to help doesn't end. Follow the tips in this list to make sure the employment experience is positive for your loved one:

- ✔ Use social stories, Power Cards, discussion, or even role-playing to address challenges in social interaction that may come up during your loved one's workday. (For more on these tools, check out Chapter 13.)

✔ Address all issues concerning needed supports with little or no effort from the employer. For example, the person under your care may have the best sorting skills of anyone you know. However, if the person faces challenges in verbal communication, dealing with frustration, and so on, you *must* plan support to minimize these challenges prior to the person starting the job. Having a misunderstanding or a tantrum on the job for any reason isn't conducive to employment success.

✔ Make sure that all appropriate colleagues communicate your loved one's job responsibilities through the communication means he uses. The method may be verbal or through sign language, pictures, or a combination of methods. Many people refer to job manuals when starting out in positions. Make sure the person under your care (as well as his support person) has and understands the reference material.

✔ If the person understands the requirements of his position, but he still can't follow directions, you should conduct a *functional behavioral assessment* (FBA) to determine the reason. An FBA looks at all the causes and consequences of challenging behaviors and helps develop systems for resolving the problem (see Chapter 11 for more on FBAs).

Some reasons for failing to follow directions may include insufficient or ineffective reinforcement, noxious sensory input, or, in rare cases, sabotage from coworkers who don't want to work with a person on the autism spectrum.

Exploring employment opportunities for those more severely affected by autism

If the person under your care is more severely affected with autism, you have to consider more formal and informal support to achieve a successful employment endeavor. With the right supports, even persons severely affected by autism can find some form of employment.

Your job is to accurately assess the individual's level of functioning and to help him pursue vocational training that will prepare him for specific workplace duties. You may connect a low-functioning individual with supported workshop environments that cater to people with significant development impairment. (For more on matching the needs of the person under your care to a job opportunity, see the section "Matching your skills and desires with job opportunities".)

Another supportive working environment that may work for your loved one is a sheltered workshop — if you're willing to relocate (see the sidebar "Sheltered workshops: Enhancing quality of life" for an explanation).

Sheltered workshops: Enhancing quality of life

Often thought of as a transitional step, a *sheltered workshop* is supposed to prepare people with disabilities for independent, competitive employment. For those persons unable to work competitively, at least some form of employment is possible thanks to the sheltered workshop. Unfortunately, you see a tendency in many places for this form of employment to become little more than a place to warehouse people with disabilities to perform repetitive, meaningless tasks.

Although popular for a period of time, sheltered workshops have been in decline in the United States. However, they still thrive in places around the world. Located about 35 kilometers northwest of Tokyo, Japan, Keyaki-no-Sato is an excellent model of how a sheltered, residential workshop can provide meaningful and productive employment. (For more information about the workshop, see www.disabilityworld. org/04-05_04/il/japan.shtml.)

I (co-author Stephen Shore) visited Keyaki-no-Sato and was impressed with the cleanliness, order, and teamwork between some severely affected people with autism. Above all, I was impressed with people living with dignity, purpose, and happiness in their lives.

An Advocate Off the Ol' Block: Getting Involved with Your Community

Community involvement is a part of leading a productive and fulfilling life. In fact, some studies indicate that community involvement is an important variable in leading a long and healthy life. Involvement in the community takes place on many levels, ranging from global to regional to your neighborhood. Getting out into the community can be as simple as taking a field trip to a local pizza joint or as complicated as spending several days on a trip to a point of interest.

Involvement in the community also leads to the formation of additional communities, a positive for any adult with autism who wants more socialization. For both autistic and non-autistic people alike, community involvement gives you a positive sense that you're part of something larger and more valuable than your individual being. Additionally, community involvement allows you to develop a broader and stronger potential support system that you can lean on during rough times.

Communities form around interests such as ballroom dancing, computers, and causes like autism awareness and breast cancer. In this section, we take a look at some of the benefits of community involvement and how you can join the vast number of communities that are as diverse as the autism spectrum itself.

Don't think the community is as large or as important as we make it out to be? You need to widen your scope in thinking about your community. People of a particular race, nationality, or culture can share common experiences of coming from a certain geographical location or share language, thought, beliefs, religion, or other binding factors. Some people with autism enjoy attending houses of worship, which tend to feature highly structured services and other events. Your geographic community (or neighborhood) may have interesting activities and opportunities for involvement. The possibilities are everywhere!

Becoming a part of your community

Involvement within a community usually begins with an activity. For example, if you're a musician or are interested in music, you can join a community band or get with like-minded music lovers and attend concerts (as long as your senses can handle it). One of the reasons I (co-author Stephen Shore) teach people with autism how to play musical instruments is to provide a gateway to joining a community band or orchestra. I've spent many enjoyable evenings playing in a community ensemble.

If you have athletic interests and skills, you can join a club or team in your community. If team-oriented, ball-type sports are difficult for you, you can look for more individual activities that can still be accomplished in groups. You can bicycle with a local organization, join a jogging group hosted by a sporting-goods store, or get with a group of people and attend a local sporting event. Other types of community-based events can include going to movies with roommates, coworkers, or friends; having picnics in a park; joining a book club; and participating in fundraising or awareness walks.

Activity based events are much more successful for people with autism than socially based events. The activity forms the reason for the gathering and provides the structure that people with autism commonly need. Socially oriented activities (like a gala event or a singles' dance) tend to be less structured. If you must attend a less-structured, socially based activity, you can do your best to create a structure. Take a look at the sidebar in this section for one example of how to do this.

If you're looking to increase your social involvement, you may want to begin with simple social gatherings with peers that you know. It may be worth taking time to build up to big events, such as dances, with many strangers in attendance. It may also be helpful to develop a few positive peer relationships with other people on the autism spectrum and then work with these people to move toward increasing social involvement.

Inserting structure where you find none

One time, my wife and I (co-author Stephen Shore) were invited to a barbeque dinner within the Chinese community that primarily involved people talking to each other. I didn't know many people, and I felt uneasy about the lack of an activity to structure the event.

Fortunately, I discovered that no one knew how to operate the gas grill to cook the food. Neither did I! However, I quickly learned how to operate the device, and soon I structured all my

interactions around preparing the food. Things were going well, so I became emboldened.

A few years ago, I read in a body-language book that a common male-bonding gesture is to playfully punch the shoulder of another fellow. I tried it out, and soon a bunch of Chinese guys and I were busy talking, and we all had a good time.

I attribute the success of this event to my being able to find a structured activity within a relatively unstructured event.

Looking within the autism community

Many people consider people with autism as a community. Within this large, overarching community, you can find many smaller communities that provide an opportunity for communication and the exchange of ideas. Such communities include autism conferences, Internet-based communities, and organizations run for and by autistic persons. The following sections outline these communities in more detail.

Attending autism conferences

Autism conferences are places that provide opportunities to meet people and build life-long friendships. Large autism conferences, such as the Autism Society of America's annual national conference (www.autism-society.org), can have attendances of 1,500 to 2,000 people and between two- and three-dozen autistic people taking part. In addition to giving presentations and helping to plan the conferences, autistic persons quickly form their own communities — the ASA's conference features an Autism Town Meeting and a space referred to as the "Persons with Autism Room." People not on the autism spectrum are permitted to enter only on invitation and when escorted by an autistic person.

Another particularly friendly event for people with autism is the annual MAAP Services conference (*MAAP* stands for *M*ore advanced individuals with *A*utism, *A*sperger Syndrome, and *P*ervasive Developmental Disorder). Like with the ASA, MAAP puts special effort into respecting and accommodating for the needs of people on the autism spectrum. Take a look at the Web site www.maapservices.org for information on the next conference.

Considering Internet-based interaction

Computer-based communication seems particularly suited for many people with autism. Because interactions are word-based and not face-to-face, you don't have the distraction of attempting to decode nonverbal cues. Additionally, face-to-face conversations are somewhat temporary, meaning that words are spoken, and you have to aurally decode and remember them during a conversation. This process can be very difficult or even impossible for autistic people who have auditory processing or attentional issues. Words on a computer screen don't have to be spoken, and you can read them as many times as you need.

Although cyberspace can be a great place to meet people, you need to realize that people you meet online are strangers. To stay safe, keep the following tips in mind (for more info on possible sites to visit on the Net, check out the Appendix):

- **Keep personal information private.** If you wouldn't give a stranger on the street your phone number and address, don't give them to someone you just "met" online. Also, don't share personal information about your friends (including phone numbers and addresses) with your new online friends.

- **Make sure the person's purported identity is accurate.** It's very easy to make up an entire fictional personal profile online, just as it's difficult to prove who another person is without actually seeing the person. However, you should do your best to try.

- **Tell a trusted adult if someone makes you nervous online.** Don't be afraid to let someone know that you're uncomfortable with something someone said to you or told you to do.

- **Consider checking with a trusted friend before you send any pictures of yourself to an online acquaintance.** Sending a picture of yourself over the Net may seem harmless, but you should double-check with someone just to make sure the person agrees that it's safe.

- **Keep your password secret.** Create a unique password that you can remember. Use letters, numbers, punctuation marks, and different cases wherever possible to make the password unpredictable.

- **Meet an online friend *only* in a public place.** If you choose to meet a person for the first time face to face, do so in a public place that contains many people. Also, make the initial meeting — and possibly several of the meetings thereafter — short and casual. For example, you could meet the person for a cup of coffee in a café.

Consider bringing a friend or other trusted person with you upon meeting an online acquaintance in person for the first two or three times.

Trying out autistic-run organizations

One of the more well-known autistic-run organizations is Autism Network International (`ani.autistics.org`). In addition to running a listserve (an Internet-based communication tool; see the Appendix) for people with autism, ANI holds an annual conference known as *Autreat*. The event focuses on the positives of living with autism rather than cures, interventions, or striving for "normalcy."

Finding businesses and other organizations that show interest in involving people with autism on a daily basis can be very helpful. Becoming involved with such organizations may lead to work, volunteer opportunities, and other activities than can boost your involvement in the community.

For caregivers: Encouraging an adult with autism to get involved

Diversity (which is abundant in autism) brings richness to a community. As with education and employment (see the previous sections of this chapter), a person with autism may need accommodations and support from an aide or a coach to feel the motivation to become involved in the community. Caregivers of individuals at all functioning levels should encourage community involvement. Even low-functioning individuals with autism can find some aspects of community involvement that foster a sense of belonging and boost self-esteem.

The level of accommodation and support needed can range from *almost none* to *intensive*. When deciding on the level of help necessary, keep in mind that the goal of inclusion within the community is to have both the person with autism and the community benefit from the person's involvement.

Some communities have drop-in centers that hold activities for people with disabilities. However, these options have both pros and cons. A positive aspect is that they provide support for people with autism and other disabilities. A drawback is that these events separate people with these differences from the larger community.

Encouraging community involvement can come in many ways, including actions indicating that community involvement is important. In addition to actions, kind words that promote community involvement can also help a person's concerns about becoming active.

Here are some areas to consider when you want to support a loved one's involvement in the community:

✔ **Transportation:** For some people, transportation may mean both a ride to the event and social, behavioral, or other support at the event. Others may only need to travel on a public bus instead of driving or even walking.

✔ **Communication:** You may need to provide persons with no or limited verbal ability other means of communication, such as sign language or graphically-based tools, in addition to an aide or other support person. You may want to encourage some situations, such as jogging with a club or going to a ballgame, that require only minimal communication. (See Chapter 10 for more on communication assistance.)

✔ **Social:** Because autistic people have trouble with nonverbal cues and figurative language, the social aspect of community involvement can be challenging. You can encourage involvement by helping the person under your care become more familiar with these types of communication. (Take a look at Chapters 10 and 13 for more information about helpful tools.)

✔ **Behavioral:** Challenging behaviors are often one of the greatest concerns of people in the community. You need to know the behaviors well in order to successfully navigate around activities and events containing antecedents to challenging behaviors.

Like with employment situations, neurotypical people involved in community activities need to know that you'll provide support to handle any challenging behaviors and that you don't expect them to interact or intervene in challenging situations.

Chapter 15

For Adults with Autism: Fostering Friendships and Romantic Relationships

· ·

In This Chapter

▶ Establishing and nurturing relationships

▶ Stepping foot into the dating world

▶ Achieving the highest level of intimacy

▶ Helping caregivers give relationship support

· ·

*I*n general, our culture has three levels of close acquaintance: friendships, romantic relationships, and sexual relationships. All three levels are challenging for everyone, but they can be even more challenging for you, a person with autism. You have to work that much harder to make and maintain true friendships due to your differences (both because of your needs and others'). But don't be discouraged. You'll find that all your work will pay off when you make friendships and (hopefully) find love.

In this chapter, we explore some ideas on how to help you succeed in areas that are extremely important in establishing relationships. We help you figure out how to make friends, and we identify the prerequisites for maintaining friendship with the possibility of it deepening into an intimate relationship. We show you the ropes on how to start dating. Finally, we discuss moving on to a sexual relationship when you and your love interest are ready and willing.

 As a bonus in this chapter, we provide information in each section to help caregivers educate their dependents on the topics of friendship and intimacy. Some people on the autism spectrum aren't able to maintain relationships without some help, and we want you to be as prepared as possible to assist them. We also provide dating and sex-education information so you can help the person with autism in your life find love.

Developing Friendly Relationships

People in a friendly *relationship* share one or more common interests as a bond. With most people, this friendship develops through socially oriented gatherings that initially emphasize unrelated small talk about the weather, bosses, coworkers, and so on. These surface conversations can develop into meaningful discussions about common interests after the people involved establish a degree of mutual comfort.

But for you, a person on the autism spectrum, developing friendships can be difficult as you struggle with understanding the fine points of social communication. Many people on the autism spectrum have difficulty with *pragmatics* (using language in its proper social context), nonverbal communication (such as body language), and subtle social interaction. However, by using tactics such as watching modeled appropriate social communication and studying the specific social cues that others readily pick up without intense study, you can become familiar with the expectations of friendly relationships and gain the confidence to actively pursue friendships. We show you the way in this section.

Although it may be more difficult for persons with autism to make friends, the friendships autistic individuals make are strong relationships based on honesty and trust. A person who befriends an individual with autism must be an understanding person who isn't afraid to relate to people who other more shallow people may avoid.

Understanding the circle of relationships

Being aware of the different types of relationships is important for people both on and off the autism spectrum because failing to understand the nature of your relationship with another person can lead to uncomfortable situations and hurt feelings. Most persons off the spectrum learn the rules of social interactions through observation, but as a person on the spectrum, you may not be able to glean the rules through observation alone due to a possible impairment of interpreting non-autistic spectrum social skills — a hallmark of autism. What you need is direct instruction. Take a look at Figure 15-1 to see how you can group different categories of relationships, and check out the following list, which outlines some of the different types of relationships, ordered from the most distant to the most intimate:

 ✔ **Stranger:** This group is made up of people you've never spoken to and very rarely see. *Examples:* A waitress at a restaurant, a person sitting in a park, fellow commuters to the workplace.

✔ **Acquaintance:** You see these people more regularly, but you have the opportunity to make small talk on a strictly irregular basis. *Examples:* Neighbors, some classmates, some coworkers.

✔ **Friend:** You've known these people for a while. You talk about personal things, and you go to events that involve common interests (see Chapter 14 for some examples of these events). Some friendships can become very deep. You and your friends may tease each other, but you don't make fun of each other or cause any harm. *Examples:* Neighbors, classmates, or coworkers who you've established relationships with and people you meet through common interests.

✔ **Family and significant others:** You have the closest bond with these people, and you usually spend the most time with them while growing up. *Examples:* mom, dad, siblings, boyfriend, girlfriend, fiancé, spouse (most people make a shift toward the latter four as adults; see the following sections in this chapter).

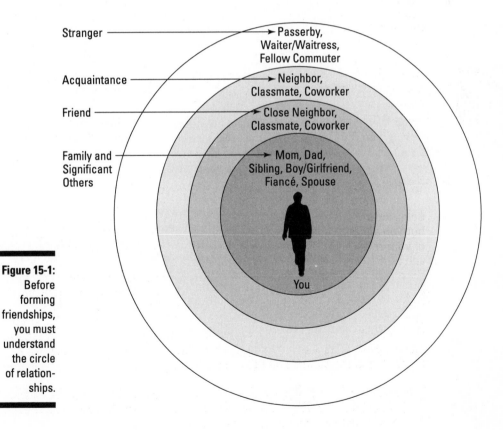

Figure 15-1:
Before forming friendships, you must understand the circle of relationships.

Stranger ——————→ Passerby, Waiter/Waitress, Fellow Commuter

Acquaintance ——————→ Neighbor, Classmate, Coworker

Friend ——————→ Close Neighbor, Classmate, Coworker

Family and Significant Others ——————→ Mom, Dad, Sibling, Boy/Girlfriend, Fiancé, Spouse

You

Making first contact

The more people you meet, the more likely you are to make friends. But you can't always wait for another person to initiate the relationship. You shouldn't be afraid to make first contact when you feel comfortable with a situation. The following sections give you tips on how to make the first contact and generate small talk and where to go from there.

Engaging in small talk

When making first contact with a person you're interested in becoming closer to, try to make small talk as much as possible. You can always ask a person how he or she is doing. Other common topics of small talk can include a discussion of the weather or about how work/school has been going. When making small talk, follow these tips to keep the other party interested:

- Always try to make some eye contact and look interested in what the person is saying.

- Smile when someone else smiles at you.

- Don't get upset if the small talk ends and the person walks away; you don't want to force someone to continue to talk when he or she wants to move on and do something else.

If your friendship is meant to be, the other person will show interest in talking with you. The key part of any relationship is what "friend" means. A friend is someone who shows genuine interest in you and what you have to say. All you can do is make the effort to try to begin talking with someone and see what happens from there.

You may have difficulty talking to someone new for the first time because people on the autism spectrum tend to have great difficulty with the small-talk stage and commonly jump right into discussions about interests. The key is to figure out when this type of conversation is appropriate. You can feel more comfortable jumping right into common interests at clubs and other gatherings based on an interest or passion. At work or school, you may decide to discuss common interests only after someone else brings up a topic you're interested in. This way, you make sure that you're not just injecting your own interests into conversations when others may not want to talk about what you enjoy. Be careful, though, not to dominate the discussion of mutual interests. Give those around you a chance to get word in.

When meeting new people, many businesspeople record a few facts about those people for future conversational material. Try this tip as you meet new people.

The initial stage of talking to others in order to make friends may not be the best time to disclose your autism. You may just want to act as you naturally do, and if you come off as "different" to others, the others must decide if they're accepting of who you really are, regardless of diagnosis.

Settings for making (or moving on from) first contact

The following list gives you some suggestions on increasing your circulation within your community. You can follow these bits of advice after you make first contact with an acquaintance, or you can make first contact during one of these activities.

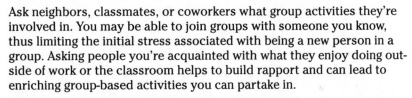

- ✔ **Get involved with activity-based clubs and groups.** People on the autism spectrum tend to fare better in activity-based events (such as at a bicycle club gathering, a computer-user group, or on a nature walk) rather than at socially oriented gatherings (office parties, family reunions, bars, and so on). Activity-based events provide a structure in which you can practice social interaction and form friendships. You can become comfortable in the group setting by participating in the structured activity before much interaction has to take place.

  Ask neighbors, classmates, or coworkers what group activities they're involved in. You may be able to join groups with someone you know, thus limiting the initial stress associated with being a new person in a group. Asking people you're acquainted with what they enjoy doing outside of work or the classroom helps to build rapport and can lead to enriching group-based activities you can partake in.

- ✔ **Invite others to join you for specific, structured activities.** Find out if neighbors or classmates enjoy activities you're comfortable with, such as playing a computer game, bicycle riding, or other passions you have. The interaction will be more successful than having someone over to just "hang around." (See Chapter 14 for some other activity tips.)

  Avoid activities that may present you with sensory issues. If you have trouble with loud noises and crowds, for example, you should avoid meeting potential friends at loud, crowded concerts. (For more on common sensory issues, see Chapter 10.)

- ✔ **Volunteer to work with older or younger groups of people.** People with autism often get along better with persons of other age groups. Younger people have less-sophisticated requirements for their interactions, and older people often have the patience to help *scaffold* (or structure) an interaction.

For caregivers: Helping your dependent establish friendships

Helping a person on the autism spectrum make and maintain friendships can be difficult, but it isn't impossible. And if the person you care for is willing to go out and meet people, you should be willing to do whatever it takes to help (and willing to motivate if the person is a bit hesitant). If the person you care for is low functioning and has trouble getting out and meeting people, you can still support him in trying to socially interact with the people he sees on a regular basis. Here are a few ways to get your dependent started:

✔ **Find activity-based events to attend.** Help your child find groups he may want to join based on his special interests, like a science club or a jogging club. You can also arrange for social time with neighbors or classmates who have similar interests.

Try to use connections with local autism support groups as a way to get information about other parents/caregivers interested in finding social groups for the person with autism they care for.

✔ **Help him to be a good friend.** You can help him understand the subtle nuances of communication that people off the autism spectrum take for granted. Here are a couple notes for caregivers (see the section "The most important part of boyfriend or girlfriend is 'friend'" for more tips):

- **Set up a hygiene schedule.** Some people with autism may not recognize their "ripe" smells and the need for a shower. Others may be overly sensitive to the use of a washcloth and certain soaps — especially the scented variety. Setting up a visual or word-based schedule for hygienic activities is helpful. You should also find cleaning products that aren't overwhelming to the senses of the autistic person.

- **Show him how to have agreeable disagreements.** Disagreeing need not be a blood sport. It may be helpful to develop a social story or Power Card that describes what to do when a disagreement occurs. (See Chapter 13 for more details on these tools.)

✔ **Explain the concept of "appropriate touching."** Use the circle of relationships diagram in Figure 15-1 to help determine developmentally appropriate types of touch. For example, a 4-year-old child hugging everyone he sees is cute. When a 24-year-old does the hugging, however, it has different meanings. Teaching the person to substitute handshaking for hugging will serve him later on in life.

For further information on helping people with autism increase their time spent in the community to develop friends and relationships, check out Teresa Bolick's book *Asperger Syndrome and Adolescence: Helping Preteens and Teens Get Ready for the Real World* (Fair Winds Press).

Recognizing (And Overcoming) the Challenges of Dating

The second level of friendship introduces the sometimes uncomfortable but definitely enjoyable level of intimacy into a relationship. The sheer number of books on dating indicates that intimacy can be challenging for many people, including you. Some of your major challenges likely stem from your ability (or inability) to express the subtle verbal and nonverbal types of communication that indicate a person's desire to have a relationship with another person. You also may have trouble determining what level of relationship another person desires. Don't worry, it isn't just you; most people on the autism spectrum have difficulty perceiving and accurately decoding these cues.

For people on the autism spectrum, the greatest success in dating comes by first looking for a friend (see the previous section). If you discover sufficient compatibility with a person, perhaps you can move on to an intimate relationship that stems from your friendship. This section helps you take the next step, if you so desire.

The challenges posed by a lack of interpersonal skills in people with autism make it even more important that a good friendship precede any attempt to go on a date. Deepening the relationship with another person by engaging in more activities of common interests, actively listening to the other person, and sharing your needs and desires makes it easier when the time comes to let the other person know of your interest in dating.

Asking for a date

You may have issues that neurotypical people don't face, such as difficulty understanding body language and other nonverbal cues, but you share something in common with every other adult interested in dating: You get nervous. You can minimize much of the challenge that comes with asking a person out for a date by not actually using the emotionally charged word "date." Think of dating as an extension of engaging in an activity with a friend or a person who you would like to get to know better as a friend (a task made easier if you get to know the person before you ask him or her out on a date). The request can be as simple as asking the other person if he or she would like to go out for a movie, get a snack or meal, meet for coffee, or engage in another activity of interest.

You can ask the other person on a date face-to-face or via the phone, e-mail, or other form of communication. Keep your communication brief and to the point. Using e-mail or instant messaging may be easier for you because you face no distractions from attempting to decode nonverbal communication. Asking in person or on the phone is usually faster, however. It may be wise to avoid using chat rooms to ask people out on dates because the people you chat with may not be people you know very well. Try to avoid randomly asking people out on dates if you haven't met them and hardly know them.

Simple is best. A sample telephone or Internet conversation could go like this:

> **Lovely Lady:** *Hello?*
>
> **You:** *Hi! This is Jimmy Peterson. How are you?*
>
> **Lovely Lady:** *I am fine. And you?*
>
> **You:** *I am good. There's a great concert this weekend at the Centrum, and I would like to go. Would you like to go with me?*
>
> **Lovely Lady:** *Sure! When is the concert?*
>
> **You:** *The concert is at 7 p.m. this Friday.*

At this point, you make plans to meet at an agreeable place, set up a time, and so on. Now, suppose the response is negative, indicating that the person is busy. Here's a possible response:

> **Handsome Hunk:** *I would like to, but I'm unable to go.*
>
> **You:** *Well, it was nice talking to. See you in school (if you go to the same school).*

Dating tip: Don't confuse a girlfriend with a squeeze machine

I (co-author Stephen Shore) am not sure I can consider this story as a dating experience, which I suppose is part of the problem. After spending a good amount of time over several weeks with a woman in college, I found out that she *really* liked hugs and backrubs. I was elated!

Now, in the non-autistic world, this preference was a code indicating that she wanted to have a more intimate relationship. But my autistic interpretation was that I had a friend who also doubled as a Temple Grandin–type deep-pressure-squeeze machine (a device developed by Temple Grandin to provide the deep pressure

her body craved). After several weeks, she invited me to her house to sleep over. And that's exactly what I did, slept — even in the same bed with her.

Soon, she seemed very frustrated and was crying. It took a lot of talking for me to realize that not only did she want to be my girlfriend, but also she thought we had been dating steady for at least a month or two!

I never perceived her nonverbal communications indicating that she wanted to be my girlfriend. Fortunately for me, I no longer need to worry about how to date, because I've been married for over 16 years.

Many requests for dates do get turned down, so if it happens to you, you're in good company. The other person may truly be busy, or he or she may just not want to hurt your feelings by rejecting your offer. Don't get down about it. Remember, the other person is missing out on spending time with you!

You should follow the three-strikes rule, which states that you can ask the other person out on a date (nicely) a total of three times. If the "Nos" add up to three, you should assume that the person doesn't want to date you, and you need to leave him or her alone. To do otherwise invites the possibility of being accused of stalking or harassment.

Behaving appropriately during the date

Congratulations on the accepted date offer! When you go on your date, make sure you enjoy yourself and go slow. You're likely nervous. The other person is probably just as nervous as you are. Try to kick off a date by starting conversation about topics both of you share mutual interest in to lower the inevitable stress level (see the section "Engaging in small talk" earlier in this chapter). If things are going well, you may want to gently take your companion's hand while you make conversation or enjoy a movie to show your affection. Observe how the other person responds. If he or she holds on to your hand as well, you know that things are moving along. If your companion pulls away, he or she isn't ready for a closer relationship. That may be as far as you want to go for a first date.

On the other hand (no pun intended), the person you're dating may hold his or her hand out to you. If you're comfortable taking that hand to hold, you can do so. If you're not ready to hold hands at that time, or if holding hands causes you unbearable sensory issues (see Chapter 10), feel free to say so in a simple manner. "I would rather not hold hands at this time." You can use a sentence like this for any activity, such as kissing, hugging, or sex, if you just don't feel ready.

If things continue to go well on your date, and you both agree to go on another date, repeating the handholding may be a good idea. If the handholding goes well the second time around, you may want to go further. Strongly consider asking for permission before you move on to kissing, petting, and sex. It may not seem very romantic, but given the challenges you may face in nonverbal communication, it's better to be safe than sorry. (For more information about sex and autism, see the section "Taking It to the Next Level with Sexual Behavior" later in this chapter.)

If you plan on going out alone on a date, make sure you feel comfortable being alone with the person. If you go out with someone you may not be comfortable with alone, consider having someone you know and trust come along with you on the first date or try to arrange a double date, where you go on the date with another couple. Double dates can ease the stress associated with being alone with someone.

How do I tell if we are boyfriend/girlfriend?

Determining the exact stage of intimate relations can be confusing for everyone. However, because of my autistic tendencies, I (co-author Stephen Shore) could never accurately decode when a relationship was at a particular stage. By the time I met the girl who would become my wife, I had devised my own social narrative to help me realize when I had reached the intimate stage.

Essentially, I decided that if a woman displayed the three behaviors of hugging, kissing, and initiating handholding, she wanted to be my girlfriend. At that point, my response would be one of the following: yes, no, or I need further investigation and analysis.

My wife and I have recently celebrated our 16th wedding anniversary, so I reckon that "yes" was the right answer. I was lucky because no person tried to take advantage of my lack of knowledge in the area of intimate relations. Well, some persons may have, but my total lack of awareness may have protected me in what could've been a dangerous situation.

The good news is that you can overcome the challenges of relationship classification with open and direct communication about relationships, dating, and sexuality. Using the information in this chapter, along with the other sources we mention, you can learn how to develop safe and fulfilling relationships with others both on and off the autism spectrum!

Opting for full or no disclosure

Making the decision to disclose your autism to a date is an important one. We feel that you should keep your autism spectrum disorder on a "need-to-know basis." And just when is that time? When the effects of being autistic significantly impact a relationship and you feel a need for better mutual understanding and trust (usually after a number of dates when your bond is growing stronger), you should disclose your condition at your discretion.

One good way to disclose your condition is to use the following four steps:

1. **Talk about your strengths and challenges.**

   Take time to discuss possible things you struggle with, such as social conversation, sensory issues, or issues of repetitive behavior. Couple that with a discussion of your strengths, which may include having a good memory, being a good worker, or being a kind person.

2. **Sort your strengths and challenges out in terms of how you possibly use your strengths to work through some challenges.**

   Explain how you try to compensate for your struggles by emphasizing your strengths. For example, you could talk about how you use your memory strength to keep track of what people are interested in so you can have introductory topics to discuss. This activity compensates for your troubles in starting up new conversation.

3. **Bring the conversation toward other successful persons with your set of characteristics. You can also mention people with differing characteristics.**

   For example, you can mention Temple Grandin, an autistic woman who emphasized her strengths and was able to get a PhD, find a good job, and even write books about what she overcame. You can even throw out Thomas Jefferson's name — the founding father is theorized to have had Asperger Syndrome (see Chapter 5 for more on this type of autism).

4. **Trot out the label.**

   As an introduction, you may want to mention that scientists, educators, and others are studying people with varying characteristics, and it just so happens that your characteristics line up with (insert your label here).

Each disclosure situation is different. It may be possible to get through the 4 Steps in 10 to 15 minutes, or it could take a number of days or possibly longer. You can also choose to make a partial disclosure if you aren't ready for full disclosure. In this case, you can mention the specific area where a characteristic of autism may be affecting the situation. For example, you may ask to leave a room lit with fluorescent lights because "I have sensitive eyes."

Try to be confident when you attempt disclosure. Remember, you're describing to someone who you are. If the person gets upset about who you are, he or she isn't the kind of person you want to be intimate with.

One way you can "prime" the disclosure discussion is to give the person you're dating an autobiography of a person with autism that best resembles your situation. You can find many good autobiographies on people with autism. We recommend that you read any of Temple Grandin's books. She always talks clearly about the struggles and rewards of coping with autism.

For caregivers: Moving on to dating

Entering the dating world is an anxiety-producing process, and people with autism are no exception. The person in your life with autism may experience rejection, feel like an outsider, or just feel different from her peers, and situations in adolescence and dating often bring out those feelings even more intensely. When the person in your life is ready to move from a friendship to a romantic relationship, you can help her succeed by answering questions, initiating discussions, and being generally supportive. Some low-functioning children on the spectrum may not be able to understand dating or romantic relationships. If you care for a low-functioning person, you must realize that friendships can still occur, but a friend doesn't necessarily have to be a boyfriend or girlfriend. For high-functioning individuals who demonstrate an understanding of dating and a desire to date, here are a few of our favorite tips for caregivers:

✔ Be a sounding board. Give her the chance to try out that first telephone invitation (see the section "Asking for a date").

✔ Discuss appropriate behavior for the date (see the section "Behaving appropriately during the date").

✔ Role-play certain dating situations, such as conversations at dinner or the movies, and discuss any confusing areas.

Make sure that the person with autism doesn't confuse your supportive role-playing identity with actual dating. Also, you should discuss the physical aspects of situations rather than the actual physical contact. Physical contact in a role-playing situation is very confusing to people with autism (and those without) and may be damaging (and illegal).

✔ Conduct "touching" discussions about appropriate actions and receiving touch from others. Some points of discussion include the following:

• If you don't want someone touching you in a certain place, you shouldn't touch another person in that place.

• The person with autism should have a "safe person" she can discuss any concerns with. She should see the "safe person" as someone who wants to help her rather than punish her.

• Encourage self-advocacy before your loved one begins dating. Being aware of one's comfort level and letting others know in a way they can understand requires skills in appropriate self-advocacy.

A person with autism should know that some persons, such as doctors or nurses, may have to touch parts of her body without permission. Make sure she doesn't confuse this behavior with sexual behavior.

Taking It to the Next Level with Sexual Behavior

Intimate relations can be challenging for you, a person on the autism spectrum, because you run into plenty of unspoken expectations that most people seem to understand without discussion. Confusion with nonverbal cues can be comical, such as when someone yawns and you think the person is choking and pound on her back to help her breath, or it can be harmful, such as when a person doesn't understand the need to stop a behavior. To address this challenge, we recommend you take time to review some important aspects of the *hidden curriculum* for developing intimate relationships. *Hidden curriculum* is a term used to describe social information that everyone knows, but no one is taught. For more about hidden curriculum, see Chapter 5. For now, go through the following sections to discover more about the hidden curriculum through the scope of engaging in sexual behavior as an autistic adult.

The most important part of boyfriend or girlfriend is "friend"

No set of rules governs how long you have to know a person before you try to cultivate a boy/girlfriend relationship. Acquiring a boy/girlfriend may occur after you've known the person as only a friend for some time. As a person with autism, it may be easier for you to develop boy/girlfriend relationships with people you're already comfortable with as friends. On the other hand, you may meet someone for the first time and know right away you want him or her to be your boy/girlfriend. In either situation, the most important part of the boyfriend or girlfriend relationship is being a "friend."

Teresa Bolick, a psychologist specializing in helping children and young adults on the autism spectrum, has some pointers for developing and maintaining the most important prerequisite to intimate relations — friendship. These tips describe some of the most vital components of being a good friend and, in turn, boy/girlfriend. Here are the tips:

- **Listen as carefully as you can.** People like to be listened to, and listening is a vital skill in being able to relate to others. Two of the key indicators you can use to ensure that your significant other knows you're listening are eye contact and the turning of your body toward the person talking. You may need some direct instruction in this area to demonstrate that you're paying attention.

  You may find eye contact difficult or impossible. Many people on the autism spectrum who can make eye contact report that they don't receive any useful information for their efforts. For this reason, we recommend that if eye contact is difficult, look in the vicinity of the other person's eyes. For instance, you can focus on the person's nose, mouth, or forehead areas.

- **Practice proper hygiene.** Set a schedule to take care of basic personal hygiene needs, and stick to it. Even if you don't notice your breath or body odor, others may, including your love interest.

  If you're turned off by smells coming from your significant other, you need to first classify the smells. You should say nothing if you think she doesn't intend to smell that way (if she has body odor, for example). If you think she chooses to smell that way and it bothers you (she wears strong perfume, for example), you should explain nicely that the smell bothers you.

  Sensory issues often play a large part in the lives of people with autism. If you're overly sensitive to smells, you should find a mild, scent-free soap that works for you. If you're particularly sensitive to the feel of loofahs or washcloths, experiment with different materials, including soft linens found in the baby departments of stores, to find something that works for you. It's also possible to wash yourself clean by using only your hands. (Co-author Stephen Shore has a beard because shaving feels like a power sander scraping across his face.)

✔ **Share life experiences and feelings.** This step is vital for moving from the acquaintance and friendship stages to the significant-other stage. In short, you develop and accumulate experience-sharing interactions by spending time together.

✔ **Shoot for agreeable disagreements.** All people disagree from time to time, but you have to find a way to respectfully disagree. Look for ways to respect the person and treat her kindly, even if you don't agree with her point of view.

✔ **Friendship counts.** Research shows that the most successful long-term, intimate relationships are between people who are friends first. Place a premium on friendship instead of rushing to the physical aspects of a relationship.

✔ **Show interest.** People are flattered when you ask them questions about how they like to spend their time, what hobbies they enjoy, and what thoughts they have about current events. Strive to have the other person do more talking than you.

✔ **Stay on an even keel.** Being overexcited or "running on empty" interferes with your efforts to make friends and develop intimate relationships.

✔ **Stop means stop/No means no.** In this case, the literal interpretation of language by people on the autism spectrum is an asset. Many problems occur when a person tries to second-guess the other person's "no" as being a tease or really meaning "yes" during discussions of intimacy. You have to assume that if someone says "no," he or she does mean "no."

Engaging in sexual activity

If you and your significant other feel comfortable with the idea, sex can be a wonderful way to express love and appreciation.

Sex by definition is a sensual experience. The hyper and hyposensitivity of people with autism can affect their sexual activities. For example, hyposensitivity can cause problems in obtaining necessary stimulation for achieving orgasm. Others may find the experience of sex overstimulating. Tactile sensitivities may require wearing clothing on some parts of the body while engaging in sexual activities. (For more on dealing with sensory issues, see Chapter 10.)

If the other person doesn't want to have sex, you must immediately stop. Although it may not seem fair, anytime the other person wants to stop holding hands, kissing, petting, making out, or having sex, you must immediately cease. To do otherwise invites a charge of sexual assault! You also need to be familiar with the appropriate contraception devices you can use to avoid the life-changing effects of unintended pregnancy.

Sexual experience isn't limited to sexual activity with another person. You can also sexually gratify yourself with self-touching, often referred to as *masturbation*. Masturbation is an activity you should keep private, just as you keep sexual activity with another person private. Touching yourself in sexually stimulating ways around other people can make them very uncomfortable, and, more importantly, doing so is against the law. If you want to experience sexual activity by touching yourself, find a private place to do so where others can't see you.

For caregivers: Exploring sex education for people with autism

Maybe you've heard the myth that people on the autism spectrum aren't interested in intimate relationships and sex. Visiting an Asperger support group (which tend to be predominantly male) and watching what happens when a female with Asperger Syndrome walks in can quickly dispel this myth. Maybe people just don't want to admit, because of societal taboos, that folks on the autism spectrum — especially those who can't self-report — have sexual function. But sex is a basic need integral to all persons. Sexuality influences thoughts, feelings, actions, and interactions. It affects mental and physical health. And intercourse is but a small part of sexuality. Just as with the rest of the human population, people with autism are interested in intimate relations and sex to varying degrees.

Some research indicates that 81 percent of adults with autism ages 16-40 demonstrate some signs of sexual interest. Unfortunately, perhaps due to a lack of or improper education on the topic, a third engage in masturbation in public areas, and close to half use objects in connection with this activity. Masturbation is especially prevalent (and problematic) in low-functioning persons on the spectrum, who may only express their sexual urges through masturbation. Persons on this end of the spectrum often have the least understanding of socially acceptable behavior, including where and when masturbation can be appropriate.

Some experts observe that most learners with developmental disabilities receive sexuality education only *after* having engaged in some behaviors that are considered inappropriate, offensive, or potentially dangerous. Waiting to address the issue of sexual education for autistic persons is somewhat akin to closing the barn door after the horse has run.

One complicating factor in the sexual education of people on the autism spectrum is that social differences, between those on and off the spectrum, eliminate a primary information source in this area — other peers not on the autism spectrum. Therefore, people on the spectrum often don't get the normal information (or they get misinformation, in some cases) about sex from non-spectrum peers.

People on the spectrum talk about sex

One of the best ways to gain insight on how people with autism feel about intimate relationships and sex is through firsthand accounts. Two groundbreaking books, written by people on the autism spectrum, are *Autism-Asperger's and Sexuality*, by Jerry and Mary Newport (Future Horizons), and *Sex, Sexuality and the Autism Spectrum,* by Wendy Lawson (Jessica Kingsley Publishers). These books are easy to understand and chockfull of useful and important advice.

Therefore, it's up to you, the caregiver, to educate your dependent on matters of sex. Providing education about sex won't likely change the amount of sexual activity a person with autism has. What it will do, though, is allow him or her to direct sexual urges more appropriately. Use the advice in the following pages to channel your child's sexual energy so he or she can live a full and happy sexual life.

If the person under your care has difficulty successfully interacting with his environment (sometimes referred to as *low-functioning*), it can be even more beneficial to offer sex education. Even if he has difficulty communicating and otherwise successfully interacting with his environment, he has sexual urges. If you don't provide the proper education, he will satisfy his urges in some way, which may be less than desirable, or he may become very frustrated. Don't skip this important topic for people on this end of the spectrum.

Teaching about sex and managing behavior

Because the education that non-spectrum people get from peers, the media, and others tends to be missing for people on the autism spectrum, direct instruction is very important. Teaching a person with autism about sex is like teaching any other subject: You need to make accommodations for the abilities and learning style of the person on the autism spectrum (see Chapter 11). You can manage inappropriate actions such as masturbation in public areas like any other challenging behavior.

Lynn Mitchell of the Cody Center identifies these important considerations and concepts when teaching people on the spectrum about sex:

✔ **Think ahead and be proactive.** Address sexually related challenges that your child may face as he enters adulthood — ideally, before they occur. Some of these issues include masturbation, sexual abuse, personal safety, and sexually transmitted diseases. You should also consider reproductive topics such as pregnancy, childbirth, and parenthood.

When a high-functioning female with autism begins to menstruate and show some sexual interests, she needs to know that sex can result in pregnancy. You need to talk with your autistic adolescent or adult about birth control measures if you think he or she may be interested in becoming sexually involved with another person.

You can also discuss sexual orientation in an informative way. You shouldn't present the topic as if you want to make the person with autism make a choice. Your goal is to inform the individual that some people are attracted to individuals of the opposite sex, some are attracted to both sexes, and others are attracted to the same sex.

✔ **Adjust your teaching style.** Most people with autism benefit from a concrete, calm, supportive, and serious manner. As with other areas of education, you may need to educate in small manageable pieces of information (see Chapter 11).

Most people with autism are visually oriented. As a result, having simple diagrams and possibly three-dimensional models of both male and female reproductive organs can be helpful. Local autism societies or other organizations serving individuals may be able to hook you up with materials that are useful for teaching sex education to individuals with developmental disabilities.

✔ **Topics to cover.** Peter Gerhardt, president of the Organization for Autism Research (www.researchautism.org), identifies ten central concepts to cover in sex education:

- Public versus private behavior

- Good touch versus bad touch

- Proper names for body parts

- Slang names for body parts

- Personal boundaries

- Masturbation (see the following section, "Redirecting masturbation")

- Social skills and relationship building (see the section "Developing Friendly Relationships")

- Avoiding danger and abuse prevention

- Dating skills (see the section "Recognizing [And Overcoming] the Challenges of Dating")

- Personal responsibilities and values

Redirecting masturbation

Almost all people engage in masturbation, and people with autism are no exception. Where the exception does pop up is in the appropriateness of the act. Most people learn (from their peers, family, media, and their own observation) when masturbation is appropriate (and when it isn't appropriate), but persons with autism and other conditions may need more direct instruction.

Inappropriate masturbation is one of the more challenging behaviors some people with autism present. Societal taboos about teaching how and when to masturbate add to these difficulties. Fortunately, after you get past the taboos, you can manage masturbation just like any other behavior.

Here are some guidelines Peter Gerhardt, President of the Organization for Autism Research (www.researchautism.org), suggests for redirecting this behavior for more appropriate situations:

✔ Interrupt the behavior as early in the chain as possible.

✔ Remind the individual about the appropriate parameters of time and place.

✔ Redirect the person to

• An activity requiring the use of both hands. Reinforce the individual for appropriate discrimination or use of hands.

• An activity requiring preferred levels of attention, focus, or physical activity — in other words, another mutually exclusive behavior.

• The appropriate place for the activity. Consider scheduling "alone time" in the person's room if appropriate, and avoid redirection to places other than an individual's bedroom. Although the bathroom may be a tempting target, what would happen if the individual converts the behavior to bathrooms in other peoples' homes and other public locations?

These tips are good practices in redirecting any undesired behavior. Try the strategies with other challenging behaviors.

Chapter 16

Special-Needs Planning for the Future

. . . .

In This Chapter

▶ Reviewing the parameters of trusts and estates

▶ Funding your at-home program

▶ Finding an attorney or planner

▶ Understanding why you need a will

. . . .

*W*e hate to be the bearers of bad news, but here it is: You're going to die someday. You, like all parents or guardians, have to plan for the likelihood that your child will outlive you.

Many parents find planning for their autistic child's special needs — for both the present and the future — overwhelming or intimidating. You don't know what's going to happen, so you decide to wait and see. Before you know it, the weeks turn into months, and the months turn into years. One day you may realize that time's running out and you haven't done anything.

Children grow up quickly. Many, many situations get in the way of special-needs planning in the short term, and a perfect time to plan doesn't exist. Your best bet is to get started and adjust the details of your plan as time passes. You won't be sorry if you overplan, but you will be sorry if you wait too long. If you don't plan ahead, your child may end up with a minimal income or be disqualified from government services entirely. Get started soon, and you will be glad that you did.

In this chapter, we cover the decisions you need to make such as what to leave your child in your will, who will be your child's guardian after you are gone, how to choose people to help you make the decisions, and how to think about your child's future care, supervision, security, and quality of life. We wrote this chapter with help from some experts in financial planning, and we try to address the most vexing questions.

Avoiding Common Financial Mistakes

We don't want you to be caught up short by not having done everything you can do financially for your child, so we asked Nadine Vogel, the mother of two disabled children and founder of MetDesk, a division of MetLife Insurance that helps parents with special-needs planning, to help you avoid the most common financial mistakes parents make. Here's what she told us:

- ✔ **Not drafting documents properly.** Many parents use otherwise competent financial professionals who don't know about special-needs laws. Professionals without this knowledge may make mistakes that can harm your child's financial future, such as drafting a will or life-insurance policy incorrectly. You need an attorney who specializes in special-needs planning to draft a will for your estate.

- ✔ **Not coordinating your financial life.** Parents or well-meaning relatives may unknowingly make your child the beneficiary of investments, for instance, that negatively affect your child's benefit eligibility. See the section "Keeping eligibility for government services in mind" in this chapter.

- ✔ **Not having enough information about laws impacting your child.** For example, parents may assume they're automatically the guardians of their 18- or 21-year-old child (your state determines the legal age limit), when they haven't actually gone through the legal procedure needed to obtain legal guardianship. You don't want to find out the hard way that you can't see your adult child's medical results under current federal law without the child's written permission. Your lawyer or local disabilities group should be able to help you with the laws in your state and county.

And, of course, the biggest mistake of all is not planning, which is why you're reading this chapter. MetLife conducted a survey that found that 60 percent of parents don't expect their special-needs children to become financially independent, yet the majority of parents hadn't written a will. Don't wait until it's too late! (For more info on drafting a will, see the section "Writing Your Will" later in this chapter.)

Putting Plan to Paper: Getting Started

To make decisions about your child's future, you'll need to think about several issues we discuss in this section, including his earning abilities and your financial situation. If you spend some time thinking about these issues initially, you will be better able to focus your planning. Ask yourself the following four questions:

✔ What's my child's prognosis to be able to support himself and manage his financial affairs? What's his earning potential?

✔ What government benefits does he receive now, and what is he eligible to receive?

✔ How am I doing, financially?

✔ What is the best living environment for my child?

The answers to these questions will help you to determine what will be in your will or family trust, whether your child will use government assistance, and who will take care of him after you are no longer able to.

Taking account of your child's prognosis

In order to plan for your family's financial future, you have to think about your child's prognosis. This task is difficult, especially if your child is young. Maybe your child will be much more independent than you can ever imagine, in which case you'll be happy to toss out these plans. You can start planning for college, in that event. On the other end of the spectrum, your child may need constant care and attention, in which case your planning may make all the difference. The best course of action is to be conservative right now and plan for the worst-case scenario. A professional evaluation may be necessary for younger children because you don't have objectivity. For adult children, you're probably aware of what he or she can do.

Now consider his or her earning potential. Can your child contribute financially, and if so, how much? Is he or she self-supporting at the present time, or can you envision such a scenario? Even if your son or daughter is employed, his or her job may not cover all the necessary living expenses.

In addition, although the person may be self-sufficient in personal care and the ability to work and earn an income, many people with special needs are easily influenced and manipulated. They may have difficulties with simple money and budget matters requiring assistance.

Don't forget college. Your child may wind up going to college, even if you didn't expect that to happen. In that event, you want to ensure that the assets you have allocated for planning can be transferred. Don't automatically dismiss the college option. This issue will continually creep up throughout the child's school career, so you need to be prepared for it.

Keeping eligibility for government services in mind

State and federal benefits are available even if your child works, but many parents of autistic children and adults with autism are unaware of these qualifications. Government benefits can help your child while you're alive as well as after you're gone.

Parents need to be mindful of eligibility requirements when financial planning, because a person with autism can lose his or her eligibility by inheriting too much. (Such benefits are *means-tested,* meaning the government takes into account your child's income or assets.)

For example, the federal Supplemental Security Income program (SSI) and Medicaid help pay for basic needs such as food, clothing, and medical care if your child has less than $2,000 in assets. Another major government benefit is the Social Security Administration's (SSA) Social Security Survivor/ Retirement Benefit. If a parent dies, or becomes disabled and/or retires, the person with autism may be eligible for cash benefits and Medicare. No means test exists for these benefits, and some people qualify for SSI, SSA, Medicaid, and Medicare simultaneously.

There are earned and unearned income caps that vary among the states for various government programs. The person must qualify medically based on his or her condition. IQ and previous employment are also considered for some government programs. Child support and adoption subsidies over the allowed limit can result in ineligibility or termination. Make sure you get the details from your state's government office.

Other government benefits such as Social Security Disability Insurance (SSDI) don't have financial eligibility requirements — regardless of what you leave to your son or daughter. After your child qualifies, the Social-Security payments will keep coming.

A helpful government organization is NICHCY, or the National Dissemination Center for Children with Disabilities (in case you're wondering, the name changed but the acronym didn't). This organization provides information on types of disabilities, research, and laws that apply to autism and other disabilities. You can contact NICHCY in writing at P.O. Box 1492, Washington, DC, 20013, by phone at 800-695-0285, by fax at 202-884-8441, or online at nichcy.org. You can download a host of government publications, in English and Spanish, there for free. (See the "Writing Your Will" section later in this chapter for more details about planning by the government's rules.)

Sizing up your estate

You need to know what you have to provide for your child later. Maybe you think "estate" is too grand a word for your paltry assets, but that's the legal term you hear when speaking with legal professionals. To size up your estate, write down every asset that you own; you may be pleasantly surprised!

When listing your assets, don't forget the following:

- ✔ Equity in your home and any other real estate
- ✔ Investments, such as stocks and bonds
- ✔ Pensions, annuities, IRAs, 401(k)s, and other retirement vehicles
- ✔ Appreciable art and antiques
- ✔ Life insurance policies that have a cash value

Considering living arrangements and guardianship

Where will your child live after you're gone, and who will be her guardian? Difficult as this prospect may be, you need to think about who will make the best decisions for her. You should name this person (or people) in your will. This key decision needs to be made immediately, because it greatly affects your child's future.

The guardianship decision means that you must consider the following: Who will provide daily care and supervision? Who will monitor doctors' visits, diet, medication, and therapy? What experience do future care providers have in caring for a person with autism? And who is qualified to attend the Individualized Education Program (IEP) meeting (see Chapter 12 for more about IEPs)? The "Designating guardianship" section later in this chapter provides more information about guardianship.

Involving an Attorney and/or Financial Planner

If you want to hire a professional to help with your family's special-needs planning, the best place to start is to make sure the person you choose has some experience in this area. Special-needs law is a specialty area that even an experienced trusts-and-estates attorney or seasoned financial planner may not know.

Most importantly, your advisors should never tell you what to do. They must listen to what you want for your loved one now and in the future. Their job is to fulfill your wishes through planning and document preparation. If anyone starts telling you to do this and do that, the smartest thing you can do is leave.

However, a growing number of specialists *are* entering the special-needs field — some even have personal experience with disabilities in their families. The best way to contact a professional with experience in the field may be to get a recommendation. Keep in mind, however, that planning is a team project. No individual can do it all alone. Here are some ways to get recommendations for professionals:

- ✔ Contact a local disabilities group to find someone familiar with special-needs issues.

- ✔ Call your local bar association or other trade group.

- ✔ Ask other local parents for referrals.

- ✔ Ask your insurance company, investment advisor, or other financial services company if it has services targeted for special-needs kids. MetLife, for example, has MetDesk, which has a toll-free number on its Web site (www.MetLife.com; choose the link for Individuals, and then click on Special Needs Planning). This organization gives free referrals to special-needs attorneys, support groups, and local disability advocates.

When you contact a professional, ask questions about his or her experience and philosophy, and don't feel that you're obligated to hire anyone whom you interview. Also, don't overlook the nonfinancial aspects of the prospective relationship. This kind of business relationship, where family members are involved, can present emotional decisions that require more than technical expertise. If the person is inexpensive but insensitive, you may find dealing with him too stressful to be worth the savings.

Here's what you can look for when interviewing prospective planning professionals:

- ✔ **Experience in working with special-needs families.** If you find the professional through a recommendation, you may already have this information. You may be able to find somebody new to this area who could work out fine, but why take a chance?

- ✔ **Expertise.** To do financial planning legally, no specific paper credential is required. Designations you may see are CPA, JD, MBA, CFP (Certified Financial Planner), but the most important expertise is familiarity with federal, state, and county laws regarding disabilities. The laws change frequently, and you need someone who's caught up.

There is one professional designation that signifies extensive expertise specifically in special-needs planning. The designation is Chartered Lifetime Assistance Planner (ChLAP), which is awarded to graduates of the National Center on Life Planning (NCLP), a nonprofit organization in Northridge, California, that provides planning services and has established a national training program and resource center for attorneys and other professional advisors on the subject of special-needs planning.

✔ **Communication skills.** Your lawyer/planner should be able to explain the laws and financial terminology in layman's terms, respectfully and not condescendingly, so that you know exactly what she's doing. It's your money! If you can't communicate well with the person, you should move on.

✔ **Personal sensitivity and tact.** The decisions you make about your child are fraught with emotional issues, and you need somebody who understands that and can deal with it.

✔ **Accessibility.** Who do you want doing the actual work: the person you interview or an intern? Does the person have a policy on returning phone calls? What about e-mail?

One other consideration is price. Ask the attorney/planner to estimate her fee in writing. If you think the fee is in line with the amount of work she'll be doing and what you expect to pay, good. If the fee sounds like more than you can afford, find out how reasonable it really is. But this is not the time to shop for a bargain. Choose your planner based on ability, not the fee. Fees are often negotiable, or you can ask to work out a payment plan. Most professionals who work with special-needs families know they face financial pressures and are more than willing to work with you. Also consider how the advisor is being compensated. Is the service being provided based on a fee, sale of product, or both? You need to know up front how it will work.

When working with a team of advisors (attorney, tax consultant, financial advisor), have a planning agreement prepared by each team member specifically stating the services to be provided and the cost before you commit. Some planners may take credit cards as a convenient option. If your child is on SSI or SSA programs, you may use these funds to pay fees.

Writing Your Will

If you have a child or close relative with autism, you need a will . . . it's that simple. Why, you ask? If you die *intestate* (or without a will), your state's laws determine where your assets go, and you don't want the government making such important decisions for you!

Although the laws vary from state to state, they generally mandate that all of your assets go to the surviving spouse. If there is no surviving spouse, then it goes to all surviving children in equal shares. Creating a will (or a living trust) that allocates your assets is the only way to be sure that all your family members distribute your assets in the manner that you decide.

You can always change or revoke your will before your death if circumstances change. Make the best decision you can with the information you have now. Being safe is better than doing nothing. Also, as your attorney will remind you, be aware that your will doesn't control all your assets. Items such as life insurance (with your spouse as beneficiary) and joint property go to your spouse upon your death, no matter what your will says. Additionally, investment vehicles such as IRAs, 401(k)s, and annuities pass by beneficiary designation and must be changed. You don't want your child to receive a direct death benefit payment after both of his parents have died.

Also, make sure grandparents' wills aren't drafted in such a way that the grandchild with autism could receive an inheritance. This situation could happen if the parent dies before his parents (the grandparents of the autistic child).

We recommend that you hire a professional attorney to prepare your will. Wills are a technical subject, and creating a will isn't a do-it-yourself proposition. The advice we give you in this section is general advice, not legal advice, but it should help get you going in the right direction.

Setting up a special-needs trust

Many parents set up a special-needs trust in their will to make sure their child has money for recreation, travel, and education while maintaining his right to federal assistance if anything happens to you. If dividing your assets amongst your children affects your autistic child's ability to receive benefits, you leave your child out in the cold after you're gone.

The information we provide in this section is for you if you decide not to will your money to your disabled child. The special-needs trust is designed to keep his assets safe. You need a lawyer, qualified paralegal, or legal document preparer to draw up this trust. The person who prepares your will should know how to do this.

Deciding if a special-needs trust is right for your child

If your autistic child can manage her own finances, you need to determine whether she may one day need to depend on government benefits such as Supplemental Security Insurance (SSI), subsidized housing, personal attendant care, or Medicaid. You need to think long-term. If you think she may need these types of services, a trust may be the way to go.

Special-needs trusts come in different forms. Evaluate whether you are getting the correct document by discussing the following questions with a professional:

- ✔ When are you planning to fund the trust?
- ✔ Have any other family members stated that they want to leave some of their assets to the special-needs trust?
- ✔ Is the trust being funded by a court settlement?
- ✔ Do you want to use the trust funds now?
- ✔ Do you want to transfer your child's assets to the trust?

With the wrong type of trust, you risk the loss of government and other benefits. Some trusts are state specific. Do your homework on this before signing anything.

Of course, if your child is highly functioning and not eligible for means-tested benefits, you may want to leave her part of your estate. Plan based on your child's abilities today, not what you hope for. You can always change your plan.

Considering ways you can fund the trust

Parents frequently fund special-needs trusts through life insurance. Life insurance is a common vehicle because it helps people of modest means "create an estate." It's also very important to know the type of life insurance policy you are purchasing. Make sure it will fund the trust upon your death.

If you and your spouse are retired or close to retirement, and your children are adults, you may have pensions, a home with high equity, and no financial responsibility to other children. In this case, you don't need insurance. Rental properties, mutual funds, stocks, inheritance, and gifts from others — any income-producing asset — will suffice.

Putting your special-needs plan in play

Setting up a special-needs trust requires many considerations on your part, including disinheriting your child, writing a letter of intent, and appointing a trustee.

Disinheriting your child

Strange as it may sound, disinheriting your autistic son or daughter may be the kindest step you can take if your assets aren't enormous (like most of us!) and your child isn't completely self-supporting. In these cases, the federal and state governments are obligated to support your child. You disinherit your child by not leaving him financial assets in your will, or you leave him a token amount such as $1 to show that you have not forgotten him. As Jaime Parent, father of an autistic adult who speaks frequently on financial planning for disabilities, says, "Your child owns nothing." Parent, who lives in Maryland, also highly recommends purchasing a life insurance policy for your own peace of mind. Other advocates suggest that it is unnecessary if you have other assets to fund the child's trust.

When you disinherit your child, you must make sure that Grandma, cousin George in Toronto, and your child's best friend don't make him the beneficiary of their wills or of any insurance policies. You need to explain that their generous and well-intended gifts could end up hurting your child by disqualifying him from the benefits he depends on. You better check your own policies, too, while you're at it! Let's say Grandma leaves your child $5,000 during your lifetime. He can't just write out a check to you once he's receiving government benefits, because authorities will ask questions about any questionable transactions. They may want to reduce his benefits by the amount of the gift, something you'd probably like to avoid.

In the worst-case scenario, money received by a child with autism can be transferred out of his or her name without affecting benefits, if you have the right type of trust. If the amount is small (say under $10,000), reimbursement or prepayment of rent (if the child is over 18) is one way. If the amount is over $10,000 from an inheritance or a legal settlement, an OBRA93 Special Needs Trust may be appropriate (OBRA93 stands for Omnibus Budget and Reconciliation Act, which was created in 1993). This type of special-needs trust is funded by the person with autism. It is the most restrictive type of trust and has a payback provision to the government after the beneficiary dies. The fact that it allows your child to remain on SSI and Medicaid overrides any of its provisions.

When you fill out government forms, you want to be able to say that your child has no assets at all, not a checking account containing $2,000, for example. If he has one, agency officials will monitor the account to make sure it stays under $2,000. Your best course of action is to clean out the assets entirely, as tough as that may seem.

Writing a letter of intent

Another part of the special-needs trust process is writing a *letter of intent* — a statement that sets out your wishes for your child's care for a future caregiver (who may be a different person from the trustee). It shouldn't even be mentioned in any legal document so it isn't construed to be a part of it, which enables you to write anything and not worry about legal language. Nobody other than the care providers can prepare this letter because the advisors don't have intimate knowledge of the person. The letter of intent is a document that is ever-changing as the person grows and matures. You can make changes without having to use an attorney, notarize signatures, and have witnesses each time. Your special-needs planner may have a template that you can follow when drafting the letter. The following should be included in this letter:

- Information on your child's physical and mental condition — this is the most important part of your letter

- Medications, physicians, food allergies, and medical history

- Your aspirations for your child's future

- Your beliefs about issues such as dating and marriage, religion, living situation, work, and academic plans for your child

- Your child's interests, hopes and dreams, hobbies, social habits, likes and dislikes

This information helps the future caregiver manage your child's daily activities after you're gone. But don't wait to give the letter of intent to people — it's invaluable now to other family members, friends, teachers, school nurse, therapists, and government support coordinators. It tells them everything they need to know now about your child. You can sometimes obtain templates for these letters from special-needs planners.

Appointing a trustee

You also need to appoint a trustee. You charge the trustee whom you name in your will with managing the funds in the special-needs trust. That person may be a relative, a family friend, or possibly a professional trustee. You can obtain professional referrals from places such as MetLife or Merrill Lynch. Trust companies include Wells Fargo, Chase Manhattan, Harris Trust, Mass Mutual Trust Company, Heartland Financial, and Northern Trust.

Before naming an institution as a trustee, you must meet with a representative and know their fees, services, and minimum amount it will manage. Often there is a minimum you must meet to qualify.

Families have the option of naming a trusted friend or family member as a cotrustee with a financial institution. Or you may elect to name family or friends without an institution. Trustees can hire professionals for investment, tax, and management advice.

You must carefully design the trust so that the trustee (who has complete authority over its funds) doesn't allow the beneficiary (your child) too much income so that his benefits are jeopardized. This is a great example of why you need an attorney who understands special-needs planning and is familiar with your state's trust laws (see the section "Involving an Attorney and/or Financial Planner" earlier in this chapter).

The trust must also stipulate the following:

- What happens to the trust funds after the beneficiary dies, along with funeral arrangements for the beneficiary

- Who becomes the trustee if the original trustee dies

✔ That the funds supplement, not replace, other benefits (Items that don't reduce federal payments include medical care, telephone bills, education, and entertainment.)

✔ That the trust not be used to pay family debts

Other decisions that you need to make with respect to the special-needs trust and your will, with the help of an attorney, are as follows:

✔ Choosing a revocable or irrevocable trust. This means whether you can remove funds from the trust while you're still alive, in the event of an emergency. A revocable special-needs trust with assets in excess of $2,000 will result in the loss of or ineligibility for government benefits. The trust must be irrevocable in order for the assets not to be considered to belong to the person with autism. Don't put money in the special-needs trust if you think you may need it back! You can't take it back or use it for anyone else in an irrevocable trust.

✔ Choosing a living or testamentary trust. *Living* means you and others can fund it now and use it; *testamentary* means it goes into effect after the parents' deaths. The problem with testamentary is that no one (for example, your child's grandparents) can name a testamentary trust as beneficiary if they don't know when it will be in effect.

✔ Determining how to take care of the autistic child without excluding her siblings in your will.

Giving a morally obligated gift

If your child needs a great deal of help and disinheriting him seems too harsh (see the section "Putting your special-needs plan in play" for more on the topic of disinheriting), consider this option for your will: You can gift one of the child's siblings with what's called a *morally obligated* gift. This gift indicates that you give the money to one of the siblings and trust her to share it with your autistic child in the way that you spell out before your death.

Obviously, you must trust that your child will carry out your wishes if you do this. A morally obligated gift isn't legally enforceable, and that's the rub. Use this only as a last resort. If you go this route, you can still leave items to your autistic child that may have personal value to him, as long as they don't exceed $2,000 in worth.

Your son or daughter, if mentally competent, can hire whatever assistance he or she needs to help with managing the gift.

Even if your autistic child's sibling is responsible, however, he may have difficulty carrying out your wishes. He may become ill or disabled, or he may go bankrupt. He may have to make difficult choices. He may die or divorce, putting the money into other hands. Because of these risks, if your autistic child needs lifetime care, morally obligated gifts may put siblings under too much pressure. It may take a little more work in the beginning, but we recommend a trust as the strongest option, regardless of how trustworthy your child is.

Designating guardianship

The topic is hard to even think about, but you need to decide who you want to take care of your child if something happens to you before she's of legal age or if she's incapable of making her own decisions when she turns 18 or 21. (If you're around when she reaches the age of maturity, and she's incapable of making her own decisions, you may want to consider having yourself declared her legal guardian. If she can make her own decisions for the most part, you have a dilemma.)

When choosing a guardian, make a list of everyone you know, eliminate the ones you know you don't want, put the others in the order you want them to serve, and then ask them in succession. You can use this same method when choosing successor trustees.

If your child isn't able to read and understand on an adult level, can't drive a motor vehicle, and can't manage her affairs, you're helping her by becoming her guardian. You shouldn't beat yourself up about it. You aren't taking her freedom from her. Some states are even beginning to pass legislation that allows adults with guardians the right to vote and drive.

We asked Bart Stevens, owner of Bart Stevens Special Needs Planning, LLC — a provider of fee-based planning services (on the Web at www.bssnp.com or toll free at 888-447-2525) — and author of *The ABC's of Special Needs Planning Made Easy* (The Stevens Group, LLC, Scottsdale, Arizona), for his suggestions on guardianship. This is what he said:

> ✔ The first step is to evaluate, with the help of professionals, your child's abilities. Pay close attention to her when she performs typical activities such as dressing, bathing, toileting, preparing meals, and so on. Evaluate your child and make the decision that is in your child's best interest. You can always rescind guardianship at a later time or apply for it as well.
>
> If all parties agree that the child isn't capable of performing these activities, full legal guardianship may be appropriate.

Many states offer the option of limited guardianship specifically for healthcare, finances, education, and so on.

✔ Another option is that the person with autism can execute a living will and power of attorney for healthcare, finances, and legal matters. This doesn't take away any rights. If the person with autism has no assets, the courts may appoint an attorney at no charge, and court costs may be waived. The person can change and/or terminate the living will at any time. The person can also override any decisions made by the person with power unless otherwise stated.

Friends and/or family can fill any of the guardianship positions. Some states offer public and private fiduciary services when you can't find anyone to serve. You may choose one or more guardians to serve together. Also, if the person with autism moves to another state of residence, a guardian has to repetition to maintain guardian status. Successor guardians must also go through the petition process. States vary in their guardianship procedures.

Part V
The Part of Tens

"My daughter is autistic, but don't worry, once she calms down she'll act just like you minus the contemptuously judgmental glare."

In this part . . .

Parents and teachers of children with autism compile plenty of lists. Lists of behavioral symptoms, lists of medications, lists of foods to avoid, lists of goals and accommodations, and so on. Other lists can include support groups and friends you can call when you just need to reach out and talk to someone. We're not immune to the list craze, so we provide you with some top-ten lists in this part.

We include some good tips on how to manage uncomfortable or difficult conversations with tact, and, possibly most importantly, we give you ten things to do following an autism diagnosis.

And toward the end of the book, you find an Appendix containing additional resources to aid in your efforts to help the person with autism you support lead a fulfilling and productive life (even if that person is you!).

Chapter 17

Ten Tactful Responses to Challenging Questions or Comments

Sadly, people with autism often face social disapproval — not because they look different, but because they look so "normal." Unlike other disabilities, autism doesn't clearly disable a person on the outside. People with autism are expected to behave "normally," which can make life difficult for them and for their parents. Parents face unwanted, awkward choices: Do you explain to others that your child is special, or do you hope that they won't judge you or invade your privacy if your child does something disruptive?

We're here to help ease your discomfort, if only momentarily. This chapter gives you tips for handling some common uncomfortable situations you may encounter, whether you're a person with autism or the caregiver of one.

"What Special Talent Does He Have?"

You think you've finally found somebody who's sympathetic and nonjudgmental to talk to. You're happily conversing, and then out of nowhere comes the dreaded "What special talent does he have" query. People usually deliver this question in a friendly way, but suddenly your child is reduced to the status of circus performer and conversation piece.

Whether your child has a "special talent" isn't really relevant here. The point is that you don't want to reduce him to being capable of only that ability. Would your companion ask you that about your other children? Would he or she be comfortable with you posing the same query? The implication is upsetting and annoying.

Was the person's motive rudeness? No, it was simple ignorance. The person's friendliness attests to his or her goodwill. So you may want to give the benefit of the doubt. Here are some gentle ways to educate somebody asking this question:

✔ "Some autistic children have special talents and some don't, just like the rest of us. What's *your* special talent?"

✔ "I don't know, but I can tie my tongue into a knot."

✔ "We don't think of him that way. We think everything he does shows talent, considering how hard he has to work to overcome his disability."

✔ "He puts up with dumb questions from strangers." (Just kidding! Stop! You should run this through your head to make yourself smile before moving to one of the previous suggestions.)

"Why Can't You Control Your Kid?"

Variations on the control-your-kid theme are numerous: "What kind of parent lets his/her child misbehave that way?" "Didn't you teach her any manners?" "Let me have your child for a weekend . . . I'll straighten her out!" Or just a plain-old, judgmental Bad-Parent Look.

People with autism often perceive the world very differently from others, which results in unexpected differences in behavior. Although the lighting in a department store may simply seem garish to some, it may be totally overwhelming to a person who sees fluorescent lighting like a strobe light. The result is a sensory-overload tantrum. Can you blame the person? Most people would be uncomfortable shopping in a store lit with strobe lights. (For more on sensory issues, see Chapter 10.)

Also, most people can filter and prioritize incoming sensory data, which allows you to ignore sounds, lights, and other information that isn't important in a given situation. Many people with autism lack this ability. They have an experience comparable to watching a television set that receives all 500 or more channels at once with the volume at full blast.

When someone asks, "Why can't you control your kid," the implication is that you're a failed, weak, negligent parent, which is why your child doesn't behave. Please don't be tempted to believe this if you get this kind of feedback. When other people misunderstand or misjudge you, it can be painful and frustrating. However, if you know that you're doing the best job you can for your child, you don't have to let these emotions get to you.

"Asperger Snausperger. He Looks Fine. He Just Needs a Better Attitude."

Hearing criticism from others about your parenting is more likely if you have a child with Asperger Syndrome than with kids who have more severe forms of autism. Children with Asperger's appear to be like everybody else, which means they don't get cut much slack for unusual behavior.

So what can you do about other parents who criticize your parenting? What about people who refuse to acknowledge your child's diagnosis? You can point out that most people used to think the earth was flat and that evil spirits caused epilepsy. It may be better, however, to give them something to read about autism. Education can be the best revenge.

Some parents and people with autism carry wallet-sized cards or pamphlets you can purchase from the Autism Society of America (`www.autism-society.org`) and other organizations to hand to ignorant strangers. If people refuse to listen, quietly move on. They've made their choice. You can help educate only those who have open minds.

"Who Did He Inherit It From?"

A person who asks "Who did he inherit it from?" reveals ignorance more than anything else. This question makes you feel defensive, as if you must explain something you don't even fully understand yourself. You wish others would think about the implications of what they say before opening their mouths.

You can say, "Yes, current research indicates that autism has a strong genetic factor, which then gets triggered by something else." But you're not responsible for explaining the causes of autism to the world, especially because research hasn't established causation anyway (see Chapter 3). You have enough on your plate. Just say, "I don't know," and leave it at that.

You can also go for a humorous response if you like. Both parents can eagerly claim genetic responsibility. Or if only one spouse is present, you can state — with a smile — "Although my spouse claims responsibility, I know that the genes come from MY side."

"Why Should Your Child Get Special Treatment?"

People usually don't wonder outright why your child gets special treatment, but that can be implied when parents try to arrange special services for their children, such as accommodations in school or behavioral, educational, or developmental programs (see Chapters 9 and 10). The best defense is to know your rights. Under the law, your child has the right to an education, and if his education costs more than others, that's irrelevant. (See Chapter 12 to find out more about your rights.) What's relevant is that he gets the help he needs.

Similarly, children with disabilities don't fall under the same laws regarding school disciplinary procedures, nor should they. If they don't understand in the first place that a behavior is against the rules, autistic kids can't be held to the same standard. Their behavior is different from willful misbehavior. The school isn't giving special treatment, it's using common sense. We present a good Functional Behavioral Assessment in Chapter 11 that will usually reveal the sensory, pragmatic, or other underpinnings of challenging behaviors.

As with many other questions, education may be the best response. Do your best to educate others about the obstacles presented by autism as well as the contributions to society by people with differences, such as Albert Einstein and Thomas Edison.

You don't have to justify your child's treatment. A child with autism should get what he needs because he needs it. Simple as that. The Individuals with Disabilities Education Act, the Americans with Disabilities Act, and common decency say so.

"Are You Kidnapping That Child?"

When an autistic child acts up in public, it may look like her parents are abusing or even kidnapping her. Security may even approach the parents on the child's behalf.

Keep your cool and consider your objective when responding to accusations from strangers. If you get upset, you solidify someone's negative judgment of you. A soft answer may disarm the most narrow-minded busybody. A person who's really concerned will probably back off.

This situation happened to Dennis Debbaudt, a private investigator, when his autistic child was in the midst of a full-blown tantrum as he carried him through a mall parking lot. Dennis has devoted his life to helping policemen, firefighters, and other first responders with his book, *Autism, Advocates, and Law Enforcement Professionals: Recognizing and Reducing Risk Situations for People with Autism Spectrum Disorders* (Jessica Kingsley Publishers).

The "Bad-Parent" Look

The bad-parent look can be among the hardest things to deal with because it's just a look (or sometimes just body language), but it implies that you're lower than a politician with a racketeering indictment and deserving of zero respect. And your options for response are limited because the judgment is indirect. How can you respond when nothing is actually said? Maybe you don't want to respond, but you feel like you should set the record straight.

Ask yourself what you hope to accomplish. Are you responding for yourself or for your child? Are you too worried about what others will think if you say something or if you don't say anything? Are you missing a chance to educate others about autism if you don't? We can't give you a right or wrong answer.

The trouble with responding calmly in these situations is that you have the added drama of dealing with your child while trying to appear under control. This makes a neutral, nondefensive tone difficult to convey.

One way to deal with the situation is to ask, "Pardon me?" or "May I help you?" as sweetly as humanly possible. A judgmental person will be so embarrassed that he or she will just mutter something incomprehensible and scoot away.

"Is She Still in Her Own World?"

The question "Is she still in her own world?" is an all-time candidate for insensitivity. In fact, due to sensory hypersensitivities, many people with autism are so much more aware of the world around them that it's painful. Imagine being able to hear the ticking of every electric clock in the house or being driven to distraction from the crinkling of a plastic bag that someone is stuffing under the kitchen sink.

Our friend Kassiane Sibley, a person on the autism spectrum, recommends a couple routes to take in response, each with a bit different tone. Here's the first, more . . . ahem . . . bold response: (Staring blankly) "Who else's world would she be in? I mean, really. It's not like they beam us all off the planet at age 22. Do they? If they did I missed my flight. Darn."

She takes a more educational approach with this response: "Or, alternatively, you can explain how autistic people tune out because they are overwhelmed by a world that is too loud, too bright, talks too fast with weird figures of speech . . . and so as a protective mechanism, people on the spectrum often tune out. Autistic people like precise language. Asking if an autistic person is in his or her own world has a pretty good chance of getting hackles up. That's why he or she is glaring at you silently instead of answering although he or she may be perfectly verbal."

You have multiple ways to answer the same question, so have fun!

"They Grow Out of It, Don't They?"

A person who says, "They grow out of it, don't they?" says it out of innocence, or out of ignorance, perhaps. Although it isn't your personal duty to educate everyone you meet about autism, you can combat flagrant misconceptions. In this situation, we recommend a neutral reply to the effect that autism remains a lifelong challenge for those who have it.

"But She Doesn't Look Autistic . . ."

People diagnosed with autism, Asperger Syndrome, or Pervasive Developmental Disorder — Not Otherwise Specified (see Chapter 2) don't look any different than anyone else. They may exhibit differences in behavior or movement, but aside from the possibility of children with Asperger Syndrome having slightly larger heads, outsiders can see no defining features.

The lack of physical differences results in confusion to people not in the know. They expect more from your child than he or she may be able to give. Autism is a difference in how the brain is wired, not of the body. Possible responses can range from brief education about the brain being wired differently to talking about other conditions such as heart disease and diabetes not resulting in any physical differences.

Chapter 18

Ten Things to Do after a Diagnosis

*W*hen you first receive the diagnosis of an autism spectrum disorder (ASD) for your child, whether you suspect it or not, the news can be a major shock. In this chapter, we offer ten tips for getting started after diagnosis, captured at one of our favorite Web sites, www.autisminfo.com. (Thanks to Brad Middlebrook, an occupational therapist, for his permission to adapt the tips for our readers.) Although each step may logically progress from one to the next, you may want to do more than one simultaneously.

Learn and Read as Much as Possible

When you begin researching, the glut of available information and advice can be overwhelming. You may find that the information seems very complicated, but press on. The more you read and discover, the easier it will be to understand new information. Even the complicated medical information will begin to make sense. Think of the task of researching as putting together a huge puzzle. But always remember to consider the source of any information you find. Also, try to keep an open mind by not focusing on one intervention or therapy exclusively. No treatment works for everyone. Search until you find the right combination for your child.

For not much money, you can stay informed by checking out and subscribing to newsletters offered by major autism organizations such as the Autism Society of America (ASA), Unlocking Autism (UA), the Autism Research Institute (ARI), and Cure Autism Now! (CAN!). We list the organizations and publications in the Appendix along with other helpful resources you can use to expand your research. You can also ask your local library to buy more books on autism.

If it seems like you're getting more familiar with your computer than your family, you may be spending too much time online. You need to strike a balance between researching and networking and spending time with your family.

Network with Other Families

Many parents of children with autism preach that other families in similar situations provide the most important support system of all. If you're active in the autism community, which we recommend (see Chapter 14), you'll meet numerous parents at support groups and conferences who are going through the same struggles and are happy to share their experiences. This camaraderie can greatly reduce the sense of isolation you may be feeling. You can find leads to support groups through the Appendix in this book, as well as through parents of other children diagnosed with autism and therapists and other professionals.

If you can't make it to conferences or support-group meetings, you can purchase audiotapes or watch Web casts of many conferences. But do make every effort to attend these sessions. The people you meet can be even more helpful than the presentations you attend.

Test, Test, Test

Test your child early to get a baseline picture of where he or she is. A clear picture of your child's biological condition provides a roadmap for treatments and therapies to follow. If you can't afford all the tests you need up front, prioritize them — with your medical providers' help. (See Part II for more testing and medical information.)

Investigate Sources of Financial Aid

You must continually pursue avenues of financial aid. Autism can quickly exhaust your resources, but, fortunately, funding and assistance do exist. Financial aid is generally available at the county level for children under the age of 3. You need to apply for the Medicaid waiver, known in some states as the Katy Beckett deeming waiver. If you don't ask, you won't receive. (See Chapter 16 for more.)

Keep good financial records. Any organization that gives you funding may want a reasonable accounting from time to time. And avoid using the words "autism" or "PDD-NOS" with insurance companies. If you're treating biological abnormalities such as a yeast overgrowth, abnormal immune markers, or diarrhea, have the doctor code the treatment as such. Many HMOs specifically exclude autism in their policies, but your child deserves treatment for his health problems, just as any neurotypical child would get.

Consider Major Lifestyle Changes

Treating autism can seriously drain your financial resources. Depending on your situation, you may have to enact major change (such as changing your job or downsizing your home). Of course, you should consider all your options before doing something drastic; you may need to make only short-term sacrifices to allow for the funds that you'll need to treat your child. The good news is that the costs you have are often not permanent; they're upfront costs that may not last for more than a few years.

If you have a spouse or significant other, you need to support each other and establish a division of responsibilities. You need to understand the time commitment associated with caring for an individual with an autism spectrum disorder. Take time to think about how this added responsibility will impact your life and possibly your relationships with others. You may need to take steps to reorganize where you devote your time in order to make increased allowances for treating someone with autism.

Autism treatment takes sacrifice, but the hard work pays off. Many parents will tell you that the emotional rewards you experience — regardless of your child's progress — are much more lasting than any hobby or house can bring.

Set Up an Educational/Behavioral Program in Your Home

If you can afford it, a structured one-on-one program that focuses on education and behavior works for many children with autism (see Chapter 9). Just make sure the program is reputable, and be certain everyone involved with the program shares your expectations and goals. Have your tutors and consultants read and sign a contract you put together that specifically states what they'll do and what you'll do. A contract puts everyone on the same page, literally.

Begin Therapies

The medical professional who diagnoses your child may refer him to other specialists for therapy, including speech, occupational, and physical therapy. These therapies help your child gain communication, social, and physical skills (see Chapters 9 and 10). Insurance providers, including Medicaid, often cover the cost.

Address Your Child's Diet and Nutrition

Dietary sensitivities affect many people with autism. Consider trying diets (such as the wheat-free and dairy-free diets explained in Chapter 8) that have helped many children respond with better behavior within about 3 to 4 weeks.

Based on medical testing and your doctor's recommendations, you also should start your child on vitamin and mineral supplementation geared for his needs. It's likely your child isn't meeting his body's nutritional needs (many autistic people have nutritional deficiencies). Be sure to consult with a nutritionist and pediatrician who have expertise in autism. Find good ones you feel comfortable with and trust, even if they don't live in your area. (For more on supplementation, see Chapters 7 and 8.)

As you clean up and possibly restrict the diet of your child, try doing the same for yourself. Autism drains you physically, especially if you're not in good health. Find time to exercise and eat right to improve your health — both you and your child will benefit.

Don't Give Up

Attitude is everything! From the start, try to be a morale booster for your doctors, therapists, teachers, and family. Remember, autism shouldn't preclude you from laughing and having fun together as a family. Educate your doctors who aren't familiar with autistic patients, and encourage them to read about autism. Provide up-to-date information to those who can help you.

Many of the treatments and interventions take time to produce results. Be patient. Work hard every day after the diagnosis, and demand that others work hard as well. It *will* pay off.

Get Out and Relax

After you find out everything you need to do for your child, you may be tempted to give up everything you do for yourself and put the focus solely on your child. But making time for yourself and relaxing are necessary. You must take care of yourself to be of any good to your child. Encourage your spouse to take time to recharge as well.

Appendix

Where to Go for More Help

Maybe your goal for this book is to gather as much info as you can to provide your autistic child with the best treatment possible. Maybe you want to pick out the best doctors, diets, and treatment plans medicine has to offer. Maybe you, an autistic adult, want information on making the transition to interdependence. For these goals and many more, our book is all you need! However, autism research advances almost daily, and doctors discover more and more as time passes about this condition and how to help people with autism recover function to lead fulfilling and productive lives. Therefore, you should have additional resources at your disposal to keep up with the times.

In this Appendix, we provide a classified list of additional resources that will help you discover more about the autism spectrum as you continue to support and nurture the people with autism you know and love. Consider this compilation the beginning of a journey, where we lead you to many other useful resources that we can't include here due to limited space.

Even if you don't agree with some of the philosophies promoted by some of these organizations, keep in mind that it can be useful to know what people and organizations are doing and thinking about in the diverse world of autism. As with other challenges you face in life, you should consider multiple sources according to your needs.

Finding Other Helpful Texts

This section provides a list of publishers that specialize in autism-related books, research journals, and magazines.

Temple Grandin's recommended reading

Dr. Temple Grandin, a university professor who has autism, has plenty of expertise and personal experience with autism, which gives her a unique perspective on the information available. With this in mind, we asked her to come up with a list of books that she personally recommends — books that provide parents and teachers with more detailed practical information beyond what may be included in *Understanding Autism For Dummies*. Dr. Grandin struggled to narrow down the list, but here are her top choices. (You can read more about Dr. Temple Grandin in her classic *Thinking in Pictures,* 2nd Edition [Vintage Press].)

✔ *Asperger's Syndrome: A Guide for Parents and Professionals,* by Tony Attwood, with a forward by Lorna Wing, PhD (Jessica Kingsley Publishers). This book provides practical insights and advice for working with both children and adults. (Watch for Tony's upcoming book due out soon: *The Complete Guide to Asperger's Syndrome,* which features more of Tony's expertise in areas such as the development of social skills and relationships and career advice.)

✔ *A Treasure Chest of Behavioral Strategies for Individuals with Autism* (Future Horizons), by Beth Fouse and Maria Wheeler, special education teachers with years of practical experience in solving difficult behavior problems. This book should be especially useful if you work with children or older individuals with poor verbal skills.

✔ *Behavioral Intervention for Young Children with Autism: A Manual for Parents and Professionals* (Pro-Ed, Inc.), edited by Catherine Maurice, Gina Green, and C. Luce. Maurice successfully used behavioral treatments to teach her child language with the Lovaas method (see Chapter 9). The clear instructions for teaching young children are very valuable, but Temple recommends that you skip the biased editorializing.

✔ *Navigating the Social World: A Curriculum for Individuals with Asperger's Syndrome, High Functioning Autism and Related Disorders* (Future Horizons), by Jeanette McAfee, MD. The author provides simple-to-use exercises and lessons for teaching all-important social skills, such as greeting and meeting new people.

✔ *Biomedical Assessment Options for Children with Autism and Related Problems,* published by the Autism Research Institute (ARI), a San Diego–based research and advocacy group, and written by John B. Pangborn, PhD, and Sidney M. Baker, MD. (It's also known as the DAN [Defeat Autism Now] Protocol and is available from ARI's Web site, www.autismwebsite.com/ari/index.htm). This text contains the latest scientific information on the use of nutrients, special diets, vitamins, and other non-drug treatments.

✔ *Taking the Mystery Out of Medications in Autism/Asperger Syndrome* (Future Horizons), by Luke Tsai, MD. This is an easy-to-read overview of medications used to treat disorders that often occur in conjunction with autism spectrum disorders (we discuss medications in Chapter 6).

✔ *Autism: An Inside Out Approach* (Jessica Kingsley Publishers), by Donna Williams, a gifted writer and artist who has overcome the communication challenges of her autism and an abusive childhood. This book is a must read for people working or living with nonverbal, low-functioning individuals with autism and for those seeking to understand their own sensory problems. Williams has written other, better-known books, but this one provides the best descriptions of her very severe sensory problems.

Specializing in autism spectrum disorders

These publishers provide other helpful texts about autism:

- ✔ **Autism Asperger Publishing Company** (www.asperger.net): A premier source for easy-to-read research-based books that focus on providing practical solutions for interventions that help people with Asperger Syndrome and high-functioning autism. This company also hosts autism-related conferences.

  15490 Quivira Rd., P.O. Box 23173, Shawnee Mission, KS 66283
  877-277-8254

- ✔ **Future Horizons** (www.futurehorizons-autism.com): The oldest of the autism publishers provides a range of books pertaining to the autism spectrum. The publisher also hosts numerous autism conferences.

  721 West Abram St., Arlington, TX 76013
  800-489-0727

- ✔ **Jessica Kingsley Publishers** (www.jkp.com): The largest publisher of autism and other psychologically oriented books for parents and professionals.

  116 Pentonville Rd., London N1 9JB
  +44 (020)7833-2307

  400 Market St., Suite 400, Philadelphia, PA 19106
  866-416-1078

Special-education publishers

Check out these books and other materials on autism:

- ✔ **DRL Books, Inc.** (www.DRLbooks.com): Publishes books focused on educating children with autism and other developmental disabilities.

  12 West 18th St., Suite 3E, New York, NY 10017
  800-853-1057

- ✔ **Paul H. Brookes Publishing Co.** (www.pbrookes.com): Books, tests, curriculum, and other materials made primarily for teachers and other professionals who deal with autism and other disabilities regularly.

  P.O. Box 10624, Baltimore, MD 21285
  800-638-3775

- ✔ **Pro-Ed** (www.proedinc.com): This company creates tests, resource and reference texts, curriculum, and materials for therapy for children with autism and other disabilities.

  8700 Shoal Creek Blvd., Austin, TX 78757
  800-897-3202

- ✔ **Woodbine House** (www.woodbinehouse.com): An outfit that publishes books for parents, teachers, children, and professionals who interact with autistic and other special-needs individuals.

  6510 Bells Mill Rd., Bethesda, MD 20817
  800-843-7323

Research journals and magazines

You may find the following autism journals and magazines helpful:

- ✔ **The Advocate** (www.autism-society.org): Published quarterly by the Autism Society of America, *The Advocate* publishes research and articles of interest regarding the entire autism spectrum.

- ✔ **Autism Asperger Digest** (www.autismdigest.com): Devoted to presenting advice from the world's experts on autism (including those with autism), the *Autism Asperger Digest* gives you practical information you can put to immediate use.

- ✔ **The Autism Perspective** (www.theautismperspective.org): Published by Nicki Fischer, the focus of *The Autism Perspective* is on providing clear and unbiased contributions from people with autism, parents, researchers, and others supporting those on the autism spectrum.

- ✔ **Autism Spectrum Quarterly** (www.asquarterly.com): A cross between a journal and a magazine, this publication provides researched-based information about autism with the readability of a magazine.

- ✔ **Journal of Autism and Developmental Disorders** (www.kluweronline. com/issn/0162-3257/contents): A research-based journal focused on publishing evidence-based, peer-reviewed articles on the latest research on the autism spectrum.

Surfing Informative Sites on the Web

The Internet is a wonderful place to find resources for and information about autism. However, material written for the Web may not undergo vigorous review for accuracy. Be sure to verify what you read on the Web.

Connecting with advocacy organizations

This section provides a list of organizations devoted to supporting the autism community and related causes.

- ✔ **Advocates for High Functioning Autism, Asperger Syndrome, and Pervasive Developmental Disorders** (www.AHA-AS-PDD.org): Through publications and conferences, this organization provides objective, up-to-date, reliable, evidence-based info that enables you to thoughtfully evaluate any proposed treatment for persons with autism.

- ✔ **Asperger's Association of New England (AANE)** (www.aane.org): This organization offers information, support groups, educational teacher in-services, and conferences.

- ✔ **Autism One** (www.autismone.org): A parent-oriented group focused on biomedical issues, education, advocacy, adult issues, and fundraising for autism. Autism One holds an annual conference in May in Chicago.

- ✔ **Autism Research Institute (ARI)** (www.autismwebsite.com/ari/index.html): This institute is dedicated to broadcasting results of research on the causes, prevention, diagnosing, and treatment of autism.

- ✔ **Autism Society of America (ASA)** (www.autism-society.org): The oldest and most comprehensive autism organization features several state and regional chapters. In addition to providing information on autism and engaging in governmental advocacy, this organization hosts national and regional conferences on autism.

- ✔ **Autism Speaks** (www.autismspeaks.org): Having recently joined forces with the National Alliance for Autism Research (NAAR), co-founders Suzanne and Bob Wright strive to give a voice to all "dealing with the hardships of autism." Their focus is on funding biomedical research into the causes, prevention, treatments, and the eventual cure of autism.

- ✔ **AutismLink** (www.autismlink.com): A site that has a relatively comprehensive and nonbiased listing of support groups and treatment services available in each state. The site also links to chat rooms, listserves, and discussion forums.

- ✔ **Cure Autism Now (CAN)** (www.cureautismnow.org): Funds research for finding the causes, prevention, and treatment of (and cure for) autism.

- ✔ **Defeat Autism Now (DAN)** (www.danconference.com): This organization is dedicated to educating people primarily about biomedically based research and effective interventions for autism. It holds two annual and other regional conferences.

- ✔ **Families for Early Autism Treatment (FEAT)** (www.feat.org): A parent organization with chapters around the United States that are dedicated to the education of, advocacy for, and supporting of families of children on the autism spectrum.

- ✔ **Global and Regional Asperger Syndrome Partnership (GRASP)** (www.grasp.org): This organization strives to educate people about Asperger Syndrome and to effect positive change for people with Asperger Syndrome and high-functioning autism. The director, half the board of directors, and the entire advisory board are people with autism.

- ✔ **More advanced individuals with Autism, Asperger Syndrome, and Pervasive Developmental Disorder (MAAP)** (www.maapservices.org): Dedicated to the networking of parents, professionals, and people on the autism spectrum to learn more about people with high-functioning autism and Asperger Syndrome.

- ✔ **Organization for Autism Research (OAR)** (www.researchautism.org): Dedicated to using science to help answer the many challenges faced by parents and other family members of children with autism. The group also raises funds for autism research. OAR hosts a national conference every fall in the Washington, D.C., area.

- ✔ **Unlocking Autism (UA)** (www.unlockingautism.org): A group dedicated to raising autism awareness, funding for research, and governmental activism in an effort to help people on the autism spectrum lead fulfilling and productive lives. Check out its interactive live Web-based chat support, available from 9 a.m. to 4 p.m. (and often later!).

Perusing general-information sites

Consult these trustworthy Web sites for articles and links that will bring you up to date on the latest news concerning the autism community.

- ✔ **Autism Resources** (www.autism-resources.com): One of the most comprehensive collections of links relating to all areas of autism. The site provides FAQs, personal accounts of people with autism, info on educational/behavioral and biomedical interventions, and a continuously updated bibliography of books dealing with autism.

- ✔ **Autism Today** (www.autismtoday.com): An information and resource center filled with articles, online education opportunities, conference locales, the latest autism news, a directory, and advice from the top experts in fields of special needs.

- ✔ **Center for the Study of Autism** (www.autism.org): Affiliated with the Autism Research Institute, this site gives parents and professionals the best and most current information pertaining to autism. The site also has an introductory overview of autism translated into several languages.

- ✔ **Neurodiversity** (www.neurodiversity.com): A "diverse" online library, providing resources and advocacy for people on the autism spectrum. One fun feature: The site has a link for gift ideas for those on the spectrum!

- ✔ **Online Asperger Syndrome Information and Support (OASIS)** (www.aspergersyndrome.org): One of the largest and most reliable online information sources pertaining to Asperger Syndrome.

- ✔ **Tony Attwood** (www.tonyattwood.com.au): A massive Web site chock-full of information based on the research of the most well-known expert on Asperger Syndrome.

Having some fun

Check out these activities for kids on the spectrum:

- ✔ **JF2 Dolphin Project at Florida's Gulfarium** (www.gulfarium.com/jfdolphin.htm): An educational research program devoted to enhancing traditional therapies for people with disabilities (including autism). Interaction with dolphins helps with accomplishing therapeutic and learning objectives.

- ✔ **Surfers Healing** (www.surfershealing.org): Founded by parents of a child with autism, who seemed to find respite only in the ocean, this free camp is devoted to promoting the experience of surfing for children with autism and their families. Check the Web site for a location near you.

Gaining insight from people with an ASD

The Internet can be a marvelous tool for autistic people to share their insights about life with autism. Be prepared for a wide variety of opinions.

As we detail in Chapter 2, we consider Asperger Syndrome as part of the autism spectrum, so we include some information here from people who consider themselves to have Asperger Syndrome.

- ✔ **The Asperger Marriage Web Site** (www.asperger-marriage.info): Hosted by a man on the autism spectrum and his neurotypical wife, this site is useful for persons wanting to find out more about maintaining a successful long-term relationship with an autistic person.

- ✔ **Autism Network International (ANI)** (ani.autistics.org): Devoted to self-help and advocacy, for and by autistic people. ANI hosts an annual gathering called "Autreat" for people with autism and others who support them.

- ✔ **The Autism Picture Page** (www.picturepage.net): This page reveals the human side of life on the autism spectrum as only art can.

- **Autism Resources — Accounts of Autistic People** (`www.autism-resources.com/links/accounts.html`): A list of Web-based personal life stories of people with autism and links to other autistic autobiographical sites.

- **AutismAsperger.net** (`www.autismasperger.net`): The Web home of co-author Stephen Shore serves to build greater awareness and appreciation of the strengths autistic people have to contribute to society.

- **Autistic Adults Picture Project** (`www.isn.net/~jypsy/AuSpin/a2p2.htm`): A site made up of hundreds of pictures and mini-biographies of adults with autism. The goal of the site is to develop awareness that autistic children grow up to be adults on the autism spectrum.

- **Autistic Advocacy** (`home.att.net/~ascaris1`): A fascinating collection of essays and information by Frank Klein, an autism advocate, examining the issues of self and collective advocacy of people with autism.

- **Autistics.org** (`www.autistics.org`): Self-tagged as the "real voice of autism," this site is primarily for and by autistic people, although other members of the autism community may find useful information here.

- **Donna Williams' Personal Page** (`www.donnawilliams.net`): Author of several books on autism and known the world over for her consultations and presentations, Donna Williams welcomes you to discover more about her — and yourself.

- **Institute for the Study of the Neurologically Typical** (`isnt.autistics.org`): This site puts the "shoe on the other proverbial foot," using typical "medicalese" to describe nonspectrum behavior and characteristics.

- **University Students with Autism and Asperger Syndrome** (`www.users.dircon.co.uk./~cns/index.html`): A collection of first-person accounts by people with autism, centered on college experiences.

Chatting about autism

A chat room is an online interactive typing session with others — somewhat like instant messaging (IM) with a group of people in one IM window. Chat rooms can be excellent sources of information and support. But before joining a chat room of any sort, you need to be aware of appropriate Internet etiquette:

- **Observation is recommended.** Take some time to observe the conversation in a room for content and to find out how people communicate with each other — especially when entering an unfamiliar chat room.

- ✔ **Discussion is expected.** If you disagree with someone or with a topic at hand, you can state your viewpoint. However, it's often better to agree to disagree.

- ✔ **Safety first.** Don't reveal personal information about yourself, unless you know all the members of the chat room well. Also:

  - Be careful about getting together with people you have met only in a chat room. If you agree to meet with someone, do so where others are around, such as at an autism conference or other public location.

  - Make the initial meeting short, such as for a cup of coffee.

  - Strongly consider bringing a friend with you to meet your Internet friend for the first time or two.

Here are a couple of Internet-based chat rooms you may find helpful:

- ✔ **#asperger** (`www.inlv.demon.nl/irc.asperger`): Open only to people on the autism spectrum, this site is mostly frequented by young adults. To gain access, you need to use a browser that contains Javascript (which most current browsers are equipped with) or download International Relay Chat (IRC) software at `www.katkorner.com/ircasperger.html`.

- ✔ If you belong to the Internet service America Online (AOL), you can find a number of chat rooms relating to autism (simply look under the People menu).

Exploring listserves

Similar to an e-mail list, listserves broadcast member posts to all members and are a great way to share information and support. To join a listserve, send an e-mail to the addresses in the list that follows, or visit the Web sites we include for further information about the communities and how to join.

Like with joining a chat room, you need to be aware of appropriate Internet etiquette for listserves. See the previous section for Internet etiquette advice.

- ✔ **AUTINET** (`AutAdvo-subscribe@yahoogroups.com`): The primary goal of this listserve is to promote understanding and unity between people on the autism spectrum and parents, doctors, teachers, and others in the greater autism community. You can find more information at the site `health.groups.yahoo.com/group/AutAdvo`.

- ✔ **AUTISM** (`listserv@maelstrom.stjohns.edu`): The oldest and most well-established listserve on autism-related information.

✔ **Autism Network International** (listserve@listserve.syr.edu):
Primarily for people with autism; however, parents and others can take
part as well. You can find more information about the listserve at Autism
Network International's Web site (ani.autistics.org).

Accessing World-Wide Autism Organizations and Resources

If you live outside the United States or are just curious to see what resources
are available in other countries, you may find the links in this section useful.
The National Autistic Society in England provides the links. Here are a couple
of overarching international sites to get you started:

✔ **The International Association Autism Europe** (www.autismeurope
.org): Focused on raising awareness and political involvement in
Europe, this group's main objective is to bring forward the rights of
autistic people and their families.

✔ **World Autism Organisation** (www.worldautism.org): Dedicated to
improving the quality of life for people with autism and those supporting
them. It holds a biannual *World Autism Congress,* bringing together autistic people, researchers, and the rest of the global autism community.

For a regularly updated and comprehensive listing of countries and their
associated autism resources, visit the National Autistic Society's Round-the-
World Web site at www.nas.org.uk/nas/jsp/polopoly.jsp?d=661.

Index

Notes